Money at the N

The Human Economy

Series editors:
Keith Hart, University of Pretoria
John Sharp, University of Pretoria

Those social sciences and humanities concerned with the economy have lost the confidence to challenge the sophistication and public dominance of the field of economics. We need to give a new emphasis and direction to the economic arrangements that people already share, while recognizing that humanity urgently needs new ways of organizing life on the planet. This series examines how human interests are expressed in our unequal world through concrete economic activities and aspirations.

Money at the Margins

Global Perspectives on Technology, Financial Inclusion, and Design

Edited by

**Bill Maurer, Smoki Musaraj,
and Ivan V. Small**

*Thanks for
your contribution to all
of my classes !*

*Best !
Smoki*

berghahn
NEW YORK · OXFORD
www.berghahnbooks.com

First published by

Berghahn Books

www.berghahnbooks.com

Library of Congress Cataloging-in-Publication Data

Names: Maurer, Bill, 1968- editor. | Musaraj, Smoki, 1979- editor. | Small, Ivan
Victor, 1972- editor.
Title: Money at the Margins: Global Perspectives on Technology, Financial Inclu-
sion, and Design / edited by Bill Maurer, Smoki Musaraj, and Ivan Small.
Description: New York: Berghahn Books, 2018 | Series: The Human Economy;
Volume 6 | Includes bibliographical references and index.
Identifiers: LCCN 2017051496 (print) | LCCN 2017054657 (ebook) | ISBN
9781785336546 (eBook) | ISBN 9781785336539 (hardback: alk. paper)
Subjects: LCSH: Finance—Developing countries. | Money—Technological
innovations—Developing countries. | Poor—Developing countries.
Classification: LCC HG195 (ebook) | LCC HG195 .M655 2018 (print) | DDC
332.09172/4—dc23
LC record available at https://lccn.loc.gov/2017051496

British Library Cataloguing in Publication Data

A catalogue record for this book is available from the British Library

ISBN 978-1-78533-653-9 hardback
ISBN 978-1-78920-048-5 paperback
ISBN 978-1-78533-654-6 ebook

Contents

▦ Illustrations

Figures

Tables

Acknowledgments

This volume is the product of multiple years of research, collaboration, and discussion among a transnational and interdisciplinary network of scholars, practitioners, philanthropists, designers, and policymakers brought together through the financial and intellectual support of the Institute for Money, Technology & Financial Inclusion (IMTFI) at the University of California, Irvine. We are thankful to IMTFI for making these conversations possible and for the ongoing support for research by scholars based in the Global South. The chapters and discussions in the volume have also benefitted from the intellectual exchanges at various IMTFI conferences over the course of 2011–2016, as well as academic and practitioner conferences ranging from the American Ethnological Society to the World Bank's Digital Finance workshop and GSMA's Mobile Money for the Unbanked event. These exchanges and others taking place in different corners of the globe have made possible the sharing of knowledge and expertise among scholars living and writing in the communities that they research.

It has taken a global village to bring this volume together. We thank first and foremost Jenny Fan for her tireless and meticulous work on countless administrative tasks related to the various steps of this project—from research to writing to publishing—and for consistently over the past five years helping us navigate multiple time-zones, institutional requirements, and academic schedules. Second, we thank John Seaman for his ongoing administrative support and for his unique sense of humor. We thank in particular members of the Value and Money writing group—Sean Mallin, Taylor Nelms, Stevie Rea, Beth Reddy—for their comments on earlier drafts of the introduction of the volume. A number of faculty, students, and postdocs at the department of anthropology at UCI have provided ongoing feedback and intellectual stimulation for the conversations that run through this volume. We thank Julia Elyachar, Keith Murphy, Tom Boellstorff, Kristin Peterson, Ursula Dalinghaus, Nathan Coben, Nathan Dobson, Robbie Kett, Nick Seaver, Nima L. Yolmo, Lotta Björklund Larsen, and Janny Li for their generous input and friendship. The essays included in this volume and our thinking about the themes of the book have also been informed by conversations with a wide network of scholars and practitioners in philanthropy and industry. We thank, among others, Scott Mainwaring, Jonathan Donner, Olufunmilayo (Funmi) Arewa, Nina Bandelj, Alladi Venkatesh, Carol Benson, Jan Chipchase, Paul Dourish, Wendy March, Tatyana Mamut, Katie Porter, David Pedersen, Gustav Peebles, Frank Bean, Allison Truitt, Abhishek Sinha, Elisabeth Berthe, and the commentators in this volume for helping us thing through the implications and impact of our work within and outside the academe.

Special thanks go to Peter Wissoker for his meticulous copyediting of an earlier version of the whole manuscript and to Ryan Masteller for copyediting the final manuscript. Many thanks also to Nandita Badami for copyediting several chapters of the volume. The editorial team at Berghahn Books has made the publication process a pleasure. Special thanks go to Marion Berghahn, Amanda Horn, Burke Gerstenschlager, and Rebecca Rom-Frank for their prompt help throughout the production process. Thanks also to the anonymous reviewers of the book for their generous comments and suggestions.

Research for all chapters included in the volume received funding by IMTFI which was in turn generously funded from 2008–2017 by a series of grants from the Bill & Melinda Gates Foundation. We are very grateful for their support through the years, especially to Amolo Ng'weno, Mireya Almazan, Jake Kendall, Mohammed Mohammed, Rodger Voorhies, and Rebecca Mann. In addition, Bill Maurer's research on payments was supported by grants from the US National Science Foundation, Law and Social Sciences program (SES 0960423 and 1455859). Any opinions, findings, conclusions, or recommendations expressed in this material are those of the author(s) and do not necessarily reflect the views of the National Science Foundation or any other agency.

Last but not least, the chapters included in this volume are only the tip of the iceberg of the wealth of research around money and payments generated through the support of IMTFI. Over the years of assembling this volume together, a large network of IMTFI fellows from all corners of the world have provided continuous inspiration and expertise on the growing field of research and applications of different technologies of money and payment for the purpose of financial inclusion. Ongoing intellectual exchanges through international conferences, workshops, and working papers over the years with Deepti KC, Vivian Dzokoto, Cliff Mensah, Ishita Ghosh, Eric Osei-Assibey, Carly Schuster, Pradeep Baisakh, Tony Omwansa, Lakshmi Kumar, Gianluca Iazzolino, Syed Aiman Raza, Svetlana Tyukhteneva, the authors of this volume, and many others have been invaluable as we continue to follow and analyze the rapidly chang-ing worlds of remittances and payments facilitated by new technologies. There are many other fellows and fellow travellers who informed our conversations and nourished our imagination, and while we cannot do justice to all of them by name, we hope that this volume will direct atten-tion to this growing and ongoing body of research on money, technology, and financial inclusion, of which these chapters are only a sample.

Introduction

Money and Finance at the Margins

SMOKI MUSARAJ AND IVAN V. SMALL

A rotating credit-association meeting filled with food, music, laughter, and community spectators. Migrants who negotiate state borders by foot and sim cards. Traders creatively swapping between international and socialist currency spheres. A complex semiotic world of visual bargaining cues in a busy street market. Creative technology uptake and adaptation among visually impaired members facilitating participation in a women's savings group. Such are the types of lively stories that animate this volume on technology, inclusion, and design – stories drawing on everyday practices around money, value, storage, savings, and transfers among oftentimes marginalized communities across the Global South.

Money, commonly conceived of in its various material currency forms, offers critical insight into a range of practices surrounding notions of value, including the diverse ways it is managed by individuals, groups, and societies. Recent technological innovations – from dispensing cash transfers via ATM to the ability to store, transfer, and cash out credit via mobile phones – have had a significant impact on much of the world's population. In the process, such mediums have targeted and brought to light often financially "invisible" populations, whose marginal capacity for participation has left them either dismissed or forgotten in mainstream economic arenas: those living under the global poverty line of two dollars per day, often referred to as "the unbanked." And yet, their economic activities are significant and complex, and quite visible for those who choose to look.

The authors in this volume who look at such financial activities represent a variety of interdisciplinary academic, design, and policy backgrounds, bringing together fields of research and practice. Each of the chapters addresses changes in the uses and meanings of money that occur through more general political and economic but also technological transformations. Indeed, technology is a central point of inquiry in the volume. Across a range of locales, the authors examine how recent and ongoing technological developments in the money sphere – in particular the digitalization and thus dematerialization of money – have dramatically altered practices of and attitudes toward monetary storage, accounting, exchange, and transfer.

These intriguing developments are the subject of concerted discussion among academics as well as researchers and policymakers. In order to contextualize our contributors' work, we will turn to three of the topics at the core of these discussions: (1) new understandings of money and finance in economic anthropology and sociology, especially as pertains to studies of low finance; (2) everyday uses of new financial technologies aimed at poverty reduction and financial inclusion; and finally, (3) forms of collaborations between academics and practitioners in industry and philanthropy relating to new designs of money for inclusion.

Money, Value, and Wealth in Contexts of Low Finance

In recent years, the financial lives of the so-called "poor" have come to constitute a field of interest in development economics (Banerjee and Duflo 2011; Rutherford 2000) as well as a new market for global capital (Roy 2010). Proliferating alongside multiplying microfinance initiatives, exemplified in the initial success of Muhamed Yunus's Grameen Bank, this literature draws attention to the complex financial lives of "the poor" in various parts of the Global South. In particular, the landmark publications *Poor Economics: A Radical Rethinking of the Way to Fight Global Poverty* (Banerjee and Duflo 2011) and *Portfolios of the Poor: How the World's Poor Live on $2 a Day* (Collins et al. 2009) have laid new ground in thinking about low finance – that is, the various strategies and resources that the unbanked (people excluded from formal financial institutions) mobilize in their everyday financial lives. This line of research asserts that "the poor" also engage on a daily basis in financial activities such as saving, loaning, hedging risk, and investing. While recognizing the agency of the unbanked in their daily lives, however, such studies are narrower in their approach to notions and forms of money, limiting the definition to legal tender and stripping away any recognition of its broader cultural, social, and moral meanings (see for example critiques by Guérin, Morvant-Roux, and Villarreal 2013: 11; Schwittay 2011: 385).

A long tradition in anthropology and sociology of money has critically engaged with the definition of the classic functions of money in economic theories (as a means of exchange, unit of account, means of payment, store of value), further diversifying the ways of thinking about money as a commodity *and* a token (Hart 1986), as a mediator of sociality and intimacy (Zelizer 1997), as "a memory bank" (Hart 2000), and as "a relationship" (Maurer 2015a).[1] Further, economic anthropologists have for some time now challenged the ways that notions of "value" and "wealth" are defined in economic theory and policy by exploring how such notions are produced and deployed differently in variant cultural contexts (Weiner 1992; Munn 1986; Guyer 1993; Graeber 2001; Shipton 2007, 2009). Rather than thinking about value in purely economic terms, for instance, a number of old and recent classics in economic anthropology explore various forms and regimes of value (Appadurai 1986; Guyer 2004; Roitman 2005; Truitt 2013) as defined, negotiated, and transformed by people on the ground.

This book builds on these notions of money, value, and wealth to expand the discussion around the practices and meanings of financial transactions at the margins of global capital. The chapters in this volume span a wide range of money objects or objects used *as* money – from cattle to cash to mobile – and provide a rich tableau of practices and institutions that format and operate around such objects. Coming from diverse disciplinary backgrounds, the authors in this book nonetheless share a similar ethnographic sensibility to the study of money and finance. The book is attuned to money's "repertoires, pragmatics, and indexicality" (Maurer 2006: 30) as well as to people's creative uses of different forms of money in their everyday lives. The authors examine how people in diverse cultural and socioeconomic settings understand and use monetary repertoires for various purposes (for instance, to make social payments or to accumulate savings, pleasure, and/or prestige); how they differentiate (earmark) different kinds of money based on their materiality, provenance, and/or use; how they combine and move across different financial institutions and monetary repertoires as they seek creative ways to save, loan, and invest. Further, the book identifies the variety of institutions that enable and/or are enabled by such monetary repertoires; the chapters ask how formal and informal banking institutions intertwine in and may govern people's daily financial transactions; how money mediates social and cultural rituals, obligations, and events; and how various financial practices are subject to sociocultural institutions such as rank, class, and gender. These ongoing projects continue to underscore the interplay between multiple forces and actors – states, markets, people – in shaping the meaning and uses of money in everyday life.

In addition to highlighting complexity and diversity of the forms and functions of money, the book offers a more expansive approach to the very notions of value and wealth – economic, social, cultural – as defined, created, and applied by actors on the ground. The chapters explore the incredibly diverse practices of wealth creation by people living on less than two dollars a day—from storing wealth in piggy banks and ROS-CAs (rotating savings and credit associations) or as foodstuffs and jewelry (Tankha; Bajracharya; Villarreal, Guérin, and Kumar), to making payments (financial, social, cultural) via lottery networks operators (Echeverry and Cuartas) or mobile-money services (Nandhi, Kusimba, Kunyu, and Gross). Further, several of the chapters highlight the creative acts of conversion, performance, and play that permeate transactions with non-bank financial institutions such as rotating savings associations in the Kathmandu Valley (Bajracharya), shared store-credit cards in Chile (Ossandón et al.), or mobile-money ritual payments in Kenya (Kusimba, Kunyu, and Gross).

Recent works in cultural and social studies of finance contest a long-established narrative on the encroachment of the economic over the social and cultural worlds, advocating instead for a turn to practices, pragmatics, and performativity of economic concepts and objects (Maurer 2006, 2007; Callon 1998; Callon, Millo and Muniesa 2007; MacKenzie 2008; Zaloom 2009). Rather than fixing a particular notion of value, the ethnographic lenses turn to the repertoires, moralities, and materialities of money (Bloch and Parry 1989; Akin and Robbins 1999; Guyer 2004; Musaraj 2011; Truitt 2013), and to the practices and processes of valuation and value transformation in the marketplace and beyond (Çalışkan and Callon 2009, 2010; Kjellberg and Mallard 2013). Key ethnographic accounts look closely at the particular technologies, discourses, and economic theories that create and perform financial markets (see Zaloom 2006; Mackenzie 2008; Ho 2009; Holmes 2013). While introducing a whole new way of thinking and studying financial markets, these studies by and large focus on centers of global finance, on official and regulated markets, and on professional entrepreneurs/traders/bankers. One exception to this approach to finance is the growing literature on remittance transfers among migrant communities that bridge the Global North and South. This literature has contributed key anthropological insights into the generative capacities of the remittance economy in mobilizing, shaping, and transforming localized and transnational relations, imaginaries, and desires (see, among others, Levitt 2001; Glick-Schiller and Fouron 2001, Coutin 2007, Chu 2010; Small 2012; Pedersen 2013; Kwon 2015; Paerregaard 2015). We follow along the footsteps of this literature and advocate for an anthropology and sociology of low finance that may well provide unique analytical insights into the uses and meaning of money and finance beyond the bank and the trading room.[2] Such approach would make a contribution not just to scholarly debates but also to policymaking.

One of the crucial shortcomings of traditional approaches to economic development and microfinance is the assumed separation between the formal and informal sectors and a clear preference of the latter over the former. The very notion of "informal economy" was first introduced by anthropologist Keith Hart in his study of economic practices among low-income populations in the slums of Accra, Ghana (1973). The term was adopted by the International Labor Organization and took on a life of its own in development circles; however, it quickly departed from the intended purpose (the claim that the poor in urban Accra were, indeed, economically active, albeit formally unemployed).[3] Economic anthropologists have long challenged both the idea of that separation as well as the hierarchy of values imposed on these two categories. This has been supported by ethnographic research from various parts of the Global South that explores how informal practices are always already intertwined with formal institutions (Roitman 2005; Elyachar 2003, 2005; Han 2012; Lucia 2014; Wilkis 2014) and the ways that the informal is used to circumvent the structures of exclusion integral to those institutions.

In this book, we maintain the focus on finance at the margins but caution against the formal/informal binary. We use the term low finance to refer to economic transactions that take place mostly (though not entirely) outside of formal banking systems and official regulatory regimes, are mostly mediated by cash in soft currencies (see also Guyer 2011), and that often entail multiple financial platforms and mediums of payment and exchange.

A number of the chapters in this book provide insight into the intertwined spheres of low and high finance, exploring the specific forms of inclusion/exclusion and ways people have navigated around financial barriers. Chapters by Taylor and Horst, Villarreal, Guérin and Kumar, Mesfin, Echeverry and Cuartas, and Bajracharya, for instance, discuss the multiple forms of wealth that various groups of the unbanked in Haiti, the Dominican Republic, India, Mexico, Ethiopia, Colombia, the Philippines, and Nepal mobilize as a means of everyday financial survival and asset-creation. These accounts take a closer look at the financial lives of people living on less than two dollars a day, going beyond the model of "financial diaries" (Collins et al. 2009) by examining, instead, the various financial resources that are economic as well as other functions. Thus, these authors note how women in India, Mexico, Kenya, and Nepal mobilize various social, economic, and cultural resources in order to generate multiple forms of wealth. These resources include social and kin ties (among family, neighbors, women's groups, political patrons) as well as different types of capital (cash, jewelry, mobile money, government grants). Their desired forms of wealth, or assets (Guyer), include savings (in cash or other valuables) (Tankha; Villarreal, Guérin, and Kumar; Mesfin), economic opportunities (Taylor and Horst; Echeverry and Cuartas), pleasure (Bajracharya), and prestige (Villarreal, Guérin, and Kumar; Mesfin).

A common thread that runs through a number of these chapters is the intertwining of financial technologies and social ties in the everyday practices of wealth-creation. As Jenna Burrell points out in her commentary, this theme runs against the grain of assumptions prevalent among development and industry practitioners about the impersonal and individualistic nature of technology. By ethnographically tracing how people on the ground embed new and old monetary technologies in social interaction and cultural practice, this book seeks to address the gaps in the design of and policymaking around new technologies of financial inclusion. We explore these gaps in the next section.

Technologies of Financial Inclusion

Poverty reduction has long been a moving target for development economists and policymakers. The World Bank estimated that 1 billion people still lived in extreme poverty in 2015. Identifying effective tools for addressing poverty has been a challenge ranging from top-down infrastructure modernization projects to participatory community projects driven by methodologies (Chambers 1997) for engaging local stakeholder needs and capacities. Economist Jeffrey Sachs's famous call to an "end of poverty" (2005), taken up by the development community, identified key strategies, including the harnessing of technology for development purposes. Technology for development has become mainstreamed, as numerous program initiatives by the United Nations Development Programme, USAID, the World Bank, and other international aid organizations attest. In the money arena this has included an emphasis on the digitalization of money in a variety of sectors, from government cash transfers to mobile money. Cashlessness is viewed as a potential development strategy for increasing financial transparency, reducing corruption, and facilitating savings and transfers – particularly international and urban-rural remittances, which are widely recognized as important sources of local development financing (Ratha 2006 et al.).[4] It is in this context that we can better situate and understand the current global campaign toward financial inclusion, a campaign that resonates with earlier policies that advocated the formalization of the informal economy as a site for economic development in the Global South.[5]

We trace the history of the current global campaign for banking the unbanked to the emergence of microfinance in the late 1970s. As described earlier, following the initial success of the Grameen Bank a number of international development agencies, governments, nongovernmental organizations, and private philanthropists joined in a global campaign advocating microfinance as a means of including the "bottom of the pyramid" in regulated financial institutions (banks, credit, and, consequently, debt). More recently, such campaigns see the dematerialization of money – the movement from cash to digital payments – as a technological fix to the broader problems of poverty and financial exclusion. Thus, leading international organizations (the World Bank), government bodies (USAID), and private philanthropic foundations (the Bill & Melinda Gates Foundation, MasterCard Foundation) have embraced (and are heavily investing in) developing mobile money and other electronic and digital financial instruments under the banner of financial inclusion (see, for instance, Demirgüç-Kunt et al. 2015).

A number of chapters in this volume focus on several such initiatives for financial inclusion via digital forms of money, credit, and payments. These chapters explore mobile money as an arena of cashless interest and development potential. The ubiquity of cell phones in the developing world and the success of certain countries such as Kenya and the Philippines in creating agreements between banks, regulators, and telecom operators to use cell phones to perform functions such as storing and transferring value or applying for microloans is seen as a potential boon for those traditionally excluded from formal financial participation.[6] As the chapters in this volume illustrate, however, efforts to promote formal financial inclusion should not dismiss the diverse ways that the poor already participate quite actively and creatively in the economic arena (Rutherford 2009). Furthermore, the mapping and adaptation of existing monetary practices to new technological tools and infrastructures often have unintended consequences.

The emergence of mobile money – originally the use of airtime as a form of currency to send monetary value from person to person (P2P) via cell phone transactions – has been a particularly interesting example of a development in the sphere of finance that has been widely adopted in parts of the Global South (Mas and Morawczynski 2009; Kendall et al. 2012). The unprecedented success of Kenya's mobile-money company, M-PESA, in gaining a greater share of the market of P2P transactions than banks (Omwansa and Sullivan 2012) has prompted many in the development world to look into mobile payment technologies and services as a potential new market for microfinance initiatives. In other contexts (such as GCASH in the Philippines and EKO in India), mobile-money services seem to succeed in areas such as state cash transfers or P2P transfers among migrants (Gusto and Roque; Nandhi). But the emergence of mobile money and its success in some (but not all) countries of the Global South has raised a number of issues around money and development more generally. Thus, the success of M-PESA in particular is routinely used in industry discourse to make a case for cashlessness as a strategy for economic development, increased security, and even antiterrorism. What this particular discourse of cashlessness often fails to address, however, is the market politics that are often driving the push for mobile money – the rivalries between brick-and-mortar banks and telecom companies, the particular agent networks that emerge around mobile-money services, and potential monopolies in the telecom industry. Most importantly, while mobile money promises to expedite transfer, it is not always clear how such services might create new sources of income for the poor or how they might address deeper infrastructural problems. Does mobile money in its digital record of financial transactions create a big data trail that raises concern over issues of privacy, discretion, and governance? Or does it contribute to a financial record that might ease access to credit? Other questions are of an analytical order: Does mobile money present a new money form, and, if so, how are we to think critically about what this form enables/disables?

Several of the chapters in the book explore the application and effects of mobile money (Nandhi; Kiiti and Mutinda; Kusimba, Kunyu, and Gross; Taylor and Horst) as well as other emerging technologies such as biometric identification (Donovan) and government cash transfer programs (Gusto and Roque) for the purpose of financial inclusion. These contributions, however, present a nuanced picture of the effectiveness of new technologies in poverty alleviation. While in some cases mobile-money services facilitate the sending of remittances or even savings (Nandhi), other accounts point to persisting concerns about trust, privacy, and personal relationships to the service providers. Others raise questions about the new forms of governance enabled by such technologies (Donovan) as well as new forms of inclusion/exclusion for client populations (Kiiti and Mutinda). A number of the chapters come from practitioners in technology and development economics – the ethnographic insights that these contributions bring together are, therefore, also aimed at future policy and design.

Humanitarian Design and Collaborative Research Practices

An ethnographic approach to apprehending emerging intersections of finance and technology is also finding relevance among industry designers, who over the years have recognized the importance of catering to what is now often called human-centered (also known as humanitarian) design (HCD).[7] Human-centered design encourages an ethnographic approach to ascertaining how human behavior offers important insights into product design and adaptation that maybe be overlooked in the engineering process. One key feature that distinguishes this design approach from others is investing in ethnographic methods of research (as opposed to traditional market research) by deploying teams of social scientists and designers to engage in participant observation, tagalongs, and long-term face-to-face interactions with people on the ground. A number of these firms are now partnering with philanthropists and industry to develop tools aimed at increasing financial inclusion, often including various types of mobile-money and conditional cash-transfer applications or other technologies that would potentially solve deep structural and infrastructural problems.[8]

While subject to the "neoliberal" critique of commodifying and marketizing ethnography (after all, such firms bid for contracts in a highly competitive environment), these players nonetheless have carved out a new "assemblage" of actors that cross-cut design, development, and social sciences (Schwittay 2011; Maurer, Nelms, and Rea 2013). Such collaborations recall the concept of para-ethnography (Holmes and Marcus 2008) as well as a number of collaborative projects (Maurer and Mainwaring 2012; Riles 2013) whereby anthropologists and other social scientists engage in research with subjects in other fields who share similar methods and forms of expertise. Further, our notion of collaboration also seeks to address ongoing calls for more serious engagements with theories from the South (Comaroff and Comaroff 2011). In bringing together authors who either live and work in various parts of the Global South or have conducted extensive ethnographic research at various sites in Africa, Asia, and Latin America, we hope to expand on the few remarkable projects that have provided a space for voices outside of the Euro-American academy (Guyer 1995; Hart and Sharp 2015; Hart 2015). Such an approach recognizes that subjects of research are "epistemic partners" (Holmes and Marcus 2008) rather than radically other "informants." The epistemic and practical work that transpires through such collaborations takes shape laterally (Maurer 2005), with ethnographers and research "subjects" mutually shaping one another's forms of knowledge and, potentially, design of new products, services, and policies.

This is a challenging path to take, and many of the authors in this book attest to the methodological, cultural, and political challenges that such collaborative work entails. But it is a path that helps ensure that social theories and methods are not mired in the academy, but instead may be put to work and offer reflective insight in the wider world. Some of the projects featured in this volume experiment with a different kind of engagement with their field by, among others, actively seeking to advocate financial literacy among poor rickshaw pullers in Delhi, India (Nandhi); providing social support to marginalized indigenous populations in the Philippines (Gusto and Roque); or thinking about alternative ways to measure creditworthiness among informal workers in Colombia (Echeverry and Cuartas). As microfinance inclusion initiatives target and expand the financialization of the poor (Roy 2010), these chapters also caution against importing ready-made models of inclusion, and provide design guidelines attuned to local institutions and practices of financial resourcefulness and responsibility.

Organization of the Chapters

In order to expand this discussion on the role of money and everyday practices of its use in anthropology, policy, and industry, and to reflect fully on the materials of the volume's authors, we have organized the thirteen chapters of this volume under four main themes: "In/Exclusion," "Value and Wealth," "Technology and Social Relations," and "Design and Practice." For each section, an established scholar or practitioner in the field was invited to contribute a short essay discussing the authors' findings – including theoretical, ethnographic, and practical contributions, how the section chapters intersect with and inform each other, and the doors they open for further discussion and reflection.

The first part, "In/Exclusion," includes chapters by authors from various disciplinary backgrounds – anthropology, political science, communications, and environmental sciences – and spans three countries (Haiti, Dominican Republic, Kenya). The section explores the experiences of various groups of people excluded from formal banking institutions (migrants, refugees, persons with visual impairment). As Ananya Roy points out, read together, these chapters invite us to think more critically about "the organization and institutionalization of financial inclusion" and the everyday practices of navigating, negotiating, and contesting categories of included and excluded populations.

Part II, "Value and Wealth," brings together chapters by anthropologists, a sociologist, and an economist working in four countries (Nepal, Cuba, India, Mexico) and drawing upon a wide range of concepts and theories in the anthropology and sociology of money. The three chapters highlight complex and diverse notions of value and wealth that go well beyond economistic measures and that also include social, cultural, and political considerations. Reflecting on this section, Jane Guyer draws attention to the temporal dimension of practices of value and wealth creation. She highlights the efforts by a number of the protagonists in these chapters at creating "enduring value" in a context of uncertain "monetary temporalities." This attention to the temporalities of finance and life is especially pertinent to the everyday experiences of people living at the margins that this book explores. "'Living on two dollars per day,'" Guyer observes, is "actually not in dollars (a stable currency) nor is it daily (on a regular rhythm)." Guyer thus identifies a blind spot in the very definition of poverty in global development discourse – namely, the uncertain temporalities of finance and life for people at the margins of global capital.

Part III, "Technology and Social Relations," draws attention to the everyday uses of various financial technologies (mobile money, digital government cash grants, retail credit cards), in ways not always anticipated by the designers of such technologies or by the authors researching them (see Ossandón et al.). The three chapters in this section come from scholars with interdisciplinary backgrounds in anthropology, sociology, and science and technology studies and focus on three different countries (Chile, South Africa, Kenya). The chapters share a perspective on technology and finance as being entangled with social relations and cultural norms. In her commentary, Jenna Burrell notes that this relationship between technology and social ties "has not been given the same weight and consideration." Bringing attention to this relationship, as authors in this section do, would be of particular interest to industry and philanthropy practitioners advocating the application of new digital technologies as a solution to financial inclusion.

It is with this ethos that the authors in the final part, "Design and Practice," approach existing and future digital technology aimed at financial inclusion efforts. Authors in this section are practitioners in design, international development, and communications technology; one of them has engaged in applied social science. The chapters in this section are written in a different style; the authors draw upon their ethnographic insights for the purpose of informing better designs of financial services and products. As Blumenstock notes, the research and design proposals discussed in these chapters are "a powerful reminder of the chasm between current design and current practice." All authors in this section, while not anthropologists by training, seek to bridge this chasm by way of ethnographically informed design and policy.

The afterword by Bill Maurer further echoes this commitment to ethnographic research in discussions, assessments, policies, and designs of new technologies aimed at promoting financial inclusion. Drawing upon authors in this volume and others working on similar projects, Maurer makes a case for collaborative, grounded research that attends to the "ingenuity and the cultural and social forces at play whenever people pay." This is a call for deploying a "diversity of knowledge forms" in policy and industry researching and designing money and payment infrastructures for the poor. We hope that, by mobilizing diverse knowledge forms, the contributions and discussions of this volume will help highlight and rethink the various ways that "money" and "value" are recognized and practiced among communities at the perceived margins of the traditional economic mainstream, and further inform broader debates and agendas related to technology, inclusion, and design.

Smoki Musaraj is assistant professor of anthropology at Ohio University. She received her PhD in anthropology and MA in political science from the New School for Social Research. She is a cultural anthropologist with a specialization in economic and legal anthropology. Her research focuses on the anthropology of money and value, informal and alternative economies, speculative bubbles, corruption and the rule of law, postsocialist transformations, and societies of southeast Europe and the Mediterranean. Dr. Musaraj has published in various journals, including *Cultural Anthropology, Current Anthropology,* and *Ethnologie Française.*

Ivan V. Small is assistant professor of anthropology and international studies at Central Connecticut State University. He holds a PhD in anthropology from Cornell University and a Master of International Affairs from Columbia University. His research focuses on issues related to money, development, emerging markets, consumption and mobility in Southeast Asia – including migration, remittances, and transportation. His first book is titled *Currencies of Imagination: Channeling Money and Chasing Mobility in Vietnam* (Cornell 2018). Dr. Small has also worked and consulted for various think tanks, foundations, and nonprofit organizations including the

Smithsonian, India China Institute, Ford Foundation, and World Policy Institute.

NOTES

1. For a comprehensive review of the anthropology of money, see Maurer 2006 and Hart and Ortiz 2014.
2. For similar ethnographic approaches to the everyday pragmatics of money and finance beyond the centers of global finance, see also Hertz 1998; Elyachar 2006; Çalışkan 2010; McFall 2014; Langley 2013; Deville 2015.
3. Keith Hart has situated the emergence of the notion of "informal economy" within the context of the Cold War, and especially of the failure of states, both east and west of the iron curtain, to "deliver economic democracy in adequate measure" (2000: 148). Further, Hart notes, "the idea came out of the lives of Third World people, whose money makes them about as conventionally poor as it is possible to be in our mechanized world" (ibid). The concept was further taken up by development scholars and practitioners working within the framework of structural adjustment policies of the 1980s and 1990s.
4. Calls for cashlessness as the future of money are increasingly voiced by a wide range of actors. The Better Than Cash Alliance (www.betterthancash.org) has brought together a number of such actors that cut across industry, philanthropy, and regulatory bodies to promote "cashlessness" and "cash-lite"-ness. For reviews of these developments, see, among others, Maurer (2015b); Kendall et al. 2012; and the World Bank (2015) report *Payment Aspects of Financial Inclusion*. For critical overviews on cashlessness and financial inclusion, see Donovan (2012a, 2012b).
5. An influential study by Hernando de Soto (1989) defined the specific approach towards the informal economy that prevails among international development institutions to this day, namely, that formalizing the informal economy is beneficial to all (see Elyachar 2003, 2005 for a critical history of the use of the concept of informal economy and advocacy of formalization of the "bottom of the pyramid").
6. For an illustration of the euphoria around Kenya's story of mobile money lifting millions out of poverty, see Omwansa and Sullivan 2012. Recent efforts by the international telecommunications giant Vodafone repeatedly cast new mobile-money initiatives in countries such as Romania and Albania as "technology honed in Africa [and] exported to Europe" (Shadbolt 2015; see also Finnan 2014). A number of international organizations, private and public, publish ongoing reports that also proclaim the positive effects of mobile money on financial inclusion. Leading voices in this include reports and blogs by the Consultative Group to Assist the Poor (CGAP), the World Economic Forum, and the GSM Association (GSMA).
7. For a popularized version of "human-centered design" see Brown 2009 and the IDEO HCD toolkit. For a critical review of human-centered design and its application by design firms, see Tonkinwise 2011.

8. The design firm IDEO, for instance, has partnered with CGAP to research the impact of mobile money on low-income communities in Ghana (see project overview "New Mobile Money Solutions in Low-Income Communities," https:// www.ideo.org/projects/new-mobile-money-solutions-in-low-income-commu nities/completed). See also CGAP's study of the benefits of HCD for financial inclusion, Seltzer and McKay 2014.

REFERENCES CITED

Akin, David, and Joel Robbins. 1999. *Money and Modernity: State and Local Currencies in Melanesia.* Pittsburgh, PA: Pittsburgh University Press.

Appadurai, Arjun. 1986. *The Social Life of Things: Commodities in Cultural Perspective.* Cambridge: Cambridge University Press.

Banerjee, Abhijit V., and Esther Duflo. 2011. *Poor Economics: A Radical Rethinking of the Way to Fight Global Poverty.* New York: PublicAffairs Books.

Bloch, Maurice, and Jonathan Parry. 1989. "Introduction: Money and the Morality of Exchange." In *Money and the Morality of Exchange,* edited by Jonathan Parry and Maurice Bloch, 1–32. Cambridge: Cambridge University Press.

Brown, Tim. 2009. *Change by Design: How Design Thinking Transforms Organizations and Inspires Innovation.* New York: HarperCollins.

Çalişkan, K., 2010. *Market threads: How Cotton Farmers and Traders Create a Global Commodity.* Princeton, NJ: Princeton University Press.

Çalışkan, Koray, and Michel Callon. 2009. "Economization, Part 1: Shifting Atten-tion from the Economy towards Processes of Economization." *Economy and Society* 38(3): 369–98.

———. 2010. "Economization, Part 2: A Research Programme for the Study of Mar-kets." *Economy and Society* 39(1): 1–32.

Callon, Michel. 1998. *The Laws of the Markets.* Malden, MA: Blackwell Publishers.

Callon, Michel, Yuval Millo, and Fabian Muniesa (eds.). 2007. *Market Devices.* Mal-den, MA: Blackwell Publishers.

Chambers, Robert. 1997. *Whose Reality Counts? Putting the First Last.* London: Inter-mediate Technology.

Chu, Julie Y. 2010. *Cosmologies of Credit: Transnational Mobility and the Politics of Desti-nation in China.* Durham, NC: Duke University Press.

Collins, Daryl, Jonathan Morduch, Stuart Rutherford, and Orlanda Ruthven. 2009. *Portfolios of the Poor: How the World's Poor Live on $2 a Day.* Princeton, NJ: Prince-ton University Press.

Comaroff, Jean, and John L. Comaroff. 2011. *Theory from the South: Or, How Euro-America Is Evolving toward Africa.* New York: Routledge.

Coutin, Susan. 2007. *Nations of Emigrants: Shifting Boundaries of Citizenship in El Salva-dor and the United States.* Ithaca, NY: Cornell University Press.

De Soto, Hernando. 1989. *The Other Path: The Economic Answer to Terrorism.* New York: Basic Books.

Demirgüç-Kunt, Asli, Leora Klapper, Dorothe Singer, and Peter Van Oudheusden. 2015. *The Global Findex Database 2014: Measuring Financial Inclusion around the World.* Washington, DC: World Bank.

Deville, Joe. 2015. *Lived Economies of Default: Consumer Credit, Debt Collection and the Capture of Affect.* Abingdon, Oxon: Routledge.

Donovan, Kevin P. 2012a. "Mobile Money for Financial Inclusion." In *Information and Communication for Development 2012,* edited by Tim Kelly and Michael Minges, 61–73. Washington, DC: World Bank.

———. 2012b. "Mobile Money, More Freedom? The Impact of M-PESA's Network Power on Development as Freedom." *International Journal of Communication* 6: 2647–69.

———. 2014. "Mobile Money." In *International Encyclopedia of Digital Communication and Society:* 1–7.

Elyachar, Julia. 2003. "Mappings of Power: The State, NGOs, and International Organizations in the Informal Economy of Cairo." *Comparative Studies in Society and History* 45(3): 571–605.

———. 2005. *Markets of Dispossession: NGOs, Economic Development, and the State in Cairo.* Durham, NC: Duke University Press.

———. 2006. "Best Practices: Research, Finance, and NGOs in Cairo." *American Ethnologist* 33(3): 413–26.

Finnan, Daniel. 2014. "M-Pesa Mobile Money Brings African Technology to Europe." Radio France International, 18 July. Retrieved 1 June 2016 from http://en.rfi.fr/africa/20140818-m-pesa-mobile-money-brings-african-technology-europe-skys-limit-says-founder.

Glick-Schiller, Nina, and Georges Fouron. 2001. *Georges Woke Up Laughing: Long Distance Nationalism and the Search for Home.* Durham, NC: Duke University Press.

Graeber, David. 2001. *Toward an Anthropological Theory of Value: The False Coin of Our Dreams.* Basingstoke: Palgrave Macmillan.

Guérin, Isabelle, Solène Morvant-Roux, and Magdalena Villarreal (eds.). 2013. *Microfinance, Debt, and Over-Indebtedness: Juggling with Money.* New York: Routledge.

Guyer, Jane. 1993. "Wealth in People and Self-Realization in Equatorial Africa." *Man* 28(2): 243–65.

———. 1995. "Introduction: The Currency Interface and Its Dynamics." In *Money Matters: Instability, Values, and Social Payments in the Modern History of West African Communities,* 1–34. Portsmouth, NH: Heinemann.

——— (ed.). 1995. *Money Matters: Instability, Values, and Social Payments in the Modern History of West African Communities.* Portsmouth, NH: Heinemann.

———. 2004. *Marginal Gains: Monetary Transactions in Atlantic Africa.* Chicago: University of Chicago Press.

Han, Clara. 2012. *Life in Debt: Times of Care and Violence in Neoliberal Chile.* Berkeley: University of California Press.

Hart, Keith. 1973. "Informal Income Opportunities and Urban Employment in Ghana." *Journal of Modern African Studies* 11(1): 61–89.

———. 1986. "Heads or tails? Two Sides of the Coin." *Man,* pp. 637–656.

———. 2000. *Money in an Unequal World.* New York: Texere.

———, ed. 2015. *Economy for and against Democracy.* New York: Berghahn Books.

Hart, Keith, and Hernando Ortiz. 2014. "The Anthropology of Money and Finance: Between Ethnography and World History." *Annual Review of Anthropology* 43: 465–82.

Hart, Keith, and John Sharp, eds. 2015. *People, Money, and Power in the Economic Crisis: Perspectives from the Global South*. New York: Berghahn Books.

Hertz, E., 1998. *The Trading Crowd: An Ethnography of the Shanghai Stock Market*. Cambridge, UK: Cambridge University Press.

Ho, Karen Zouwen. 2009. *Liquidated: An Ethnography of Wall Street*. Durham, NC: Duke University Press.

Holmes, Douglas R.. 2013. *Economy of Words: Communicative Imperatives in Central Banks*. Chicago: University of Chicago Press.

Holmes, Douglas R., and George E. Marcus. 2008. "Cultures of Expertise and the Management of Globalization: Toward the Re-Functioning of Ethnography." In *Global Assemblages: Technology, Politics, and Ethics as Anthropological Problems*, edited by Aiwha Ong and Stephen J. Collier, 235–52. Oxford: Blackwell.

IMTFI. 2010. Design Principles. Retrieved 15 August 2017 from http://www.imtfi.uci.edu/files/imtfi/docs/2013/imtfi_dps_2010.pdf.

Kendall, Jake, Bill Maurer, Phillip Machoka, and Clara Veniard. 2012. "An Emerging Platform: From Mobile Money Transfer to Mobile Money Ecosystem." *Innovations: Technology, Governance, Globalization* 6(4): 49–64.

Kjellberg, Hans, and Alexandre Mallard. 2013. "Valuation Studies? Our Collective Two Cents." *Valuation Studies* 1(1): 11–30.

Kwon, June Hee. 2015. "The Work of Waiting: Love and Money in Korean Chinese Transnational Migration." *Cultural Anthropology* 30(3): 477–500.

Langley, Paul. 2013. "Introduction: Consuming Credit." *Consumption Markets and Culture* 17(5): 417–28.

Levitt, Peggy. 2001. *The Transnational Villagers*. Berkeley: University of California Press.

Mackenzie, Donald. 2008. *An Engine, Not a Camera: How Financial Models Shape Markets*. Cambridge, MA: The MIT Press.

Mas, Ignacio, and Olga Morawczynski. 2009. "Designing Mobile Money Services: Lessons from M-PESA." *Innovations: Technology, Governance, Globalization* 4(2): 77–91.

Maurer, Bill. 2005. *Mutual Life Limited: Islamic Banking, Alternative Currencies, Lateral Reason*. Princeton, NJ: Princeton University Press.

———. 2006. "The Anthropology of Money." *Annual Review of Anthropology* 35: 15–36.

———. 2007. "Incalculable Payments: Money, Scale, and the South African Offshore Grey Money Amnesty." *African Studies Review* 50(2): 125–38.

———. 2015a. "Money Talks." *Aeon*. Retrieved 2 September 2017 from https://aeon.co/essays/how-money-evolved-from-shells-and-coins-to-apps-and-bitcoin.

———. 2015b. "Data-Mining for Development? Poverty, Payment, and Platform." In *Territories of Poverty: Rethinking North and South*, edited by Ananya Roy and Emma Shaw Crane. Athens: University of Georgia Press.

Maurer, Bill, and Scott D. Mainwaring. 2012. "Anthropology with Business: Plural Programs and Future Financial Worlds." *Journal of Business Anthropology*. 1(2): 177–196.

Maurer, Bill, Taylor Nelms, and Stephen C. Rea. 2013. "'Bridges to Cash': Channeling Agency in Mobile Money." *Journal of the Royal Anthropological Institute* 19(1): 52–74.

Maurer, Bill, et al. 2013. *Warning Signs/Ways Forward: Digital Payment Client Uptake.* Irvine, CA: Institute for Money, Technology & Financial Inclusion.

McFall, Elizabeth Rose. 2014. *Devising Consumption: Cultural Economies of Insurance, Credit and Spending.* New York: Routledge, Taylor & Francis Group.

Müller, Lucia. 2014. "Negotiating Debts and Gifts: Financialization Policies and the Economic Experiences of Low-Income Social Groups in Brazil." *Vibrant: Virtual Brazilian Anthropology* 11(1): 191–221.

Munn, Nancy D. 1986. *The Fame of Gawa: A Symbolic Study of Value Transformation in a Massim (Papua New Guinea) Society.* Durham, NC: Duke University Press.

Musaraj, Smoki. 2011. "Tales from Albarado: The Materiality of Pyramid Schemes in Postsocialist Albania." *Cultural Anthropology* 26(1): 84–110.

Omwansa, Tonny K., and Nicholas P. Sullivan. 2012. *Money, Real Quick: The Story of M-PESA.* Croydon, UK: Balloon View Ltd.

Paerregaard, Karsten. *Return to Sender: the Moral Economy of Peru's Migrant Remittances.* Berkeley: University of California Press, 2015.

Parry, Jonathan, and Maurice Bloch, eds. 1989. *Money and the Morality of Exchange.* Cambridge: Cambridge University Press.

Pedersen, David. 2013. *American Value: Migrants, Money, and Meaning in El Salvador and the United States.* Chicago: University of Chicago Press.

Polanyi, Karl. 1944. *The Great Transformation: The Political and Economic Origins of Our Time.* Boston, MA: Beacon Press.

Poon, Martha. 2009. "From New Deal Institutions to Capital Markets: Commercial Consumer Risk Scores and the Making of Subprime Mortgage Finance." *Accounting, Organizations and Society* 34(5) (July): 654–74.

Ratha, Dilip. 2006. *Economic Implications of Remittances and Migration.* Washington, DC: World Bank.

Riles, Annelise. 2013. "Market Collaboration: Finance, Culture, and Ethnography after Neoliberalism." *American Anthropologist* 115(4): 555–69.

Roitman, Janet. 1990. "The Politics of Informal Markets in Sub-Saharan Africa." *Journal of Modern African Studies* 28 (4): 671–96.

———. 2003. "Unsanctioned Wealth: Or, The Productivity of Debt in Northern Cameroon." *Public Culture* 15(2): 211–37.

———. 2005. *Fiscal Disobedience: An Anthropology of Economic Regulation in Central Africa.* Princeton, NJ: Princeton University Press.

Roy, Ananya. 2010. *Poverty Capital: Microfinance and the Making of Development.* New York: Routledge.

Roy, Ananya, and Emma Shaw Crane (eds.). 2015. *Territories of Poverty: Rethinking North and South.* Athens: University of Georgia Press.

Rutherford, Stuart. 2000. *The Poor and Their Money.* New Delhi: Oxford University Press.

Sachs, Jeffrey. 2005. *The End of Poverty: Economic Possibilities for Our Time.* New York: Penguin Press.

Schwittay, Anke F. 2011. "The Financial Inclusion Assemblage: Subjects, Technics, Rationalities." *Critique of Anthropology* 31(4): 381-401.

Seltzer, Yanina, and Claudia McKay. 2014. "What Human-Centered Design Means for Financial Inclusion." Washington, DC: CGAP. Retrieved 17 August 20017 from   http://www.cgap.org/publications/what-human-centered-design-means-financial-inclusion.

Shadbolt, Peter. 2015. "Africa's Mobile Money Makes Its Way to Europe with MPesa." CNN. 5 January. Retrieved 1 June 2016 from http://edition.cnn.com/2014/11/20/tech/mobile/tomorrow-transformed-m-pesa-mobile-payments/.

Shipton, Parker. 2007. *The Nature of Entrustment: Intimacy, Exchange, and the Sacred in Africa.* New Haven, CT: Yale University Press.

———. 2009. *Mortgaging the Ancestors: Ideologies of Attachment in Africa.* New Haven, CT: Yale University Press.

Small, Ivan. 2012. "Over There: Imaginative Displacements in Vietnamese Remittance Gift Economies." *Journal of Vietnamese Studies* 7(3): 157–83.

Tonkinwise, Cameron. 2011. "A Taste for Practices: Unrepressing Style in Design Thinking." *Design Studies* 32(6): 533–45.

Truitt, Allison J. 2013. *Dreaming of Money in Ho Chi Minh City.* Seattle: University of Washington Press.

Weiner, Annette. 1992. *Inalienable Possessions: The Paradox of Keeping-While-Giving.* Berkeley: University of California Press.

Wilkis, Ariel. 2014. "Sociología del Crédito y Economía de las Clases Populares." *Revista Mexicana de Sociología* 76(2): 225–52.

Zaloom, Caitlin. 2006. *Out of the Pits: Traders and Technology from Chicago to London.* Chicago: University of Chicago Press.

———. 2009. "How to Read the Future: The Yield Curve, Affect, and Financial Prediction." *Public Culture* 21(2): 245–68.

Zelizer, Viviana. 1997. *The Social Meaning of Money: Pin Money, Paychecks, Poor Relief, and Other Currencies.* Princeton, NJ: Princeton University Press.

Part I

In/Exclusion
The Question of Inclusion

ANANYA ROY

Recently, I have found myself in a recurring debate with scholars and activists I admire greatly. As my research and scholarship increasingly focuses on the politics of inclusion, they insist that we pay attention to the entrenched and expanding contours of exclusion. As I trot out examples of various discourses and programs of inclusion – from financial inclusion to paradigms of inclusive growth to slum legalization and upgrading – they shake their heads in disagreement and even despair. "The poor are still getting screwed, and all of this is simply the latest fashion in how to dress it all up and make it look pretty," said one of them, a human rights activist, to me the other day. I do not disagree with him. Persistent poverty and growing wealth and income inequality, along with vast disparities of political power between the rich and the poor, are defining features of our present historical conjuncture. How can anyone argue against the simple and seemingly incontrovertible fact that the poor keep getting screwed?

But my interest in the politics of inclusion, manifest in my previous work on microfinance or my current work on the efforts in India to craft something akin to an urban welfare state, is not a naïve neglect of exploitation and dispossession but rather an attempt to formulate a nuanced understanding of *how* such exploitation and dispossession actually takes place, and most of all how they continue despite the devastations they usually wreak. I am also interested in the discourses and programs of inclusion because they tell us something important about the complex role of the state in governing and managing poverty and inequality. That role is too often reduced, in our critical theoretical formulations, to the handmaiden of neoliberalism. But there are many aspects of the state that such formulations ignore, notably the ongoing reinvention of the developmental state in several countries of the Global South. Financial inclusion is a key part of this renewal of development, and, in turn, the deployment of information technologies is a key part of financial inclusion. This book, with its meticulous attention to how the "unbanked" come to be included and integrated into programs of development and governance, is timely. In particular, it broaches the important question of how we study discourses and programs of financial inclusion while being attentive to the transnational geographies of global capital and the enclosures enacted by technological innovation. To this end, I suggest that we carefully consider the analytical device suggested by Taylor and Horst in their essay on financial inclusion and exclusion at the Haiti–Dominican Republic border – that of the "living fence." For them the living fence is a "metaphor," one that allows us to "interrogate and move beyond the inclusion-exclusion binary." I think this is immensely useful. As analytical tool and metaphor, the living fence allows us to understand the brutality, even violence, of enforced borders, as well as the negotiations and contestations that unfold in how these borders are lived through ordinary practices of ordinary people. As the authors note, it gets us out of the bind of having to prove exclusion or justify inclusion.

To pay attention to the "living" in the "living fence," it is necessary to consider the methodologies through which financial inclusion, associated technologies, and everyday practices are studied. The editors of this book advocate "a distinctively ethnographic approach," calling this "an anthropology of low finance." This is an important and compelling research agenda, and the various chapters in this book, especially in this part on "In/Exclusion," demonstrate its contributions. Writing against stereotypes of the financial practices of refugees, Omeje and Githigaro foreground how Somalian refugees mobilize diasporic capital to create business communities in Nairobi. This is not a story of the inherent entrepreneurial capacity of Somalian refugees but rather a historicized analysis of local and transnational kinship networks and (re)emergent cooperative forms of financial lending and pooling.

In relation to an anthropology of low finance and the metaphor of the living fence, I want to pose two questions. The first concerns the organization and institutionalization of financial inclusion. By this I mean the proliferation of programs and platforms of inclusion, some initiated as state policy, others as nongovernmental, even profit-making, endeavors. What is the relationship between these norms and rules (the word "structure" could be used here but perhaps would overemphasize a structuralist understanding of these processes) and everyday practices of low finance? I see this to be one of the main issues at stake in the essay by

Niiti and Mutinda on "vulnerable populations" in Kenya. This term signals a category, one produced through the norms and rules of governing. As their work demonstrates, governing is not only financial inclusion or poverty reduction but also the special concessions made for specially designated "vulnerable populations." Put another way, the question of inclusion necessarily raises the question of how vulnerability, disability, and disadvantage mark and categorize social difference and how such social difference is managed and governed. My second question has to do with the relationship between low finance and high finance. My own interest in financial inclusion lies in how it is implicated in what I like to call "bottom billion capitalism," the diverse efforts to integrate the world's bottom billion – the billion or so people living under conditions of extreme poverty – into new global markets. For example, many of the financial practices made visible in this part, from remittances to ROSCAs (rotating savings and credit associations), are also those that are seen to generate forms of value that can be monetized and capitalized. I thus end with the self-description provided by NextBillion.net, a website and blog dedicated to "development through enterprise": "We chose Next Billion for its dual meaning: on the one hand, the phrase represents the next billion people to rise into the middle class from the base of the economic pyramid (BoP); on the other, it indicates the next billion(s) in profits for businesses that fill market gaps by integrating the BoP into formal economies" (http://www.nextbillion.net/About.aspx). Here then, in a pithy sentence, is the politics of inclusion. As the living fence is a metaphor, so is "next billion" – for the aspirations of a global economy premised on inclusive growth, for a vision of capitalism in which socioeconomic mobility and expanding profits exist in harmony. This too demands of us ethnographic scrutiny.

Ananya Roy is professor of urban planning, social welfare and geography and inaugural director of the Institute on Inequality and Democracy at UCLA Luskin. Previously she was on the faculty at the University of California, Berkeley. She is the author of Poverty Capital: Microfinance and the Making of Development (Routledge 2010) for which she received the Davidoff Book Award of the Association of Collegiate Schools of Planning. Her most recent book is Encountering Poverty: Thinking and Acting in an Unequal World (University of California Press, 2016).

CHAPTER 1

 # A Living Fence
Financial Inclusion and Exclusion
on the Haiti–Dominican Republic Border

ERIN B. TAYLOR AND HEATHER A. HORST

Introduction

Financial inclusion is often understood to be about choice. The logic of "banking the unbanked" and providing access to services such as mobile money and microfinance is that access to a greater range of products allows poor but rational consumers to choose products that best fit their needs, lowering monetary and transaction costs and relieving the stress of meeting everyday needs. A design or cultural logic might also suggest that when products – even financial ones – are put in the hands of human beings, they take on heightened symbolic meanings. Yet, studies by social scientists have demonstrated that most people already have a significant degree of financial choice, even when formal financial products are not available (James 2014; Stoll 2012). As the financial diary studies in India and South Africa demonstrated conclusively, poor people have access to a broad range of financial tools for saving, borrowing, lending, investing, and insuring (Collins et al. 2009). Moreover, these are often socially embedded in local communities and family networks. What, then, does formalization of financial services offer to those who have already been navigating a diverse (if unbanked) financial landscape?

The introduction to this book suggests a way to address these kinds of very real questions from the perspective of the poor. It is not formalization per se that provides greater choice, but rather, as Musaraj and Small suggest, that the technologies and infrastructures upon which formal financial products operate provide possibilities that informal products generally do not. Telecommunications infrastructure permits transactions to take place at a vastly greater speed over large geographic distances than do informal products. Transaction data is disembedded from its local context, "remembered" by computers rather than being kept in the ledgers or memories of transacting parties. Consumers are theoretically freed from the material constraints entailed in cash and paper records.

And yet, the newly "banked" (or mobile moneyed, etc.) tend to continue to use informal products. As Musaraj and Small note, the division between formal and informal financial tools is a false one when viewed from the perspective of consumers. Rather than switch completely from old to new when they gain access to formal services, people often choose from among the entire array at their disposal. Formal financial services offer some superior features, but they do not replace informal services completely. In some cases, this is due to the fact that other aspects of people's lives transgress the formal/informal divide: people may, for example, be unevenly incorporated into state apparatuses, lacking identity documents for instance, or they may operate primarily in a localized informal economy and have little need for long-distance transactions.

Straddling a formal/informal divide becomes all the more complex when consumers live and work across a national border. In this chapter we present a case study of two towns on the border of Haiti and the Dominican Republic to illustrate how Haitians negotiate the restrictions and advantages of border crossing for financial inclusion. We use the term "living fence" to describe how the border simultaneously generates sources of insecurity (through state control and economic exclusions) and possibility (through its permeability and differential economies). This chapter includes the perspectives of consumers, employees, and entrepreneurs in order to demonstrate how relationships and technologies mutually shape the economic and social lives of Haitians living on both sides of the border region. The border of Haiti and the Dominican Republic is an example of what Sidney Mintz (1962) called the "living fence." Through this analysis, we problematize notions of inclusion and exclusion through demonstrating the contingent nature of the power relations embedded within the economic and social relations formed across the living fence.

The Living Fence

In what follows, we use the notion of the living fence to analyze how Haitians develop relationships and navigate through the "border" to achieve economic and social mobility, what is sometimes referred to as "inclusion." Mintz described the hedges that demarcate the boundaries of the *lakou* (homestead) in the Haitian countryside as "living fences" that keep out trespassing humans and other animals, provide shade, prevent soil erosion, and are aesthetically pleasing. Their purpose is not only exclusion; they are also decorative, inviting, and often permeable. In key ways, the border region resembles these living fences. At once porous and closed, inclusive and exclusive, the border is far more than a container; it also facilitates productive activities, and it often invites rather than repels visitors. Moreover, the border is constituted as much by the people and objects that cross it daily as by state regulation. Conceptualizing the border region as a living fence enables us to explore how it shapes and reshapes Dominican-Haitian relations, which ebb, flow, and change over time as new financial, technological, and economic opportunities enter the ecology. We focus upon the range of economic activities connected to production and consumption, including the multiple impacts of the two states, residents' use of financial products, local entrepreneurial activities, and employer-patron relations. We problematize notions of inclusion and exclusion through demonstrating the contingent nature of the power relations embedded within the economic and social relations formed across the living fence.

State Construction of the Living Fence between Haiti and the Dominican Republic

In the southwestern corner of the Dominican Republic lies the region of Pedernales. Despite being replete with natural wonders, pristine tropical beaches, and national parks, few tourists ever travel there because of its distance from the country's major cities and the relative lack of transportation infrastructure. With a population of approximately 31,000, the region is the poorest in the country. Economic activities primarily consist of agriculture, fishing, imports, and domestic commerce. The town of Pedernales is home to half of the region's total population. It is hardly a booming economy, but is it not desperately poor either. It boasts all the features one would expect in a small regional capital, including schools, a hospital, restaurants, hotels, and NGOs. It even has its own virtually constant electricity supply – a rarity in the Dominican Republic, where rolling blackouts are common. The relative affluence of Pedernales is due to its economic diversification. Apart from being a major center for agricultural trade, Pedernales houses one of the region's ports, a cement factory, and a factory that sorts secondhand clothing. Its location on the border with Haiti affords it a special economic function as a major hub on a trade route that connects Santo Domingo with Port-au-Prince via the island's southern towns: Barahona and Pedernales on the Dominican side; Anse-à-Pitres, Marigot, and Jacmel on the Haitian side.

Haitians living in Pedernales and Anse-à-Pitres depend upon access to Dominican markets to undertake economic activities as producers, distributors, and consumers, since Anse-à-Pitres lacks the diverse economic activities and large enterprises of Pedernales. Residents of Anse-à-Pitres walk to Pedernales daily to work, sell, shop, or use services that are not available on the Haitian side of the border. These include accessing some health and education services as well as the internet, bill paying, sending or receiving remittances, buying phone credit, and traveling further afield. These are not merely conveniences: residents suffer economic and social hardship when it is not possible to cross the border. Unless there are exceptional circumstances, the border crossing is open every day from eight o'clock in the morning until five o'clock in the afternoon. No identification is necessary: crossing is simply a matter of walking over the footbridge spanning the river between the two countries. As a result of this porosity, life is administratively, economically, and socially intertwined across the border, and it has been so for at least a century. In fact, from an economic perspective, the border is important to both nations. The *Dominican Today* (2013) reports that annual trade across the entire border amounts to approximately US$1.1 billion in formal transactions and US$900 million in informal transactions.

The importance of mobility to the Haitian economy is reflected in a common Kreyol proverb, "Marche cherche pa jamn domi sans soupe" (one who goes looking doesn't sleep without eating). On an island where tropical storms seasonally hamper efforts at mobility, making unbridged rivers unpassable, looking for livelihood can pose significant challenges. And yet, the proverb suggests that those who seek out livelihood will always find it. Like other countries in the Caribbean, migration has been a pervasive feature of social life, with migration for education, work, and "travel" (Duany 2011; Olwig 2012) becoming a rite of passage for many in the region (Pessar 1999). Within this context, families are often distributed across borders, with children sent or left to live with aunties and grandmothers while parents work to support them (Olwig 2013; Grasmuck and Pessar 1991). Haitians, in particular, have engaged in migration for economic and political reasons, moving for work, education, and to escape political persecution (Bartlett 2012; Schiller and Fouron 2001; Jackson 2011; Martin et al. 2002; Orozco and Burgess 2011; Richman 2005). As such, migration is a structural fact for many Haitians in the region, with remittances accounting for an estimated US$1.9 billion, or around 24 percent of the country's GDP in 2012 (Maldonado and Hayem 2013).

While in recent years the stress has been on transnational migration to the United States, Canada, Europe, and nearby countries in the region (Schiller and Fouron 2001; Richman 2005; Jackson 2011; Pessar 1995, 1997), mobility across the national border between the Dominican Republic and Haiti has long been a part of Haitian efforts to seek livelihood. This is due, in part, to its relative accessibility as a migration destination; migrants do not have to source the costs of airplane flights or risk a boat trip across the Caribbean Sea. As far back as the nineteenth century, Haitian labor has supplied *bateyes* (sugar plantations) in the Dominican Republic, particularly in the far east of the island (Ferguson 2003; Martínez 1995). More recently, Haitians have taken advantage of urban economic growth to work in construction, domestic service, and marketing in the major cities (Martínez 1999) or to engage in trade (Taylor 2014a). This migration eastward reflects the greater poverty of Haiti, where 80 percent of people live below the poverty line and 1 percent of the richest Haitians own half of the country's wealth (CIA World Factbook 2013). The poorest country in the Americas, with a nominal GDP (PPP) of US$1,164, Haiti depends heavily on international aid and remittances to prop up a fragile, agriculture-based economy. Bank branches are concentrated in major cities, making them difficult to access for the 48 percent of Haitians who live outside rural areas (CIA World Factbook 2013).[1]

In contrast, the Dominican Republic has a nominal GDP per capita of US$9,922, and 34.4 percent of its population lives below the poverty line. It is the second largest economy in Central America and the Caribbean, with a well-developed tourism industry and a significant degree of domestic production. Although still poor, its greater wealth means that the vast majority of migration flows from Haiti to the Dominican Republic, not the other way around. In fact, many residents of Pedernales told us that they rarely visit Anse-à-Pitres, despite the fact that it is so close by. Some had not crossed the border since they were children, and others had never entered Haiti at all. The vast majority of traffic across the border consists of Haitians entering the Dominican Republic to access markets, work, or visit relatives who have settled there.

Many border residents have family scattered throughout both sides of the island. It is relatively common for familial networks to span Hispaniola from Port-au-Prince to Jacmel in Haiti's south, through Anse-à-Pitres and Pedernales, and on to Santo Domingo and Higuey in the east of the Dominican Republic. These networks trace the primary paths upon which people, merchandise, and money circulate. The border region, through unifying a small part of each nation, assists in circulation along these routes through expanding access to means of mobility, improving communication, and reducing costs. As we have argued elsewhere, "while one of the primary functions of national borders is to arrest mobility, *border regions* promote mobility because they provide opportunities for economic and social arbitrage" (Horst and Taylor 2014).

However, the prevalence of mobility and circulation should not be overestimated. The situation of Haitian migrants in the Dominican Republic has always been precarious, irrespective of their legal status. *Anti-haitianismo* (anti-Haitianism) in the border region and beyond, and the Dominican state's role in promulgating it, has been well documented by historians, anthropologists, and nonprofit organizations (see Augelli 1980; Derby 1994, 2009; Gregory 2007; Human Rights Watch 2002; Turits 2002). Deportations occur frequently and without notice, including instances of children born in the Dominican Republic to Haitian parents.

In fact, living and working in the Dominican Republic is becoming increasingly difficult. In 2010, the Dominican constitution was altered to refuse citizenship to children born in the Dominican Republic to "transient" parents, meaning that the children born to parents who did not have a Dominican visa at the time of their child's birth are no longer considered to be citizens (United Nations 2013). A recent ruling by the Constitutional Court has authorized the Dominican government to review records dating back to 1929. This means that up to 200,000 other Dominicans of Haitian descent may be stripped of their citizenship and left stateless (Gonzalez 2013). This practice reflects the long history of *antihaitianismo* in the Dominican Republic (Grasmuck and Espinal 2000). For Haitian migrants, the Dominican Republic is therefore simultaneously an important source of economic growth and a constant source of insecurity.

Haitian descendants living in the border region are also subject to the High Court's ruling. For example, Fredelina lives in Aguas Negras, a small town on the Dominican side of the border. She is a single mother with three children who makes a living through selling beans in the Pedernales market and sweets around her town. She lives rent free in a vacated house, and she receives a small monthly remittance from her boyfriend, who lives and works in the east of the Dominican Republic. Fredelina and her children were all born in the Dominican Republic, but none of them have the right to apply for Dominican citizenship. So long as she stays in Aguas Negras, her life is unlikely to change significantly, but if her children wish to live in other parts of the Dominican Republic they will have to travel as illegal immigrants.

The primary reason why Fredelina's life would not be much affected if she remains in the border region is because of the flexibility with which state rules are enacted there. On either side of the border, passage is open for the most part, so long as the people crossing do not try to go far beyond the towns on either side. For example, a Dominican can cross at Anse-à-Pitres and spend a day in the Haitian town or nearby areas, but if they wish to stay any longer or travel any further, they are expected to obtain a visa from the Haitian consulate in Santo Domingo. Equally, Haitians can cross into Pedernales, and in many cases reside there permanently, but if they want to travel further afield, they need to either possess a visa or enough money to pay bribes of approximately 4,000 pesos (US$93) to reach Santo Domingo. In a certain sense, then, the further one travels away from the border, the harder it is to cross it.

Some of the most important ways in which features of the state affect the economic and financial status of Haitians have nothing to do with the actual border or with surveillance beyond it. These are also crucial to the ability of Fredelina and her children to live in Aguas Negras. Curiously, one important possession that Fredelina has is her Haitian identity card, which she was able to obtain despite the fact that she was not born in Haiti and is not a resident there. Without this card, Fredelina would need a third party to receive her Western Union remittances from her boyfriend, who lives three hundred miles away in the east of the Dominican Republic. The most important services provided by the Dominican state are healthcare and education, which are universally accessible up to certain limits. Fredelina can use Dominican hospitals and clinics at little to no cost, and she has given birth to all of her children in the Pedernales hospital. Her children have the right to attend Dominican primary and secondary schools, but they are unlikely to be able to attend a Dominican university. Without Dominican documents, their only option is to obtain a student visa and pay full fees. They may be able to enroll in a university in Port-au-Prince, but even there they face a range of economic, administrative, and linguistic barriers. For this family, the living fence in some ways resembles a cage: there is room for movement, but the legal boundaries are firmly delimited by one's ability to pay.

Financial Products and the Question of Economic Inclusion

Given the centrality of money in the experience of mobility, to what extent can a new generation of financial products mitigate different kinds of exclusions? Since the Grameen Bank launched microcredit in the 1970s, microfinance has grown to be a significant part of initiatives for socioeconomic development. The logic of microfinance is that financial inclusion can assist in the alleviation of poverty through the provision of inexpensive financial products that provide security and access to capital. Distance from bank branches, exorbitant fees, and illiteracy number among the factors limiting access to formal banking facilities. Instead, people rely on informal financial services, which can be expensive, time-consuming to use, and slow to complete transactions. This puts the unbanked at a disadvantage relative to people who do have access to formal banking, as it extracts from productive activities and leisure time and reduces consumers' options with respect to market interaction. However, while access to formal financial services certainly bestows many benefits, it is difficult to prove that these services actually alleviate poverty (Roodman 2012).

From this point of view, financial products are similar to other networking technologies, such as mobile phones. Both formal financial services and mobile phones are useful – perhaps essential – but not "silver bullets" that solve all problems of access or inclusion (see Burrell 2010; Roodman 2012; Singh 2009; Srinivasan and Burrell 2012; Taylor 2015; Taylor and Horst forthcoming). Furthermore, some researchers suggest that the people most likely to benefit from microfinance are those who have access to money in the first place (Morawczynski 2009; Morawczynski et al. 2010). A similar line of reasoning has also been argued for mobile phones. Horst and Miller (2006) have noted that the people most likely to benefit from the social networking capacity of mobile phones are those who already have well-developed networks. Whether we are discussing finance or communication, "inclusion" does not necessarily mean that social structures are broken down and the playing field leveled. Even as "inclusion" is democratized, inequality may increase because doing so provides a means for people who were already ahead of their peers to make further gains, leaving those on the bottom rung of the ladder further behind.

National borders can be particularly interesting places to observe the effects of financial services because they enable direct observation of how national differences are negotiated. Financial worlds on the border of the Dominican Republic and Haiti are complex because they bring together two different financial systems and currencies (Baptiste et al. 2010). This essentially doubles the kinds of financial products available, giving Haitians who live in the border region an advantage over Haitians living elsewhere. Financial services located in Anse-à-Pitres include Fonkoze (a microcredit institution), Western Union, and a mobile-money service (Digicel TchoTcho). Pedernales has a greater range of classic formal financial services, boasting a major national bank, a cooperative bank, Western Union, and Caribe Express. On both sides of the border, we can see that mobile phones and financial products influence the ways in which people behave and interact.

As will be described later, the main formal financial products used by Haitians living in the border region tend to be the remittance services offered on both sides of the border. On the Dominican side, money circulates between Haitians and their family living in different parts of the country. The reasons why people send money are various, and the circulation occurs in multiple directions. For instance, Fredelina received money regularly from her boyfriend in the east of the Dominican Republic. In another case, a Haitian woman living on the border sent money regularly to her children who were studying at university in Santo Domingo (see also Miner 2013).

Another one of our interviewees, Monica, had been living in a town close to Santo Domingo with her mother and her young son, but her mother would not let her work. She relocated to Anse-à-Pitres, leaving her son behind, to see if she could make a living as a Madame Sara (female Haitian vendor), selling clothes, shoes, and accessories in the binational market on the border. Her plan was to build up her business and send money to her mother for the care of her son. Monica's case diverges from what we normally think of as standard migration routes: although she had originally migrated to the Dominican Republic, she moved back to Haiti to take advantage of Dominican markets and send money eastward.

Haitians' use of transfer services in Pedernales is not without problems. Some of the Haitians we interviewed in 2010 told us that they were deeply dissatisfied with the need to use services across the border in the Dominican Republic. They claimed that they were subject to racist treatment in the Western Union office in Pedernales. Language barriers, long waiting times, and the high cost of the service were also singled out as deterrents to use. At the time of research, the Pedernales branch did not use a computer-based system, relying instead on slower phone transfers. In addition, many individuals needed to send money in US dollars from the Dominican Republic to Haiti, which increases the transaction costs. A number of residents told us that they preferred to use Caribe Express, which is also located in Pedernales but is much more "Haitian friendly." Participants told us that the benefits of Caribe Express over Western Union reflected the fact that many members of staff speak at least some Creole (or at least make an effort to communicate) and are friendlier to Haitians. In addition, there are lower costs for transactions, which are also faster. During our research, however, a Western Union office opened in Anse-à-Pitres, making many of these problems redundant.

On the Haitian side of the border, remittance routes are heavily shaped by patterns of migration and trade. Our research suggests that more than half of the residents of Anse-à-Pitres were born in a different town in the south and southeast regions of Haiti. Most residents have family still living in those towns, and children who are in school may live with relatives rather than with their parents. Since the launch of mobile money in Haiti, the process of sending money has become less expensive and faster for families whose senders and receivers both have access to a mobile-money agent (Taylor et al. 2011). Digicel TchoTcho, a Haiti-wide mobile-money service, became available on the border in February 2012. In another reversal of the stereotype of remitters, one young man we knew signed up for mobile money so that a cousin of his, who lives fifty miles away in Jacmel, Haiti, could send him money to pay her Sky television bill. It is a Dominican service and needs to be paid in Pedernales. In this case, her financial inclusion was not as a person attempting to escape poverty but as a consumer whose payments were made more efficient through this new technology. Previously, she had sent the money for free via a fleet of fishing boats that travel twice a week (on Mondays and Fridays, which are market days on the border) from Marigot (near Jacmel) to Anse-à-Pitres. The boats carry people, goods, and money, and the trip takes seven hours overnight.

Despite the infrequency and slowness of this boat service, we found few people who had signed up for mobile money by the time we left the border in May 2012. Given the virtually absolute absence of any mobile-money advertising or branding, it is not surprising that people were not using it. In fact, few people had even heard of it. It appears that, even in small towns, news does not necessarily travel that fast by word of mouth. This point is crucial when it comes to thinking about how to actively stimulate "inclusion": mobile money is a consumer good like any other, and ordinary market mechanisms for encouraging uptake can be usefully deployed to inform consumers about new choices.

Some residents use informal services in conjunction with electronic ones, suggesting that reasons for using informal services may not simply be lack of access to formal ones. For example, David has been a resident of Anse-à-Pitres since 2002. He has family in Port-au-Prince, Santo Domingo, and the United States. Because he works for the United Nations base in Anse-à-Pitres as a translator, he has an account with Scotiabank in Jacmel. He can use his Visa card to withdraw money "from any ATM around the world," but he uses the local boat service to send money to his children who are studying in Jacmel. He sends 500 gourdes (approximately US$8) once a month to pay for their daily living expenses, plus extra money at the beginning of the school semester for fees and uniforms. The boat service may be slow, but David is not in any particular rush. Learning to use mobile money, and teaching his family how to use it, would present economic and transaction costs.

What does access to this range of financial products tell us about economic inclusion? A variety of financial products are likely to increase the probability that consumers will find one that is shaped to their needs. On the border, greater options give consumers greater choice and flexibility, but other issues negatively impact their use, such as lack of access to cash and unpleasant experiences using financial services. It is clear that financial worlds are shaped by far more than consumer access to financial products. Indeed, Haitians' experiences as producers also shape their ability to take advantage of the social, economic, and financial diversity that the living fence offers.

Client-Patron Relations, Dependence, and Mobility

The ability of the border region, as a living fence, to simultaneously provide productive opportunities and pose restrictions is also observable in relations between Haitians and their employees. Because Haitians will work for far lower wages than Dominicans, they dominate the labor force in agriculture, construction, and domestic service. For example, a Haitian construction worker in Pedernales, Dominican Republic, earns around 5,000 to 8,000 pesos (US$105–170) per month, compared to 8,000 to 12,000 (US$170–254) for a Dominican. Similarly, whereas a Dominican working as a domestic servant will earn around 5,000 pesos per month, a Haitian will be paid 1,500 to 2,000 pesos (US$31–42).

However, to understand how employer-employee relations affect economic and financial inclusion, we need to investigate well beyond the price of labor. Forms of cooperative relations have existed in both nations for centuries. Apart from literature on cooperative farming, most studies of cooperative relationships in the Dominican Republic have focused on different forms of the patron-client relationships. One example is the Dominican *caudillo,* a strongman who commands the loyalty of his own army (Betances 1995; Wolf 1967). The caudillo system transferred into the national political system, especially manifesting itself during the Trujillo dictatorship, and lives on today in the form of personal promises bestowed by aspiring politicians upon their constituents (see Taylor 2013). Another, socially flatter example is the Dominican system of godparenting, in which *padrinos* and *madrinas* are expected to contribute to the upbringing of children, including, in many cases, paying their university tuition. Conversely, Haitian literature on patron-client relationships has generally emphasized their role in politics (Laguerre 1989; Nicholls 1996), and there is a vast amount of information on more horizontal relationships such as *pratik* (between clients and traders), the *kombit* (working group), and the *lakou* (household) (Edmond 2007; Mintz 1961; Pierre 2009; Smith 2001).

On the Dominican-Haitian border, patron-client relationships are visible in the productive relationships between sellers and customers and between employers and employees. Whether patron-client relationships between Haitians and Dominicans are essentially between equals or whether there is a power differential depends in large part upon access to economic resources. Wage laborers in particular may be dependent upon their patron for their basic needs, and the shortfall of what they require to survive on a day-to-day basis may be paid or donated in the form of material possessions or food rather than cash. These donations might take the form of boarding in the employer's home, giving employees old or unwanted clothes or other items, paying for employees' children's education, or buying them gifts at Christmas. Employers also may offer loans or direct gifts of cash and items such as mobile phones. Because employer-employee relations tend to incorporate sentiments of friendship, power differentials can become hidden. As with microfinance and mobile phones, inclusion does not necessarily generate greater inequality: in fact, the social affection of patron-client relations can obfuscate power differentials.

The most striking case of employer-employee patronage we found concerned a woman called Variola. Variola, now in her thirties, is from Thiotte, a town located in Haiti, approximately forty minutes' drive up the mountain from Anse-à-Pitres. When she was eleven years old, Variola's father had a stomach illness. She wanted to make money to help pay for his healthcare, so she ran away from home with a thirteen-year-old friend. The two girls spent an entire day walking down the mountain to Anse-à-Pitres, where they were accepted into the home of the older girl's aunt. After a few months, Variola found work and residence in the home of a Dominican woman in Pedernales. This woman – we'll call her Maria – taught Variola to clean and, when she was old enough, to cook as well. Their relationship became so strongly cemented that neighbors refer to Variola as "Maria's daughter."

Variola is now an adult and lives across the border in Anse-à-Pitres with her husband and their four children, but she continues to work for Maria six days per week, earning a monthly salary of 2000 pesos (US$46), just

40 percent of what a Dominican would earn for the same job. Variola's husband had a serious motorbike accident a few years ago and cannot work, leaving Variola as the only breadwinner. However, despite the fact that she does not earn enough to support her family, she does not want to ask for a raise because "Maria gives me everything, I am ashamed to ask her for more." Every day Variola takes food home for her children, and Maria buys her many of the things she needs, including her children's clothes at Christmas time. Not long before our interview, Maria bought her a Dominican mobile phone so that Variola can call Maria if she cannot come to work. Variola told us that if she doesn't have money for food and asks her boss for 200 pesos, her boss will give her 500 pesos and not expect it to be repaid. Variola asked Maria to pay her wages every Saturday, rather than in the usual monthly installments, so that she can manage her money better. Maria agreed. On Mondays Variola shops for food in the border market because it is less expensive than the local supermarkets, and it is possible to purchase small quantities.

Variola's life consists of going to work in Pedernales, going home and looking after her children, and attending church on Sunday mornings. She has only ever left the border region once. A couple of years ago, Maria's mother died, and Variola accompanied Maria to Santo Domingo in order to help with the funeral preparation. Variola got to look around Santo Domingo twice: once from the bus window on the way into town, and once from the bus window on the way out. The rest of the time she stayed in the house. She does not have good relations with her neighbors in Anse-à-Pitres, telling us that some of them despise her for deigning to sell her labor across the border as a domestic servant. They remarked to her that she was forced to "wash the panties of Dominicans" because she "didn't know how to do anything else." This is an insult given the taboos associated with washing and handling undergarments due to their close association with menstruation and the female body in the Caribbean (see, for example, Sobo 1993). Variola does have other dreams, and she is contemplating the possibility of leaving her children with relatives in Thiotte in order to migrate to Santo Domingo to work as a domestic servant. There is no reason to doubt Maria's affection for Variola. However, in some ways, Variola's situation is rather like that of a child. Instead of paying a higher wage, Maria decides Variola's consumption choices for her. Maria's approach could certainly be read as a kind of financial inclusion, but it is rather more paternalistic than conducive of financial independence.

Curiously, mobile phones were brought up quite often in our interviews with people about their work (Horst and Taylor 2014). We encountered numerous people who said their employer provided them with their first mobile phone. Not so many years ago, mobile phone handsets were far more expensive than they are now, and if it were not for the gifts or loans of employers, many people would have had to wait a long time to attain one. Even today, not everyone can afford a handset or the cost of communicating. Yet it is very much in the interest of employers for their employees to possess a phone. Indeed, Variola kept just two numbers in her mobile's address book: Maria and a friend. Variola would have liked to be able to call her mother in Thiotte without having to borrow a neighbor's phone, but she could not, because her phone was Dominican. However, Variola also states that she probably would not have thought a phone to be an important enough item on which to spend her meager income of 2000 pesos per month. Indeed, she barely uses the phone other than for work, having neither the need nor sufficient disposable income. In her case, the phone has more utility for her boss than for herself.

Evens, aged twenty-four, is a very different mobile user to Variola and experiences patronage in an entirely different fashion. Evens is a young man who divides his time between Thiotte, where he is enrolled in high school, and Pedernales, where he comes to work periodically. His only form of legal documentation is a Haitian identity card. Unlike Variola, he is highly mobile, and highly connected. More importantly, he has worked in a range of different kinds of employment, including construction, as an electrician's assistant, in a barbershop, and in a hardware store. When he works as an electrician's assistant he earns 6,000 pesos (US$126) in two weeks–six times Variola's salary. As a result, Evens has far more labor mobility than Variola, who has spent her entire life as a domestic servant in one family.

Evens has owned nine mobile phones in his life because he keeps losing them. He bought his first phone in 2007 when Digicel arrived in Haiti. His current Nokia, registered with the company Orange, was a gift from one of his employers, who runs the hardware store where he currently works on Saturdays. Evens lives above the store, and his boss gave him the phone so that he could call Evens if the shop got busy. He doesn't have any names recorded in the phone because the SIM card belongs to his boss. However, he also owns a Haitian SIM card (with Voilá), and a Dominican SIM card (with Claro). In case he also loses these, he records the numbers of all his contacts in a notebook that he carries everywhere with him. Thus while Evens depends upon favors, often work related, to retain phone access, he has found a way to retain ownership over information. In fact, his mobile phone system and the networks it represents are crucial to his maintenance of mobility, as former and new employers will call him to offer him work.

Evens leverages relationships and technologies in such a way that gaining inclusion does not mean giving up freedom. Not tied to any particular employer, he is able to negotiate his working conditions by simply getting up and leaving if they do not suit him. In this he resembles the market women who sell goods on the border and in the streets of Pedernales more than he resembles the many Haitian workers who cross the border daily to sell their labor at very low wages. The Madame Saras and Evens strike a balance between the advantages of productive relations and the independence offered by being able to negotiate one's own price in the market. For Madame Saras, this negotiation centers upon the price of commodities; for Evens, it is the price of his labor.

However, their ability to combine the benefits of market freedom and social interdependence is contingent upon the porosity of the national border. If the border is shut, they cannot pass through to trade or work. Ultimately, then, their livelihoods depend upon one source: the Dominican state. The border has shut down on various occasions, including during the 2010 cholera outbreak (Haiti Libre 2010). In this respect, Haitians face the same limitations irrespective of their dependence upon patronage relations, for the Dominican state is their overarching patron. Haitians with more skills, connections, and mobility, such as Madame Saras and individuals like Evens, are probably far better situated to adapt if the border shuts. However, the greater poverty of Haiti means that there are fewer opportunities available, and competition for positions and customers is far greater. This is why the metaphor of the living fence is so apt for the Dominican-Haitian border region: it excludes and includes in complex ways that are constantly changing. Whether these changes present obstacles or opportunities is a question that is constantly under negotiation.

Conclusion

Throughout this chapter we have sought to highlight the complexities of the financial inclusion discourse through the examination of Haitians living on the border of Haiti and the Dominican Republic. Rather than equating access to mobile phones and financial services as an all-or-nothing proposition—that people are either included or excluded—we have highlighted the ways in which exclusion and inclusion can be understood as a shifting or temporal state of being. For many of our study participants, migrating to a place where there is a larger economy and a need for labor and trade is a far better option. The infrastructures that are built to supplement the changing mobile and financial ecologies clearly provide more opportunities to experience inclusion (see also Horst 2013; Horst, Kailahi, and Singh forthcoming). As finance becomes ever more mobile, however, labor and even trade remain relatively "shackled to space" due to the need to access particular markets in particular places.

In the border zone, the living fence provides more breathing room than in other places in Haiti, but at the end of the day it is not broadly inclusive because there are many people who are not well or reliably positioned to leverage its opportunities. Even the people who are well positioned face hard limits, because their market mobility depends upon the actions of the Dominican state. In effect, the structural conditions of the border region, particularly the role of the Dominican state in controlling resources such as labor and goods, and access to markets and consumers, means that for many Haitians inclusion can only be experienced as temporary and partial. Indeed, the closure of the border every day at 5 PM highlights this in a very concrete and substantive way (Taylor 2014b).

While in many ways this is an unusual example of the tension between social, geographic, and economic exclusion and inclusion, we would like to suggest here that the notion of a living fence, with its porous and shifting boundaries that include and exclude, may be a better metaphor for describing the lived relationships that people have with a range of financial resources, industries, and institutions. At the very least, it suggests that there may be good reasons to interrogate and move beyond the inclusion-exclusion binary that has been so seminal to the early work on mobile money and microfinance.

Acknowledgments

This essay draws on research funded by the Institute for Money, Technology & Financial Inclusion at the University of California, Irvine, USA.

Erin B. Taylor is an economic anthropologist specializing in research into financial behavior. Her research focuses on material culture and financial practices. She is the author of *Materializing Poverty: How the Poor Transform Their Lives* (2013, Altamira), and the editor of *Fieldwork Identities in the Caribbean* (2010, Caribbean Studies Press). Taylor has been conducting research on squatter settlements in the Dominican Republic since 2004, and on mobile phones, mobile money, markets, and migration in Haiti since 2010. She also designed and produced the *Consumer Finance Research Methods Toolkit*.

Heather Horst is professor in the Department of Media in Communications at the University of Sydney, Australia, and an adjunct professor at the Digital Ethnography Research Centre at RMIT University, Australia. Heather's current research explores transformations in the telecommunications industry and the emergence of new mobile media practices across the Asia-Pacific region. Her recent publications examining these themes include *Digital Anthropology* (Berg 2012), *Digital Ethnography: Principles and Practices* (Sage 2016), and *The Moral Economy of Mobile Phones in the Pacific* (forthcoming).

NOTE

1. According to one BBC News report (2010), approximately 15 percent of Haitians have a bank account, a figure that reflects both the size of the informal economy (at least two-thirds of the workforce) and the underdevelopment of financial infrastructure.

REFERENCES CITED

Augelli, John P. 1980. "Nationalization of the Dominican Borderlands." *Geographical Review* 70: 19–35.

Baptiste, Espelencia, Heather A. Horst, and Erin B. Taylor. 2010. "Haitian Monetary Ecologies and Repertoires: A Qualitative Snapshot of Money Transfer and Savings." Institute for Money, Technology & Financial Inclusion (IMTFI). Retrieved 6 February 2014 from http://www.imtfi.uci.edu/imtfi_haiti_money_transfer_project.

Bartlett, Lesley. 2012. "South-South Migration and Education: The Case of People of Haitian Descent Born in the Dominican Republic." *Compare: A Journal of Comparative and International Education* 42(3): 393–414.

Betances, Emilio. 1995. "Social Classes and the Origin of the Modern State: The Dominican Republic, 1844–1930." *Latin American Perspectives* 22(86): 20–40.

"Bill Gates Offers $10m Fund for Mobile Banking in Haiti." 2010. BBC News, 9 June. Retrieved 6 February 2014 from http://www.bbc.com/news/10273158.

Burrell, Jennifer. 2010. "Evaluating Shared Access: Social Equality and the Circulation of Mobile Phones in Rural Uganda." *Journal of Computer-Mediated Communication* 15(2): 230–50.

———. 2012. "Producing the Internet and Development: An Ethnography of Internet Cafe Use in Accra, Ghana." PhD dissertation. London: The London School of Economics and Political Science (LSE).

CIA World Factbook. 2013. Retrieved 1 September 2013 from https://www.cia.gov/library/publications/the-world-factbook/geos/ha.html.

Collins, Daryl, Jonathan Morduch, Stuart Rutherford, and Orlanda Ruthven. 2009. *Portfolios of the Poor: How the World's Poor Live on $2 a Day.* Princeton, NJ: Princeton University Press.

Derby, Lauren. 1994. "Haitians, Magic and Money: Raza and Society in the Haitian-Dominican Borderlands, 1900–1937." *Comparative Studies in Society and History* 36(3): 488–526.

———. 2009. *The Dictator's Seduction: Politics and the Popular Imagination in the Dominican Republic.* Durham, NC: Duke University Press.

Duany, Jorge. 2011. *Blurred Borders: Transnational Migration between the Hispanic Caribbean and the United States.* Chapel Hill: University of North Carolina Press.

Edmond, Yanique M., Suzanne M. Randolph, and Guylaine L. Richard. 2007. "The Lakou System: A Cultural, Ecological Analysis of Mothering in Rural Haiti." *Journal of Pan African Studies* 2(1): 19–32.

Ferguson, James. 2003. *Migration in the Caribbean: Haiti, the Dominican Republic and Beyond.* London: Minority Rights Group International.

Gonzalez, Juan. 2013. "Citizenship of Haitians in Dominican Republic for Decades Threatened by Court Ruling." *NY Daily News.* October 22. Retrieved 6 February 2014 from http://www.nydailynews.com/news/world/gonzalez-citizenship-haitians-threatened-article-1.1493523.

Grasmuck, Sherri, and Patricia R. Pessar. 1991. *Between Two Islands: Dominican International Migration.* Berkeley: University of California Press.

Grasmuck, Sherri, and Rosario Espinal. 2000. "Market Success or Female Autonomy? Income, Ideology, and Empowerment among Microentrepreneurs in the Dominican Republic." *Gender and Society* 14(2): 231–55.

Gregory, Steven. 2007. *The Devil behind the Mirror: Globalization and Politics in the Dominican Republic.* Berkeley: University of California Press.

Haiti Libre. 2010. "Haiti – Cholera Epidemic: Border Closed, Important Dominican Military Device." 27 November. Retrieved 6 February 2014 from http://www.haitilibre.com/en/news-1759-haiti-cholera-epidemic-border-closed-important-dominican-military-device.html.

Horst, Heather A. 2013. "The Infrastructures of Mobile Media: Towards a Future Research Agenda." *Mobile Media & Communication* 1: 147–52.

Horst, Heather A., Sandra Kailahi, and Supriya Singh. Forthcoming. "The Value of Sacrifice: Mobilising Money among Tongans in Auckland." *Transitions.*

Horst, Heather A., and Erin B. Taylor. 2014. "The Role of Mobile Phones in the Mediation of Border Crossings: A Study of Haiti and the Dominican Republic." *Australian Journal of Anthropology (TAJA)* 25(2): 155–70.

Horst, Heather A., and Daniel Miller. 2006. *The Cell Phone: An Anthropology of Communication.* New York: Berg.

Human Rights Watch. 2002. "'Illegal People': Haitians and Dominico-Haitians in the Dominican Republic." 14(1[B]): 1–32. Retrieved 21 March 2014 from https://www.hrw.org/report/2002/04/04/illegal-people/haitians-and-dominico-haitians-dominican-republic.

Jackson, Regine O., ed. 2011. *Geographies of the Haitian Diaspora.* New York: Routledge.

James, Deborah. 2014. *Money from Nothing: Indebtedness and Aspiration in South Africa.* Stanford, CA: Stanford University Press.

Laguerre, Michel S. 1989. *Voodoo and Politics in Haiti.* London: Macmillan.

Maldonado, René, and María Luisa Hayem. 2013. "Remittances to Latin America and the Caribbean in 2012: Differing Behavior across Subregions." Multilateral Investment Fund, Inter-American Development Bank. Washington, DC. Retrieved 21 March 2014 from https://publications.iadb.org/handle/11319/5919?locale-attribute=en.

Martin, Philip, Elizabeth Midgley, and Michael S. Teitelbaum. 2002. "Migration and Development: Whither the Dominican Republic and Haiti?" *International Migration Review* 36(2): 570–92.

Martínez, Samuel. 1995. *Peripheral Migrants: Haitians and Dominican Republic Sugar Plantations.* Knoxville: University of Tennessee Press.

———. 1999. "From Hidden Hand to Heavy Hand: Sugar, the State, and Migrant Labor in Haiti and the Dominican Republic." *Latin American Research Review* 34: 57–84.

Miner, Jenny. 2013. "Migration for Education: Haitian University Students in the Dominican Republic." Pomona Senior Theses. Paper 89. Claremont University. Retrieved 21 March 2014 from http://scholarship.claremont.edu/pomona_theses/89.

Mintz, Sidney. 1961. "Pratik: Haitian Personal Economic Relationships." *Proceedings of the 1961 Annual Spring Meeting of the American Ethnological Society.* Washington, DC: American Anthropological Association.

Mintz, Sidney W. 1962. "Living Fences in the Fond-des-Nègres Region, Haiti." *Economic Botany* 16(2): 101–5.

Morawczynski, Olga. 2009. "Exploring the Usage and Impact of 'Transformational' Mobile Financial Services: The Case of M-PESA in Kenya." *Journal of Eastern African Studies* 3(3): 509–25.

Morawczynski, Olga, David Hutchful, Edward Cutrell, and Nimmi Rangaswamy. 2010. "The Bank Account Is Not Enough: Examining Strategies for Financial Inclusion in India." *ICTD '10 Proceedings of the 4th ACM/IEEE International Conference on Information and Communication Technologies and Development.* New York: ICTD.

Nicholls, David. 1996. *From Dessalines to Duvalier: Race, Colour, and National Independence in Haiti.* New Brunswick, NJ: Rutgers University Press.

Olwig, Karen Fog. 2012. "The Care Chain, Children's Mobility and the Caribbean Migration Tradition." *Journal of Ethnic and Migration Studies* 38(6): 933–52.

———. 2013. "Migration and Care: Intimately Related Aspects of Caribbean Family and Kinship." In *Transnational Families, Migration, and the Circulation of Care Work: Understanding Mobility and Absence in Family Life,* edited by Loretta Baldassar and Laura Merla, 133–39. London: Routledge.

Orozco, Manuel, and Elisabeth Burgess. 2011. "A Commitment amidst Shared Hardship: Haitian Transnational Migrants and Remittances." *Journal of Black Studies* 42(2): 225–46.

Pessar, Patricia R. 1995. *A Visa for a Dream: Dominicans in the United States.* Boston: Allyn and Bacon.

———. 1997. *Caribbean Circuits: New Directions in the Study of Caribbean Migration.* New York: Center for Migration Studies.

———. 1999. "Engendering Migration Studies: The Case of New Immigrants in the United States." *American Behavioral Scientist* 42(4): 577–600.

Pierre, Yves. 2009. "Wage Labour in an Agrarian Economy: The Case of the Central Plateau of Haiti." *Social and Economic Studies:* 149–74.

Richman, Karen. E. 2005. *Migration and Vodou.* Gainesville: University Press of Florida.

Roodman, David. 2012. *Due Diligence: An Impertinent Inquiry Into Microfinance.* Washington DC: CGD Books.

Schiller, Nina G., and Georges E. Fouron. 2001. *Georges Woke Up Laughing: Long-Distance Nationalism and the Search for Home.* Durham, NC: Duke University Press.

Srinivasan, Janaki, and Jennifer Burrell. 2012. "Revisiting the Fishers of Kerala, India." IMTFI Conference, UC Irvine, December 2012. Irvine: IMTFI.

Singh, Supriya. 2009. "Mobile Remittances: Design for Financial Inclusion." In *Internationalization, Design and Global Development,* edited by N. Aykin, 515–24. Berlin and Heidelberg: Springer.

Smith, Jennie M. 2001. *When the Hands Are Many: Community Organization and Social Change in Rural Haiti.* New York: Cornell University Press.

Sobo, Elisa J. 1993. *One Blood: The Jamaican Body.* New York: SUNY Press.

Stoll, David. 2012. *El Norte or Bust! How Migration Fever and Microcredit Produced a Financial Crash in a Latin American Town.* Lanham, MD: Rowman & Littlefield.

Taylor, Erin B. 2013. *Materializing Poverty: How the Poor Transform Their Lives.* Lanham, MD: AltaMira.

———. 2014a. "Why the Cocks Trade: What a Transnational Art Market Can Reveal about Cross-Border Relations." *Visual Studies* 29(2): 181–90.

———. 2014b. "When Crisis Is Experienced as Continuity: Materialities of Time in Haiti." *Ethnologie Française* XLIV(3): 493–504.

———. 2015. "Mobile Money: Financial Globalization, Alternative, or Both?" In *MoneyLab Reader: An Intervention in Digital Economy,* edited by G. Lovink, N. Tkacz, and P. de Vries, 244–56, Amsterdam: Institute of Network Cultures.

Taylor, Erin B., Espelencia Baptiste, and Heather A. Horst. 2011. "Mobile Money in Haiti: Potentials and Challenges." Institute for Money, Technology & Financial Inclusion. Retrieved 22 March 2014 from http://www.imtfi.uci.edu/files/images/2011/haiti/taylor_baptiste_horst_haiti_mobile_money_042011.pdf.

Taylor, Erin B. and Heather A. Horst. 2013. "From Street to Satellite: Mixing Methods to Understand Mobile Money Users." Proceedings of the Ethnographic Praxis in Industry Conference, London, 15–19 September, 63–77. London: Ethnographic Praxis in Industry.

———. 2014. "The Aesthetics of Mobile Money Platforms in Haiti." In *The Routledge Companion to Mobile Media,* edited by Gerard Goggin and Larissa Hjorth, 462–72. New York: Routledge.

———. Forthcoming. "Banking on the Market: Mobile Phones and Social Goods Provision in Haiti. In 'Unseen Connections: The Materiality of Cell Phones,' edited by B. Kobak, A. Kemble, J.A. Bell, and J. Kuipers. *Anthropological Quarterly.*

Turits, Richard L. 2002. "A World Destroyed, A Nation Imposed: The 1937 Haitian Massacre in the Dominican Republic." *Hispanic American Historical Review* 82(3): 589–635.

United Nations. 2013. "UN Urges Dominican Republic to Ensure Citizens of Haitian Origin Do Not Lose Nationality," 1 October. Retrieved 6 February 2014 from http://www.un.org/apps/news/story.asp?NewsID=46152#.WZ1sEXUjFhE.

Wolf, Eric R. 1967. "Caudillo Politics: A Structural Analysis." *Comparative Studies in Society and History* 9(2): 168–79.

World Bank. 2010. Factsheet on Haiti. Retrieved 4 February 2014 from http://blogs .worldbank.org/peoplemove/a-factsheet-on-haiti.

"Yearly Trade with Haiti: US$1.1B Formal; US$900.0M Informal." 2013. *Dominican Today.* 20 December. Retrieved 4 February 2014 from http://www.domin icantoday.com/dr/economy/2013/12/20/50021/Yearly-trade-with-Haiti-US11B-formal-US9000M-informal.

CHAPTER 2

Capital Mobilization among the Somali Refugee Business Community in Nairobi, Kenya

KENNETH OMEJE AND JOHN MWANGI GITHIGARO

Introduction

Ever since Kenya intervened in Somalia in late 2011 to contain Al-Shabaab [considered to be a terrorist organization based in Somalia but with networks across East Africa], the Somali refugees residing in Kenya have been labeled by both the state and the public as terror threats. As of early 2014, the state was conducting security swoops in the primarily Somali Eastleigh suburb of Nairobi in light of growing terror threats. These operations have resulted in gross human-rights violations within sections of the Somali refugee community (Human Rights Watch 2013; Omeje and Githigaro 2012; Maingi and Omeje 2012). Yet, despite this increased scrutiny, the refugee community remains a key player in the Kenyan business environment.

Third world refugees are often constructed as parasites and unwanted elements in their host nation (Kirui and Mwaruvie 2012; Jaji 2013). They are accused of being dependent on the state and associated with underground economies such as illicit drugs trade, arms trafficking, and so forth. This study discounts this argument and observes that contrary to negative perceptions of refugee communities like the Somalis', capital mobilization strategies have enabled many Somalis in Kenya to be astute, successful entrepreneurs. Through an examination of the capital mobilization strategies of the Somali refugee business community in Nairobi, we explain how these capital strategies have helped lead to successes in the Somali business community. The community draws on various sources of business capital both locally (Kenya) and transnationally (North America and Europe), and we examine their strategies of capital mobilization, particularly the use of remittances, through the lenses of social capital and transnationalism. In recent years, the flow of money through the *hawala* system [an informal money-transfer system via a transnational network of agents in the Muslim world] by the Somali diaspora has been estimated at about US$1.6 billion annually (Lewis 2008: 134; CIA 2015).

The prolific business exploits and transnational entrepreneurship of the significantly large number of Somali refugees in Nairobi seems to shatter the well-entrenched conception of refugees as poverty-stricken, unwanted parasites that bring undue pressure on meager state resources. The destruction of the Somali state by two decades of civil war and the onerous challenges of life in exile have not weakened or destroyed the people's community-centered values, which seem to be the pillars of their transnational business success. This research seeks to bridge this literature gap.

In terms of methodology, this study adopted two qualitative methods of data collection, namely semi structured in-depth interviews and document analysis. A total of sixty purposively selected Somali refugee respondents were interviewed. Also included in the study sample were nineteen indigenous businessmen of Kenyan origin, twelve Indian businessmen, and forty-two Kenyan police officers. The sample comprised various generations and business ventures and aspirations. Fieldwork data collection was conducted between June and September 2011. The fieldwork data was analyzed using thematic coding, interpretivist discourses, and narrativism.

Transnationalism and Social Capital Development

The collapse of the Somali state in 1991 obliterated neither the people's sense of community nor the reality of societal life. Kinship solidarity was mobilized and reconfigured to reinvent community relations within national and transnational boundaries. A major impetus for the reinvention or invigoration of the Somali transnational community has been the traditional entrepreneurial values of the people, who tend to prioritize a communitarian approach to social capital development. This is why transnationalism and social capital development are key concepts for understanding the way the Somali diaspora functions and flourishes within the context of political turbulence and a failed state at home.

Globally, transnationalism is a major concept in contemporary immigration studies. But the delimitations and nature of the phenomenon in both theory and practice remain significantly contentious. Transnationalism broadly refers to "multiple ties and interactions linking people

or institutions across the borders of nation states" (Vertovec 1999: 447).
Vertovec (1999) discusses at least six overlapping thematic uses of the
term: (1) as a social morphology focused on social formation spanning
new borders; (2) as a diasporic consciousness marked by dual or multiple identifications; (3) as a type of cultural reproduction described in
terms of syncretism, creolization, bricolage, cultural translation, and hy-
bridity; (4) as an avenue of capital for transnational corporations (TNCs),
including remittances sent by immigrants to family and friends in their
homelands; (5) as a site of political engagement both in terms of homeland politics and politics of homeland governments, and so forth; (6) as a
reconfiguration of the notion of place from an emphasis on the local to
the translocal.

Social capital is important in understanding how refugees tap into their
traditional social networks, whether for livelihood support, aid in establishing a business enterprise, or some other reason. It is both a versatile
concept and phenomenon, which can be analyzed at both the macro and
micro levels. Social capital at the community level is synonymous with
civic values and comprises a texture of values, norms, and associations
that sustain and allow for civic commitment and ethos (Putnam 1995). At
the micro level, social capital is framed around a single social actor and
focuses on resources and potential or actual advantages due to the individual's position in a network (Bolzoni 2009). In this chapter, we look at
transnational diaspora relations as a crucial form of social capital among
the Somali refugees in Kenya.

Our focus is on these Somali refugees' business activities and remittance uses. Few studies have been conducted on refugees' remittances as
opposed to migrant workers' remittances (Lindley 2010; Hernandez and
Coutin 2006; Dalakoglou 2010; Villarreal 2013). A number of factors ap-
parently account for this. First, getting data in countries experiencing
conflicts and from their scattered diaspora populations is often difficult.
Second, in some instances, it may be impossible to disaggregate the contribution made by the refugees from that of other migrants. Finally, refugees in richer countries may remit money both to their homelands and to
neighboring countries of first asylum to support their relatives, making
their contribution more diffuse than those of other migrants (Van Hear
2003). The minimal evidence available on refugee remittances does suggest, however, that these funds are used in similar ways to those sent by
economic migrants to meet such needs as daily subsistence and healthcare, among others (cf. Van Hear 2003; Lindley 2010).

Drawing from fieldwork data on money remittances among a section
of the Somali diaspora in the UK, Lindley (2009) offers an extensive anal-

ysis of the motivating factors that encourage Somalis abroad to send remittances to their relatives in Somalia and elsewhere. Her analysis is situated in the social textures underpinning remittances. She observes that the starting point for these remittances is a strong sense of familial and cultural reaffirmation derived from these acts. Key among the motivating factors to send remittances, the author argues, are reciprocity and social pressure. Dispersed Somalis feel obligated to "reciprocate" various forms of assistance accorded in the past. The assistance ranges from being brought up to facilitation of school attendance or migration overseas, and it comes from a variety of people, including parents, aunts and uncles, and others. This type of social assistance is a generalized reciprocity typical among kin but one without obligation to repay. Social pressure is also a motivation to send remittances. The Somalis, as a result of their strong kinship affiliations, feel "shamed" when they are unable to support their relatives back home. Strong social pressure is also manifested among the diaspora itself because of the overriding importance of the diaspora networks in key aspects of refugees' lives, expressed in things such as financial assistance, social contacts, networks, and so forth (Lindley 2009). Indeed, gossip about nonremittance can be devastating to their lives. Remittances in themselves help to maintain transnational connections (Lindley 2009; Dalakoglou 2010).

The other motivating factor for remittances among the Somali diaspora is the material needs of the kin back home. These needs are directly attributable to poverty, and remittances are sent to allay them (Lindley 2009). Somali recipients of these remittances can thus be conceptualized as operating in an "economy of affection" environment as described by Goran Hyden (2006). Hyden (2006: 73) posits that "the economy of affection is constituted by personal investments in reciprocal relations with other individuals as a means of achieving goals that are seen as otherwise impossible to attain." The economy of affection operates mainly in informal institutions. It engenders an expectation on the part of the less endowed that obtaining favors from someone with resources is entirely legitimate. Such favors are usually sought within local family structures, but with growing social mobility, the boundaries of this form of behavior are being extended transnationally. The inclination is to approach problem-solving by seeking out another person for help rather than finding solutions on one's own. The economy of affection can also be used to explain social status in the society.

Lindley (2009) observes that remittances among the Somali diaspora are fraught with challenges. One is that they can leave the remitters cash-strapped and financially insecure. This was particularly the case with a cross section of Somali refugees who were interviewed as part of an empirical study in London and who worked mainly in low-paying jobs and/or on state benefit schemes. The remittances would sometimes leave them without disposable income and, as a consequence, without the ability to invest abroad or at home because of their obligation to assist the less endowed members of their kinship networks (Lindley 2009). Recent studies have indeed found that the demand for remittances from the Somali diaspora has in the recent past worked against social mobility in the refugees' host country and made it extremely difficult to accumulate capital to establish businesses back home (cited in Sorensen 2004: 22). The remittance process, despite being a means of maintaining family relations in the face of long absences, continues to be characterized by challenges and tensions. One of the other notable challenges is that those who make up the Somali diaspora are sometimes unwilling to relocate back in Somalia because their kin depend on their remittances from abroad. Relatives have abused the remittance practice and taken the remittances for unintended purposes. There are cases where male relatives use the remittances to marry new wives and sire many children when they were sent to provide upkeep for their family. The Somali diaspora has also been hoodwinked in the past by relatives at home who claim to have all manner of illnesses to ensure a continued flow of remittances (Lindley 2009)

At the family level, the remittances from the diaspora have been a source of tension among married couples. This can add strain to the family in cases where the man is struggling to provide for his family. Children may also fail to understand why their parents send remittances to their relatives in far off lands (Lindley 2009). The Somali diaspora has responded with a number of strategies to resolve these tensions and address the challenges associated with these remittances. One of the coping strategies has been to get family networks (which can spread beyond the Horn of Africa) to take turns remitting set monthly amounts to their kin in Somalia and neighboring countries such as Kenya. A second strategy is to keep tabs on remittance receipts and to whom the money goes. One other strategy is to send just enough money to alleviate "hardship."

A long-term strategy to cut down on remittances entails the provision of business capital, paying for basic needs such as education for their kin and assisting their kin to migrate to the developed world. The provision of business capital to assist their kin in establishing small businesses remains the most sustainable hope in the long term for reducing remittances (Lindley 2009). This remittance approach has worked well for the Somali refugees in Nairobi who are progressively gaining a significant edge in business. Horst (2004: 6) notes a study that found remittances from the Somali diaspora to Somaliland had contributed to a vibrant private sector. Studies have indicated that remittances contribute to the development and reconstruction of Somali-inhabited lands. Another option is simply to avoid remittances altogether (Lindley 2009: 138–39). These remittances are channeled through the informal money-transfer system known as the *hawala*. But the *hawala* market remains indispensable to families who are responsible to and dependent on family ties (Lindley 2009).

The most successful migrant business communities, it is widely acknowledged, arise as a result of the very interstices enabled by transnationalism. Such ventures include shipping and cargo companies, import-export companies, labor contractors, and money-transfer houses (Glick and Schiller et al. 1995: 55).

Somali Refugees' Business Activities: Key Findings from Field Research

Our fieldwork data and observations reveal that the Somali refugee community in Eastleigh, Nairobi, and its environs are engaged in a variety of business activities. The main sectoral activities can be classified as follows:

- hospitality industry (hotels and guesthouse lodges);
- real estate (residential/business premises, notably shopping malls);
- financial services (foreign exchange bureaus, most notably the money-transfer services, such as the *hawala*);
- clothing and textiles trade;
- information technology (IT) and electronics (telecommunication services such as cyber cafes; sale of computers, electronics, and related accessories);
- assorted wholesale and retail businesses;
- transport and goods delivery (public-service commercial vehicles, long-distance haulage services, goods-clearing and forwarding, and parcel-delivery business);
- livestock trade;
- petty trade (e.g., roadside food, cloth, DVD, and children's toy vending).

Our fieldwork sources indicate a variety of options available for mobilization of business capital to the bulk of the Somali refugee community in Nairobi. Most respondents reported that a greater part of their business capital was sourced through their kinship networks. Other key sources of capital include transnational remittances, rotating savings and credit associations (ROSCAs), community contingency fund support, personal savings, business partnerships, bank loans, and recycling previous business capital (table 2.1).

In the following, we outline some of the specific details about these practices of generating capital – through social networks, banking institutions, and other financial networks – among the Somali community in Kenya.

1. Clan/Kinship Networks

Secondary data sources indicate that Somali refugees in Nairobi use social capital as leverage to acquire business capital (Lindley 2007: 5). In addition to remittances received from the diaspora, more than half of the Somali refugees interviewed in this study assert that clan/kinship

Table 2.1. Sources of Financial Capital Mobilization among the Somali Refugee Community in Nairobi

Forms	Source
Clans/kinship networks	Clan/interclans kinship networks
Remittances	From relatives in the diaspora
Conventional rotating savings and credit associations (ROSCAs) popularly known in Kenya as "merry-go-rounds" or *ayutta* among the Somali	Periodic contribution by group members; mainly prevalent among women in business
Community contingency fund	Clan-based business networks existing in the Eastleigh Somali settlement suburb
Personal savings	From employment wages and stipends in small and medium enterprises operated by their kin
Business partnerships	Business partners who are either Kenyan-based relatives or those in the diaspora
Bank loans	Formal-sector financial institutions
Recycling of previous business capital	Money raised from the sale or auctioning of total merchandise stock (and sometimes property) previously owned in Somalia

Source: Fieldwork interviews with Somali refugees in Nairobi, Summer 2011.

networks within Nairobi are important sources for their business capital. Within the community, specific funds are set up within the kinship networks to help provide business capital to needy members and also to help meet sundry social needs, especially paying for their children's education. The refugee community places a high premium on education for their children and young adults. There are two tracks of education commonly available among the refugee community; they are not strictly exclusive of each other. The first track is formal schooling (i.e. attending government-owned or private schools) while the second is the relatively informal Islamic religious education known as *madrassa*. The high priority that the refugee community gives to provision of education for their children and dependents tends to reinforce the finding in Lindley's (2009) study that the priority given to investment in education by the Somali diaspora is part of a long-term strategy to reduce their kin's dependence on them. The interviewed respondents aver that acquiring an education promotes an individual's capacity for self-sustenance. About 33.3 percent of the refugee respondents had tertiary-level qualifications (e.g., diploma, BA, and MA), and 20 percent of them attained secondary-school (Ordinary level) qualifications. Another 30 percent of the respondents reported not having any formal education, while 14 percent reportedly completed primary school. Only 3 percent of the respondents had only basic Islamic education. It is important to note that a significant majority of the respondents had secondary and postsecondary qualifications. Some 40 percent of the respondents further indicated that they had previously supported or were currently supporting members of their family to acquire both formal and Islamic education (Lindley 2009).

Be that as it may, nearly all the study respondents mentioned that they are part of, or have access to, some community contingency funds within their Nairobi-based clans and beyond. The funds obtained from these community kitties are generally interest free. The funds are managed by a constituted committee, and hardly any of the borrowers had defaulted. The explanation advanced was that defaulting would bring shame to them and also dent their reputation in the community and related business circle. Besides, respondents value the funds' continuity and as such regularly contribute to each one they belong to. In addition, some of the Somali businessmen interviewed (albeit a negligible few and relatively wealthy folks) felt a societal responsibility to generally assist their countrymen businesswise regardless of clan affiliations. However, for the vast majority of the respondents, clan affiliation is a major factor in financial and social support. This observation is consistent with findings from a similar study in South Africa where there is a significant presence of the Somali refugee business community. Drawing on fieldwork with Somali refugees in Mayfair in Johannesburg, South Africa, Sadouni (2009) asserts that clan affiliations are a pivotal consideration in providing business support. Among the Somali business community in Mayfair, the flow of financial resources works across networks within clans as opposed to across clans. This phenomenon can be directly traceable to the colonial era in Somalia when sub tribal and clan identity construction became first entrenched and then reinforced. These primordial identity constructions and permutations have continued in Somalia's post-independence era, well into the contemporary civil war era (1991 to present).

Kinship plays a vital role in supporting new Somali immigrants on their arrival to Nairobi. Typically, once the Somali refugees arrive in Nairobi they are hosted by relatives, and the duration can vary from a couple of months to a few years. Thereafter, they are either accorded apprenticeship opportunities if they lack the requisite experience to start a business activity or they are facilitated to start their own businesses immediately if they already have previous experience. These two support processes are similar to the practices observed among Somali refugees in South Africa where fresh immigrants are usually accommodated by relatives and immediately employed in their kin's businesses. Progressively, they are able to save up some money to establish their own businesses (Bolzoni 2009: 146). This aspect of community support is particularly strong and well embedded in the Somali local culture. The strong sense of community support among the Somali refugees is succinctly captured by the following expression of a businesswoman in a fieldwork interview: "Our businesses survive on community support; we cater for the business needs of the community members. We are always there for each other . . . we trust and believe in each other.'

2. Remittances

Remittances received by respondents from their kinsmen in the diaspora remain a principal source of capital mobilization for a quarter of the refugee businessmen and women interviewed for this study. It is observable that Somalis have strong, well-established, and highly supportive local and transnational kinship networks; hence, it is common practice for Somalis in the diaspora to regularly utilize the efficient *hawala* money-transfer system for remittances. Our fieldwork indicates that these remittances are utilized for various purposes, ranging from the establishment of new businesses and expansion of existing enterprises to the meeting of basic social needs. These remittances emanate from several sources – notably spouses, siblings, and cousins who are spread out transnationally. The frequency of the remittances varies from a one-off remittance to periodic remittances (monthly, quarterly, biannually, and occasionally, as the case may be). Remittances, as Lindley (2009) has well captured, are deeply woven in social textures and embedded in family cultural networks. The following narrative of an interviewed Somali refugee is illustrative of the transnational reach of their businesses and the inherent cultural trust shared among their kin. A 28-year-old male Somali refugee recalls his journey from Mogadishu (Somalia's capital) to Nairobi, and subsequently to Canada and then back to Nairobi to establish a business partnership with his brother:

> I fled Mogadishu six years ago for Nairobi in the thick of the Somali civil war. I then stayed in Nairobi for three years and shortly thereafter left for Canada where I was until recently. It has been four months since I came back to Nairobi from Canada. While in Canada I worked in a petrol station where I managed to save some money and sent it to my brother to start a motor spare parts business. This spare part business is a partnership with my brother. I trust him to run the business in my absence as I will be relocating back to Canada soon.

This narrative puts into focus the debate of who conventionally qualifies to be defined as a refugee. Some are dynamic refugees who take advantage of opportunities provided by international support agencies and kinship networks to move across national boundaries with relative ease, and who, in the process, could generate the necessary capital to start off and grow a business. It is arguable whether such mobile and progressively well-off people, forced originally from their homelands by war, still continue to fit into the conventional label of the term "refugee," or is there a point at which this category of refugee becomes transformed to "economic migrant"? Does a refugee who has been offered an asylum status by a third country, as is the case with the preceding respondent who is a Canadian asylumee, continue to be defined as a refugee in the second country (in this case Kenya) or in the third country for that matter?

2b. Remittance Uses

The members of the Somali refugees' business community interviewed for this study indicated a variety of needs that were met by remittances from their kinsmen in the diaspora. The remittances were put to uses ranging from business capital to meeting basic social needs, such as school fees and living expenses (table 2.1; figure 2.1).

Table 2.2. Remittance Usage Patterns among the Somali Refugee
Business Community

1. Business Capital (50% of respondents)
2. Living Expenses (35% of respondents)
3. Community Support (10% of respondents)
4. Education Facilitations (5% of respondents)

Source: Fieldwork data with Somali refugees in Nairobi, Summer 2011.

More generally, the members of the Somali refugee community we spoke
with indicated broad usage of remittances:

- "I receive remittances from my family members abroad through *ha-wala* for paying my rent and buying food . . . I prefer the services of *dahabshill* [an informal money transfer operator]."
- "I have family members abroad. They send money regularly. I used previous remittances for my business capital."
- "My first wife and children are in Canada . . . ; they support me regularly when I need to expand my shop by sending remittances that also pay for school fees for my two nephews here in Kenya . . ."

Figure 2.1. Somali refugees' remittance usage patterns.

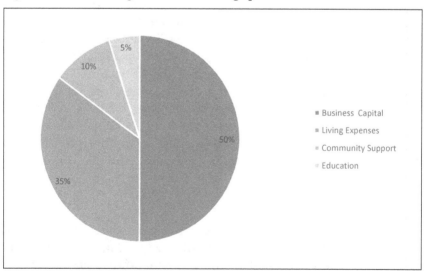

Source: Fieldwork data with Somali refugees in Nairobi, Summer 2011.

3. Rotating Savings and Credit Associations' (ROSCAs)

Goran Hyden's (2006) economy of affection thesis has been used to explain the rise of self-help efforts all over Africa, such as "rotating savings and credit associations," or ROSCAs. ROSCAs often emerge in places where formal credit markets are slim or nonexistent, and therefore they are conceived to fill existing gaps in financial inclusion (Gugerty 2007: 251). They are utilized for a variety of social and business-oriented needs. Examples of social needs would be money or credit required for conducting marriage ceremonies, settling hospital bills, paying tuition fees for wards in school, etc., while the business-oriented needs are mostly (re) investment capital. But the financial schemes are not restricted to developing economies and underprivileged people as they have also been found to exist in some developed countries where most individuals have access to formal banking institutions (Gugerty 2007: 251).

On the African continent, ROSCAs have existed since ancient times. Among the Yoruba of southwestern Nigeria, *esusu* (savings), a ROSCA variant, is an ancient institution. *Esusu* operates as mutual self-help organizations that assist scheme members in meeting a number of obligations such as funerals, weddings, religious ceremonies, businesses, and so forth. *Esusu* has historically permeated all sectors of the Yoruba social life, and the credit scheme does not stratify between the rich or the poor in its membership (Adebayo 1994). Fieldwork data from the Somali refugees' business community in Nairobi indicate that they operate a specific variant of ROSCAs mainly tied to business investment and expansion.

A majority of the Somali women entrepreneurs interviewed in this study (70 percent) reported their membership in and utilization of ROSCAs. The most popular type of ROSCA reported by these women entrepreneurs is known in their local Somali language as *ayutta* (literally translated as "merry-go-round"). This type of ROSCA involves members making either daily or weekly contributions, with the raised amount benefitting group members on a periodic, rotating basis. When a ROSCA member receives their periodic disbursement (usually of the full or substantial percentage of the total contributions over the set period), they usually use the proceeds to expand their business. To this end, a respondent remarked,

> I belong to an *ayutta* with some of my friends. Every month, each member contributes US$200. We are ten of us. In a month two *ayutta* members are each given US$1,000. This assists us in boosting our businesses. When one is in an *ayutta*, you are not charged any interest on the money paid out unlike

a bank that would have to charge one an interest or commission for this kind of support.

The monthly contribution of US$200 is an interesting pointer to the volume of trade turnover of some of the Somali-owned businesses in Nairobi, including small- and medium-scale enterprises operated by women.

According to our respondents, defaults among ROSCA participants are rare among Somali female entrepreneurs ostensibly because the schemes are so deeply embedded in social structures. Defaulting would damage one's reputation and credit history, something that would not be good if the person should require any form of financial support for purposes of business expansion in the future. Particularly because membership in the Somali ROSCAs is informed by friendship ties and clan affiliations, defaulting would compromise reputation and standing in this closely knit business community. Portes and Manning (2005: 160) posit that in most ethnic enclave economies, like the Somali, members do not generally default on payments in ROSCAs once they have received their own payout, largely due to their appreciation of community support for their business success. There are therefore some intrinsic sociocultural motivations for the Somali women entrepreneurs to contribute to their ROSCA kitties.

ROSCA membership among the Somali refugee business community is more prevalent among the women in comparison to men on a ratio of three to one, according to our data. This is similar to findings from a study conducted in Fujian and Zhejiang in southern China between 1994 and 1997 that sought to account for gendered cleavages in business and why more women than men organize ROSCAs, or what is termed as *hui* (association) in the local Wu Chinese dialect (Tsai 2000). The local Kenyan business operators (mostly ethnic Kikuyu) we interviewed indicated that they embrace ROSCAs and practice their principles more or less like the Somali refugee community. The Indian business community based in Nairobi, however, does not have a ROSCA tradition. Kenyan local business operators actually term their variant of ROSCAs "merry-go-rounds," the English translation of the Somali women's *ayutta*. Like groups elsewhere, the motivation to join ROSCAs in the local Kenyan community is in part informed by the relatively high cost of borrowing in the formal financial market. Typically, members contribute set amounts daily or weekly, which are then periodically disbursed to each member on a rotating basis. For the indigenous Kenyan entrepreneurs, ROSCA membership is spread across the gender divide, implying that both men and women could and do belong to the same ROSCA group. Beneficiaries utilize the proceeds from their ROSCA earnings for a variety of obligations and needs. These include settling children's school fees, buying household furnishing/property (e.g., furniture, refrigerator, television set, vehicle, plots of land) and business investments. Membership of the local Kenyan ROSCA is largely based on friendship and trust as opposed to kinship.

In addition to their material benefits, ROSCAs are seen by members as important forums for business information sharing. There exists however a segment of local Kenyan business operators who will not risk joining or forming any ROSCAs principally as result of negative experiences in the past. This category of respondents cites cases of dishonest members who default on their contribution to the kitty after receiving their payout.

4. Community Contingency Fund Support

Members of the Somali refugee business community in Eastleigh establish various microcredit-oriented contingency funds for a wide array of needs, especially business assistance. These contingency funds are grassroots self-help schemes mainly organized along clan or lineage lines. Members contribute a flexible amount of cash monthly to the kitty. The actual amount contributed depends on a member's financial means and ability. Respondents mentioned that the contingency fund can, among other purposes, be accessed as credit by anyone in need of setting up a new business (e.g., new immigrants) or expanding existing business enterprises. The fund is managed and disbursed by a committee drawn from the subclan or clan concerned. Fundamentally, the contingency fund operates more or less like some of the conventional ROSCAs already discussed. According to one of the respondents,

> Our clan pools resources on a monthly basis for the community contingency fund. We have created this fund to assist new comers or clan members that might require assistance in any way, e.g., medical bills, wedding expenses, traveling abroad, business needs, etc. Each member of the fund contributes a certain amount voluntarily. In my own case, I contribute 10,000 Kenyan shillings monthly [about US$115]to the fund. We have a committee that is responsible for the kitty and its disbursement.

Similarly, by virtue of its close community ties, the Somali refugee business community in Nairobi can mobilize to raise funds at short notice in order to assist any community member in need. The donated amount can then be used by the beneficiaries as they deem appropriate, but quite often the donations are meant for starting a business or settling bills like accommodation rents and medical expenses. "We come from a closely knit community," asserts a passionate respondent. "If one has a problem, for example, if they are unable to pay their bills or in desperate need to start a small business, the community can be easily mobilized for a *qaran* [fundraising activity]."

Furthermore, the Somalis in the diaspora (including the refugee community in Nairobi) regularly use remittances to facilitate community-based and emergency aid projects in their home country. Horst (2004) found this was also true among the Somali diaspora in Minneapolis in the United States, where diaspora-led community projects are mainly facilitated by Somalis originating from a certain region or clan linking up to support the development initiatives of those at home, and in the process clans often become the unit for mobilization of resources. These community-development projects are generally for providing, expanding, or improving public infrastructures such as water supplies, electricity, roads, schools, and healthcare delivery.

5. Personal Savings

Personal savings by the Somali refugees are another source of business capital mobilization reported by respondents. These savings are either mobilized from formal employment or from the stipends earned from apprenticeship opportunities provided by their kinsmen. Some 10 percent of the Somali respondents indicated that they sourced their business capital from savings. The Somali refugee community in Nairobi is known to offer apprenticeships to new business entrants in their small and medium-sized enterprises. The skills acquired in their apprenticeships give them a practical head start in their chosen business ventures as they learn and understand, among others skills, how to run a business. They are then able to progressively tap into their kinship networks to access available opportunities, including credit and capital to nurture and expand the nascent business enterprises they set up. The following excerpt on the role of savings in starting up a business narrated by a 28-year-old Somali female who is a proud owner of a cosmetic shop is illustrative:

> I have been running this cosmetic shop since 2008. Before then, for three years I used to do cloth vending for my aunt who came to Kenya much earlier. I raised a significant sum of my business capital by saving commissions from the vending trade. It was relatively easy for me to save because I stayed with my aunt and therefore never incurred daily living expenses such as rent, bus fare or food. In starting my own business, I took a small loan from my aunt to top up my savings. I repaid the loan in installments without interest.

This story exemplifies the value of personal savings that can then be complemented by borrowing from established social networks. It is also important to note how this young Somali tapped local social capital to advance her business interests. Doing so enabled the respondent to save because her accommodation costs were met. The fact that the emerging entrepreneur was able to acquire an interest-free loan was and is a great business enabler to her and the entire Somali refugee business community.

6. Business Partnerships

Our interviews indicate that the Somali refugee community has also adopted business partnership as a form of capital mobilization. In these cases, partners contribute an agreed-upon amount that can then be translated to a stake or share in the business venture. By opting for joint business ventures, partners are able to harness expanded business opportunities resulting from a pool of business capital. From our fieldwork report, the Somali refugees' business partnerships are spread across different national boundaries, and this is a significant indication to why their businesses thrive and succeed. Given their vast diaspora network, the Somali business entrepreneurs tend to have wide access to business capital and trade information, and therefore significant advantages over, for instance, their local Kenyan counterparts. One of the factors that explain the Nairobi-based Somali refugee community's business success story is their ability to mobilize business capital from their kinship networks across the globe. Notions of trust that are deeply embedded in their kinship networks also work to their advantage. About 10 percent of our respondents are engaged in either local or transnational partnerships with their kinfolk, and these ventures are built on significant levels of trust among community members. About two-thirds of the respondents engaged in these business partnerships are male, and the rest female. "I have family members in the US who are partners in my business," asserts a refugee businessman, "and they send remittances regularly whenever there is a good business opportunity to invest in." A Somali refugee mobile-phone dealer in Eastleigh described the evolution of his business partnership from a formative stage:

> This shop is a partnership between me and my distant cousin in Dadaab [North Eastern Kenya]. I sincerely cannot tell how we are related but back in Somalia we lived in the same extended family homestead. . . . I approached members of my clan here in Nairobi and was able to raise 30 percent of the capital and my cousin raised 70 percent . . . ; we then got my cousin's friend

to partition a small space for us at the frontage of his shop where we sell phones. At the end of the month, we pay a little fee to the shop owner.

In other words, friendship and the idea of someone from "home" (and not necessarily from an immediate clan affiliation) can play a role in business. The important inference to be derived here is the existence of trust that can transcend even well-entrenched clan affiliations among the Somali people, and that trust can prove useful in business. Indeed, the quote avers that one of the business partners is far away from Nairobi in Dadaab, northeastern Kenya, and thus has entrusted this respondent to run his 70 percent share of the business.

Another respondent affirmed that "most Somalis partner with relatives and kinsmen in business; for example, in the raising of capital, clan considerations come into play. . . . In my own case, I am in partnership with a fellow *Hawiye* [clan]. This has to do with trust in one's clan." The preceding two respondents' accounts point to the important roles that trust, kinship, and friendship play in business networks among the Somali refugee community.

7. Bank Loans

During our fieldwork, approximately 5 percent of the interviewed Somali businessmen indicated that they have utilized bank-loan facilities to either set up new business ventures or to expand existing ones. To qualify for the bank credits, they usually call on their wealthier kinsmen to act as their guarantors at the bank. A majority of the respondents (including those who have never opted for bank loans) reported preference for Islamic banks in the event that they are seeking business financing. This preference is rooted in their Islamic religious philosophy that prohibits interest (*riba*) in credit disbursements.

8. Recycling of Previous Business Capital

Some 4 percent of the Somali refugee businessmen (women did not report this trend) interviewed in this study observed that they sourced their business capital by selling off the total business stock and property they previously owned in Somalia and migrating to Nairobi to start an entirely new life in a similar or different line of business. One Somali refugee businessman recounted how he sold his thriving business enterprise in Somalia shortly before the country was engulfed by civil war in 1991 and used the proceeds to establish a new business in Nairobi.

The businessman had to rely on his relatives' networks and guidance to gain a business foothold on his arrival in Nairobi. According to the respondent,

> I used to be an entrepreneur in Mogadishu where I had a clothes shop and a wholesale business about twenty years ago. I left Somalia before the civil war broke out on a full scale. I had a bad feeling that my business would not survive if I stayed longer. I immediately sold my business and crossed into Kenya and in particular to Eastleigh where I had cousins that operated businesses at the famous Garissa Lodge. I lodged in a hotel with my family before my new business venture could take off. I presently own three mini-marts and a textile shop.

A number of the Somali refugees currently doing business in Nairobi had been engaged in businesses prior to the outbreak of civil war in their homeland. This category of respondents further indicated that their main motivation for migrating to Nairobi was for the purpose of continuing their businesses. It is also indicative, from the respondents' accounts, that a number of them branch off into new forms of businesses on arrival in Nairobi and that they are always guided by the feasibility advice of their host kinsmen as they make such strategic decisions.

Conclusion

Far from being vulnerable parasites on the Kenyan state, people, and economy, the Somali refugee community is a self-sustaining powerful force in the business front – thanks to their extensive mobilization of financial capital and sprawling investments achieved over the years through solid kinship networks. The kinship-based community spirit and sentiments shared by Somalis, which is at the root of their business success in the diaspora, has functionally survived the collapse of the Somali state. The people in the diaspora have built a largely self-regulating, transnational business community in which honesty, trust, hard work, reciprocity, and mutual support are key driving values. The destruction of the Somali state by two decades of civil war and the onerous challenges of life in exile have neither weakened nor destroyed the people's community-centered values, which seem to be the pillars of their transnational business success. The key to building such a huge transnational business empire in Nairobi is the role of the refugees' kinsmen in the more developed countries (notably Europe and North America) who are an important source of business capital through remittances.

This is a unique form of war-induced, cooperative diaspora. The people in the diaspora not only send remittances to help their kin establish businesses but in some cases they come on board as absentee partners. Within the local refugee community in Nairobi, various clan-based self-help support networks and organizations are used to aid one another in business and social life, especially weaker parties and new arrivals. There are productive support schemes, including the provision of accommodation, apprenticeships, business capital, credit referencing, obtaining consignment of goods on credit, interest-free loans, revolving membership-based credits, etc., to help individual members of the community kickstart, grow, expand, and diversify their business. Formal-sector credits are also sought from banks, preferably Islamic banks because of the diverse advantages they hold for this predominantly Muslim community. It is remarkable that members of the community do not default in repaying any disbursed credit or reciprocating any transactional obligations and commitments among themselves even when there is no written or binding agreement, as is often the case.

Acknowledgments

The authors gratefully acknowledge the University of California Irvine–based Institute for Money, Technology & Financial Inclusion (IMTFI) for funding this empirical research project. The IMTFI director Professor Bill Maurer and program administrator Jenny Fan deserve special mention for their immense support.

Professor Kenneth Omeje is a senior research fellow at the John and Elnora Ferguson Center for African Studies (JEFCAS), University of Bradford, UK, and research fellow, Center for African Studies, University of the Free State, Bloemfontein, South Africa.

John Mwangi Githigaro is lecturer in peace and conflict studies at St. Paul's University, Limuru, Kenya. John is a recipient of the 2017/18 Social Research Council's Next Generation in Social Sciences research fellowship.

INTERVIEW LIST

1. Interview with Somali refugee female trader on 15 July 2011 in Nairobi. Interview was conducted by a member of the project fieldwork team.

2. Interview with a Somali refugee male trader on 12 July 2011 in Nairobi. Interview was conducted by a member of the project fieldwork team.
3. Interview with Somali female trader on 11 July 2011 in Nairobi. Interview was conducted by a member of the project fieldwork team.
4. Interview with Somali refugee businessman on 19 July 2011 in Nairobi. Interview was conducted by a member of the project fieldwork team.
5. Interview with Somali refugee male trader on 22 July 2011 in Nairobi. Interview was conducted by a member of the project fieldwork team.
6. Interview with Somali female refugee trader on 12 July 2011 in Nairobi. Interview was conducted by a member of the project fieldwork team.
7. Interview with Somali male refugee trader on 14 July 2011 in Nairobi. Interview was conducted by a member of the project fieldwork team.
8. Interview with Somali male refugee taxi driver on 14 July 2011 in Nairobi. Interview was conducted by a member of the project fieldwork team.
9. Interview with a Somali refugee female trader on 12 July 2011 in Nairobi. Interview was conducted by a member of the project fieldwork team.
10. Interview with a Somali refugee female trader on 11 July 2011 in Nairobi. Interview was conducted by a member of the project fieldwork team.
11. Interview with a Somali refugee male trader on 19 July 2011 in Nairobi. Interview was conducted by a member of the project fieldwork team.
12. Interview with Somali refugee businessman on 19 July 2011 in Nairobi. Interview was conducted by a member of the project fieldwork team.
13. Interview with Somali male refugee trader on 22 July 2011 in Nairobi. Interview was conducted by a member of the project fieldwork team.

REFERENCES CITED

Adebayo, Akanmu G. 1994. "Money, Credit and Banking in Pre-colonial Africa: The Yoruba Experience." *Anthropos* 89: 379–400.

Aggarwal, Rajesh K., and Tarik, Yousef. 2000. "Islamic Banks and Investing Financing." *Journal of Money Credit and Banking* 32(1): 93–120.

Bolzoni, Magda. 2009. "Refugees and Asylum Seekers in Cape Town: Situation, Challenges, and Perspectives." In *A Game of Mirrors: Economic Development and Social Cohesion in Piedmont and South Africa,* edited by B. Filippo and O. Elana, 125–52. Torino: Italy: Frame-lab.

CIA. 2015. "Somalia." The World Factbook. US Central Intelligence Agency. Retrieved 15 July 2015 from https://www.cia.gov/library/publications/the-world-factbook/geos/so.html.

Dalakoglou, Dimitris. 2010. "Migrating-Remitting-'Building'-Dwelling: House-Making as 'Proxy' Presence in Postsocialist Albania." *Journal of the Royal Anthropological Institute* 16(4): 761–77.

Gugerty, Mary K. 2007. "You Can't Save Alone: Commitment in Rotating Savings and Credit Associations in Kenya." *Economic Development and Cultural Change* 55(2): 251–82.

Hernandez, Ester, and Susan Bibler Coutin. 2006. "Remitting Subjects: Migrants, Money and States." *Economy and Society* 35(2): 185–208.

Horst, Cindy. 2004. "Money and Mobility: Transnational Livelihood Strategies of the Somali Diaspora." *Global Migration Perspectives,* 9 October, Amsterdam Institute of Metropolitan and International Development Studies. Retrieved 16 May 2012 from http://www.gcim.org.

Human Rights Watch. 2013. *You Are All Terrorists: Kenyan Police Abuse of Refugees in Nairobi.* New York: Human Rights Watch.

Hyden, Goran. 2006. *African Politics in Comparative Perspective.* Cambridge: Cambridge University Press.

Jaji, Rose. 2013. "Somali Asylum Seekers and Refoulment at the Kenya–Somalia Border." *Journal of Borderlands Studies* 28(3): 355–68.

Kirui, Paul, and Mwaruvie John. 2012. "The Dilemma of Hosting Refugees: A Focus on Insecurity in North Eastern Kenya." *International Journal of Business and Social Sciences* 3(8): 161–71.

Lewis, Ioan M. 2008. *Understanding Somalia and Somaliland: A Guide to Cultural History and Social Institutions.* New York: Columbia University Press.

Lindley, Anna. 2007. "Protracted Displacement and Remittances: The View from Eastleigh, Nairobi." *New Issues in Refugee Research,* Research Paper 143: UNHCR.

———. 2009. "The Early-Morning Phonecall: Remittances from a Refugee Diaspora Perspective." *Journal of Ethnic and Migration Studies* 35(8): 1315–34.

———. 2010. *The Early Morning Phone Call: Somali Refugees' Remittances.* New York: Berghahn Books.

Maingi, Joy, and Omeje Kenneth. 2012. "Policing Refugees in Fragile States: The Case of Kenya." In *Policing in Africa,* edited by D. J. Francis, 73–94. London: Palgrave Macmillan.

Omeje, Kenneth, and Githigaro, John. 2012. "The Challenges of State Policing in Kenya." *African Peace and Conflict Journal* 7(1): 64–87.

Portes, Alejandro. 1998. "Social Capital: Its Origins and Applications in Modern Sociology", *Annual Review of Sociology* 24: 1–24.

———. 2000. "The Two Meanings of Social Capital." *Sociological Forum* 15(1): 1–12.

Portes, Alejandro, and Manning, Robert. 2005. "The Immigrant Enclave: Theory and Empirical Examples." In *The Urban Sociology Reader,* edited by J. Lin and C. Mele, 152–63. Oxon: Routledge.

Putnam, Robert D. 1995. "Bowling alone: America's declining social capital." *Journal of Democracy,* 6: 65–78.

Sadouni, Samadia. 2009. "God Is Not 'Unemployed': Journeys of Somali Refugees in Johannesburg." *African Studies* 68(2): 235–39.

Schiller, Nina G., Basch, Linda, and Blanc Cristina S. 1995. "From Immigrant to Transmigrant: Theorizing Transnational Migration." *Anthropological Quarterly* 68(1): 48–63.

Small, Ivan V. 2012. "Embodied Economies: Vietnamese Transnational Migration and Return Regimes." *Sojourn: Journal of Social Issues in Southeast Asia* 27(2): 234–59.

Sorensen, Ninna. 2004. "The Development Dimension of Migrant Transfers." Danish Institute for International Studies (DIID) Working Paper 16. Retrieved 18 June 2012 from http://www.diis.dk.

Tsai, Kellee S. 2000. "Banquet Banking: Gender and Rotating Savings and Credit Associations South China." *China Quarterly* 161: 142–70.

Van Hear, Nicholas. 2003. "Refugee Diasporas, Remittances, Development, and Conflict." *Migration Information Source*, June 1, 2003.

Vertovec, Steven. 1999. "Conceiving and Researching Transnationalism." *Ethnic and Racial Studies* 22(2): 447–62.

Villarreal, Magdalena. 2013. "Indebted Mexicans in the Californian Mortgage Crisis." In *Microfinance, Debt, and Over-Indebtedness: Juggling with Money,* edited by Isabelle Guèrin, Solène Morvant-Roux, and Magdalena Villarreal, 46–63. New York: Routledge.

CHAPTER 3

The Use of Mobile-Money Technology among Vulnerable Populations in Kenya

Opportunities and Challenges for Poverty Reduction

NDUNGE KIITI AND JANE WANZA MUTINDA

The significant role that technology can play in human development is undeniable. Increasingly, development practitioners argue that mobile technology has become a key ingredient for addressing poverty in developing countries (Handapangoda and Kumara 2013; Mbogo 2010; Boateng et al. 2012; Wallis 2011). Yet, technology can also be a tool or instrument that facilitates exclusion of certain populations within a society, hindering the very process of development it was set out to achieve (Papaioannou 2011). In reviewing literature, questions of how technology is benefiting marginalized populations, whether based on gender (Wallis 2011; Boateng et al. 2012) or issues around disability (Seale et al. 2010), are increasingly raised.

The opportunities and challenges of technology were highlighted in a qualitative study that investigated the use of mobile-money services (e.g., M-PESA and Zap) and platforms by vulnerable populations in Kenya, and the impact on them, as tools for poverty reduction. Among the twenty-one women's groups that were part of the first phase of the study, we found that mobile-money technology can facilitate social networks and economic development with limited and less pronounced challenges. However, during the second phase of the study, the experiences of persons with visual impairment were extremely different. The findings showed that stigma, fraud, lack of privacy, dependency, pin number security, and overall inaccessible technology limited their ability to fully benefit from the mobile-money services, often perpetuating poverty or loss.

The United Nations Development Programme (UNDP) posits that "a nation's ability to solve problems and initiate and sustain economic growth depends partly on its capabilities in science, technology and innovation" (2005a: 20). In Kenya, mobile-money technology has been hailed as the most revolutionary innovation of this century. Buku and Meredith have enthusiastically embraced this change:

> The recent and widespread availability of affordable mobile phone tech-
> nology in developing countries has paved the way for the development of
> a number of mobile money and electronic remittance services. One of the
> most successful of these services is Safaricom's M-PESA program, launched
> in the East African nation of Kenya in March 2007. Since then, the program
> has successfully enrolled 15.2 million users, transferred more than US $1.4
> trillion in electronic funds, and contributed significantly to poverty allevia-
> tion and financial inclusion efforts in rural Kenya. (2013: 375)

But studies have also shown that there is a correlation between social and digital exclusion. Individuals who tend to be socially excluded, whether it's based on some form of social stratification, will frequently be vulnerable to the digital divide (Seale et al. 2010; Warshauer et al. 2004). The question is, how can we ensure these mobile-money technologies are more inclusive rather than exclusive? Drawing on research with women's groups and persons with visual impairment (VI), this chapter examines some of the opportunities and challenges posed by this revolution.

In the Eastern Province of Kenya, poverty and inequalities are stagger-ing. According to the Central Bureau of Statistics, the Eastern Province is one of the poorest regions of the country (as cited in UNDP and UNIFEM 2005). This problem especially affects women. These gaps and inequal-ities are evident in access and control of resources, economic opportu-nities and power, and political voice. In her gender-focused research, carried out in Makueni District, Ndambuki found that poverty, among other issues, was defined by politicians and community leaders as the greatest challenge facing Kamba women (2010). This, she argues, supports other studies by researchers who posit that women's participation in the political arena is often undermined and limited by economic pressures (Ndambuki 2010; Nasong'o and Ayot 2007).

Additionally, when it comes to property ownership, men own 95 per-cent of all land holdings in Kenya, while women own only 5 percent (UNDP and UNIFEM 2005). The government of Kenya describes that one of the main problems in achieving gender equity is the unwillingness of some communities to change entrenched cultural beliefs, such as land ownership by women (as cited in UNDP and UNIFEM 2005). Since the ownership of land and property often facilitates access to collateral and other resources, this challenge frequently translates into high levels of poverty, mainly concentrated among women in rural areas. Recognizing women's limited and sustainable economic improvements, Vinya wa Aka Group (VwAG)[1] used their experience as a catalyst to train and empower women in the rural areas of the Eastern Province of Kenya, covering districts such as Machakos, Makueni, Mwingi, Kitui, Embu, Mbeere, and Meru.[2] VwAG is a registered women's group, from Eastern Kenya, whose members hold residence in both urban and rural settings. Hennink, Kulb, and Kiiti describe this group as

> a Kenyan women's group that initiated an expanded community-based model of microcredit which goes beyond a basic ROSCA to include mechanisms for investment and social support. Vinya wa Aka is not affiliated with any formal microfinance institution (MFI) scheme or banking institution. It thereby challenges the traditional top-down model of development by recognizing the bottom-up model, based on the ABCD framework that builds on community assets utilized by women's groups. This approach reduces dependency on external aid and technical assistance and may be more sustainable in addressing community development. (2013: 1029–31)

In development, training has often been used as a tool for capacity building and empowerment (Eade 1997). Because women are often vulnerable to external "shocks," the training facilitated the ability of women to create wealth with the aim of reducing poverty within their families and communities. This included investing in high returns using sectors like the Nairobi Stock Exchange, mutual funds, endowment funds, and bonds. It was during this process that mobile-money technology increasingly became popular in Kenya.

Within the women's groups, evidence showed that mobile-money technology played a role in facilitating group contributions, loans, and other social aspects of the group process. However, the extent of the mobile technology's impact was not clear. This observation was a catalyst to the first phase of the research, which investigated the use of mobile-money technology among the twenty-one women's groups in Eastern Kenya. One of those women's groups was made up of individuals with visual impairment. Their special and expressed distinct needs, in relation to mobile-money technology, facilitated the second phase of the research, among persons with visual impairment.

Why Persons with Visual Impairment?

Although the statistics have not been confirmed, Kenya has a fairly large population of persons with visual impairment, reported at just over half a million (Kenya Union of the Blind, 2009). Research has shown a direct correlation between poverty and persons with a disability. There is often a causal effect, which prompts the question: does poverty lead to the disability, or does the disability perpetuate poverty?

Research studies in three countries have drawn attention to the poverty/ visual impairment link (Kuper et al. 2008). Poverty is often shown as a cause or consequence of poor health (ibid.) affecting the most vulnerable populations. For example, childhood blindness is correlated with socio-economic development (Njuguna et al. 2009). In Kenya, only 21 percent of children with visual impairment attend school (Ministry of Education 2009). Additionally, visual impairment has a gender aspect in Kenya. Statistics show that visual impairment impacts 55 percent females and 45 percent males (Kenya Union of the Blind 2009). Health, education, or gender, when ignored, can affect poverty especially among the visually impaired.

There is an increased need for people with visual impairment to have access to technology available to the general public. Failure to provide access will only continue to deepen the divide between the sighted population and those with visual impairment (Gill 2002). Additionally, poverty hinders accessibility, which is more pronounced among vulnerable populations. A study carried out in Kenya confirms that M-PESA[3] services tend to benefit individuals of higher, socioeconomic status (Mbiti and Weil 2011, increasing the negative implications for persons with visual impairment. Seale, Draffan, and Wald have argued that "unequal access to technologies serves to exacerbate social stratification, whilst equal access can reduce marginalization" (2010: 445).

Theoretical Frameworks Informing the Study

The concept of "empowerment" has been central to the work of Vinya wa Aka and a motivation to train and share knowledge with the women in the rural part of Eastern Kenya. Public health specialist Nina Wallerstein defined empowerment as a process that

> influences people's ability to act through collective participation by strengthening their organizational capacities, challenging power inequities and achieving outcomes on many reciprocal levels in different domains: psychological empowerment, household relations, enhanced social capital and cohesion, transformed institutions, greater access to resources, open governance and increasingly equitable community conditions. (2006: 29)

Anthropologist and development practitioner Deepa Narayan builds on this idea by suggesting that empowerment is increasing the assets and capabilities of poor people (2002: 14). A research study, carried out by MAP International[4] and Emory University, found that empowerment is often linked with human agency (Hennink et al. 2009). In his book *Development as Freedom,* economist and Nobel Prize winner Amartya Sen talks extensively about human agency and freedom. He defines agency as the opportunity for people to make choices and to act to improve their situation in life through various avenues. This means people have the freedom to define alternatives and not be externally restricted to any single course of life (Sen 1999). However, extensive literature illustrates that a clear understanding of empowerment must also consider the relationship between power and agency in a given situation (Gaventa 2004; Freire 1984; Alsop and Norton 2004). What often drives the "push-and-pull" factors for empowerment within societies is the imbalance of access or power.

Development economist Sabina Alkire builds on these ideas and argues that agency is not just one-dimensional but must be considered with respect to different dimensions of well-being (Alkire 2007). This concept of a multidimensional approach to well-being parallels the model used by Vinya wa Aka to help women address issues of poverty through resource mobilization and investment. A key part of this empowerment is the access and use of mobile-money services.

Thus, this study has extensively used the concept of empowerment to inform and guide the process and analysis. VwAG approaches their work from the Freirean perspective that

> [p]eople have ideas and are able to engage in critical reflection. This perspective thrives on the fact that if people are given the opportunity to understand and express themselves, they can offer solutions. Freire argues that this process of critical reflection, dialogue, and conscientization ultimately leads to awareness-raising among individuals and the community. It is the process of the facilitator which embraces the true reality of the community. (Kiiti and Nielsen 1999: 66)

This reality is very relevant for women and persons with visual impairment in Kenya, whether it is the opportunity for empowerment or the challenge of disempowerment.

Mobile-Money Services and Poverty Reduction in Kenya

In Kenya, the use of mobile-money services has become increasingly diversified as the growth rate has dramatically risen. For example, two of the largest services are M-PESA (Safaricom) and Zap money (Zain). M-PESA is "an electronic payment and store of value system that is accessible through mobile phones" (Mas and Morawczynski 2009: 1). Zap money has been called a "mobile wallet" because it provides more functions, not just the money-transfer service (Mas and Radcliffe 2010). In rural Kenya, M-PESA has extended financial services to large portions of the population that have no access to the banking industry (Mas and Radcliffe 2010). The predications are that these services will expand and become accessible to parts of the country that have often been excluded from financial, banking, or other services.

In his book *The Poor and Their Money,* Stuart Rutherford (2009) highlights the importance of the poor and vulnerable having access to appropriate money-management services. He also goes on to argue that practitioners need to learn from these examples. These basic "merry-go-round" models of savings, sometimes known as rotating savings and credit associations (ROSCAs), don't often address or document what Collins, Morduch, Rutherford, and Ruthven (2009), in their book *Portfolios of the Poor: How the World's Poor Live on $2 a Day,* describe as the surprisingly sophisticated financial lives of the poor. This process often includes creating complex portfolios of saving and borrowing within their context. Additionally, the merry-go-round approach, with its economic-driven outcomes, doesn't always capture the wealth and dynamic interactions from the social, cultural, educational, psychological, emotional, and spiritual aspects. This makes it very difficult to really measure the extent that mobile-money services impact poverty.

All twenty-one women's groups trained and mentored by VwAG were working to address poverty from a social, economic, and psychological perspective. Most of the groups were engaged in some form of investment (mainly shares and land ownership), savings accounts, merry-go-round, social/spiritual support, and microfinance projects mainly in rural areas. Currently, all the groups have savings accounts – as a group and many as individuals – and some form of financial investments. Additionally, most of the groups continue using the merry-go-round system for sharing resources and reducing poverty within their families and communities. The groups are also extensively involved with community outreach.[5]

Most of the visually impaired respondents were from rural areas but living in more urban settings because of work or their schooling. In general, it would be hard to access and engage the visually impaired in rural areas because of stigma, discrimination, and other barriers.

All study participants, registered for mobile-money technology services, used M-PESA. There was emphasis that M-PESA was the initial service introduced to rural and urban areas, which led to its growth and popularity. This was expressed by most groups:

> We use M-PESA . . . M-PESA was the one which came first and earlier. You
> found that many people were in Safaricom, so . . . there was no other option
> other than registering with M-PESA.
>   . . . Many people are in Safaricom since it was the first one in Kenya.

Very few (less than 5 percent) of the participating study respondents actually used other mobile-money technology services. Typically, they had another service for a specified purpose (e.g., business option) or as a "backup" line while still maintaining M-PESA as the main functional service.

Women's Groups

M-PESA facilitated women's group payments, especially for members in urban areas or away from their groups, mostly in the rural areas. Women highlighted various aspects of this, emphasizing efficiency as essential to group planning:

> People are able to pay their dues on time even if they are not present.
>   It enables us to plan . . . what we want to do with that money and what-
> ever we wanted to do is done.
>   . . . So, M-PESA has helped us because I am able to send my money on
> time, in good time.

Some of the groups used M-PESA for microfinance transactions, whether for purchasing or selling a product for their businesses. This involved facilitating development projects or small-group businesses like crafts, school, or ginnery, especially in the rural context. There was strong support and use of M-PESA as a service that promotes more economic transactions in the rural areas, thus leading to rural development and, arguably, the reduction of poverty. Group members from extremely rural and remote areas confirmed this:

> On the side of purchasing goods, it's like we have been freed from traveling
> by vehicles. We just send the money and the goods are delivered to us . . .
> you have paid for everything including transport.

M-PESA also facilitated and strengthened social support systems and networking. Women's groups are often expected to attend social events planned or organized by members of their groups. When attendance is not feasible, M-PESA can serve as a tool to help demonstrate support:

> [W]e sent [money] through M-PESA and we organized [supported] those who
> were to attend. It was all through the phone . . . the mobile phone.

Moreover, members of these groups used M-PESA to help absent family:

> M-PESA is safe for transacting and efficient means of sending money when faced with emergencies. For example, when someone gets sick, you can source money and get it in time, hence you help save a life.
>
> . . . [W]e now feel that Safaricom has helped us because if I want to talk to my mother this minute, I can talk to her. I send her money, if she doesn't have sugar, she buys sugar. So, it has brought us closer to our parents and our children and the people who are . . . who are far away.
>
> There are changes in our families because I have been sent money by my child who stays in Nairobi [capitol city] . . . he will send it to me through the phone and I go withdraw it so that I can solve the problem.

A group leader shared her experience getting support from other members of her women's group when her husband was hospitalized:

> Like in my case, my husband fell sick and was suddenly referred for urgent surgery. When finally my husband was discharged, it was about 1 PM and I did not have enough money to offset the hospital bill. So I called Hannah [not real name] and by 5:30 PM, I had the full amount of money because of the mobile phone.

From a basic usage standpoint, the women emphasized that M-PESA is convenient, safe, accessible, efficient, and affordable. The fact that M-PESA creates opportunities for employment was also viewed as a positive aspect of the service. From the research, it is clear that mobile-money services are central to the success of these women's groups. As one group member put it, "The use of M-PESA has been extremely beneficial to many people." Many of the group members expressed that they couldn't imagine not having M-PESA as a service now.

However, the use of M-PESA did not just provide opportunities; it also came with challenges for the women's groups. These included fraud, network problems, cost, services for special populations, and group communication dynamics.

Several of the women had lost money to fraud. The most common type of fraud was receiving a call or SMS from an individual who claimed to have sent money to the wrong M-PESA account by mistake. They usually request the money be sent back to them. One woman described a personal experience of how she was almost robbed through M-PESA:

> For example, last week I got three SMS messages continuously; same number, difference of one minute. They were saying to confirm that I had received . . . 5,525 Kshs. . . . so your M-PESA now is 8,000 Kshs. And in my phone I had I think either 2,500 Kshs. So immediately, I knew it was a . . . it was a hoax.

Some of the elderly women emphasized that sometimes their main challenge is their inability to read, meaning they have to give out their personal information, which could be used for fraud. This issue was also expressed by the women's group with sight challenges.

Network issues often arise. The women's groups that VwAG works with are mainly based in rural areas where network reception limits access to service, slowing down transactions. One woman explained the challenge they often face: "'The network is low,' so you are told, 'there is no network.' . . . Today there is no M-PESA. So you find you wanted to send that money quickly, but it can't go because of . . . the network."

The general cost of M-PESA services seemed to be accepted. The issue was mainly highlighted because of the level of poverty, especially in rural areas. Even though the service is greatly appreciated for its convenience and security, the charge is often viewed as an expense that could be available for more pressing issues. One woman put it this way, "If you send money through the M-PESA to the treasurer, you should send with the money [sic] for removing it [transaction fee]."

It was evident that M-PESA services can impact group communication and interaction both positively and negatively. On one hand, it allows for money to be sent to facilitate planning of meetings or other activities. On the other hand, some groups argued, this can also perpetuate the lack of meeting attendance, thus limiting the social aspects and components of the group. This affects the sociopsychological support that comes from group interactions. Some women stated it well:

> Many people feel that they can fail to attend the group meetings and they send the money and it's fine with them [group members].

> Yes, some members would take advantage of that in that they don't have to attend the meeting as long as they send the money [using M-PESA].

> Somebody will be feeling, ah, let me send using M-PESA. Even if you put some penalty of failing to attend [group meeting], a person may send the penalty and fail to attend . . .

So, while some group members weren't concerned by missed meetings, for others it negatively affected the group dynamics. Although there were numerous challenges mentioned, the groups made it clear that, as one respondent put it, "the positives are more than the negatives."

Persons with Visual Impairment (VIs)

Persons with visual impairment (VIs) experienced many of the same benefits as the women's groups, especially the convenience of using mobile-money services. However, VIs tended to have more pronounced negative experiences when trying to use this technology. In general, the VIs mentioned that having a disability was in and of itself very expensive, especially when compounded by societal ignorance and stigma.

Persons with disability felt that the Kenyan culture of ignorance, stigma, and discrimination was extremely harmful to them and held them back from accessing development opportunities. Our informants told us that many Kenyans consider disabled people to be shameful or useless. Indeed, they are often cast aside and hidden. Several interviewees mentioned being shunned by their communities, peers, and even families because of their disabilities.

> Where I come from, there has been difficulties in people accepting me even sometimes when I am walking and I get lost, if I ask somebody, most of the times they don't talk to me, even when I want to buy something from the shop, it's a problem. When I come to the side of my family, up to now, they have not accepted me.

> Well, it is not very easy to integrate with people who have sight, even where you were born. You find that when the people realize that you have a disability, especially visual disability, you are told not to do so many things . . . so sometimes you tend to withdraw even when you go out from the home to the community it's like a spectacle . . . so to integrate properly is not easy.

> Up to now, they [family] think I am a curse to them because they have never seen a blind person like me in their lineage.

Some interviewees mentioned specific instances of abuse, discrimination, or other ill treatment that were ignored or accepted by the public. This exemplified the lack of accountability many VIs have found in Kenya concerning the treatment of persons with disabilities or challenges. Many interviewees mentioned that people are not trained to work with VIs. The following comments by VIs illustrate specifically how the transport sector often don't accommodate and properly behave toward them:

> The vehicle [public transportation] . . . sometimes I don't find it friendly, user friendly because some people, the touts or conductors . . . they don't have the polite language.

> [T]he passengers should be informed . . . because for instance if you want to get a seat in a bus, you may move and pass a seat and yet the passenger is there, the conductor who should be showing you . . . they are not sensitive . . .

Interviewees were very specific about distinguishing between people in professional settings being unaware of how to work with VIs and the ignorance among the general public.

Throughout Kenya, many people do not understand what a disability is and often do not know how to react to a visually impaired person. This does not always result in discrimination but tends to make situations awkward and create challenges for VIs in working with or getting to know or trust people, as well as in using technology. To use mobile money as a VI is difficult because the mobile-money system requires sight. In order to use mobile-money services, VIs are forced to rely on other people, even strangers or well-meaning individuals, to handle their mobile-money banking. This fosters dependency, perpetuating their vulnerability:

> First, it's so much challenging because when you want to send money you have to be assisted, that is the first thing we experience. Secondly, is the usage. If you want to confirm the amount that you have sent or you have received, you have to use another person. So you find that you are so much dependent on people who have no visual impairment because the mobile that we have is the cheap one in the market. . . . They don't have that software informing you.

> There might be a challenge if you are a totally impaired person to use M-PESA . . . unless you have a phone that is jaws [audio program] enabled, it might be a problem because this is where you need help from people. . . . Some of the information you are working on when you are doing M-PESA is private.

As a result of these obstacles, several different types of fraud can occur in the process of using mobile-money services. One of the most frequently mentioned issues was that VIs have to share their pin numbers with others in order to use mobile-money services. The story of Esther (not her real name) illustrates how this is a major security issue, as the pin number allows access to all of the money and other data in a person's M-PESA account. While in her house, Esther's "friend" said he could help her transfer funds. After he got her pin number, he transferred the money, which was meant for her child's education, to his own account. As this story illustrates, because they cannot see, VIs are thus more likely to be ripped off through scams. This makes the need for audible phones more urgent.[6]

Mobile-Money Technology and Link to Poverty

The participants in the study clearly inferred a link between mobile-money services and poverty alleviation. The women's groups tended to see it as helping reduce poverty, while the VIs saw it as potentially increasing poverty. One women's group member from a semiarid area said, "[M-PESA] is making things better such that the poverty is not so high." For the most part, many participants, especially from the women's groups, identified using mobile-money services as a tool for socioeconomic support for the individual, family, and community. Mobile-money services helped users address several issues that affect livelihoods or well-being, such as health, agriculture, microfinance and business, education, food security, and emergencies. Even though the women, especially those from extremely rural areas, faced challenges – such as fraud and network issues – while using mobile-money technology, they were not as pronounced as they were for more vulnerable populations such as VIs. Persons with visual impairment often experienced fraud and network challenges differently.

Without citing numbers or statistics, many interviewees tied disability to poverty. This was particularly the case of the VIs. In terms of health and education, persons with visual impairment tend to generally have higher hospital and medical bills. Schooling for the blind is expensive, as are school materials and the cost of living away from home, as many blind schoolchildren do. Further, to get around, they need special equipment, or they must hire guides. Many interviewees mentioned that it is a challenge for persons with visual impairment to afford living independently to any degree, whether at school or in the context of the family. Of particular relevance for this volume, poverty was sometimes perceived as being perpetuated by the use of mobile-money technology, especially because of the cost and accessibility:

> Sometimes if you want assistance from a person, some do cheat and they might withdraw more or less the money you want. So there is cheating in terms of the person you are asking for assistance.

> We have an economic [barrier]. . . . These phones for visually impaired, maybe the mobile that speaks, is very expensive.

> One is that they are expensive. . . . [T]he economic . . . expensive nature of the mobile services makes it a barrier. You may find that if you want to access . . . the most appropriate services, they are very expensive.

> When it comes to M-PESA, even though you don't want to disclose your information to someone, you have to when using this service. There is no privacy because you have to rely on another person.

Interviewees brought this point up, exemplifying it through stories and their own experience, because they believe that perhaps poverty reduction would help prevent more people from becoming visually impaired. Many VIs struggle with poverty and frequently need assistance. One person with visual impairment said it this way: "Poverty and visual impairment are brothers." Mobile-money technology, they argued, could help in shifting this reality.

Discussion

M-PESA, Safaricom's mobile-money service, provides up to 80 percent of the mobile phone market in Kenya (Buku and Meredith 2013). The benefits of M-PESA, highlighted in the research, paralleled those in the literature. This service caters to a large portion of the population that has no access to banking (Mas and Radcliffe 2010) and clearly builds on the urban-rural linkages in Kenya (Mas and Morawczynski 2009). This parallels the study findings.

Among VwAG and the twenty-one women's groups, for instance, the mobile-money service has become a core component of the group's management, communication system, savings and investment. Many of the group's members now make their monthly or loan payments using a mobile service, predominantly, M-PESA. As we have seen, this has resulted in several things. First, it has provided access to more banking and saving options. Second, it sometimes has limited the social networking or personal interaction that is often foundational to any human transaction as group members have chosen to skip monthly meetings and instead send their payments using mobile-money services. This illustrates the complexity of anthropologist Bill Maurer's point that money has a role in social engagement or interaction (Maurer 2006). Third, access to mobile services has added a level of efficiency within the group, helping to streamline banking procedures and payments of assets or other services. For group members who live overseas or outside of Nairobi, the use of mobile-money systems has proven convenient and efficient.

However, as people with sight take advantage of all that mobile-money services have to offer with limited barriers, the challenge to make this technology accessible and relevant to persons with visual impairment is still very real. In discussions with VIs, they emphasized how they still feel vulnerable because they get their personal information, like pin numbers, stolen or they face discrimination when trying to access transportation to go to mobile-money outlets. "Every day, millions of people around the world who have a disability, are faced with frustrating – even impossible-situations. . . . [T]hese people should enjoy the same services and opportunities in life as everyone else" (Pedlow et al. 2010: 147). As one of the employees of an organization working with VIs argued, "Mobile banking is supposed to work for everyone, so it is paramount to provide access to these resources."

At the policy level, the focus must be on rules that facilitate inclusiveness and effectiveness of mobile-money technology for all citizens. However, merely specifying inclusivity leaves unanswered questions, especially for those with visual impairment. What does "accessible" mean, what accommodations are reasonable, and who will bear the financial costs and responsibility of implementation (Gill 2002), whether for women's groups or persons with visual impairment? As the research illustrates, the women's groups, whether in rural or urban areas, have less pronounced difficulties in the usage of and accessibility to mobile-money services. For Kenya, the real challenge is ensuring that policies facilitate inclusiveness and access for persons with disabilities or other concerns.

For the visually impaired, the approach to mobile-money technology must be informed by a justice or human rights approach. As previously discussed, VIs face discrimination and injustices that make them more vulnerable when trying to use mobile services. Additionally, mobile-money technology must be interdisciplinary, holistic to include "products, resources, methodologies, strategies, practices and services . . . to promote functionality for visually impaired people with regard to autonomy, independence, quality of life, and social inclusion" (Alves et al. 2009: 148). Finally, as highlighted in the study, mobile technology must be undergirded by training and support services (Resnikoff et al. 2004) to ensure it is effective and inclusive. This was emphasized by VIs so that they can receive better treatment and customer service.

Afterword

According to Kenya's constitution, "A person with any disability is entitled to access . . . appropriate means of communication . . . materials and devices to overcome constraints arising from the person's disability" (Government of Kenya 2010: 63). As this research highlighted, many individuals are also willing to be part of the solution. This is how one person expressed their desire:

> So we have to stand strong although we have the disability. We have to stand and show society that disability actually is not inability. We can do it if we are given the opportunity and not sympathy.

A highlight of the workshop we ran for persons with visual impairment was a testimonial by an M-PESA agent who was himself visually impaired. He expressed this bottom line on why he took on the challenge of becoming an M-PESA agent: "[W]e are only impaired, not disabled." To the policymakers and service providers, he emphasized the need for mobile-money technology that facilitated acceptability, availability, accessibility, and adaptability. Yet, persons with disabilities continue to be significantly marginalized in terms of both policy and practice (Nkansah and Unwin 2010).

There are many guiding documents that can help inform policy and practice. At the national level, these include the Kenyan constitution, National Plan, and the State of Disabled People's Rights in Kenya – 2007; and at the international level, the UN Convention on the Rights of Persons with Disabilities – 2006. Governments, NGOs, and institutions must focus on ensuring policies that are fair and inclusive, especially for individuals with challenges. As one member of a focus group in rural Kenya put it, "I am blind, so the service providers should formulate policies that are user friendly for persons with disability."

At the workshop for persons with visual impairment, the presence of policymakers and service providers did not go unnoticed. Participants did begin to hear a shift in policy and practice. One of the mobile-money companies committed to developing software to ensure text to speech for VIs. They also mentioned that customer services for VIs would improve through a special customer-care line that would be launched. There was a commitment to developing an interactive voice recording or an "audible" feature so mobile-money technology is more accessible for persons with visual impairment. These are small, but promising, steps.

Acknowledgments

The researchers would like to thank the Institute for Money, Technology & Financial Inclusion (IMTFI) for their support to carry out this research. Our gratitude is also extended to the many civil society members, especially the women's groups from Eastern Kenya and the persons with visual impairment, service providers, and policymakers who graciously gave their valuable time to share their experiences and knowledge. Our research assistants in both Kenya and the United States did a terrific job in ensuring a solid research process through their interviews, transcription, and translation.

Ndunge Kiiti is a visiting professor at Cornell University with the International Programs, College of Agriculture and Life Sciences (IP-CALS) and Cornell International Institute for Food, Agriculture, and Development (CIIFAD). She is also an adjunct faculty at Emory University's Rollins School of Public Health, Department of Global Health, in Atlanta, Georgia. Her research on mobile money, empowerment, and health has been published in journals including *Journal of Development, Journal of Devel-*

opment in Practice, and *Journal of Development Communication.* Dr. Kiiti has a PhD in communication from Cornell University, Ithaca, New York, which included a one-year study in international health at the John's Hopkins School of Public Health, Baltimore, Maryland.

Jane Wanza Mutinda holds a PhD in environmental studies from Kenyatta University with an emphasis on gender and development. She is currently a senior lecturer and former chairperson in the Department of Environmental Studies and Community Development, Kenyatta University. She is currently serving as a deputy director in the the Directorate of Public and Students Complaints. She has done research and published papers in the areas of environment and sustainable development, gender and development, and mobile money technology.

APPENDIX 1: Research Description and Methodology

In the two-phase research, the aim was to, more comprehensively, study, document and disseminate the impact of mobile-money services on vulnerable populations – specifically women and persons with visual impairment who tend to be marginalized within societies. During the first phase, data were collected among twenty-one women's groups who had been trained by VwAG in the rural part of Eastern Kenya.[7] The second phase illuminated the experiences of persons with visual impairment in Kenya, especially as it intersected with poverty and mobile-money technology. Individuals and institutions impacted by visual impairment were identified using the snowball method.

In both phases of the study, data was collected using diverse methods, mainly qualitative in nature, considering the literacy rates in rural and urban areas. Focus-group discussions were carried out with six to eight members of each of the study populations. A total of thirteen focus groups were carried out: six with the women's groups and seven among individuals with visual impairment.[8] In-depth interviews focused on selected members of the particular population, mainly leaders for women's groups (N=21) and representatives and leaders from institutions or organizations working with persons with visual impairment (N=27).[9] Participatory observations of groups' monthly meetings or other events were done mainly to observe the use of mobile-money services. An extensive literature review mainly included library research and documents from government offices, nongovernmental organizations (NGOs), and service providers.

In terms of documentation, the first part of the study was a process of capturing and profiling the users of the mobile-money services. The process was also designed to assess and document the impact, both positive and negative, of the mobile-money services on the individuals or groups. The second part included data coding and analysis using thematic codes. In the third part of this research, we shared and disseminated the findings, mainly through workshops targeting the research participants, representatives from the study populations, service providers, and policymakers.

The workshop processes aimed to achieve three purposes. First, the goal was to disseminate some of the preliminary thematic findings from the research on mobile-money services. Second, the service providers and policymakers had the opportunity to respond to some of the issues and challenges highlighted in the research. This provided an opportunity to begin addressing the findings. The workshop formats worked effectively for sharing and influencing policy because they engaged the individuals who were impacted by their services. Finally, the third goal was to provide a networking opportunity for participants. For the women's groups, this was a frequent request throughout the VwAG training and research process. The research team observed and followed all ethics and etiquette requirements.

NOTES

1. *Vinya wa Aka* means "The strength of women" in Kikamba, the group's local language or "mother tongue."
2. At the time of research, the regions were called "districts." With the Kenyan government restructuring, these are now referred to as "counties."
3. M-PESA: M=Mobile; Pesa=money in Swahili.
4. MAP (Medical Assistance Program) International is a global health and development organization headquartered in Brunswick, Georgia.
5. Community outreach projects include environmental conservation (tree planting); counseling/mentoring youth in and out of school; community health education; financial support for local institutions and initiatives; and working with people challenged by disabilities.
6. As one participant put it, "On the negative side, eh, sometimes now because of this challenge of being visually impaired, most of the times . . . the phones which are available nowadays, they are not audible, they don't talk."
7. On an average, the women's groups can range from ten to thirty members in a group. A few of the groups have more members.
8. Additionally, focus groups were held with students from the academic institutions, mainly at the college level. However, at the Thika School for the Blind, focus-group discussions included students at the primary and secondary levels.

9. The individuals interviewed included members of the one women's group, Cheerful Sisters; nongovernmental organization leaders who were impacted by visual impairment themselves; principals; and top officials of the academic institutions.

REFERENCES CITED

Alkire, Sabina. 2007. Measuring Agency: Issues and Possibilities. *Indian Journal of Human Development* 1(1): 169–75.

Alsop, Ruth, and Andrew Norton. 2004. "Power, Rights, and Poverty Reduction." In *Power, Rights and Poverty: Concepts and Connections,* edited by R. Alsop. Washington, DC: World Bank, 37–58.

Alves, Cassia, Gelse Monteiro, Suzana Rabello, Maria Gasparetto, and Keila Carvalho. 2009. "Assistive Technology Applied to Education of Students with Visual Impairment." *Rev Panam Salud Publica/Pan American Journal of Public Health* 26(2): 148–52.

Banks, Ken. 2013. "A Personal Portrait of SMS: Innovation and Application for Progress." *Harvard International Review*: 38–43.

Boateng, Richard, Robert Hinson, Rakiya Galadima, and Longe Olumide. 2012. "Preliminary Insights into the Influence of Mobile Phones in Micro-trading Activities of Market Women in Nigeria." *Information Development* 30: 32–50.

Buku, Mercy, and Michael W. Meredith. 2013. "Safaricom and M-PESA in Kenya: Financial Inclusion and Financial Integrity." *Washington Journal of Law, Technology and Arts* 8(3): 375–400.

Collins, Daryl, Jonathan Morduch, Stuart Rutherford, and Orlanda Ruthven. 2009. *Portfolios of the Poor: How the World's Poor Live on $2 a Day.* Princeton, NJ: Princeton University Press.

Eade, Deborah. 1997. *Capacity-Building: An Approach to People-Centered Development.* Herndon, VA: Stylus Publishing LLC.

Freire, Paulo. 1984. *Pedagogy of the Oppressed.* New York: Continuum Press.

Gaventa, John. 2004. "Participatory Development or Participatory Democracy? Linking Participatory Approaches to Policy and Governance." *Participatory Learning and Action* 50: 150–59.

Gill, John. 2002. "The Development of Information and Communication Technology Systems to Include People with a Visual Impairment." *Visual Impairment Research* 4(3): 133–41.

Government of Kenya. 2010. The Constitution of Kenya. National Council for Law Reporting with the Authority of the Attorney General, Nairobi, Kenya.

Handapangoda, Wasana, and Ajantha S. Kumara. 2013. "The World at Her Fingertips? Examining the Empowerment Potential of Mobile Phones among Poor Housewives in Sri Lanka." *Gender, Technology and Development* 17(3): 361–85.

Harper, Simon, Yeliz Yesilada, and Tianyi Chen. 2011. "Mobile Device Impairment . . . Similar Problems, Similar Solutions?" *Behaviour and Information Technology* 30 (5): 673–90.

Hennink, Monique, Ndunge Kiiti, Mara Pillinger and Ravi Jayakaran. 2012. "Defining Empowerment: Perspectives from International Development Organizations." *Development in Practice* 22(2): 202–15.

Hennink, Monique, Carolyn Kulb, and Ndunge Kiiti. 2013. "Vinya wa Aka: An Expanded Microcredit Model for Community Development." *Development in Practice* 23(8): 1029–41.

Kenya Union of the Blind. 2009 http://kub.or.ke/.

Kiiti, Ndunge, and Eric Nielsen. 1999. "Facilitator or Advocate: What's the Difference in Shirley White?" In *The Art of Facilitating Participation: Releasing the Power of Grassroots Communication,* edited by S. A. White. New Delhi: Sage Publications, 52–67.

Kuper, Hannah, Sarah Polack, Cristina Eusebio, Wanjiku Mathenge, Zakia Wadud, and Allen Foster. 2008. "A Case-Control Study to Assess the Relationship between Poverty and Visual Impairment from Cataract in Kenya, the Philippines, and Bangladesh." *PLOS Medicine* 5(22): 1716–28.

Mas, Ignacio, and Olga Morawczynski. 2009. "Designing Mobile Money Services: Lessons from M-PESA." *Innovations* 4(2): 77–91.

Mas, Ignacio, and Daniel Radcliffe. 2011. "Mobile Payments Go Viral: M-PESA in Kenya," 1 March. Capco Institute's *Journal of Financial Transformation* no. 32: 169–182.

Maurer, Bill. 2006. "The Anthropology of Money." *Annual Review of Anthropology* 35: 15–36.

Mbiti, Isaac, and David N. Weil. 2011. "Mobile Banking: The Impact of M-PESA in Kenya." National Bureau of Economic Research, Working Paper No. 17129. Cambridge, MA. Retrieved 16 September 2017 from http://www.nber.org/papers/w17129.

Mbogo, Marion. 2010. "The Impact of Mobile Payments on the Success and Growth of Micro-Business: The Case of M-Pesa in Kenya." *Journal of Language, Technology and Entrepreneurship in Africa* 2(1): 182–203.

Ministry of Education. 2009. Report: Enrolment of Visually Impaired Pupils. Nairobi, Kenya.

Narayan, Deepa. 2002. *Empowerment and Poverty Reduction.* Washington, DC: World Bank.

Nasong'o, Shadrack, and Theodora Ayot. 2007. "Women in Kenya's Politics of Transition and Democratization." In *Kenya: The Struggle for Democracy,* edited by G. R. Murunga and S. W. Nasong'o. London: Zed Books, 164–196.

Ndambuki, Jacinta. 2010. "Discursive Representation of Women's Interests and Needs in Makueni District – Kenya." Unpublished thesis. Johannesburg: University of the Witwatersrand.

Njuguna, Margaret, Gerald Msukwa, Bernadeth Shilio, Cillasy Tumwesigye, Paul Courtright, and Susan Lewallen. 2009. "Causes of Severe Visual Impairment and Blindness in Children in Schools for the Blind in Eastern Africa: Changes in the Last 14 Years." *Ophthalmic Epidemiology* 16: 151–55.

Nkansah, Godfred, and Tim Unwin. 2010. "The Contribution of ICTs to the Delivery of Special Educational Needs in Ghana: Practices and Potential." *Information Technology for Development* 16(3): 191–211.

Papaioannou, Theo. 2011. "Technological Innovation, Global Justice and Politics of Development." *Progress in Development Studies* 11(4): 321–28.

Pedlow, Robert, Devva Kasnitz, and Russell Shuttleworth. 2010. "Barriers to the Adoption of Cell Phones for Older People with Impairments in the USA:

Results from an Expert Review and Field Study." *Technology and Disability* 22: 147–58.

Resnikoff, Serge, Donatella Pascolini, Daniel Etya'ale, Ivo Kocur, Ramachandra Pararajasegaram, Gopal Pokharel, and Silvio Mariotti. 2004. "Global Data on Visual Impairment in the year 2002." *Bulletin of the World Health Organization* 82(11): 844–52.

Rutherford, Stuart. 2009. *The Poor and Their Money: Microfinance from a Twenty-First Century Consumer's Perspective.* Rugby, UK: Practical Action Publishing.

Seale, Jane, E.A. Draffan, and Mike Wald. 2010. "Digital Agility and Digital Decision-Making: Conceptualising Digital Inclusion in the Context of Disabled Learners in Higher Education." *Studies in Higher Education* 35(4): 445–61.

Sen, Amartya. 1999. *Development as Freedom.* New York: Anchor Books.

UNDP and UNIFEM. 2005. "Needs Assessment of the Millennium Development Goal 3 on Gender Equality and Women Empowerment-Kenya, February 2005."

Wallis, Cara. 2011. "Mobile Phones without Guarantees: The Promises of Technology and the Contingencies of Culture." *New Media and Society* 13(3): 471–85.

Wallerstein, Nina. 2006. "What Is the Evidence on Effectiveness of Empowerment to Improve Health?" Copenhagen, WHO Regional Office for Europe (Health Evidence Network Report). Retrieved 19 May 2016 from http://www.euro.who.int/__data/assets/pdf_file/0010/74656/E88086.pdf.

Warschauer, Mark, Michele Knobel, and Leeann Stone. 2004. "Technology and Equity in Schooling: Deconstructing the Digital Divide." *Educational Policy* 18(4): 562–88.

Part II

Value and Wealth
What do Value and Wealth Do?
"Life" Goes On, Whatever "Life" Is

JANE I. GUYER

All theories of value and wealth are necessarily predicated on identifying qualities of lastingness, through time. To invoke the most mundane and theory-neutral concept for this range of phenomena, an "asset" is formally defined as "a resource controlled by the entity as a result of past events and from which future economic benefits are expected to flow to the entity" (Wikipedia, 11 Oct. 2014). For important political and social comparative reasons, however, emphasis has tended to be placed on the processes by which every component of this definition is created and preserved, with greatest focus on the ongoing social distribution of the resources themselves and their modes of "control." Focusing, as the authors in this part do, on daily life among relatively poor people, I want to draw out of their rich ethnography the capacity of endurance through time, from "past events" to "future benefits," as itself a foundational asset and a scarce resource, above all in the kind of worlds they describe, where daily life is quite unpredictable. Under current economic and political conditions, it is through ideologies of state and market that the formal sector alone is rendered as the central zone of the rational management of assets through time. In fact, a larger and larger proportion of money-mediated life is lived in unstable modes of employment, alongside downsized welfare states, and with policy interventions in legal status and ownership. "Living on two dollars per day" is actually not in dollars (a stable currency) nor is it daily (on a regular rhythm).

The quality that these essays place before us is the creation of duration itself: not as a function of need but as a practice of value in relation to the erratic temporalities of life, as lived in many registers: pleasure and pain, different relationships running on different rhythms, and immediacy in relation to varying benchmarks of past and future. The "margins" with which the book is concerned are not just geopolitical or social. There are "gains and losses in the margins of time" (Guyer 2014), where different temporalities of monetary circuits fail to coexist in plausible ways, and where the capacity to delay, defer, or otherwise manipulate monetary calendars is immensely powerful. This is the main theme of Amato and Fantacci's (2013) argument that it is the modern state that has lifted off the original meaning of "finance," from Latin *finis,* meaning "end."

In an idealized "traditional" world, it is either God or Custom that makes rhythms fit together. In an ethnographic paper on budgets in Cameroon (Guyer 1989), I explored how people turned "seasonal incomes" into "daily diets," through a variety of smoothing means: not always uncontentious but nevertheless available. In a recent paper (Guyer 2014), I address the promissory monetary economy, which is not, in this case, conceptualized under the same terms as debt. The failure of formal-sector temporal rigidities to accommodate to life was invoked as the reason to defer to custom (as depicted in Yoruba) whose etymology refers to choice: within an archive of received ideas, like a common-law legal system, where the participants search to find a particular resolution that "doesn't make everything worse."

These "margins-of-time" concerns emerge in fine ethnographic detail in all three of the chapters in this section, in different ways. There are circuits of the two currencies in Cuba and complex relations between them, mediated by legacy concepts from political experience. Tankha writes of the lower-level nonconvertible currency being managed through "long term social relationships among 'equal' Cubans with the same rights of access to socialist state services and products," whereas the convertible currency is applied to "unequal, fleeting and calculative relationships with foreign tourists." Clearly the quality of *enduring* value is located differently in the two circuits: in the first circuit, in a sociality that is constantly implicit in transactions with both others and the state, and in the second, in a foreign power's money that needs no long-term cultivation. It just *is.* This dual currency regime whereby people are able to move from one circuit to the other in diagonal (chiastic) trajectories appears to offer exactly the temporal nimbleness that single unified systems do not. Hence, perhaps the people's embrace of its ambiguities, such as the "the fact that 'la lucha' (the struggle) [. . .] is both enduring as well as fickle in its every day appropriations." Hence also, perhaps, people's worry about merging the two.

The image of "juggling" is particularly powerful in the chapter by Villarreal and Guérin. No one can "juggle" anything without a superlatively precise and responsive sense of timing. Here the enduring value lies in the experience of two women in mediating otherwise impossibly disturbing interferences in the temporalities of money and life. Carola's "prestige," which derives from her skill and bold confidence in the temporal management of money, as accrued over time, eventually becomes an asset in the formal banking sector. Saraswathi is involved in a "diversity of financial arrangements," using tactics as strategies "sustaining her relationships and her social identity." The authors trace out how their calculative management mediates the diversity of the temporality of others while sustaining asset value for themselves (through "gratitude" and "respect"). Both of these women respond rapidly to "emergency needs," ranging from "buying food from the ration shop" to paying for the major ritual markers of life: "marriages or funerals." The asset value of both of their careers, to themselves and to others, is precisely their capacity to support the enduring commitments of others that have to be mediated in money, across a whole variety of unruly temporal regimes. As they write, it is not so much the tangible assets that these women hold that give them an enduring value but rather the "processes of capitalization" in which they have shown such repeated evidence of skill: being "constantly" available for "opportunistic" mobilization of various monetarily calculated goods.

The fascination of *dhukuti,* with respect to wealth and value, lies in the high profile accorded to pleasure – over need or relationships or investment. Clearly, in this context, sustaining a sense of the pleasure of life is one of the most important activities that money can open up, and *dhukuti* is an established (enduring) practice that allows and fosters a "secure" means to multiple "goods" (in all senses of that term) that make the satisfaction of desire possible. Bajracharya points out that the narrow and coercive limitations of neoliberalism make a regularized practice of seizing risk, for purposes of joy, a site of enduring value.

These are fascinating chapters, from which one can gather how the *capacity* to sustain life – whatever that indicates – over time becomes an asset through which value is created, in almost the classic definition of the term asset, as quoted earlier.

Jane I. Guyer is professor emerita at Johns Hopkins University. She has held positions at Northwestern University, Harvard University, and Boston University. In 2008 she was elected to the National Academy of Sciences. She is author of several books, including *An African Niche Economy* (Edinburgh University Press 1997), *Money Struggles and City Life* (Heinemann 2002), and *Marginal Gains* (Chicago University Press 2004). Her research career has been devoted to economic transformations in West Africa, particularly the productive economy, the division of labor, and the management of money. Theoretically she focuses on the interface between formal and informal economies, and particularly the instabilities that interface gives rise to.

REFERENCES CITED

Amato, Massimo, and Lucca Fantacci. 2011. *The End of Finance*. Oxford: Polity Press.

Guyer, Jane I. 1989. "From Seasonal Income to Daily Diet in a Partially Commercialized Rural Economy (Southern Cameroon)." In *Seasonal Variability in Third World Agriculture: The Consequences for Food Security*, ed. David Sahn, 137–50. Johns Hopkins University Press.

———. 2014. "Coordinating Money Flows in Rural Economies: Eighteenth-Century England and Twenty-First Century Nigeria." Paper for the panel on Enlightenment's third pillar: solidarity and solidarity economies. Association of Social Anthropology Meetings, Edinburgh.

CHAPTER 4

Dhukuti Economies
The Moral and Social Ecologies of Rotating Finance in the Kathmandu Valley

SEPIDEH AZARSHAHRI BAJRACHARYA

"Credit-savings and work gives us enough to live. With *dhukuti* we can get the things the heart desires!"

This was what a woman of the untouchable "sweeper" caste in the old-town neighborhood of Patan – one of three city municipalities that gird the capital city of Nepal, Kathmandu – told me when I asked her about a financial practice I saw her taking part in one dusty afternoon in August 2009. I was sitting in on a credit-savings meeting organized by women in this neighborhood when I noticed two transactions taking place at the same time. The unnamed exchange involved much higher quantities of cash and no material record. When I asked about it, the women told me they were "playing *dhukuti,*" which they described as a practice involving a group of people contributing a certain monthly sum of money, the total amount of which is given to a member whose turn it is to receive the money. They organized and ran the transaction "on their own," unaffiliated with, or mediated by, any establishment. One woman talked about the gold earrings she was able to buy and wear to the last wedding she attended when I asked what they gained from the practice. Another spoke about the motorbike she recently bought her eldest son. Yet another pointed to her new house and said she had just recently purchased a TV.

The moral, social, and economic ethos embedded in this financial practice is unlike those of transactions linked to the semiformal and formal economies – credit and savings collectives, banks, and privatized finance institutes. People associated these institutions with failed infrastructure, corrupt politicians, and need ("enough to live"); they associated *dhukuti* with mobility, freedom, and pleasure ("the things the heart desires"). They discussed *dhukuti* as bureaucratic, institutionally guided, and communally determined; other institutions were considered as self-initiated, informal, temporary, and contingent. What moral, social, and economic relations and practices did collectives such as *dhukuti* assume and provoke? How were they integrated into people's, and specifically these women's, lives? How did they compare in people's minds and practices to financial practices associated with the formal and semiformal banking structures?

In the course of research, I found *dhukuti* prevailing as a social and economic phenomenon across a wide urban terrain. I witnessed it being played in different ways by multiple collectives and collectivities, a difference and multiplicity productive of various social, financial, and economic values and relations. From March 2011 to April 2012, I worked closely with women and men from several lower-caste and middle-class communities in Patan City to study the moral communities and social practices generated around financial practices such as *dhukuti*; practices that involved the informal exchange, circulation, and investment of new forms of income, finance, and consumption in urban Nepal. Contrary to prevailing depictions of such collectives as examples of social consensus and local solutions to the formal and failed economies of developing states by either pleasure-seeking or need-strapped subjects, I found the practice of *dhukuti* representing a system of value and exchange productive of past and emerging social distinctions; a flexible, creative, and overlapping use of formal and informal economies that thrived on affective economies of risk and uncertainty, and an ethos of pleasure as need.

Dhukuti

Dhukuti translates as "treasury" in the Nepali language. It indicates the place and/or container where cash and durables such as gold and jewelry are stored. It often conjures the image of a "safe" – a heavily padlocked box hidden in the domestic chambers of a home. But *dhukuti* also refers to a financial transaction and social phenomenon, which, in keeping with its literal reference, designates a sequestered arena and accumulation of capital that thrives beyond the purview of formal financial arrangement. Unlike its reference to an actual place where capital is locked, hidden, and handled by the patriarch or matriarch of a family, however, the second reference signals a mobile, conditional, and temporary exchange, transaction, and phenomena of capital investment accumulated, circulated, and bartered *outside* the home, among those to whom one is *not* related as kin.

In this sense, *dhukuti* represents an urban Nepali version of what is commonly known as a ROSCA, or a rotating savings and credit association: an indigenous financial institution affiliated with the informal financial sector of postcolonial communities (Geertz 1962; Ardener and Burman 1995; Gugerty 2007). As with most ROSCAs, *dhukuti* designates a pool of money based on the monthly contribution of a specific sum by each member of the collective that is acquired in turn by each contributing member. The collective dissolves once the participant list is exhausted and each person in the group has had a chance to receive the collected sum. Beyond these basic ground rules, however, *dhukuti* abides different styles and methods of playing, as well as varying terms of participation and conduct.

Economies of Need and Pleasure

Dhukuti is a financial practice linked to new forms of wealth that have come about since the 1970s when two economies – what I for discursive purposes refer to as "economies of need" and "economies of pleasure" – emerged and intersected within the Kathmandu Valley. "Economies of need" refer to the structures, discourses, institutions, and practices associated with the post–World War II development-aid industry. Following a regime change in 1950 and political and economic infrastructural initiatives in the 1970s, Nepal and select populations – women, children, rural, illiterate, lower- and untouchable-caste/class populations – were targeted by rural- and urban-based government, bilateral, and nongovernmental development projects, organizations, and interventions as "need-based" subjects (Fujikura 1996). The bureaucratic infrastructures that were implemented and that emerged in the name of progress and modernization as a result of these targeted interventions lay the basis for, and continue to be integral to the financial, social, and political backbone of, contemporary urban Nepal (Pigg 1992; Des Chene 1996). Simultaneous with this need-based infrastructure, the 1970s marked an influx, distribution, and availability of consumer goods and services. These were available to all Nepalis regardless of their caste, class, or gender orientation, a privilege denied by law under the previous regime (Liechty 1997). The infrastructure for this "economy of pleasure" signaled an increased privatization of industry and finance.

Scholarship about these emerging and intersecting neoliberal economies of value in the developing world tends to assume or prioritize the functions of one against the other. Either neoliberalism is seen as the outcome of a need-based structure of finance and political investment relevant to traditionally marginalized categories of caste and gender or it is seen as a means of leveling class-based aspirations and desires: need versus desire, caste versus class, local versus global. The literature on

ROSCAs follows this trend. When thought of as a need-based economy, these collectives are often portrayed as indigenous banking systems – insurance schemes, and/or savings/credit options – adapted by traditionally marginalized groups who lack access to formal banking facilities (Geertz 1962; Besley 1995; Anderson and Baland 2002; Guha and Gupta 2005). As depictions of consumer, pleasure-based economies, ROSCAs are often described as efficient and immediate means of accumulating large amounts of cash, direct means of purchasing durable goods that bypass inflated, inefficient, and corrupt collateral and bureaucratic procedures considered typical of developing world economies (Besley et al. 1993; Liechty 2003). Both perspectives assume these collectives to be products of negative economies: it is the absence of reliable banking systems and the presence of financial risks and insecurities predictive of developing economies that lead to the prevalence and need for ROSCAs. Under conditions of formal democratic government and efficient, reliable, and accessible banking, practices such as *dhukuti* need not, by these standards, exist. The practice, in other words, speaks to the failures – the crises, uncertainties, and tragedies – characteristic of late neoliberal developing economies.

My research on *dhukuti* calls for a different perspective. It addresses the need for ethnographically nuanced perceptions that do not assume the logic of a failed economy, or privilege one set of binary classifications (need vs. desire, formal vs. informal, local vs. global, caste vs. class) over another. In this chapter, I argue that the playing of *dhukuti* indicates overlapping and embedded intersections of need and pleasure-based economies that confirm past and newly emerging identifications and aspirations of class, caste, and gender. *Dhukuti* did not privilege the use of informal financial practices against institutionally available ones, either by those assumed to be in need (lower-class poor) or those seeking pleasure (high and middle classes). Rather, it was privy to a method and manner of barter that signified integrated, multiple, and contingent notions of person and value. Rather than representing a negative economy of poverty or corrupt privilege, I argue that *dhukuti* reflected an economy productive of various intersecting systems and scales of value and community. It generated conditions of possibility within which people actively and affectively constructed and imagined their financial, social, and political pasts, presents, and futures. The impacts of what are too often polarized as need- or pleasure-based economies were simultaneously felt in the Kathmandu Valley, where new infrastructures for developing responsible needs-based sources and investments in income have emerged alongside globally charged and locally manifest landscapes of consumer goods and practices in the form of what I call "economies of pleasure as need."

I begin my discussion with four ethnographic scenes that describe three ways of playing *dhukuti* among four different social collectivities: a group of middle-class women, lower "butcher"-caste entrepreneurs, high-end business-class men and women, and salaried untouchable "sweeper"-caste women. I was introduced to three types of *dhukuti* in the course of research: what people called "rotation," "lottery," and "releasing and eating." "Rotation" referred to a list of participants who received the collected amount in order of listing; there was no loss or gain in playing rotation style, as it designated a direct and predictable course of exchange. "Lottery" indicated the selection of a winner through the process of picking a name from a collective "pot." "Releasing and eating" referred to a bidding game wherein those seeking a claim on the monthly sum ("eating") challenged each other to subtract or "release" successively higher sums from the collected amount. The released bid was subtracted from the total amount received by the winning bidder; the "released" sum was, in turn, distributed among the remaining participants. I follow the ethnographic depictions of these different styles of playing with a discussion of social and moral hierarchies, formal and informal terms of exchange, and affective economies of need and pleasure.

Dhukuti Scenes

Scene One

Around 4:00 in the afternoon, Rabina called to tell me the *dhukuti* she was playing was about to begin. Half an hour later, we were walking up three flights of stairs, into a living room lined with plump, magenta-colored sofas and a TV playing a Bollywood song scene. Approximately fifteen women sat on the floor laughing and chatting. Rabina introduced me to the organizer who told me this was the last of five *dhukutis* she had organized for this day. They were playing "lottery" style. Every month she gathered the participants at her house to select one of the remaining names from the "pot." "Then we sit to eat snacks and tea," she laughed. She said they played "small-scale" – twenty participants, all women playing a cumulative sum of 10,000 Nepalese rupees (about $100 USD), based on an individual monthly contribution of 500. She said she began organizing *dhukuti* on a whim, "just like that"; as her children got older it became a way to "pass time." Before organizing *dhukutis,* she used to spend the time alone at home, watching TV drama series, until her children and husband returned from school and work. *Dhukuti* had become a way to make friends, and it provided her with a little side money she could use "here and there." It gave her something to do. "It is a lot of fun," she said. "I've met so many new people and made so many friends playing!"

Scene Two

Rabina's husband called around 10:00 AM to inform me that a *dhukuti* was scheduled to begin around 1:00 that afternoon. I met him in front of a four-story cement house along the ridges of the Ring Road—the wide paved road that separates Kathmandu's dense urban core from its rural and suburban peripheries. He told me the *dhukuti* involved twenty men playing a sum of 200,000 rupees (nearly $2000 USD). We walked to the second floor of the building where ten men sat on the floor. Rabina's husband introduced me to the organizer—a plump, middle-aged man sitting in the middle of the room next two stacks of cash. "We are all brothers," he told me as I took a seat next to him. "I am doing a kind of social service here. Everyone came to me and asked me to start a *dhukuti*. Business has been slow, and everyone has the need for cash." I asked him if that meant they were brothers by kin. He shook his head and said they were "brothers by occupation," by which he meant they were *Khadgis*, people of the lower "butcher" caste who owned meat shops in the area. Some of them were far cousins, but mostly, he said, they were "friend-brothers," *sathi bhai.*

After a few minutes, the organizer announced that they would begin playing. He brought out a plastic container filled with orange ping-pong balls. A heavy silence filled the room as each man took out one ball after another. A woman standing in for her husband who had not been able to attend the meeting in person came out shyly from behind a door and pulled out the winning white ball. With the game over, two women started distributing small plates of fried snacks and little glasses of orange soda.

Later, an informant—a woman of the same caste—referred to the men as "B-grade" *Khadgis*. When I asked her what she meant, she explained that "A-grade" *Khadgis* were those who had "name and honor." They did not keep to their caste-ordained profession of butchering but rather owned small trade shops or drove taxis for income. In other words, they were part of the modern rather than traditional caste-bound economy. B-grade *Khadgis*, by contrast, were those of lower grade who stood by their caste trade; they owned meat shops. She said these *Khadgis* had recently become wealthy due to the rising demand for meat in the city. But she warned me not to be fooled by appearances. "When you look at them, they look like they are high class because they have money and get ahead playing *dhukuti*. Actually," she said, "they are lower grade. High grade by money only. They are 'show-*Khadgis*.' They come from new money. They have money, but they don't have name."

Scene Three

I met Rabina and her husband at 9:00 PM in a fast-food kebab restaurant at a busy junction in the city. As we entered, Rabina whispered that the restaurant had been booked specifically for the *dhukuti* event. Middle-aged men and women in glittering tunics and tight jeans, faces painted with makeup, hair clipped and gelled, sat in groups of three and four at various tables. Rabina said ten *dhukutis* were being played at the same time. "They play in the millions. It is frightening!" she laughed. She pointed to the organizer: a slight middle-aged woman in tight jeans and a colorful long tunic, with hair drawn into a tight bun and ears dangling golden earrings. She said this woman played *dhukuti* like a business. "This is her profession," she told me. "Her whole family is involved. Her son and daughter-in-law keep the accounts, and her husband manages the scene." She said the gathering happened once every month, "hotel style," and that they played by a bidding system called "releasing and eating" (*chorera khane*). She was playing at the smallest scale: a *dhukuti* of 100,000 rupees (about $10000 USD) that involved ten people. When I commented on the small number of participants, she said that this was because all of the *dhukutis* being played here "played fast," within ten months to a year.

A waiter came by our table and asked us if we were ready to order. Rabina's husband told me to order whatever I wanted. "The food is the best part," he said. "Tandoori chicken, steamed dumplings, fried noodles, biryanis, kebabs, patties, and milk sweets, eat whatever you want." He said the bill was charged to those receiving the monthly collection. "Food commission," he laughed. "People fast on the day of playing so they can come here and eat as much as they can. You can taste the dumplings and kebabs in your stomach for days later!"

An hour later, the playing began. It took all of ten minutes. A woman at our table made a bid to "release" 30,000 rupees (around $300 USD)Her bid was surpassed by someone sitting at another table who bid to "release" 50,000 rupees (around $500 USD). Rabina's husband said they were not planning to bid for their money. They would wait till the end. They had no urgent or immediate need for the money. He said these *dhukutis* were mostly played by "business types" who didn't think twice about releasing large amounts of money and who needed the immediate cash.

Later, when I mentioned the event to an acquaintance, she shook her head and exclaimed that this kind of playing was "frightening," a sentiment similar to that of Rabina's husband. She said that playing of this sort was associated with high-end businesspeople and that it had become a kind of "fashion" in the city. I asked her why Rabina and her husband were playing this way since they owned a small meat shop that barely stayed afloat. She said Rabina and her husband played "for fun," and that "it was like watching a movie for them."

Scene Four

Sunita – a low, butcher-caste *Newar* – and I walked toward a neighborhood along the margins of the city, one affiliated with those of untouchable "sweeper"-caste identification known as *Dyahlas*. We had arranged to sit in on a monthly credit-savings meeting. As we walked through a narrow cobbled road, Sunita explained that all the cement houses towering over us, the TVs and cabinets, and the latest fashions and earrings the women in this community displayed came from their income as salaried and pensioned sweepers at the municipality, a job they had secured for the last fifteen years. She said that fifteen years ago a "German Project" had made an agreement with the city to hire these women as pensioned and salaried sweepers. "They have come into a lot of money since then," she said.

The credit-savings meeting was held in a room designated the "youth club." I noticed two cash transactions taking place at the table where four women sat huddled over several account booklets: one involved cash exchanges of 100-rupee notes; the other consisted of 1,000-rupee notes. When I inquired about the stacks and exchange, the women shyly responded that the first involved the credit-savings registry; the second was related to a *dhukuti* organized by one of the *Dyahla* women in charge of overseeing and keeping credit-savings accounts. The *dhukuti* consisted of sixty participants playing a monthly sum of 2,000 rupees (around $20 USD). She said they played by "rotation." Every month, the next person on the list received the money.

Sunita bit her tongue: "Sixty people!" she exclaimed. "That's five years of playing!" The woman said that most of their *dhukutis* played for that long. When I asked her what they got out of playing, she pointed out the window. "You see all the houses around you? Where do you think they come from?" I told her I thought they might use the money they received from their salaried jobs and credit-savings collections. She laughed. "Credit-savings and work gives us enough to live," she said. "With *dhukuti* we can get the things the heart desires."

As we walked away, Sunita said there was a lot of trust among these women. That was why they could afford to play for such a long stretch of time and with such large numbers of people. They all knew and trusted each other. "Nobody is going anywhere. . . . It is easy with them," she said. "They don't even have to get together for a separate event. They just give their money on time when they have it, and they take it when it is their time to receive the money. With them it is easy like that!" She said they were smart with their money. They worked hard, knew how to handle their money responsibly. She said, "They have a lot of love [*maya*] for their money. They are not like the women of our caste who don't work and act carelessly with their money."

"Love" came up again when I spoke to one of the *Dyahla* organizers. When I asked her why she didn't play by the lottery system as I had witnessed at other *dhukutis,* she said, "We don't play that way here." When I mentioned the bidding system, she shook her head and said she didn't understand how people could play that way. "Don't they have love for their money?"

> We have to work day and night for the money we earn. It doesn't just come like that, you know. We have too much love for our money. We have to suffer so much to make it. It doesn't come just like that, you know. And anyway, we don't need the money to make hundred of thousands' worth investments. We just use the money here and there, to buy this or that. I was able to finish building my house with the money I got last. My son has been asking for a motorbike. I am thinking I might buy it for him with this round of *dhukuti* money.

Social and Economic Capital

"Any form of capital – material or nonmaterial – represents an asset or a class of assets that produces a stream of benefits. The stream of benefits from social capital – or the channels through which it affects development – includes several related elements, such as information sharing and mutually beneficial collective action and decision making." (Bastelaer and Grootaert 2001)

This reference to social capital in a Social Capital Initiative Working Paper published by the World Bank Social Development Family Environmentally and Socially Sustainable Development Network speaks to how social capital has assumed an institutionalized framework for assessing and conceptualizing economic development in the Global South. From

this perspective, the social affects the quality of the "development" –
the terms of material economic exchange. By extension, social capital
connotes a specific relationship between the social and the economic
whereby financial and economic progress (the increase and accumulation of material assets) is considered best achieved under conditions and
platforms of social consensus and collectivity – "information sharing and
mutually beneficial collective action and decision making."

The collectives I witnessed dispute the assumption that the social and
economic constitute separate entities. They also challenge the notion
that the social, in the form of social capital, assumes equivocal conditions of collective harmony and consensus that necessarily lead to beneficial economic (read: national and market-based) progress. The values and
qualities associated with collectives such as *dhukuti* indicate economic values as *simultaneous* with the social. Furthermore, they reveal social values,
or what the paper infers as social capital relating to economic capital
according to locally girded and globally impacted conditions of *difference
and distinction* rather than consensus and harmony. What might appear
as social consensus and financial productivity from a perspective that
assumes the separation of the social and financial, and privileges a concept of social consensus based on the voice of the majority, conveys terms
of difference and discrimination when regarded from the perspective of
the underrepresented and silent minority. The social and financial capital
accrued from *dhukutis* were productive of continuing and emerging communal and individual differences in class, caste, and gender; the type and
manner in which people played *dhukuti* was intimately connected to how
they identified themselves and others along multiple and varying terms
of social distinction.

The first *dhukuti* I described involved a group of women whose values
and aspirations catered to a new class of woman associated with the period following the 1980s and 1990s (Liechty 2001). For these urban lower-
middle class women, *dhukuti* did not represent a significant source of income or a means to fulfill a significant household, financial, or consumer
need. They depicted *dhukuti* as a pastime, something they could afford
to do at this point in their married lives while their children attended
school and their husbands worked. Playing did not interrupt the flow
of their domestic lives; it was flexible, and it allowed them to attend to
their domestic duties uninterrupted, affording them social mobility and
a social milieu that identified them to themselves, and each other, as
urbane and modern. The organizer called it "fun." Playing involved a
type of social gathering and networking ("friendship") and an attitude toward financial investment and savvy ("time pass") that contributed to her

sense of herself as a "suitably modern" urban middle-class woman (Liechty 2003).

For the men in scene two, playing enabled them to access substantial amounts of cash without engaging financial protocols – high interest rates, collateral, and bureaucratic procedures – associated with the formal and semiformal financial economy. But the practice was specific to and emergent from their relationship to each other as "brothers" by caste and occupation. The organizer referred to it as a kind of social service. He called the participants "brothers." The reference did not identify them as brothers by kin; their brotherhood was based on caste, class, occupational, and neighborhood affiliation. There was a class dimension to the gathering as well – many of my informants of similar caste identified these men as low-grade *Khadgis* who had become wealthy by engaging the felicitous benefits of a trade without name or honor.

The restaurant *dhukuti* did not rely on or create the social intimacies of friendship or brotherhood. The players were associated with professionalism and "high-end business." People connected to each other in terms of the organizer who was known (and somewhat feared) for her professional competence. Each *dhukuti* was made up of a small number of participants – not more than ten or fifteen – indicating quick turns of playing that lasted no more than ten to fifteen months. This enabled people to access funds quicker without the risk of playing for extended periods with those to whom they bore no social ties or obligations. The playing involved a bidding system known as "releasing and eating" – a monthly auction played out publicly at the scene of gathering. Playing constituted a mandatory presence and a social event that was expensive, formal, and decadent. An entire restaurant had been booked for the event. People arrived dressed in fineries and expecting to dine on kebabs, biryanis, samosas, and tandoori meats.

But as with the other *dhukutis,* playing here did not just confirm a preordained class bracket as much as it seemed to cater to an *aspiring* modernity. Rabina and her husband owned a small meat-selling business. They could not afford, nor did they identify with, the high-stake playing they associated with the other participants, none of whom they knew personally. There was a spectator quality to their playing. They seemed to play in order to take part in what this gathering and playing represented – a desired and possible financial and social horizon. Their playing marked their participation in an urban class of financial and social exchange and possibility that did not describe their current reality as much as one they imagined. They were present as spectators – "like watching a movie" that was "frightening."

The *dhukuti* played among the untouchable-caste *Dyahla* women I discussed in the scene four, by contrast, consisted of sixty to seventy participants known to one another by kin, neighborhood, and work affiliation. Playing happened by "rotation" – the most conservative of the three playing systems that implied no financial gains or losses and a predictable time frame for how much and when funds were received by each participant. When I asked why they played by this system, women referred to their attachment, or what a few called their "love," for their money. As one woman put it, "We have to work day and night for the money we earn. It doesn't come just like that." The transactions took place exclusively in cash, derived from salaries they received at the first of each month. By contrast, the women I described in scene one used money borrowed from their husbands or credit accumulated in the course of playing other *dhukutis*. These women did not express anxiety or attachment to the money they played. They did not think about love or labor when talking about *dhukuti*. Playing was an extraneous way to "time pass" and make friends – a perspective that identified them as modern and urban women.

There were gender and caste implications to the affectations associated with *dhukuti* as well. In the area where I worked, both residents and nonresidents of the Pode Twa neighborhood of Kathmandu said *dhukuti* playing was a financial practice that flourished here more than in any other caste neighborhood. I was told this was because *Dyahla* women had come into "new wealth" in the past ten to fifteen years. These were opportune circumstances, based on the economy of need that had taught them how to be diligent and crafty with money. One of my informants continued her reasoning by contrasting these women with higher-caste women from the neighborhoods surrounding Pode Twa. Unlike *Dyahla* women, she said the higher-caste women were negligent with money and clueless about saving and investing techniques. She said this was because they did not need to work: "When they need money, they ask their husbands." In other words, unlike *Dyahla* women, these women didn't need to play *dhukuti*. Handling money – earning, saving, using, investing, risking money – was *lower-class activity*, something only wage-earning women had the need and inclination to understand.

Another telling material difference between this *dhukuti* and the others I described was the lack of a distinct event. The recognized date for paying and receiving *dhukuti* dues was simultaneous with an ongoing and recognized financial transaction – the credit-savings meetings that took place on the tenth of every month. Most women in the neighborhood already had an active credit-savings account, and it seemed a matter of convenience for them to take care of both dues at the same time. Others seemed to maintain their accounts before and after the gatherings in agreement with the organizer who took responsibility for gathering and distributing the right sum to the right people. The higher-caste Newar with whom I attended this meeting called it "easy" playing based on trust. She meant ease and lack of risk as financial ethos identifying those who did not have the option of being frivolous with their money, and who therefore stuck to their own kind – the conservative and nonmodern class and caste of woman who had gained her sense of savvy and enterprise by laboring hard for her money.

The argument is often made or assumed that late capitalism and twentieth-century globalization has promulgated class as the most relevant and dominant category of status (Harvey 1989; Jameson 1991). With regard to the developing world, the claim is that late capitalist culture has, for better or for worse, superseded "traditional" forms of distinction such as caste, gender, or race and replaced it with the terms of class (Fuglesang 1994). A similar case has been made for Nepal: "As more and more of everyday life revolves around the social imperatives of the money/market economy, the moral (and economic) logic of caste is subordinated to the economic (and moral) logic of class" (Liechty 2003: 8). But the *Dyahla* women and *Khadgi* men I worked with hardly escaped the mark of caste or gender while participating in new acquisitions and investments of wealth and class. Differences in "grades" and "types" of men and women were conveyed along past and newly recognized hierarchies of class, as well as those of caste and gender.

Engaging the Informal and Formal Financial Landscape

Dhukuti's popularity as an urban phenomenon relied on its affiliations – real and imagined – with the informal financial economy. It catered to ideas and practices of flexible and immediate transaction: the collection of large amounts of money overlooking legal and bureaucratic procedures, processes, collateral protocols and logistics associated with the formal banking sector. It was also accommodating of those in need of immediate capital. People either bid high enough to receive an allotted sum or they attempted to strike a deal with the organizer. People were also likely to play successive or multiple *dhukutis* at once – a practice described by many as a way to invest and secure their money. The assumption here was that money that stayed still – unmoving and materially evident – was likely to disappear.

The flexible, mobile, and circulatory affects and associations were critical to the practice. *Dhukuti* playing accommodated the routines of everyday life. People tended to play *dhukuti* in the hours when they were not working. The *Khadgi* men's collective gathered after 1:00 PM, when they closed their shops to come home to eat lunch, and before 4:00 PM, when they reopened them to afternoon and evening business. The collective of middle-class women played *dhukuti* in the hours when their husbands and children were not at home. The restaurant *dhukuti* took place after 9:00 PM when its members had returned from work. *Dyahla* women played *dhukuti* during other meeting times, or casually, "in passing."

But contrary to prevailing perception, people did not play *dhukuti* at the expense of formal or semiformal financial transactions. There was consistent overlap in people's use of *dhukuti* and more established means of financial exchange and investment. Urban Nepalis seemed adept at engaging in various cash and credit transactions through the multiple financial mediums and resources that spanned the urban financial landscape. They rarely expressed the need or desire to limit their use to one sector at the expense or privilege of another. I witnessed the people I worked with as being in flexible, creative, and frequent exchange with varying informal and formal means of investment and exchange.

Rabina and her husband bear this point. The couple took part jointly and separately in three of the four *dhukutis* I have described. In the course of research, they admitted to taking part in five other *dhukutis*. They also claimed to have savings accounts in one national bank, two finance companies, and a few credit-savings associations. The notebook in which Rabina's husband documented his *dhukuti* accounts was the same one in which he maintained accounts for his banking ventures and meat shop.

The Pleasures of Risk and Uncertainty

ROSCAs, and the informal economy they represent, are often depicted as indicating the failures and inefficiencies of formal financial structures in the developing world. It is, in other words, the conditions of uncertainty and risk characteristic of banking systems in developing economies that lead to informal economies and the flexible manner people use to engage formal economies. In the face of a democratic and functional structure of finance, institutions, the logic is that collectives such as *dhukuti* would be redundant; they would cease to exist. The playing and presence of such collectives thus entertain a failed economy – the consequence and reflection of underdeveloped economic, social, and political conditions of uncertainty and crisis.

Late neoliberal terms and logics of uncertainty are certainly critical to our understanding of *dhukuti* exchange. People often narrated the volatility of banking markets and infrastructures and their desires for consumer goods, products, and mobility as reasons for resorting to varying and flexible means of financial investment. But the pleasure element – the enchanted ethos – embedded in how people formulated their needs and desires is equally critical to how we understand these collectives.

By now it might have struck the reader that *dhukuti* appears to share the same vocabulary as gambling – an expressive vocabulary indulgent of play, risk, and thrill. People spoke about "playing" *dhukuti*. The bidding system was referred to as "releasing and eating." They shook their heads, bit their tongues, laughed, and spoke about it as "frightening." The events and relations surrounding *dhukuti* were anticipated with as much, if not more, commotion and excitement as the actual financial transactions. People talked with clear delight about the consumer goods and items they imagined being able to buy or they had purchased. They spoke in low whispers about the specter of illicit and ephemeral barter surrounding the practice and its participants. People came dressed in their fineries as if attending a gala or celebratory social event.

The *Dyahla* women I worked with spoke with great satisfaction about the sophistication and savvy they used to invest, circulate, and accumulate their money. They conveyed pride in the trust that served as a basis for the type of *dhukuti* they played; they spoke at length about their playing as ethical and economical, in contrast to the "business" and "fashion" type *dhukutis* they characterized as irresponsible and unethical. They called on their expertise with accounts and money; the account books they kept with meticulous care, able to juggle multiple financial transactions with ease and craft. They spoke engagingly about the consumer items and services they might purchase or anticipate. In every case, the intimacy people expressed with regard to the money, practice, and social relations involved in *dhukuti* revealed affective terms of personal, communal, and consumer pleasure.

By this measure, *dhukuti* cannot be reduced to a negative practice related to a disenchanted modernity that simply results from the risks and uncertainties inherent in the structure of a poorly developing economy. The practice was not just derivative of and subject to these external terms but seemed to actively produce and indulge elements of illicit and fashionable being that were specific and critical to its participation. It indicated the simultaneity and intersection of need and desire, or what we might think of as economies of need *as desire.*

Acknowledgments

Research for this project was funded through a generous grant awarded in 2011 by the Institute for Money, Technology & Financial Inclusion (IMTFI). I would like to thank all the women and men who revealed their lives and opinions to me in the course of research; I hope I have done some measure of justice to what they shared with me here. I would also like to thank Bill Maurer, Ivan Small, and Jenny Fan for their support and suggestions throughout the process. The errors, weaknesses, and omissions are of course my own.

Sepideh Azarshahri Bajracharya is assistant professor of anthropology in the Department of Sociology and Anthropology at Lewis and Clark College. She received her PhD in social anthropology from Harvard University in 2008. Her work focuses on the politics of communal, economic, and medical violence in urban Nepal. Recent publications include "Measures of Violence: Rumor Publics and Politics in the Kathmandu Valley," *Journal of Material Culture* 20(4) (December 2015).

REFERENCES CITED

Anderson, Siwan, and Jean-Marie Baland. 2002. "The Economics of Roscas and Intrahousehold Resource Allocation." *Quarterly Journal of Economics* 117(3), 963–965.

Ardener, Shirley, and Sandra Burman. 1996. *Money-Go-Rounds: The Importance of Rotating Savings and Credit Associations for Women.* London: Bloomsbury Academic.

Bastelaer Thierry van and Christiaan Grootaert. "Understanding and Measuring Social Capital: A Synthesis of Findings and Recommendations from the Social Capital Initiative" *Social Capital Initiative Working Paper #42,* The World Bank Social Development Family Environmentally and Socially Sustainable Development Network, April 2001.

Besley, Timothy. 1994. "Rotating Savings and Credit Associations, Credit Markets and Efficiency." *Review of Economic Studies* 61(4), 701–719.

———. 1995. "Nonmarket Institutions for Credit and Risk Sharing in Low-Income Countries." *Journal of Economic Perspective* 19(3).

Besley, Timothy, Stephen Coate, and Glenn Loury. 1993. "The Economics of Rotating Savings and Credit Associations." *American Economic Review* 83(4).

Des Chene, Mary. 1996. "In the Name of Bikas." *Studies in Nepali History and Society* 1(2): 259–70.

Fuglesang, Minou, and Stockholms Universitet. *Veils and Videos: Female Youth Culture on the Kenyan Coast,* 1994.

Fujikura, Tatsuro. 1996. "Technologies of Improvement, Locations of Culture: American Discourses of Democracy and 'Community Development' in Nepal." *Studies in Nepali History and Society* 1(2): 271–311.

Geertz, Clifford. 1962. "The Rotating Credit Association: A Middle Rung in Development." *Economic Development and Cultural Change* 10(3).

Gugerty, Mary Kay. 2007. "You Can't Save Alone: Commitment in Rotating Savings and Credit Associations in Kenya." *Economic Development and Cultural Change* 55(2).

Guha, Samapti, and Gautam Gupta. 2005. "Microcredit for Income Generation: The Role of ROSCA." *Economic and Political Weekly* 40(14).

Harvey, David. 1990. *The Condition of Postmodernity: An Enquiry into the Origins of Cultural Change.* Oxford England: Blackwell.

Jameson, Fredric. 1999. *Postmodernism, or, the Cultural Logic of Late Capitalism.* Post-Contemporary Interventions. Durham, N.C.: Duke University Press.

Liechty, Mark. 1997. "Selective Exclusion: Foreigners, Foreign Goods and Foreignness in Modern Nepali History." *Studies in Nepali Society and History* 2(1): 5–68.

———. 2001. "Women and Pornography in Kathmandu: Negotiating the 'Modern Woman' in a New Consumer Society." In *Images of the Modern Woman in Asia: Global Media/Local Markets,* edited by Shoma Munshi. London: Curzon Press.

———. 2003. *Suitably Modern: Making Middle-Class Culture in a New Consumer Society.* Princeton, NJ: Princeton University Press.

Pigg, Stacy. 1992. "Inventing Social Categories through Place: Social Representations and Development in Nepal." *Comparative Studies in Society and History* 34(3): 495–513.

Tsai, Kelley S. 2000. "Banquet Banking: Gender and Rotating Savings and Credit Associations in S. China." *China Quarterly* 161.

CHAPTER 5

Chiastic Currency Spheres

Postsocialist "Conversions"
in Cuba's Dual Economy

MRINALINI TANKHA

Introduction

Soon after the triumph of the revolution in 1959, Ernesto Guevara was appointed president of the National Bank of Cuba. Guevara had an open aversion to money and believed that its institutionalization only accentuated greed, competition, dissolute wealth, and class differences. He advocated for money solely as a unit of account, reflecting his vision of a new collective consciousness in society that privileged moral incentives over material rewards for labor (Guevara 2003 [1964]: 192). In his role at the National Bank, Guevara demonstrated his contempt for money by audaciously signing newly minted Cuban peso currency notes (figure 5.1.) solely with his Argentinean pseudonym *Che*, meaning "friend" or "pal" (Crompton 2009: 71). Ricardo Rojo, Guevara's longtime friend, wrote, "[T]he day he signed *Che* on the bills, [he] literally knocked the props from under the widespread belief that money was sacred" (1968: 106). In Cuba today, the *Che*-signed bills have become numismatic relics of a bygone era – souvenirs sold for a small fortune to foreign tourists in an increasingly dollarized economy. Guevara's symbolically charged act of signing Cuban currency notes solely with his nom de guerre is, however, simultaneously far-flung from as well as intimately intertwined with present-day practices of money in Cuba.

In this chapter I examine the structure and workings of Cuba's dual-currency system consisting of two national currencies: the Cuban peso and the Cuban convertible peso. I demonstrate how the dual-currency system emulates classic anthropological accounts of precolonial societies that separated and hierarchically ordered spheres of exchange based on different kinds of monies, commodities, and labor, allegedly in service of

Figure 5.1. 1960 Cuban peso bill signed by Ernesto "Che" Guevara.

Photo by author.

maintaining egalitarianism. But, unlike past iterations, Cuba's currency spheres display incoherencies in economic and moral imperatives due to contradictions between the state's market-oriented economic reforms since the 1990s and its official socialist political ideology. I reveal how systemic dissonance, between what is profitable economically and what is desirable morally, is accentuated, alleviated, as well as strategically circumvented in discursive financial practices of the informal economy. Even though the flow of currencies across spheres is widespread, the modalities, cultural idioms, and relations of exchange within which they are embedded are more obstinate. Lingering socialist notions of communal labor, reciprocity, solidarity, and collective struggle are selectively and strategically invoked to morally cleanse illicit economic practices driven by pursuits of private profit. Cuba's dual economy therefore presents a chiastic structure in its repetition of what are now considered antiquated economic forms as well as in the inversions and crisscrossing of its currency spheres. This chiasmus manifests through the "conversions," or flows between the distinct currency spheres that also distinguish the multiple and complex ways inherited Che-esque socialist categories continue to cast a curious shadow on wealth and value creation, social relationships, and economic moralities in contemporary postsocialist Cuba.

Cuba's Special Period Economic Reforms

The myriad ways in which Cubans encounter money, even today, is shaped by the enduring weight of memories from the Special Period crisis of the

1990s when Cuba lost its main export market and source of subsidized imports,[1] which up to that point had primarily consisted of former Soviet Bloc countries, under the COMECOM (Council for Mutual Economic Assistance). With the collapse of the Soviet Union, the Cuban government had to undertake a major restructuring of the economy in order to competitively reinsert itself into the international economy (keeping in mind the US embargo against trade with Cuba). A series of liberalizing reforms were implemented, such as diversifying agriculture to provide food security; promoting tourism; inviting foreign direct investment (FDI) through joint ventures with overseas companies; legalizing some self-employment opportunities mainly in the form of small restaurants and rooms for rent in homes catering to foreign tourism; and courting remittances from the Cuban diaspora.

To facilitate these economic reforms, there was also a shift in monetary policy that legalized the use of the US dollar (USD)[2] in Cuba to facilitate the government's private enterprise initiatives and its tourism agenda, and to allow easy transfer of remittances. The Cuban convertible peso (CUC) was also introduced at this time (in limited use) and had a value equivalent to the USD. Tourists coming to Cuba could either use USD or convert their foreign currency into CUC. The USD and CUC were used only in foreign investment, tourism, and foreign joint-venture initiatives such as tourist hotels and restaurants, tourist taxis, self-employment enterprises and specific "dollar stores" that sold mainly imported "luxury" items. This isolated the development of foreign sectors from the instabilities and disequilibria that dominated the rest of the economy (Alejandro 2012: 41). Moreover, with the USD becoming legal tender, émigré contacts became important financial assets, and in the year 2000 remittances were estimated to be $720 million (Ritter 2004: 9). Even though possession of the USD had been criminalized by the penal codes of 1979 and 1987, a widespread black market for USD had developed since the onset of the Special Period (Ritter and Rowe 2002). This justified the USD's legalization, allowing the government to gain access to the hard currency that would otherwise circulate illegally (Eckstein 1994, 2004; Henken 2000; Monreal 2002). This reasoning was explicit in the official name for the dollar stores – *Tiendas para la Recuperación de Divisas* (TRDs) or "stores for the recuperation of hard currency." However, in June 2004 the Bush administration tightened sanctions by further restricting USD remittances to Cuba. The Cuban Central Bank responded to this "economic war" in November 2004 by passing Resolution No. 80/2004 that discontinued the USD as legal tender. The CUC then replaced all of the USD's legal economic functions. The current exchange rate[3] between the two currencies is US$1 = 1CUC,[4] and an additional 10 percent tax is imposed when converting USD into CUC. This gave the Cuban government an immediate way of controlling and collecting all the hard currency entering or circulating inside in the country, since restrictions prevent other forms of hard currency from being used for buying and selling. This reduced the hard currency in circulation in the hands of Cuban citizens and immediately transferred it to the state treasury where it could be used for foreign trade. Apart from the CUC, the Cuban peso (CUP) or *Moneda Nacional* (national money) also circulates in the Cuban economy. Unlike the CUC, the CUP is supposed to be used mainly by Cuban citizens for staples such as fruits and vegetables, electricity, gas, local taxis, medicines, and other *locally* produced "nonluxury" items that are sold in *bodegas* (subsidized ration shops) or other CUP shops.

The Cuban government thus created a dual economy by enclaving the access to and uses of the CUC and CUP. The more "capitalist" CUC is used mainly for imported and higher-quality goods and services by either foreigners or Cubans (with access to foreign remittances or employment opportunities in foreign joint ventures or tourism) in activities that evoke market-like values such as competition for tips and bonuses and maximizing private profit through small private-entrepreneurship or foreign collaborations. The "socialist" CUP, on the other hand, is used mostly for locally produced subsistence and lower-quality products and state services (such as ration shops, health, education, housing, etc.) provided largely only to Cubans in institutions that are regarded as the bastions of Cuban socialism. These currency spheres resound but also cleverly distort Keith Hart's (1986) renowned notion of heads and tails embodied by the coin. For Hart, every coin has a head standing for the state and political authority and a tail representing the market. In Cuba, this state-market dialectic, that for Hart mediates the way money functions in society, is deliberately split and transposed onto the two distinct currencies – the CUP head and CUC tail.

In principle, the CUC and CUP are freely convertible,[5] however the unequal exchange rate (1CUC = 24CUP) and differential access to these currencies has exacerbated disparities between foreigners and Cubans as well as among Cubans with access to remittances and jobs in tourism versus those employed by the state. In addition, since Havana is the epicenter of tourism, this has exacerbated already severe regional economic imbalances in the country and induced internal migration to the capital. The dual currency system has, therefore, dramatized everyday life encounters and tensions between the state's socialist ideology and its insertion into a global capitalist economy.

Cuba's Official Chiastic Currency Spheres

The Cuban government's official separations between the CUP (nonluxury, subsistence, local, socialist) and the CUC (luxury, wealth, foreign,
capitalist) seem to be a striking throwback to early anthropological accounts of exchange in precolonial societies (Barth 1967; Bohannan 1955;
Firth 1939; Malinowski 1922; Salisbury 1962) where objects and social relationships were arranged and assigned to different hierarchically ordered
transaction spheres. Most of these ethnographies reflected the separation
of the exchange of *subsistence products* from the exchange of *valued objects*
or repositories of wealth (Sillitoe 2006: 6). In his work on the Tiv of Nigeria, Paul Bohannan argued that there were three *hierarchically ordered*
exchange spheres functioning to prevent certain goods from being accumulated or redistributed in morally unacceptable ways. The first subsistence sphere was governed by the "morality of the free and uncontrolled
market" (1959: 125); the second sphere was not associated with the market but with prestige; and values in the highest sphere of wealth characterized by rights in human beings (mainly women) were expressed in
terms of kinship and marriage. In Cuba, the hierarchical economic ordering of the CUC and the CUP spheres, based on principles of subsistence
and wealth, is reminiscent of these past theories of exchange. However,
given Cuba's political rhetoric and continued promise of socialism, there
is also an arresting inversion of past anthropological models because the
economically higher sphere of wealth is governed by "ethically dubious
market principles," and the economically lower CUP sphere of subsistence is associated with prestige and more enduring "kinship-like" values
of solidarity, egalitarianism, and reciprocity advocated by the socialist
state.

Much like some accounts of precolonial societies that describe how
exchange spheres also uphold and recreate constellations of economic interests and relations of political power (Ferguson 1985; Parmentier 2002),[6]
the Cuban state officially advocates for separate currency spheres in order to safeguard state power. The deliberate compartmentalization of
tourist and non-tourist spheres protracts the rate of transition and curbs
the possible threats to the socialist state arising from its market-oriented
tourism initiative. President Raúl Castro in a speech given on July 26,
2007, said,

> [W]e are currently studying the possibility of securing foreign investment,
> of a kind that can provide us with capital, technology or markets, to avail
> ourselves of its contribution to the country's development . . . upon well-

defined legal bases which preserve the role of the state and the predomi-nance of socialist property. (Castro 2007)

The CUP and CUC currency spheres therefore act as a way to legitimize the various transactional motivations and strategies ensuring the longevity of state socialism demonstrated by its continued stronghold over property as well as education, health, and the armed forces. This is true especially in the parity rate maintained between the CUP and CUC for public firms and enterprises to subsidize their inputs and imports, while the exchange rate for retail purchases by the Cuban population is 1CUC = 24CUP. For instance, a special state-run employment agency provides Cuban workers to foreign firms through subcontracts. The foreign companies pay the employment agency in USD, and the agency pays the workers a wage in CUP, equivalent to merely 5 percent of the actual contracting fee (Henken 2005: 373). As mentioned previously, the 1990s liberalizing reforms (and by extension the dual-currency spheres) were posited as short-term "diversions" (Appadurai 1986) to assuage the Special Period crisis that in the long term would be channeled toward protecting state socialism and socioeconomic egalitarianism. This evokes the tension Parry and Bloch identified as a key feature of money; its entrenchment in the symbolic construction and negotiation of two transactional orders that realize short-term, individual, and competitive interests on the one hand and long-term interests of reproducing the moral and cosmic order on the other (1989: 24)[7]. In Cuba, short-term and long-term interests are thereby fulfilled by separate spheres of activity that are negotiated through the use of two distinct currencies.

Enclaving of exchange not only maintains state power but also ar-ticulates the sociocultural idioms that ought to be preserved in society. Several ethnographies show how spheres of general-purpose money and special-purpose money (cattle, beads, cloth, wampum, cowry, etc.) have historically been separated to arrest money's leveling quality and pre-serve the flow of value in a direction where its reflection is meaning-ful to the *existing* cultural schema (Akin and Robbins 1999; Hutchinson 1992; Saul 2004; Shipton 1989). One might say then that Cuban currency spheres are vindicated through a kind of "revolutionary mystique," ac-tively evoked by the state. For instance, the text of the 1993 self-employ-ment law clearly articulates the state's interest in heavily controlling these activities in order to "prevent the values of entrepreneurship from contaminating those values and practices fostered by socialism" (CEPAL 1997: 501 quoted in Gordy 2006). In May 1994, Fidel Castro in a press con-ference at the 15th International Tourism Convention in Varadero stated:

> We have not relinquished the idea of building socialism. We have not relin-
> quished our goals. We are simply adapting to our current reality. . . . Many
> have questioned the influence tourism might have upon the minds of our
> people, upon their basic traits . . . Cuba's ties, culture, and contact with the
> world are growing. We will be all the more pure if we are able to preserve
> our virtues amid the contamination certain things might bring with them.[8]

These discourses of diseased hedonistic values associated with tourism
and the CUC sphere sullying the fabric of a virtuous socialist society are
ubiquitous in Cuban political rhetoric of the 1990s and were used to justify the separation of currency spheres. The main problematic in Cuba,
however, is that the CUP subsistence sphere largely reflects the unadul-
terated "morally superior" values of state socialism directed toward the
maintenance of collective assets, whereas the CUC sphere of wealth em-
bodies market-oriented values of individualized consumerism creating
an incongruous structure of separation in which economic and moral
incentives are in conflict with one another.

Others have postulated that exchange spheres are segregated and hierarchically ordered based on successively higher levels of skilled labor expended in the production of their corresponding exchange objects (Firth
1939). In Cuba there is an "inverted pyramid" (de la Fuente 2001; Monreal,
2002 Henken 2000) of distorted labor hierarchies in which the service
work of tourism comprises the economically higher CUC, whereas the
specialist professions (professors, doctors, lawyers, etc.) constitute the
economically lower CUP currency sphere.[9] The disjuncture between material reality and socialist ideology has led to "serious reductions of real
living standards, particularly for people in the peso [CUP] economy, such
as pensioners, employees in state enterprises and workers in education,
medicine and public service" (Ritter 2004: 10). This contradiction is one of
the more palpable manifestations of the dual economy, and the inverted
labor pyramid has intensified those very inequalities[10] and ambivalent
socialities that state discourses claimed the dual currency spheres would
make sluggish and subvert in the long run. Rather than providing an
antidote, currency spheres have exacerbated disparities between foreigners and Cubans, as well as among Cubans, and have also stimulated the
emergence of new exchange relations. Some scholars have argued that
spheres of exchange differentiate between types of exchange relations
where higher economic spheres involve activating and strengthening social relationships and alliances (Munn 1986; Piot 1991). In Cuba this is
turned upside down, as the economically lower CUP sphere of exchange
is characterized by long-term social relationships among "equal" Cubans
with the same rights of access to socialist state services and products,

whereas the unequal, fleeting, and calculative relationships with foreign tourists are confined to the CUC sphere of wealth. This also preserves distinct modalities of exchange (Akin and Robbins 1999) and channels the flow of money based on dichotomies of sharing/reciprocity vs. competition/profit maximization associated with the CUP and CUC spheres respectively.

Therefore, Cuba's official currency spheres reverberate with past accounts of exchange spheres in their functions of safeguarding matrices of power and arresting the rate of social change, and in the ways that binaries of money, objects, social relationships, labor, and modalities of exchange are schematized. The structure of Cuban currency spheres, however, displays a chiastic quality in the ways these categories are hierarchically ordered due to the contradictions between Cuban socialism and its market-oriented agenda and the resulting slippage between economic and moral incentives. One of the key issues regarding the functioning of exchange spheres is how to theorize movements and currency flows within and across spheres. Paul Bohannan's (1955) central claim was that "conveyances" (exchanges within each sphere) were morally neutral, but "conversions" (exchanges between spheres) were morally charged. Conversions were *do kwagh* (desirable) only when converting to a higher sphere of wealth and were considered to be investments. Bohannan's critics instead described hybrid ways of thinking about conveyances and conversions during cultural contact that accommodate new economic opportunities while attempting to preserve historically specific cultural schema and notions of morality. Practices of money in Cuba, especially in the informal economy, reveal the broader structural contradictions of everyday life and also display hybrid "conversions" between currency spheres. These practices demonstrate that while the objects and currencies of exchange flow seamlessly within and across exchange spheres, the accompanying social relationships and modalities are more stubborn and morally charged.

Social Practices of Money

Autonomous activities in the informal economy provided many Cubans a more immediate solution to the Special Period economic crisis. This continues to be true even in the twenty-first century. Between 1989 and 1993 there was an estimated increase in the black market from 2 billion pesos to 14.5 billion pesos (Eckstein 1994: 124). A widespread informal economy emerged in Cuba to compensate for the government's defaults in food and household supplies; housing/property bartering; religious ceremonies; gambling in clandestine dogfights and cockfights; covert emigration strategies; and trade in illegally imported items such as clothes, shoes, electronics, etc. Activities *por la izquierda* (literally "by the left" but meaning "on the sly") or *por debajo de la mesa* (under the table) and their relationship to changing conceptions of Cuban personhood have therefore become the subject of inquiry for many scholars (Fernández 2000; Leon 1997; Pérez-López 1995) during this contested period of transition in Cuba.

Boundaries of *La Lucha* (the Collective Struggle)

Informal-economy activities in Cuba are often firmly embedded in local and transnational social networks such as familial, neighborhood (*barrio*), friendship, or occupational relations as well as family connections abroad providing respite and alternatives to official routes of the dual currency spheres. During the Special Period, as part of *"La Batalla de Ideas"* (the battle of ideas) launched by the Cuban government in the 1990s, Fidel Castro urged Cubans to *luchar* (struggle), *inventar* (invent solutions), and *resolver* (get things done to survive) as ways to assuage experiences of economic crisis. These cultural idioms, especially *la lucha*, in addition to reinterpreting revolutionary imagery of struggling against colonialism and imperialism, also invoked a larger social collective of participants with shared experiences of the constraints and tribulations of Cuba's shortage-ridden dual economy. Therefore, foreigners and tourists were considered to be ontologically outside of *la lucha* because they were not subject to the same limitations and bottlenecks that pervaded everyday economic life on the island.

For instance, on my first trip to Cuba, I tipped a street musician in a combination of CUC and CUP. He was enraged when he saw the CUP bill. He was so insulted that he threw it on the floor, spit on it, and said to me, "You are tourists and can afford to pay in CUC. I would not play for you if you were going to pay me in pesos [CUP]." He stormed off but came back a few minutes later and picked up the CUP bill. This is an extremely significant moment because it displays the anxieties toward the crosscutting of the CUC and CUP spheres of exchange, which in turn symbolizes the ambivalence toward the overlapping of the modalities of exchange associated with these two currencies rather than the currencies themselves. The CUC capitalist sphere of exchange defines the social relationship between the musician and myself (the tourist) as an essentially unequal one, and in that instance I had made a mockery of this hierarchy by trying to enter the CUP socialist sphere reserved for fellow Cubans who face similar hardships of scarcity and instability in Cuba's dual economy. The separations in the CUC and CUP modalities of exchange are therefore closely associated with the kinds of goods and services being exchanged (or the kind of labor being expended) as well as the social relationships of exchange in which they are enmeshed.

On the other hand, Victor, thirty-two, worked in the imported meats and cheeses counter at one of the biggest CUC supermarkets in Havana. Victor habitually stole Spanish ham, chorizo, salmon, gouda and cream cheese (all rare treats for many Cubans) for his own consumption as well as for resale to family and friends at lower prices in CUC. Sometimes Victor would even give away small quantities of cheese and cold cuts to loved ones. Like many, Victor had wanted the job precisely because of the added perks of access to these CUC goods that could later be sold in the informal economy. The theft and resale of food and other products in the informal economy was frequent but also entailed a range of socioeconomic stakes and excited various clashing moralities. Common stolen products bought and sold in the informal economy include foreign cheese, meat, and other food from CUC shops, restaurants, and hotels; meat from CUP and CUC butcher shops; car parts from state mechanics; packaged food and household items from warehouses; and electronic spare parts from state IT departments. Victor was largely considered *buena gente* (good people) because even though he stole food items from his workplace for private profit, he was also generous and careful not to con his fellow Cuban friends and relatives who were all part of the same collective *lucha*. While Victor does not make conversions with respect to the CUC objects of exchange, he brings these CUC goods of wealth into the realm of more enduring, reciprocal gift relations (Mauss 2000 [1950]) and kinship – not unlike the modalities and social relationships among *socios* (buddies) normally associated with the CUP sphere. Despite the fact that there is some private profit for Victor, the socio-moral and economic imperatives line up more effortlessly[11] to preserve the social networks of *la lucha*, thereby dissolving some of the chiasm associated with the formal structure of currency spheres in Cuba.

This also underscores the tacit boundaries between Cubans and foreigners and implies that swindling foreigners (outsiders) does not carry the same negative valence as fleecing *socios*. Since foreigners do not operate under the same conditions as the informal economy, they are not considered part of the collective *lucha*. Private profit extracted from foreigners is a modality of exchange contained within the formal, more anonymous "capitalist" CUC sphere of exchange, making it a conveyance and hence morally neutral. However, unlike Victor, other informants were harshly criticized when they undercut the camaraderie and reciprocity of la lucha in their informal economy activity through fraudulent pursuits of self-aggrandizement at the expense of those considered part of that imagined social configuration. Therefore, while informal economy exchange resiliently undermines the formal directed flow of objects and currencies through dual exchange circuits, the informal policing of cultural frontiers between foreigners and Cubans and the corresponding conversions between relations and modalities of exchange also confirms official discourses of separation, rendering their boundaries meaningful and relevant.

La Doble Moral (Double Morality)

In the earlier instances, conversions through stealing from the workplace were not a source of moral transgression because of the ways the goods were redistributed through social networks in the informal economy. Castro's official call for fortitude during the Special Period crisis by *luchando* (collectively struggling) has been appropriated to legitimize activities fundamentally contradictory to the revolutionary project. Most of my informants veiled and justified their illegal informal practices such as stealing as ways of *luchando*. *Inventar* and *resolver,* in particular, are often used as euphemisms for stealing and getting things done at any cost. For instance, Victor would always use the word *resolver* to describe CUC items "procured" at the workplace. These popular discourses that cover up a "multiplicity of sins" (Tanuma 2007) lend themselves to what many call *la doble moral* or the "double morality" of Cuban life. In the informal economy, official discourses of *luchar, inventar,* and *resolver* are hence reinterpreted and turned on their heads against the very entity that introduced them – *el estado* (the state) writ large.

This can be seen in the actions of Norman, thirty-six, who worked as an ambulance driver at one of the biggest state-run hospitals in Havana. He was often hired by friends (functioning as middlemen) to transport illegal items from the outskirts of Havana into the city in the ambulance. In addition to his state salary of 400 CUP, Norman would make additional cash in CUC for such missions. Big vehicles such as trucks and vans were often stopped at police checkpoints located at various intersections of the city and searched precisely for smuggled goods in bulk. "But no one is going to stop an ambulance . . . and you don't have to pay for gas!"

said Norman smugly. Bohannan argued that conversions "excite a completely different sort of moral reaction: the man who exchanges lower category goods for higher category goods does not brag about his market luck but about his skill in investment, his personal magnetism and his 'strong heart'" (1955: 64–65). Carefully engineered through collective organization, Norman and his friends would use the ambulance to transport stolen meat and vegetables in bulk and sell them illegally in farmers markets or to family and friends. This cunning manipulation and bold redirecting of resources from one of the pillars of the socialist state (health) for private gain was like beating the official at its own game. Moreover, Norman's position in the CUP sphere allowed him to convert key state resources (the ambulance and gasoline) into extra CUC income and profits. This kind of upward conversion to the CUC sphere to the detriment of the state (the "head" in Keith Hart's terms) with entrepreneurial bravado was not morally undesirable; it was celebrated.

Most of my informants made the fine-grained distinction between *robar el estado* (robbing the state) that was morally acceptable and stealing in general that was not. The state was considered a hostile entity due to its discriminatory dual economic policies and defaults in providing food security and supplying basic consumer goods. Participation in *la lucha* discursively carved out boundaries both between Cubans and foreigners, as suggested earlier, as well as between *el estado* and the individual Cubans collectively engaged in *la lucha*. State resources, emblematic of the CUP sphere, that were converted into informal-economy CUC profits were, hence, ironically subject to modalities of the CUC sphere where capitalist craftiness was morally appropriate and rewarded.

Multidirectional Transnational Conversions and Moral Labor

Anthropologist Jane Guyer takes issue with Bohannan's spheres of exchange for being too insular and not taking into account broader geographical circuits of exchange. Guyer suggests that Bohannan's reading of moral conversions to higher exchange spheres excludes a critical dimension of the Tiv's trading with northern and southern tribes in *tugudu* cloth and brass rods. She argues for viewing the concept of conversion as not unique to spheres of exchange and to "see" it at

> junctures in transactional pathways. Tiv currency forms symbolized not a closed transactional model but an open set of directional transactions that work stepwise toward the constitution of stores of value that had greater longevity and security than the currencies themselves. A conversion adds,

subtracts, or otherwise transforms attributes of exchange goods in ways that define the social direction of future transactional possibilities. Conversions are the compasses and landmarks on the navigational pathways of currency circulation. (Guyer 2004: 30)

In Cuba, too, conversions and conveyances are not unidirectional nor are they restricted just to the CUC and CUP spheres carved out by the state. Marisol, a medical doctor in her early forties, also worked as a chauffeur, ferrying around tourists in her small green Hyundai Santro. She had worked as a doctor in Cuba for several years, earning a salary in CUP. With the Special Period crisis however, Marisol signed-up for a five-year Cuban government mission in the hinterlands of Brazil. She said that it was the toughest experience of her life because the village was very remote, the work was harsh, and she had no means of communicating with her husband and four-year-old son. She had gone on the mission precisely to improve their living standards, because Cuban doctors serving abroad received salaries in hard currency and also got additional perks to import goods not available for purchase in Cuba. Marisol had, for instance, imported the car precisely for the purpose of starting an informal CUC taxi service for tourists to supplement her meager CUP income. On one occasion Marisol drove my family and I to the touristy town of Viñales. We went to a restaurant for lunch and Marisol asked the waitress to seat us outdoors on the patio. The waitress turned to her and said, "The patio is only for foreigners." Humiliated, Marisol came back with tears in her eyes and recounted the waitress' response. "This is just not fair. I am a qualified doctor; I have struggled and sacrificed so much for this country, even the revolution. I work hard and still I am treated like this. . . . I am not some *jinetera* [sex worker]," she said.

Marisol's story illustrates two significant ways of thinking about conversions. First, conversions need not be unidirectional or confined to Cuban territory, and second, the value of moral and hard work legitimizes these conversions. Marisol's trajectory demonstrates a series of strategized and directed conversions from her CUP income in Cuba: US dollar income from services rendered transnationally sent back as remittances; her return to a CUP income in Cuba; her informal CUC income made possible by the foreign car she bought in US dollars in Brazil. These sustained stepwise conversions are the means by which Marisol provided for herself and her family. Unlike Bohannan's idea of upward or downward conversions, Marisol's example demonstrates how conversions can be multidirectional and activate transnational nodes of exchange to ensure future specificity, thereby counteracting, to some extent, the chiasmus of domestic dual-currency flows.

When the waitress states that Cubans cannot sit on the patio, she also questions Marisol's short-term competitive motivations, à la Parry and Bloch, by treating her like a "common hustler" seduced by making a quick buck off of foreign tourists. In her retort, Marisol invokes the larger socialist moral order that puts a premium on hard work – making it even more egregious to be denied access because she is an educated professional and not a *jinetera* who performs socially inappropriate labor. Dovetailing Karl Marx's (1967 [1867], 1988 [1844]) critiques of alienated wage labor under capitalism, Che Guevara considered work to be the most cherished weapon of the revolution and called for a new culture of work concerned with collective labor and a new consciousness that was created only "when man begins to look upon work as a moral necessity, not just a material necessity" (Guevara 2003 [1962]: 146). Marisol, therefore, uses these enduring revolutionary concepts of hard work as well as *la lucha* to justify and to some extent veil the fact that she is absconding from her job as a doctor to earn CUC profits from driving foreigners to touristy locales. This encapsulates how the chiastic nature of the dual currency spheres gets accentuated in social practice and how postsocialist perceptions of moral degradation continue to haunt upward economic conversions.

Conclusions

Rather than viewing capitalism and socialism as monolithic polar opposites, several ethnographies have advocated for the importance of looking at their continuities and coexistence under postsocialism (Dunn 2004; Humphrey and Mandel 2002; Lampland 1995; Verdery 1991, 2003). Caroline Humphrey and Ruth Mandel assert that under postsocialism we are not dealing simply with the "clash of two mutually alien economic systems, 'the market' and the 'socialist planned economy', but with a much more complex encounter of a number of specific, culturally-embedded, and practical organizational forms" (2002: 2). The source of anxiety under postsocialism emerges from how interactions between the market and existing socialist moral, cosmological, and semiotic systems are reconciled. Accounts of exchange and multiple currencies (Lemon 1998; Pine 2002; Rogers 2005) also show how practices of money, in particular, become an arena for negotiating such postsocialist angst and ambivalence.

Cuba is currently the only country to operate under a system of dual national currencies. While this system might soon be abandoned, the everyday frictions and hybrid socialist moralities that impinge upon practices of money will perhaps linger on. I have demonstrated the ways discursive informal-currency practices in Cuba simultaneously erode, evade, and reify the economic, ideological, and moral binaries (state/market, socialist/capitalist, collective/individual, Cubans/foreigners, redistribution/accumulation, competition/reciprocity, etc.) constitutive of the state's formal exchange spheres. Informal-economy conversions are ensconced in regimes of value that are formally stipulated as opposing but in fact exist simultaneously while overlapping and jostling for relevance in practices that not only challenge but also bolster and recharge socialist discourse with new signification – confirming the continued importance of the *Che* bank notes.

Fissures in economic and moral imperatives etched in the architecture of CUP and CUC exchange spheres also get exposed, evaded, and resolved in cross-sphere conversions that can be multidirectional and transnational. Michael Herzfeld uses the concept of *disemia* to characterize the juxtaposition of official and "vernacular" cultural forms. He argues that the omnipresent availability of a more semiotic code allows for its manipulation but also its reaffirmation in the pragmatic articulations of what he calls "cultural intimacy" (1997). In Cuba, informal exchange as the "vernacular form" blatantly subverts official currency spheres in pursuits of private profit, but these activities are performed in cultural idioms that also evoke, fine-tune, and reproduce Cuban revolutionary principals such as social solidarity as a tool for collective struggle (*la lucha*), even though the official itself becomes the target of the contemporary vernacular *lucha*. The discursive power of *la lucha*, however, lies in the fact that it is both enduring and fickle in its everyday appropriations because it can, in one hiss, include or exclude, moralize or immoralize, condemn or embrace, spawning the double morality of Cuban life. "Although the tactics and targets change, the *lucha* itself, with its emphasis on personal and collective sacrifice, never ceases" (Fagen 1979: 11). *La lucha* in some senses emulates the Janus-faced nature of modern money itself (Simmel 1978 [1900]): as abstract and concrete, as a promoter of alienation and freedom, and as a dialectic of both the state (head) and market (tail). It is the nexus of *la lucha* and money and their double articulations that punctuate the contemporary Cuban postsocialist socioeconomic arrangements directing and diverting flows of currencies along discursive circuits of exchange and meaning.

Acknowledgments

This research was supported by the International Dissertation Fellowship at the Social Science Research Council; the Institute for Money, Technology & Financial Inclusion at the University of California Irvine; and the Mellon Dissertation Research Grant, Sachar Award, Jane's Travel Grant, and Research Circle on Democracy and Cultural Pluralism at Brandeis University. I am grateful to Elizabeth Ferry, Mark Auslander, Dave Jacobson, Robert Hunt and Ivan Small for their comments on different versions of this chapter. I also thank Smoki Musaraj, Ivan Small, and Bill Maurer for putting this collection of essays together. All translations and subsequent errors are my own.

Mrinalini Tankha is assistant professor of anthropology at Portland State University. She was previously a postdoctoral scholar at the Institute for Money, Technology & Financial Inclusion at the University of California, Irvine. Her research focuses on macroeconomic monetary policy as well as everyday social practices of money and finance. She has done ethnographic work on the rise and imminent demise of Cuba's dual-currency system and is currently doing research on Cuba's emerging digital economy.

NOTES

1. Most notably of oil and petroleum.
2. Possession and exchange of USD by Cubans was previously illegal. There were some shops selling imported items in USD, but only foreigners were allowed to enter these spaces.
3. During my fieldwork in 2009–11, the exchange rate was US$1 = 0.9259CUC, plus a 10 percent tax. This changed in January 2011 as part of the economic reforms of the Sixth Congress of the Cuban Communist Party.
4. Retrieved 16 September 2017 from http://www.bc.gob.cu/English/exchange_ rate.asp.
5. Although all *cadecas* (currency exchange bureaus) convert CUC into CUP, there are only particular *cadecas* that convert CUP into CUC, and these are very sparsely scattered across Havana and often refuse to make the transaction. This makes the conversion from CUP to CUC an extremely tedious process. Moreover, there is a loss incurred when buying CUC at the exchange rate of 1CUC = 25CUP.
6. James Ferguson (1985) argues that the "Bovine Mystique" in Lesotho erects a one-way barrier restricting livestock-to-cash conversions in order to preserve the power/livestock nexus, despite the introduction of general-purpose money.
7. Parry and Bloch draw heavily on Emile Durkheim's idea of the two courses of life – the profane or the individualistic short-term ordering of things versus the sacred or the long-term spiritual realm of collective representations and social reproduction (Durkheim 1995 [1912]: 38).
8. Full text: http://lanic.utexas.edu/project/castro/db/1994/19940526.html (retrieved 1 October 2013).

9. Privileged tourism workers receive relatively lucrative hard currency rewards whereas professionals are remunerated in state controlled salaries of merely around 250-600 CUP per month (Ritter and Rowe 2002).
10. These inequalities are also racialized, and the state has been accused of promoting tourism apartheid. Afro-Cubans have largely been kept out of the tourism sector or relegated to positions of "harsh labor" (de la Fuente 2001: 78). Moreover, most Afro-Cubans don't have access to remittances because most Cubans in the diaspora tend to be white.
11. This mirrors more closely past anthropological accounts of exchange spheres where higher spheres reflected the strengthening and expansion of reciprocal social relationships.

REFERENCES CITED

Akin, David, and Joel Robbins (eds.). 1999. *Money and Modernity: State and Local Currencies in Melanesia.* Pittsburgh, PA: University of Pittsburgh Press.

Alejandro, Pavel Vidal. 2012. "Monetary Duality in Cuba: Initial Stages and Future Prospects." In *Cuban Economic and Social Development: Policy Reforms and Challenges in the 21st Century,* edited by Jorge I. Domínguez et al. Series on Latin American Studies. Cambridge, MA: David Rockefeller Center for Latin American Studies, Harvard University: 39–53.

Appadurai, Arjun. 1986. "Introduction: Commodities and the Politics of Value." In *The Social Life of Things: Commodities in Cultural Perspective,* edited by Arjun Appadurai. New York: Cambridge University Press: 3–63.

Barth, Frederik. 1967. "Economic Spheres in Darfur: ASA Monograph 6." In *Themes in Economic Anthropology,* edited by Raymond Firth. London: Tavistock: 149–174.

Bohannan, Paul. 1955. "Some Principles of Exchange and Investment among the Tiv." *American Anthropologist* 57(1): 60–70.

———. 1959. "The Impact of Money on an African Subsistence Economy." *Journal of Economic History* 19: 491–503.

Castro, Raúl. 2007. "The Unity of the People: Principal Weapon of the Revolution." *Granma International* 42(31): 3–5.

Crompton, Samuel. 2009. *Che Guevara: The Making of a Revolutionary.* New York, NY: Gareth Stevens Publishing.

Dalton, George. 1965. "Primitive Money." *American Anthropologist* 67(1): 44–65.

de la Fuente, Alejandro. 2001. *A Nation for All: Race, Inequality and Politics in Twentieth-Century Cuba.* Chapel Hill: University of North Carolina Press.

Dunn, Elizabeth. 2004. *Privatizing Poland: Baby Food, Big Business, and the Remaking of Labor.* Ithaca, NY: Cornell University Press.

Durkheim, Emile. 1995 [1912]. *The Elementary Forms of Religious Life,* trans. Karen E. Fields. New York: The Free Press.

Eckstein, Susan. 1994. *Back from the Future: Cuba under Castro.* Princeton, NJ: Princeton University Press.

———. 2004. "Dollarization and Its Discontents: Remittances and the Remaking of Cuba in the Post-Soviet Era" *Comparative Politics* 36 (3): 313–30.

Fagen, Richard. 1979. *The Transformation of Political Culture in Cuba.* Stanford: Stanford University Press.

Ferguson, James. 1985. "The Bovine Mystique: Power, Property, and Livestock in Rural Lesotho." *Man* 20(4): 647–74.

Fernández, Damián. 2000. "Cuba and lo Cubano, or the Story of Desire and Disenchantment." In *Cuba, the Elusive Nation: Interpretations of National Identity,* edited by Damián Fernández and Madeline Cámara Betancourt. Gainesville: University Press of Florida: 79–99.

Firth, Raymond. 1939. *Primitive Polynesian Economy.* London: Routledge.

Gordy, Katherine. 2006. "'Sales + Economy + Efficiency = Revolution'? Dollarization, Consumer Capitalism and Popular Responses in Special Period Cuba." *Public Culture* 18: 2.

Grossman, Gregory. 1977. "The Second Economy of the USSR." *Problems of Communism* 26 (September October): 25–40.

Guevara, Ernesto. 2003 [1962]. "A New Culture of Work." In *Che Guevara Reader: Writings on Politics and Revolution,* edited by David Deutschmann. Melbourne: Ocean Press: 143–152.

———. 2003 [1964]. "On the Budgetary Finance System." In *Che Guevara Reader: Writings on Politics and Revolution,* edited by David Deutschmann. Melbourne: Ocean Press: 184–211.

———. 2003 [1965]. "Socialism and Man in Cuba." In *Che Guevara Reader: Writings on Politics and Revolution,* edited by David Deutschmann. Melbourne: Ocean Press: 212–229.

Guyer, Jane. 2004. *Marginal Gains: Monetary Transactions in Atlantic Africa.* Chicago: University of Chicago Press.

Hart, Keith. 1986. "Heads or Tails? Two Sides of a Coin." *Man* 21: 637–56.

Henken, Ted. 2000. "Last Resort or Bridge to the Future? Tourism and Workers in Cuba's Second Economy." *Cuba in Transition: Papers and Proceedings of the Eleventh Annual Meeting of the Association for the Study of the Cuban Economy (ASCE).* Miami. August. Volume 10: 321–336.

———. 2005. "Entrepreneurship. Informality and the Second Economy: Cuba's Underground Economy in Comparative Perspective." *Cuba in Transition: Association for the Study of the Cuban Economy*: 360–375.

Herzfeld, Michael. 1997. *Cultural Intimacy: Social Poetics in the Nation-State.* New York: Routledge.

Humphrey, Caroline, and Ruth Mandel. 2002. "The Market in Everyday Life: Ethnographies of Postsocialism." In *Markets and Moralities: Ethnographies of Postsocialism,* edited by Ruth Mandel and Caroline Humphrey. New York: Berg: 1–16.

Hutchinson, Sharon. 1992. "The Cattle of Money and the Cattle of Girls among the Nuer." *American Ethnologist* 19(2): 294–316.

Kopytoff, Igor. 1986. "The Cultural Biography of Things: Commoditization as Process." In *The Social Life of Things: Commodities in Cultural Perspective,* edited by Arjun Appadurai. New York: Cambridge University Press: 64–91.

Lampland, Martha. 1995. *The Object of Labor: Commodification in Socialist Hungary.* Chicago: University of Chicago Press.

Lemon, Alaina. 1998. "'Your Eyes Are Green Like Dollars': Counterfeit Cash, National Substance, and Currency Apartheid in 1990s Russia." *Cultural Anthropology* 13(1): 22–55.

Leon, Francisco. 1997. "Socialism and *Sociolismo.*" In *Toward a New Cuba? Legacies of a Revolution,* edited by Miguel Angel Centeno and Mauricio Font. Boulder, CO: Lynne Rienner Publishers.

Los, Maria. 1987. "The Double Economic Structure of Communist Societies." *Contemporary = Crisis.* 11: 25–58.

———. 1990. "Introduction" and "Dynamic Relationships of the First and Second Economies in Old and New Marxist States." In *The Second Economy in Marxist States,* edited by Maria Los. London: Macmillan: 1–10.

Malinowski, Bronislaw. 1922. *Argonauts of the Western Pacific.* London: Routledge.

Mauss, Marcel. 2000 [1950]. *The Gift: The Form and Reason for Exchange in Archaic Societies.* New York: W. W. Norton.

Marx, Karl. 1967 [1867]. *Capital, Volume 1.* New York: Vintage Books.

———. 1988 [1844]. *Economic and Philosophic Manuscripts of 1844,* trans. Martin Milligan. Amherst, NY: Prometheus Books.

Monreal, Pedro. 2002. "Development as an Unfinished Affair: Cuba after the Great Adjustment of the 1990s." *Latin American Perspectives* 29(3): 75–90.

Munn, Nancy. 1986. *The Fame of Gawa: A Symbolic Study of Value Transformation in a Massim (Papua New Guinea) Society.* Cambridge: Cambridge University Press.

Parmentier, Richard J. 2002. "Money Walks, People Talk: Systemic and Transactional Dimensions of Palaun Exchange." *L'Homme* 162: 49–80.

Parry, Jonathan, and Maurice Bloch. 1989. "Introduction: Money and the Morality of Exchange." In *Money and the Morality of Exchange,* edited by Jonathan Parry and Maurice Bloch. Cambridge: Cambridge University Press: 1–32.

Pérez-López, Jorge F. 1995. *Cuba's Second Economy: From Behind the Scenes to Center Stage.* New Brunswick, NJ: Transaction Publishers.

Pine, Frances. 2002. "Dealing with Money: Zlotys, Dollars and Other Currencies in the Polish Highlands." In *Markets and Moralities: Ethnographies of Postsocialism,* edited by Ruth Mandel and Caroline Humphrey. New York: Berg: 77–97.

Piot, Charles. 1991. "Of Persons and Things: Some Reflections on African Spheres of Exchange." *Man* 29: 405–24.

Ritter, Archibald R. M. 2004. "The Cuban Economy in the Twenty-First Century: Recuperation or Relapse." In *The Cuban Economy,* edited by Archibald R. M. Ritter. Pittsburgh, PA: University of Pittsburgh Press: 3–24.

Ritter, Archibald R. M., and Nicholas Rowe. 2002. "Cuba: "From Dollarization to Euroization or Peso Reconsolidation?" *Latin American Politics and Society* 44(2): 99–123.

Rogers, Douglas. 2005. "Moonshine, Money, and the Politics of Liquidity in Rural Russia." *American Ethnologist* 32(1): 63–81.

Rojo, Ricardo. 1968. *My Friend Ché.* New York: Dial Press.

Salisbury, Paul. 1962. *From Stone to Steel: Economic Consequences of a Technological Change in New Guinea.* Melbourne: Melbourne University Press.

Saul, Mahir. 2004. "Money in Colonial Transition: Cowries and Francs in West Africa." *American Anthropologist* 106(1): 71–84.

Shipton, Parker MacDonald. 1989. *Bitter Money: Cultural Economy and Some African Meanings of Forbidden Commodities.* Washington, DC: American Anthropological Association.

Sillitoe, Paul. 2006. "Why Spheres of Exchange?" *Ethnology.* (January 1): 1–23.

Simmel, Georg. 1978 [1900]. *The Philosophy of Money,* ed. D. Frisby, trans. T. Botto-
more and D. Frisby. London: Routledge Press.
Sotirios, Jorge. 2009. "Cuba's China Syndrome." *Griffith Review.* Spring 25: 235–244.
Stark, David. 1989. "Bending the Bars of the Iron Cage: Bureaucratization and
Informalization in Capitalism and Socialism." *Sociological Forum* 4(4): 637–64.
Tanuma, Sachiko. 2007. "Post Utopian Irony: Cuban Narratives during the 'Special
Period' Decade." *Political and Legal Anthropology Review* (1) (30 May): 46–66.
Verdery, Katherine. 1991. "Theorizing Socialism: A Prologue to the 'Transition.'"
American Ethnologist 18(3): 419–39.
———. 2003. *The Vanishing Hectare: Property and Value in Postsocialist Transylvania.*
Ithaca, NY: Cornell University Press.

CHAPTER 6

Carola and Saraswathi
Juggling Wealth in India and in Mexico

MAGDALENA VILLARREAL, ISABELLE GUÉRIN,
AND K. S. SANTOSH KUMAR

Saraswathi belongs to the Paraiyar community (ex-untouchables – classified as Scheduled Caste [SC] by the Indian administrative system). She is considered a resource person for many in her neighborhood and among her kin, helping them in different ways, particularly regarding access to cash. Like other Indian women of this region, she proudly shows off gold necklaces, bracelets, earrings, anklets, and rings, which she wears on a daily basis. However, these have traveled to and from pawnshops and moneylenders, serving as they do to guarantee loans and access to cash. In fact, she has been known to borrow – and repay relatively quickly – the equivalent of a year and a half of her annual household income. She has also lent money to people from higher castes and even to men, both of which are socially forbidden.

Carola, on the other hand, heads a relatively affluent family in the modest Mexican village in which she lives. After the death of her husband, she inherited irrigated land and a significant herd of cattle, which she has managed to increase. She also used a government loan to buy a tractor, both for use in her own fields and to rent out to other producers. Carola possesses some jewels, but they are kept in a safe place inside her home. Only once has she had to pawn one of her cherished golden chains. She did so discreetly, so no one would know. After two months she managed to retrieve it. Her jewels are almost sacred to her, each being linked to a religious ritual or a particular gift. On special occasions she will wear earrings and a necklace, and perhaps a ring or a bracelet. But she has "good credit" with moneylenders and quite easily resorts to bank loans, often without collateral, given her prestige in the region.

In discussing the two cases, our aim is to analyze the nature of wealth in these women's everyday financial endeavors, placing the lens on circuits of value and frameworks of calculation. Microfinancial practices are thus the focus of our analysis. These involve people who "do their arithmetic" based on frameworks of calculation using monetary but also social and cultural parameters. They do not correspond to a single rationality but do remit us to circuits of valuation that give form and content to monetary transactions. This issue is of critical importance in reaching an understanding of the workings of finance and the economy.

By drawing on these two specific cases, our purpose is not to compare two persons or two locations and their activities within the past two decades: both contexts display strong differences, and both cases are unique in many respects. Following one of the basic foundations of anthropology, our purpose is rather to extract similarities related to processes governing social life (here financial transactions) and highlight differential patterns related to issues of wealth.

Like many other people in these two continents so distant from one another, Carola and Saraswathi face constraints when dealing with financial resources and capital,[1] not least of which entail gender. Also, both stand out as enterprising and bold within their respective social contexts. And despite the fact that they are attributed different socioeconomic status – Saraswathi belongs to the lowest caste in the region, and Carola is considered part of the landowning class[2] (though not necessarily classified as "high class" by socioeconomic standards) – both present interesting cases of diverse local strategies for accessing monetary resources. As we shall show, wealth does not only have to do with actual income or the amount of resources a certain person or family may possess, but it is also related to how certain material and symbolic resources are deployed and made significant in particular cultural scenarios.

Thus, in coming to grips with Saraswathi's and Carola's microfinancial practices, we engage critically with the notions of "capital" and "wealth," but we are particularly keen to delve deeper into the frames of calculation (following Callon 1998; Guyer 2004; and Munn 1986) mobilized by women in both contexts. In this effort, we seek to situate the different kinds of assets and resources used in the transactions within broader processes of valuation and complex webs of meanings and actions that contribute to the practices of calculation of value. Here we highlight noncommodity values and institutions that restructure monetary frameworks, doing so in such a way that we can further examine social, cultural, and moral dimensions of financial calculations.

The cases illustrate the complexity of financial practices undertaken by rural inhabitants and the subtlety of their calculation frameworks. We discuss the ways in which such circuits of valuation are articulated and framed in people's everyday financial practices. We highlight the relevance of noncommoditized transactions and the differential value attributed to goods, property, and money, and sustain the argument that social, cultural, domestic, ethnic, and power relations are part of the economy's constituent elements. These relations may act to mediate and structure financial practices. We also argue that beyond what is typically defined as capital, what matters in the acquisition of wealth is the process through which people are able to make "capital" work for them, to obtain something out of their resources (what we can call "capitalization"; see Villarreal 2004a) and that in turn requires permanent "juggling" (see Guérin, Morvant Roux and Villarreal 2013). Juggling is not simply a metaphor: it is used here to highlight the mechanisms through which people access wealth, engaging in constant – and risky – processes through which they combine, articulate, and sometimes substitute various forms of capital that acquire value only under the condition of their circulation and their entanglement with other forms of capital.

One commonly associates wealth with accumulation, but the point we want to make is that, rather than accumulating, people juggle their monetary and nonmonetary resources using social, cultural, and financial devices involving different types of indebtedness and forms of reciprocity. This also entails intersecting and often contradictory frameworks of calculation that are brought into play within specific transactions.

Classical authors like Simmel or Polanyi have already shown the subtle and complicated ways through which money and debt are intertwined with social relations. Over the last few decades, the sociology and anthropology of money and debt have continually been improved. Far from being a neutral veil or a dissolver of social relationships, money entails multiple meanings and repertoires (Guyer 1995). It is situationally defined, reworked, and "earmarked" to sustain social relationships (Zelizer 1994). It is constantly renegotiated in relations to wider symbolic and social orders (Bloch and Parry 1989) and does not necessarily lead to disembedded and abstract financial transactions but is embedded into a web of rights and obligations (Maurer 2006). Our analysis clearly draws on this body of research – we show that money and debt are both shaped by and constitutive of social relationships – while locating the social meaning of money and debt within a broader reflection on the nature of wealth.

Saraswathi: Moving across Financial Circuits of Household, Neighborhood, and Beyond

Saraswathi lives in a *colony* (the section of the village reserved for Scheduled Castes) in north Tamil Nadu (south India) about eighty kilometers (around fifty miles) from Chennai, the capital of the state. She is thirty-five years old and lives with her husband and two children. Her elder son is twenty-three years old and now works at a software company, in an industrial zone located approximately ten kilometers (six miles) from home. Her daughter, eighteen, has a part-time job at an NGO. We have known Saraswathi since 2003. We started by interviewing her as part of a study on microfinance. Then, over time, we forged a strong relationship. She readily allows us to enter into the intimacy of her household finance and to observe the extraordinary diversity of financial arrangements in which she is embedded, the tactics and strategies she deploys to assume her responsibilities while sustaining both a wide array of relationships and her social identity.

Her case is exceptional in many respects, but it does illustrate several interesting trends. She does not have a specific "job" – which she can afford to do, as her husband (and now her son) get regular monthly wages, a privilege that very few SC households enjoy. However, she also combines various sources of income, according to the needs and the opportunities. To describe in detail the complexity of her financial management and the diversity of debt ties in which she is involved is simply impossible. We shall restrict ourselves here to describing the three financial circles in which she is embedded – household and kin, "neighborhood," and beyond – while highlighting both the moral and political economy that shape them. With regards to moral economy, we focus on individual and collective moralities and the cultural values that pervade economic social relations. As for political economy, our emphasis is on how structural dialectics produce political and economic differentiation.

Financial Circulation within the Household and Kin

Saraswathi considers herself the main decision-maker within her household. She fully manages the household budget, and she can move relatively freely, which is far from a common occurrence given the extent of patriarchy in rural south India (although SC women enjoy much more freedom than women in upper castes, their movements and their bodies are nevertheless controlled). She gets full cooperation from her husband, which is also the exception rather than the rule: he gives her his entire salary and does not restrict her outings. It's a matter of trust, she says. But she also considers that her husband's support is an implicit compensation of his own behavior. While "arranged" marriages – i.e., following the rules of endogamy – are still the norm, they went for a "love marriage" as she was only thirteen (which is much younger than the average). They did not marry because of an early pregnancy, as is often the case, but because they loved each other.

At the same time, Saraswathi feels a permanent and strong pressure from her in-laws who live nearby. The love marriage has never been accepted, or at least it is always used as an excuse by her in-laws to scold her, she says. "All my life I will have to prove myself," she told us during one of our first discussions. She exerts considerable financial responsibilities for her in-laws: whenever they need cash, she helps them find the lender, and sometimes she even fully manages the transaction. As she has good relationships with many lenders, this has become a routine. For instance, she had fully managed the financing of her younger brother-in-law's marriage. In 2002 she borrowed and repaid 40,000 rupees (around US$780, which at that time was equivalent of approximately one and a half years of their annual household income), which she used to pay for such a marriage. She tells us this story with bitterness as she feels that her in-laws are expecting too much from her. But at the same time she likes challenges, she likes to feel useful, and she also feels some sort of pride. "Without me, they would not be able to manage, and they know it," she says. She has assumed the full repayment of the large debt for the marriage of her brother-in-law and managed to clear it off in 2006, combining her husband's wage and various sources of illicit activities, which we shall describe below, while facing a permanent dilemma. On the one hand, she decided to assume the entire responsibility of the debt (in collaboration with her husband through his salary) in order to save face vis-à-vis her in-laws. On the other, being able to raise lump sums necessarily prompts questions concerning her "morality": she is often suspected of using the charms of her body with her creditors. Her father-in-law, in particular, has always strongly disapproved of her behavior.

To pay back her debt, and in addition to her husband's wage, Saraswathi juggles various activities. Her family obligations require her to make use of enlarged networks. She used to trade saris, bought in Chennai and sold in her village. But after some time she stopped, since urban traders now come to the villages, and she is unable to face competition. She also used to run chit funds (known also as rotating savings and credit associations, or ROSCAs).[3] As a manager, she was allowed to take the first turn – which she often lent on to others or used to pay back a loan. She was also allowed to get remuneration – a percentage of other members' contributions. She has ceased her operations here too, as some of the members left without paying their dues. The rise of microfinance may also have contributed to the decline of women's chit funds. The rise of microfinance may also have contributed to the decline of women's chit funds. In case of specific need however, Saraswati still joins Roscas, but as a simple member. Saras-wathi also regularly buys and sells subsidized items from ration shops on the black market. More recently, she started selling soap, water purifiers, vitamins, and cosmetics for Amway, a multinational company organized through a pyramid scheme: traders are "independent distributors" and their income depends not only on their own sales of Amway products but on sales made by others whom they've recruited. Saraswathi uses the net-work she has built over time thanks to her involvement in village life and as a volunteer in a non-governmental organization (NGO).

Financial Circuits within the Neighborhood and Microfinance

Saraswathi developed this role of local leadership over the years. Because she has taken many steps on behalf of her disabled daughter with ad-ministrations to obtain certificates, scholarships, etc., she has acquired a real know-how with regards to the bureaucracy of public services. Also, for nearly ten years, she has been actively involved as a self-help-group (SHG) leader. SHGs typically gather from the same neighborhood twelve to twenty women who access bank loans with the support of local NGOs. They represent the dominant form of microfinance in Tamil Nadu. At the request of the head of the NGO, Saraswathi is also actively involved as a volunteer for various activities undertaken by the NGO (meetings, public events, training, etc.).

As we mentioned earlier, Saraswathi is considered a "cash reserve," mostly for SC women in her neighborhood, sometimes for SC women from neighboring villages that she meets through her NGO networks. Less frequently she also lends money to men – this goes against local norms but nevertheless happens quite frequently. She acts as a guarantor or as an intermediary – she lends money herself after having borrowed elsewhere.

Women need her – and appreciate her – because they lack contacts with lenders, physical mobility (many lenders are in town), or for mat-ters of discretion: they don't want their husbands to be aware of their financial transactions. Saraswathi says she does not charge for this kind of assistance but obtains indirect benefits, the first being improved cred-itworthiness among local lenders and better borrowing conditions. The very fact that she acts as an intermediary for other female borrowers allows her to borrow more and at lower costs. "Respect" and "gratitude" from local women is another indirect benefit.

This is a matter of status, as she is very much respected locally. Women's gratitude also means that they are available in case of need. Saraswathi ad-mits with a charming smile that she can "control" them, which means that she can mobilize them to sustain the patronage networks in which is she is actively involved. This is the case of the NGO at which she volunteers. Many NGOs use a patronage system[4] and require their "beneficiaries" to attend many events on which they build their legitimacy. Saraswathi also mobilizes her female networks to sustain relationships with upper castes from whom she regularly borrows and who frequently need help and labor. Finally, she also maintains close relationships with local authorities: here too she regularly brings women for public events, such as political meetings or municipal assemblies, for which it is always difficult to find participants. In return she enjoys privileged access to resources of various sorts, and she gets better access to administrative services, both for her and her network. In 2008, for instance, we saw her helping neighbors to approach the district collector about a problem with a property title.

Last, but not least, acting as a "cash reserve" allows Saraswathi to control group loans (deciding who gets what or appropriating part of the loans for herself), and nobody questions it. For instance, when the group received the first external loan in 2008, it was officially distributed to five women, but, in fact, Saraswathi personally used three of the five loans. On top of that, she fully oversees not only her own loans but also those of her daughter and her sisters-in-law. These are "internal arrangements" as she says, referring to the multiple services she provides to them. For her house she borrowed 70,000 rupees in 2010 – far more than what she is eligible for – otherwise she uses SHG loans mainly to "roll money" (paying back past debts).

Financial Circuits beyond the Neighborhood

In 2009, Saraswathi's husband got a permanent job at the Department of Transport, and one year later her son started working at a software company. These two events have considerably strengthened the creditworthiness of the household while giving rise to new social needs. Permanent employment grants a very specific social status that very few SC enjoy, provided, however, that living standards fit to it: building a new house is a first step.

Saraswathi took the initiative of renovating her house and did it gradually. While many homes in the hamlet are made of thatch and mud, hers was made of concrete, and she extended it significantly, first by adding rooms and later by adding a floor. In December 2010, she had already borrowed INR 400,000 rupees (USD 6,200), and was planning to borrow INR 200,000 (USD 3,100) more to complete the house and organize the housewarming party. She borrowed the 400,000 rupees from various sources:

she pledged the jewels of her brother's wife (around 30,000 INR, or USD 470); she borrowed INR 70,000 (USD 1100) from her SHG, INR 50,000 (USD 780) from her lover, INR 45,000 (USD 700) from her uncle, INR 100,000 (USD 1560) from two banks (50,000 each) – thanks to a friend who acts as an intermediary – and around INR 70,000 (USD 1100) from two people belonging to upper castes. In a context where banks strongly discriminate against SC and where upper castes still exert some control over low castes through debt, both practices – going through intermediaries to access bank loans and borrowing from upper castes – are extremely common. Her husband also got a 30,000-rupee (USD 470) loan from his company. At the same time, she started a chit fund. The monthly contribution is INR 1,500 and the total lot will be INR 100,000 (USD 1560); she planed to use it to pursue the house renovation. Compared to the household income – now around 8,000 INR per month – the debt service is extremely heavy, but she managed thanks to the diversity of repayment temporalities of each lender. Three lenders required strict monthly repayments: the chit fund, her husband's company, and the banks. Others asked only for the interest, and the capital could be paid at the end (pawnbroker, upper castes), while others didn't charge interest but may ask for the repayment any time in case of need (brother, uncle).

As noted above, the relationship she has with the two people from upper castes is typical of a patron-client relationship. She regularly pays back interest (around 2 percent per month) and occasionally part of the capital, which allows her to re-borrow. But money is just one aspect of the cost. She has to render multiple services, such as buying food from the ration shop – many upper castes want to benefit from subsidized products without going there – or domestic tasks, in particular at the time of ceremonies, be it marriages or funerals. Being able to bring other women as labor is crucial here. Her husband, as an electrician, is also frequently requested for the maintenance of appliances, from televisions to motor pumps. Being available at any moment to render free services and showing "gratitude" and "respect" are a tacit agreement with her creditors.

Like the wedding of her brother-in-law, Saraswathi manages the repayment by combining her husband's and son's wages with her own sources of income while regularly borrowing small sums here and there: pledging her jewels or those of her neighbors, her aunt, or her sister-in-law – the circulation of jewels, which act as quasi-liquid items, is extremely dynamic. She also borrows from local upper-caste women, from the NGO manager, and from ambulant lenders – but this option is a last resort because of the cost (up to 10 percent interest per month, while other lenders usually don't charge more than 3 percent). Being a chit-fund member also allows her to borrow from the manager up to 5,000 rupees for short periods. When she is unable to meet her repayments, she decides whom to pay first according to financial and social considerations. She tries to repay the most expensive debts first, but she also has to maintain her creditworthiness as well as her "status." With regards to the debts contracted for her house, her first priority is the loan taken by her husband in his workplace. He has a very good position and cannot afford any criticisms. The next priority is the personal loans she received from the NGO manager. "I don't want to be degraded in front of the women of my network," she says, and she also tries to dissimulate these debts. She doesn't want to be accused of being motivated only by money in her commitment to the NGO, as she was told once. At the time of one of our last visits, she also pointed out that one of her priorities in loan settlement was now with her sister-in-law (her husband's sister). The sister-in-law had recently accused Saraswathi of having made progress in her life only through Saraswathi's husband, and Saraswathi felt humiliated and irritated by this reproach. She now tries to limit dependence as much as possible.

Saraswathi clearly states that she fears most the criticisms that come from her inner circle. She says she does not care about private lenders even though they are often very aggressive and their rates can be exorbitant. Nor does she bother to be available to her "patrons." Her priority is to sustain her status and her rank in her own family and community.

Carola: Negotiating Land, Identity, and Community

Carola, on the other hand, is, as we have mentioned, a relatively affluent 43-year-old widow. The sole fact that she lives in the remains of the old *hacienda* (house of the landowner – who generally also wielded political power – in colonial times) speaks of a position within the small village in western Mexico. The *hacienda,* parts of which she has had to renovate since it was deteriorating, has the advantage of being quite spacious, with enough room for storage; more importantly, it is located alongside some of the best agricultural land in the village, which belonged to her until she sold a section of it for urban plots. In addition to owning land and cattle, her deceased husband had been a policeman in Guadalajara, the large metropolitan capital of the state, and he had not been liked because of his despotic and arrogant behavior toward workers and neighbors. Carola's father-in-law, who was deeply involved in *ejido* (a community established as a sociolegal entity linked to land ownership) politics, was hated and feared. Her own parents live in El Grullo, the capital of the municipality, which is only ten kilometers (about six miles) from Ayuquila. However, she is known as a charitable woman and has built good relationships and alliances in the village and with the regional and state authorities. One of her strongest economic resources stems from the land and cattle she inherited, but she had also worked in the United States for a period and had managed to earn a bit of cash. We had been looking forward to meeting her, since we had heard a lot about her in the village. She was *comadre* (co-mother in ritual kinship) of many people who spoke of her with respect and affection. As one of her *comadres* described her, "She is respected in the village, she has a smile for everyone, her dress is always impeccable and she helps out the poor when she can. It's not that she's rich, her sons own everything."

Circuits within the Ejido

Communication with Carola came quite easily, and she immediately told us how happy she had been with her husband, how many good relations he had with important people in the state government, and what a shock it had been for her when her husband was killed in the same village, near a tree that she later had cut down in order to forget the dreadful incident. She narrated her difficult life, how she did not receive help from her family and had to migrate to the United States and work as a housemaid to a stingy woman who counted the slices of bread she ate. She had left her seven children in Ayuquila, with a woman whom she paid to look after them, and was planning to bring them to the United States with her, but she heard that her parents-in-law had taken them to their house and had said that they would not let them go with their mother. She thus returned to Ayuquila with the small amount of money she had managed to earn, fetched her children, and recovered the land that she had rented out to her father-in-law. It was not easy to reorganize her networks: she had hoped that her godfather[5] – who was influential in politics – was going to support her to start her enterprises, but she was turned down when she tried to approach him through his secretary.

Carola's harsh father-in-law was often in the way in her endeavors – he even tried to take the land away from her. But she managed to soften him by inviting him for meals, not disagreeing with him openly, and supporting him when possible during political meetings. She advised her children to be kind to their grandfather and urged her son to help him with his cattle and associate himself with him in other economic enterprises. She also looked up old friends, offered an attentive ear to their problems, and gained support for herself. This proved useful in order to counter the gossip that had risen in the village about her having found other men in the United States. Such rumors were particularly harmful, because land could be taken away from her if the *ejido* members received any indication that she could remarry. For them, a remarriage almost inevitably implied that the new husband would acquire rights to her land.[6] Land was scarce and such situations were to be avoided.

Carola managed to convince the *ejidatarios* (members of the *ejido*), as well as her close kin and friends, that she had no plans of finding a new partner. She kept her land and later managed to obtain a permit from the municipality and the *ejido* to sell part of it for urban plots, since it was located on the outskirts of the village. Furthermore, her brother-in-law's wife, upon his death, donated his land to Carola, and later she bought (through her son) another piece of land from her father-in-law, who no longer lived in Ayuquila.

She claimed that her sons helped her. One of them was married but lived in the village and assisted with the work, and another regularly sent her small amounts of money from the United States. She quickly explained that all she had belonged to them – the *casino*[7] she had just built was for her son (who at that moment was in the United States), the land was in their names, and the two pickup trucks and old tractor were also theirs. She attended *ejido* meetings not only as an *ejidataria* (possessing as she did twenty-one hectares, or fifty-two acres, in the hills near the village) but also as a representative of her son in the United States. He was registered as an *ejidatario,* although he had never worked the land, and required that someone stand in his name to pay dues and vote in critical issues. Carola commented that he would come soon to manage the *casino.*

Later, we heard her repeat the story several times. She often used the image of subordinated widow to gain favor and portrayed her own enterprises as belonging to her sons, although we observed that she made decisions and managed the enterprises herself. This implied visiting regional authorities to obtain permits for parties and the sale of beer, organizing events in the *casino* and then selling drinks there, buying and selling cattle, contracting workers when it was required, and coordinating the use of the tractor and the pickup trucks. She also confided that she did not yet have everything in her sons' names, as they were young and could make irrational decisions. However, self-identifying as a single woman, who yearned for the support of her deceased husband and whose only interests were to sustain her family and assist those in need, helped her gain prestige and favor. In addition, she often subtly reminded others of the fact that she had good relations with important people, and used other contacts with influential people of the region to achieve her aims.

She thus managed to establish reasonable contracts for renting out part of the land, to acquire credit for buying more cattle, and to obtain permits from the municipality and local authorities for selling *ejido* land, which was not an easy task as it entailed a lot of paperwork and lobbying in government offices. Her good nature and willingness to help others won the approval and sympathy of neighbors and friends, also outside the village. Local authorities and important families in the region knew her well, and she would sometimes visit them when collecting funds to assist people in need – as was the case of the families who were left homeless after a flood in the early 1980s – or to procure funds for church or charity.

Circuits within the Village

Carola was quite well known in the municipality, and she did have access to some political networks, which helped her acquire permits to sell land or credit when she needed to. Often such ties were not effective in themselves, but they could be used to build her image as someone who was "well connected." Participating in *ejido* meetings was crucial, since important decisions were made there; for example, those concerning land rights – she had to make sure her sons were not left out of the land tenure census – and *fiestas,* which could now take place in the *casino* and provide her some profit from the sale of beer and soft drinks. However, she never presented herself as a successful entrepreneur but used her sons' names instead, and often spoke of herself as ignorant in terms of bureaucratic paperwork and legal issues. By downplaying her capacities in defense of her interests, she enrolled others as advocates for her.

As a cattle owner, Carola was in many ways a "traditional entrepreneur," although she did venture into building new enterprises, such as the *casino*, and had, at one point, migrated to the United States (like many other locals). A significant number of people either combined work outside the region with their local activities or migrated for long periods of time, but most migrated to the United States (mostly to California), both as families and as individuals, and only a few went to seek work in Guadalajara or in nearby cities. Venturing to migrate entailed having the basic resources and proper connections. Like a number of the other migrants from the town, it was not lack of food on the table that motivated Carola to engage in this journey. Rather, her decision was made out of frustration with slow agricultural profits and the need for extra income to enhance her entrepreneurial endeavors.

There were few wage opportunities for women in the region, although they worked hard from morning to evening. A bad reputation associated with working in the tomato fields discouraged many from seeking employment in them, although they sometimes worked in local *ejidatarios'* plots, particularly if they were relatives. Most helped their husbands, fathers, or sons with their own crops. A few worked as housemaids – generally outside the village – or sewed, washed, and ironed for others. Such activities were beneath Carola's status. Although she had worked as a housemaid in the United States, in Mexico such jobs were considered of low status, in addition to the fact that they did not pay well. Women resorted to selling beauty or home products from catalogues, or they earned income vending *tamales,* homemade bread, and special cooked food set up on small tables outside their home at night. Those who had achieved an education worked as teachers or secretaries in the nearby towns of El Grullo or Autlán. But Carola was an entrepreneur and, although she never worked in the fields herself, she did hire men to carry out such jobs and look after the cattle for her. She oiled her social networks and, when she needed a loan, she had good credit with local savings cooperatives and banks. She was well known by local state officers and, when they needed a "representative" for charitable or other programs, she was often called upon. This did not in itself represent an income in any way, but it did provide prestige and access, which were useful in her entrepreneurial endeavors. For one, it placed her in the "givers" rather than the "receivers" category – the latter were expected to be less well off.

But this all changed in the early 2000s as land had become less valuable. With the introduction of the North American Free Trade Agreement (NAFTA), the price of meat and maize decreased significantly. Carola could not have repaid the loans she had acquired to buy cattle even if she sold all of her herd. Like many other cattle owners, she defaulted on her payments to the government bank, which, practically bankrupt, was later closed. Luckily it took with it the identities of defaulters and the associated taint and Carola remained in very good terms with the local savings cooperatives as well as with private banks. Also she continued operating the *casino* with relative success, as well as selling some plots from the land that was closest to the village. To locals, these ventures signposted wealth.

Circuits of Valuation and Frameworks of Calculation

The position of Carola and Saraswathi is exceptional in many aspects. In Saraswathi's case, not only does her husband enjoy a good professional status but also he is extremely cooperative. Her dynamism and her social skills – the good manner she has with people – are probably uncommon. Carola inherited land and cattle, but she also possesses social skills, which are instrumental to maintaining her social status and allow her access to financial resources.

And even though Saraswathi's case is not the rule, the way she juggles money and social ties is illustrative of several broad trends. First of all, Saraswathi's case shows how sophisticated the management system of a household budget can be: she does not have direct access to formal banking, and she is almost illiterate, but this does not prevent her from calculating very meticulously her finances. Calculativeness is often considered the preserve of the economic sphere and economic theory. Calculation is thought to look only to satisfy personal interest on the basis of quantifiable indicators and units of measure. History and ethnography show that calculation goes far beyond economic acts, however. Its reasoning and rationale are complex and embedded within social settings (Weber 2001).

Although neither of the two women could, strictly speaking, qualify as "poor," they are generally thrown into this category because of their sites of residence and, in Saraswathi's case, her caste. However, their cases show that those in disadvantaged positions are not just hungry stomachs desperate to make ends meet. They seek to advance or hold on to particular individual and group identities. They are part of a variety of entitlement and obligation networks that they may seek to reinforce, appease, or flee (Guérin 2014). Calculations serve multiple – and often conflicting – purposes. As illustrated by Saraswathi's case, these may be making ends meet, respecting social structures, positioning oneself in local social networks and hierarchies, or asserting or attempting to assert one's individuality. In the case of Carola, it meant downplaying her position to a degree and making sure that others – men in particular – viewed her as nonthreatening.

In fact, the two women had to tread carefully so as not to step on men's toes, and particularly to safeguard their dignity and prestige. Carola constantly reminded others that she was a widow who missed her husband very much and was not really an owner, since everything was in her sons' names. Saraswathi went to great lengths to be on good terms with her in-laws and to make sure that she appeared as a good woman and mother. Both women were active in social and charitable activities. These cases clearly show how, as women, they felt obliged to "make up" for the fact that they were not strictly complying to gender roles.

And despite the fact that Carola's land and cattle and Saraswathi's gold and new house could classify them as wealthy, the ways in which their symbolic value was deployed and made significant was critical to their use as a form of capital, that is, as assets that contributed to the production of monetary gain. Hence, it was the processes of capitalization, more than what could have been labeled "capital" itself, that made for certain forms of wealth. It is clear that Saraswathi's assets did not measure up to the amounts that she juggled with. Yet, she managed to "produce" and circulate a significant quantity of monetary gain. This begs the need to revisit the notion of "capital" and "accumulation" and to take into account the active processes that are triggered in what we have come to consider "wealth" (Villarreal 2004a, 2009a).

Financial ties are central to these processes because of their social meaning. Debts first and foremost constitute social ties between individuals, transmitting feelings and emotions such as dignity, prestige, respectability, or, conversely, shame or humiliation. They are embedded into broader entrustments and obligations (Shipton 2007). As we have argued elsewhere, borrowers and lenders resort to specific frameworks of calculation, defined here as the sets of conceptual tools that are available and mobilized by individuals in specific situations to appreciate risk, make financial decisions, and arbitrate between various financial tools (Villarreal 2009a). Calculation frameworks have sociocultural, legal, and normative components. Calculation tools are not necessarily sophisticated or formal but have multiple cognitive, routine, and social dimensions (Coquery et al. 2006).

Calculation frameworks stem from social interactions and are thus intertwined in individuals' social positions, and here for instance we have seen how gender, caste, and class were instrumental in shaping Saraswathi's decisions and arbitrations. Even if her husband enjoys a good position, because of their caste status they are not eligible for bank loans and need an intermediary. Far from being an exception, SC discrimination regarding access to bank loans is a well-known fact (Chavan 2007). The relationship she has with upper castes is also no exception. Thanks to migration and low-caste social movements, traditional patron-client relationships based on the control of land are fading away. In the region where she lives, SC enjoy a much better position than elsewhere in the state. They have been able to organize themselves politically, many (men) work in Chennai and its surroundings, and in this way they can partly escape the dependence from upper castes locally. However the social hierarchy still persists, and creditor/debtor clearly remains a marker of social hierarchy.

This is something Carola keeps in check most of the time. She does lend out money to close friends and family, but she makes sure it is perceived as "help." She does not want to be identified as a lender. The power relation is still there, but it is "purified" in the name of support and goodwill, which also places a degree of pressure on the borrower to repay quickly and return "the favor" in some way.

The way Saraswathi and Carola deal with financial responsibilities within the household and with their kin shows to what extent financial transactions are inseparable from emotional and affective considerations. As argued by Viviana Zelizer (2005), when the economic meets the private sphere, it is not simply money, goods, or services that are exchanged but also feelings, emotions, and status. All the members of a household are involved in a continuous and intensive process of negotiation of their respective relations and positions, and financial transactions play a key role here. Even if Saraswathi's financial responsibilities within her kin are probably exceptional, the way she uses them to negotiate her position is typical of the imbrications between financial transactions and the social positioning of family members: any economic transaction is an opportunity to organize and reorganize the nature and significance of family relationships as well as the place and the status of all who are implicated.

The role of Saraswathi within her self-help group and the NGO also reflects a broader reality. While these microloans are typically presented by their promoters as a way to start microenterprises and to eradicate informal debt, in practice their main effect is to help women – or their husbands and in-laws – to better manage their cash flows: microcredit is mostly used either for consumption or to pay back past debts. The emergence or the strengthening of the women intermediaries who use their group to position themselves within local networks of patron-client ties is another unexpected effect (Guérin and Kumar 2017), and Saraswathi is a good example of this. We have followed the implementation and the evolution of the SHG movement in different parts of Tamil Nadu over the last nine years, and our assessment is similar in all the places where we have worked: the most visible effect of SHGs is the emergence of one or up to three women leaders per group. Some were already in a position of local leadership, while for others, SHGs offer new opportunities. In all cases, the (relative) control they exert on monetary flows, on the members of savings and credit groups, and on the multiple services they offer allows them to participate in local circuits of wealth distribution. The arrival of multinational companies such as Amway, which draw on "independent distributors," strengthen preexisting female circuits.

In Mexico, microlending and microfinance organizations have blossomed, mostly in response to the increasing demand for financial services. But in the municipalities of Autlán and El Grullo, where Ayuquila is located, credit and savings associations have a long history. Locals often preferred to resort to these instead of banks, including the rural government bank when it was still in operation. And government programs have introduced low-interest loans for groups of women who are willing to start an entrepreneurial activity as a group. Many such groups were advanced in the region, but most were short lived, mainly due to the difficulties in competing within established capitalist markets. However, there emerged from these enterprises, like in the case of India, a number of women leaders who, in the process, learned about the workings of government institutions and also engaged in different entrepreneurial activities. Such leadership tends to place them in convenient positions to access and negotiate social and financial resources.

In highlighting practices involving capitalization rather than simply trying to measure and weigh capital, calculation itself acquires great relevance. As the two cases show, the value attributed to certain assets is pondered through economic, but also social and cultural, considerations of different sorts.

Juggling Wealth in India and in Mexico: As a Way of Conclusion

The cases of these two women show how, in both countries, social and financial resources are closely intertwined and how wealth is socially produced.

Moral standards for women are clearly relevant to the frameworks within which they are able to calculate, make decisions, and negotiate. It is not that these two women are "representative" of two countries (in fact, in southeastern Mexico we found more similarities with the contexts Saraswathi was facing: see Morvant 2013 and Angulo 2013), but discussing their cases in parallel does show similarities in the processes they undergo and reveals interesting features of the workings of money and the nature of wealth.

One of these is the issue of juggling, which entails a constant mobilization and reallocation of resources, both tangible and intangible. Such resources need to be opportunistically picked up, translated, and introduced in circuits of valuation. This is what Saraswathi and Carola do with their financial, social, and symbolic resources. Their management system highlights the prevalence and sophistication of "juggling" practices. Juggling literally involves throwing, catching, and keeping several things in the air at once, demanding speed and dexterity, but also risk-taking. These three facets are excellent in evoking the nature of financial practices: like many others, Saraswathi combines multiple financial tools in the context of ongoing borrowing, repayment, and reborrowing practices (one borrows from one place to repay elsewhere). She swaps roles between debtor and creditor, and here, too, this practice is frequently observed, even among women who are much poorer than Saraswathi. Carola also engages in juggling with monetary and nonmonetary resources, taking on risks. However, she tends to conceal such maneuvering in order to sustain a morally accepted gender status.

Juggling with debt is a matter of temporalities, as lenders impose different time scales. It is also a matter of space, as borrowers multiply the locations and the circles of debt. But as we have seen here, social motivations also count. Juggling practices often reflect deliberate choices, strategies, or tactics aimed at multiplying and diversifying social relationships and strengthening or weakening the burden of dependency ties. Monetary and financial ties are embedded into preexisting social relationships, which in turn may evolve or change through the medium of money and debt. We have seen that the multiple logics of debt are under constant tension, with subtle, complex reasoning and tradeoffs. This leads to a plethora of complementary, and often incommensurable, nonsubstitutable financial practices.

Finally, we want to emphasize that debt and wealth are also interlinked. Following José Ossandón's (2012) depiction of commercial circuits of credit card debt, we can speak to the ways in which Saraswathi, whose possession of monetary capital is limited, can extend access to credit to her kin, friends, and neighbors. Such commercial circuits (see also Zelizer 2011) are also present in the case of Carola, whose prestige allows her access to credit within certain networks. Using the concept of circuits allows us to focus on processes, wherein relations are constantly reconstructed rather than fixed. This is the case, for example, of power relations. A debt relation entails power, but it does not automatically place the debtor in a powerless position, as we have seen in the case of Saraswathi. Wealth is, as both cases clearly illustrate, relational. Attribution of wealth is articulated within processes wherein resources are mobilized and leveraged. This can only be done within fields where their value is acknowledged and can be negotiated according to certain conventions and expectations (Villarreal 2004b, 2009b). In India, caste constitutes an important factor in the process of labeling certain resources as wealth. In Mexico, class is not only determined by the amount of resources an individual or family possesses but by the context in which they are owned and the future opportunities forecast for his or her persona. Juggling wealth thus entails mobilization of social categories, expectations, and moralities as much as it does attributing ownership and negotiating financial assets.

Far beyond our two cases, we believe that the concepts used here – juggling, calculation frameworks, relational wealth – must be taken into account when analyzing economic dynamics, whatever the context. These practices are not practices carried out by the "poor," "informal," or "traditional" economies; they are the core of social interdependency and explain in great part both wealth and impoverishment processes.

Acknowledgements

This chapter draws on fieldwork initiated within the RUME project (Rural Employment and Microfinance: Do Processes Matter? http://www .rume-rural-microfinance.org) and continued within a grant from the Institute of Money, Technology and Financial Inclusion. Both projects aimed at comparing economic practices in two small regions economically dynamic both in agriculture and non-agriculture: Autlán Valley in Jalisco (Mexico) and Villipuram and Cudallore Districts in Tamil Nadu (India).

Magadalena Villarreal is a researcher and senior professor at the Center for Advanced Research and Postgraduate Studies in Social Anthropology (CIESAS) in Guadalajara, México. She received a PhD in anthropology from Wageningen University, the Netherlands. She is coeditor of the volume *Microfinance, Debt and Over-Indebtedness: Juggling with Money* (Routledge 2013) and author of *Antropología de la Deuda: Crédito, Ahorro, Fiado y Prestado en las finanzas cotidianas* (CIESAS 2004).

Isabelle Guérin is senior research fellow at the Institute of Research for Development – CESSMA (Centre d'études en sciences sociales sur les mondes américains africains et asiatiques) and associate at the French Institute of Pondicherry. She is specialized in the political and moral economics of money, debt, and finance. Her current work focuses on the financialization of domestic economies, looking at how financialization produces new forms of inequalities and domination but also alternative and solidarity-based initiatives. Her work draws most often on original data and combines ethnography and statistical analyses. Her latest publications in English include *The Crises of Microcredit,* coedited with Marc Labie and Jean-Michel Servet (Zed Book, 2015); and *Under Development: Gender,* coedited with Christine Verschuur and Hélène Guétat-Bernard (Palgrave 2014). She regularly publishes articles in various journals that reflect her interdisciplinary approach: development studies (*World Development, Journal of Development Studies, Development and Change, Journal of International*

Development), political economy (*Journal of Agrarian Change*), and anthropology (*Current Anthropology*).

K. S. Santhosh Kumar is a research associate in the field of sociology. He has worked with many different researchers over the past eighteen years, with a specific focus on women's empowerment in the field of health and economic development. Presently, his special areas of interest are the role of credit and debt in women's daily life and decision-making.

NOTES

1. Including here different kinds of capital, such as human, social, material, and monetary.
2. Caste and class both make reference to social status. Yet they speak to different socio-historical backgrounds and entail diverse socio-economic considerations. Caste is part of a hierarchical structure that is inherited and traditionally involves endogamy. Class tends to follow a social assessment of wealth.
3. Chit is a tamil term that means "paper", and refers to the fact roscas, although informal forms of saving and credit, can use some form of written document from their members (and even if most don't). Chit funds are a kind of Rosca, that is, a group of individuals who agree to meet for a defined period in order to save and borrow together. Each member contributes the same amount at each meeting, and one member takes the whole sum once. This is often qualified as "turn", or "share", or "pot".
4. There is, in this case, as is common both in the Indian and the Mexican social scenarios, a great number of patron-client relationships taking place. Yet, what is interesting about Saraswathi's case is that it clearly shows the ways in which she deals with such relationships and at times uses them to her advantage.
5. García Barragán, a general who was quite influential in the region, had been *padrino* (godfather) at her wedding. *Padrinos* in Mexico are not only associated with baptisms but can be designated as such in different formal ceremonies, including weddings, graduations, etc.
6. Although the Law of Agrarian Reform formally allows widows who remarry to continue possessing the *ejido* land they had inherited in their name, in everyday practice men often take control over it (see also Arizpe and Botey 1986)
7. What local people referred to as *casino* was actually a large building in the village where parties, dances, and other events were held. As owner of the building, Carola could organize such events, benefiting sometimes from entrance fees but especially through the sale of beer and other drinks.

REFERENCES CITED

Angulo, Lourdes. 2013. "The Social Costs of Microfinance and Over-Indebtedness for Women." In *Microfinance, Debt and Over-Indebtedness: Juggling with Money,* edited by I. Guérin, S. Morvant-Roux, and M. Villarreal, 232–52. New York: Routledge.

Arizpe, Lourdes, and Botey Carlota. 1986. "Las políticas de desarrollo agrario y su impacto sobre la mujer campesina en México." In *La Mujer y la Política Agraria en América Latina*, edited by León and Carmen Diana Deere, 48–72. Bogotá: SigloXXI-ACEP.

Bloch, Maurice, and Jonathan Parry, eds. 1989. *Money and the Morality of Exchange.* Cambridge: Cambridge University Press.

Callon, Michel, ed. 1998. *The Laws of the Markets.* Oxford: Blackwell Publishers.

Chavan, P. 2007. "Access to Bank Credit Implications for Dalit Rural Households." *Economic and Political Weekly* (4 August): 3219–24.

Coquery, Natacha, Menant, François, and Florence Weber, eds. *Écrire, compter, mesurer: Vers une histoire des rationalités pratiques*, Paris: Éditions rue d'Ulm.

Guyer Jane, ed. 1995. *Money Matters: Instability, Values, and Social Payments in the Modern History of West African Communities.* Portsmouth, NH: Heinemann.

———. 2004. *Marginal Gains: Monetary Transactions in Atlantic Africa.* Chicago: University of Chicago Press.

Guérin, Isabelle. 2014. "Juggling with Debt, Social Ties, and Values: The Everyday Use of Microcredit in Rural South India." *Current Anthropology* 55(9): S40–50.

Guérin, Isabelle, and Santosh Kumar. 2017. "The Uneasy Relationship between Market and Freedom: Is Microcredit a Source of Empowerment or Domination for Women?" *Journal of Development Studies* 53(5): 741–55.

Guérin, Isabelle, Solène Morvant-Roux, and Magdalena Villarreal. 2013. *Microfinance, Debt and Over-Indebtedness: Juggling with Money.* New York. Routledge.

Maurer, Bill. 2006. "The Anthropology of Money." *Annual Review of Anthropology* 35: 15–36.

Morvant-Roux, Solène. 2013. "International Migration and Over-Indebtedness in Rural Mexico." In *Microfinance, Debt and Over-Indebtedness: Juggling with Money*, edited by I. Guérin, S. Morvant-Roux, and M. Villarreal, 170–92. New York: Routledge.

Munn, Nancy D. 1986. *The Fame of Gawa: A Symbolic Study of Value Transformation in a Massim (Papua New Guinea) Society.* Durham, NC: Duke University Press.

Ossandón, José. 2012. "The Economy of the Quota: The Financial Ecologies and Commercial Circuits of Retail Credit Cards in Santiago, Chile." Retrieved 15 June 2014 from Blog.imtfi.uci.edu/2012/11/the-economy-of-quota-financial .html.

Shipton, Parker. 2007. *The Nature of Entrustment: Intimacy, Exchange and the Sacred in Africa.* New Haven, CT: Yale University Press.

Villarreal, Magdalena. 2004a. "Striving to Make Capital Do 'Economic Things' for the Impoverished: On the Issue of Capitalization in Rural Microenterprises." In *Development Intervention: Actor and Activity Perspectives*, edited by T. Kontinen, 67–81. Helsinki: Center for Activity Theory and Developmental Work Research (CATDWR), Institute for Development Studies (IDS) and University of Helsinki.

———. 2004b. *Antropología de la Deuda: Crédito, Ahorro, Fiado y Prestado en las Finanzas Cotidianas.* México City, México: D.F. CIESAS, Porrúa y la Cámara de Diputados.

———. 2009a. *Mujeres, finanzas sociales y violencia economica en zonas marginadas de Guadalajara.* Guadalajara: IMMG/IJM.

———. 2009b. "Erratic Hopes and Inconsistent Expectations for Mexican Rural Women: A Critique of Economic Thinking on Alternatives to Poverty." In *On the Edges of Development: Cultural Interventions,* edited by B. Kum-Kum, J. Foran, A. Durian Priya, and Munshi Debashish, 124–142. New York: Routledge.

Weber, Florence. 2001. "Settings, Interactions and Things: A Plea for Multi-integrative Ethnography." *Ethnography* 2(4): 475–99.

Zelizer, Viviana. 1994. *The Social Meaning of Money.* New York: Basic Books.

———. 2005. *The Purchase of Intimacy.* Princeton, NJ: Princeton University Press.

———. 2011. *Economic Lives: How Culture Shapes the Economy.* Princeton, NJ: Princeton University Press.

Part III

Technology and Social Relations
Infrastructures of Digital Money

JENNA BURRELL

Financial practices of saving, investing, borrowing, and lending exist beyond the reaches of the modern state: in rural and remote regions, in urban sub- or para-economies that intentionally evade state oversight, and among populations referred to lately as "the unbanked." There money passes along an infrastructure of interpersonal relations and group membership. Such an infrastructure functions to distribute (or redistribute) accumulations according to shared notions of fairness. It aids individuals to mitigate risk, smooth transactions, and serve their own self-interests. It helps collectives to pool resources and put them to best use. This infrastructure is shaped by all the qualities and characteristics of human relationships, which can be intimate, affective, changeable, and idiosyncratic.

Where do digital technologies figure into this domain of so-called "informal" finance? In the evolving conversation about enhancing the finances of the poor, a mistaken assumption, I would argue, is to treat such technologies as antithetical to the personal and informal, to imagine that it is their nature to formalize, to replace affective sensibilities with systemization, to substitute fuzzy personal judgment with documentation and unassailable proof. The computational basis of digital technologies has been taken up by analysts directing attention away from the role they have come to play as essential tools of rich human communication. The mobile phone, for example, is key in establishing and sustaining social relations through the subtleties of voice and language. This capability is surely not apart from everyday financial practice but is integral to it.

In research and policy efforts that focus on technology as a tool of financial inclusion, a financial practice based in social relations has sometimes been cast as irredeemably inadequate. But we should question whether such a financial practice is indeed irredeemable. Although formal finance (urban-oriented, bank-based, and state-regulated) has likewise been cast as falling short, particularly in reaching and serving "the poor," it is nonetheless viewed as possible to improve upon. Digital technologies are often positioned as the key to extending formal finance and its benefits to the poor and marginalized. However, the way digital technologies could enhance a finance situated in social relations has not been given the same weight and consideration. The chapters in this part offer an even-handed account of finance grounded in social relations and the opposing or supporting role of technology in these financial forms.

Kevin Donovan's account examines debates surrounding the implementation of a social grant program by the South African government through a third party, Cash Paymaster Services (CPS), firmly a domain of formal finance. In the administration of the grants, CPS claimed to accomplish goals of financial inclusion since bank accounts were created for grantees, and it was into these accounts that the grants were deposited. They proposed to offer other financial services, loans in particular, using the grant money (and access to the bank account) to secure repayment. The validity of this claim of "inclusion," the interests it served, and the power dynamics entailed in the new system were hotly contested and debated among government representatives, pro-poor civil society groups, CPS, and other stakeholders.

Donovan's account offers important insights about social relations between payer and payee and the problems introduced by their "formalization"; he identifies a shift from an interpersonal relationship to a relationship with a remote firm. CPS claimed that formalized loans were an improvement on the reliance upon "informal" moneylenders called *mashonisas* whom they cast as exploitative. Yet, civil-society groups working on behalf of grantees argued that the *mashonisas* as members of the same community as their borrowers were thereby subject to the oversight and sanctions of that community. Furthermore, the technological distancing of grantees from their grants also involved a streamlining of claims by third parties to these funds through automated deductions, "erecting intermediaries that separated the poor from their money and who were thus positioned to profit from, and arbitrarily interfere in, their affairs." With the *mashonisas*, the grantee at least had a chance to exert some control over repayment.

Kusimba et al. get at the heart of finance via social relations and of the mobile phone as an enhancement to such practices. The authors consider relations among kin in particular and their role-based duties defined, in part, by income and employment status, age and birth order, generation, and gender. When a family head needs surgery, mobile phones become critical tools in the time-pressured rush to pool funds from family at home and abroad. Thus the phone contributes to "strengthening traditional economic support networks." And thus, "the real 'inclusion' twenty-first century information and communication technologies (ICTs) provide is into a culture of entrustment (Shipton 2007) that is surely centuries old." Kusimba and her colleagues observe how with mobile money services, the mobile phone is employed to underline or further concretize social ties through the transfer of material support. Mobile money is not an economic add-on to a social tool, but in a cultural context where material transactions (money transfers) are seen as a fundamental indicator of the quality of the social relationship, this functionality is an amplification of the sociality of the tool.

Finally, Ossandón et al. provide a perspective from Chile where access to credit has been driven by retail stores, offering store credit cards, rather than through banks or other traditional financial institutions. Focusing in particular on evolving anthropologically rooted methods for the study of financial practice, the authors aim at improving the accuracy of such accounts. This leads them to employ the monthly invoice sent to customers as a tool to provoke and ground conversation. And in the course of the research they discover something unexpected: that the store credit cards of individuals are routinely lent out to many others. Thus the records represent a network of actors, including family, even friends. These records highlight another dimension of a finance of social relations, emphasizing, as Kusimba et al. do as well, the mistake of an overly individualized examination of financial practices to the neglect of collectives, or more aptly as Ossandón et al. describe "payment circuits" whereby actors are linked together through practice by a shared format of payment.

"Technology" in the form of devices, systems, and largely invisible infrastructures is variously and broadly conceived and considered in the chapters in this part. All challenge the enduring notion of technology as an external change agent, a disruption to culture. Instead it is something that is co-constructed *through* such processes.

Jenna Burrell is an associate professor in the School of Information at UC Berkeley. She is the author of *Invisible Users: Youth in the Internet Cafes of Urban Ghana* (MIT Press 2012). She has a PhD in sociology from the London School of Economics. Before pursuing her PhD she was an application concept developer in the People and Practices Research Group at Intel Corporation. For over ten years she studied the appropriation of information and communication technologies (ICTs) by individuals and groups on the African continent. Her most recent research considers populations that are excluded from or opt out of internet connectivity in urban and rural California.

CHAPTER 7

"Financial Inclusion Means Your Money Isn't with You"

Conflicts over Social Grants and Financial Services in South Africa

KEVIN P. DONOVAN

Introduction

Throughout sub-Saharan Africa, governments and donors have significantly expanded the use of cash transfers to alleviate poverty and address other developmental needs such as education and health (Garcia and Moore 2012). These programs to "just give money to the poor" have been called a "development revolution" for their positive influences and administrative simplicity (Hanlon et al. 2010). Typically, these provide small cash grants at regular intervals to poor or vulnerable populations, most often to directly alleviate poverty but also to boost education or health. In addition to the direct goals of these initiatives, the aid industry has begun to explore ancillary benefits and opportunities.

Leveraging cash transfers to incorporate the poor into the formal financial sector is one secondary effect that has attracted notable attention, especially from the "financial inclusion" community that advocates improving access for the poor to credit, savings, insurance, and payment facilities (for an overview, see Schwittay 2011). For example, the World Bank's financial access unit, the Consultative Group to Assist the Poor (CGAP), has argued that "these payments have the potential to become a vehicle for extending financial inclusion and improving the welfare of poor people" (Pickens et al. 2009). Since at least 2012, this discourse has shifted to emphasize the benefits of electronic payments for economic efficiency and inclusion. For example, the Gates Foundation – which funds much of the financial inclusion movement – has argued that "because most poor households conduct most or all of their financial transactions in cash [it] perpetuates the poor's marginalization from the formal economy. . ." (Gates Foundation 2012). Electronic payment systems (from debit cards to mobile phones) are considered more efficient and less expensive, and as a result, donors and governments have sought to shift toward them. Financial and technology providers, too, have been supportive, not least because of the opportunity to grow their market through transaction fees and data mining.

South Africa has one of the world's largest cash transfer programs (known locally as "social grants"). During 2012–13, the South African Social Security Agency (SASSA) deployed a new payment system from its contractor, Cash Paymaster Services. The new infrastructure provided nearly 10 million grant recipients with a formal bank account and a MasterCard-branded debit card that could be used throughout the country. At first glance, this appears to be the type of financial inclusion that proponents believe will empower the poor; yet, instead of uniting stakeholders with its promise, the new system signaled peril to some grant recipients, key members of South Africa's pro-poor civil society, and elements of the government – many of whom raised alarm. These critics feared that increased provision of financial services – especially loans – to the grant recipients would undermine the emancipatory purpose of the grants. In particular, they worried that the new payment system was unfairly biased toward lenders, especially the use of automatic deductions from bank accounts for the purpose of repayment. Early evidence suggested widespread confusion amid the newly financially included, many of whom were not receiving the full amount of their grant. As one community advocate told me, "financial inclusion means your money isn't with you." For this woman who dedicated her work to securing the rights of the poor in South Africa, financial inclusion was potentially a means of empowering grant recipients, but she worried about this particular instantiation. Financial inclusion was erecting intermediaries that separated the poor from their money and who were thus positioned to profit from, and arbitrarily interfere in, their affairs.[1]

As a researcher at the University of Cape Town during this time, I was keenly following the new grant payment technology.[2] The system's potential to include millions of low-income South Africans in the financial sector intrigued me, not least due to my previous work on the use of mobile money for financial inclusion (Donovan 2012). Thus, in mid-2012 I began interacting with a community of civil society organizations and government officials engaged with the social grants.[3] Many of these individuals had lengthy experiences fighting for social justice in South Africa, including the expansion of social grants following the end of apartheid.

Their knowledge of the daily struggle that many in South Africa confront was intimate and their ties to those communities strong, but they had less experience with the world of financial inclusion, banking, and information technology. As such, I found myself partaking in something akin to what Maurer (2005) calls "lateral reason," reasoning *with* and *between* communities, rather than *about* others. In addition to my interviews and observations, I was often called on to share insights from my historical work or comparisons with other countries. This chapter on the debates over the relationship between social grants and financial services reflects this nine-month engagement in 2012–13 as well as my research on other aspects of cash transfers.

South Africa's Social Grants

The genesis of what is today South Africa's largest redistributive effort was a concern in the 1920s about the so-called "poor white problem" that led to the introduction of old-age pensions (Seekings 2007). Over time this nascent welfare state would grow, including through the expansion of pensions to the African population in the 1940s and their eventual monetary equalization in the waning days of apartheid (Seekings 2008). Today, the social grants are a crucial government initiative and have been expanded to include nearly 16 million beneficiaries in four main categories. As Bähre's (2011) illuminating discussion depicts, the grants are a crucial form of the "redistributive economy" in post-apartheid South Africa. As of March 2013, there are half a million foster care grants, 1.2 million disability grants, 2.8 million old-age pensions, and 11.3 million child support grants.[4] Residents qualify through an income-based means test, as well as the particular requirements of the grant (e.g., above sixty years old for the pension).

At the time of the 1994 democratic transition, the administration of the grants was a provincial responsibility, but the internal fragmentation of South Africa under apartheid created a situation of starkly uneven bureaucratic capacity. Beginning in the second half of the 1990s, the failures to deliver social grants in the face of so much need became the subject of significant public outcry, leading to a series of government commissions aimed at creating a system of "comprehensive social security" (RSA 2002). Eventually this led to a process of bureaucratic standardization and centralization, most notably through the establishment of the South African Social Security Agency (SASSA) in 2005 as the sole entity responsible for the delivery of grants (see Donovan 2015).

Although SASSA has been a marked improvement, the media and politicians still frequently castigate the social grants program as subject to significant fraud and corruption by wayward bureaucrats and dishonest citizens. In response, in 2012 SASSA contracted with Cash Paymaster Services (CPS), a subsidiary of the Net1 technology group, to provide a uniform, national payment system that would rely on biometric identification to combat fraudulent access to the grants. In addition to this primary goal of removing dual or undeserving recipients from the grants program, the new payment system was to offer enhanced convenience to grant recipients who would be issued with a MasterCard-branded debit card, able to function at thousands of shops. The debit cards would connect to a formal bank account offered by a Net1 partner, Grindrod Bank.[5] The service providers were quick to emphasize the opportunity this represented for the poor, such as Dries Zietsman (2012) of MasterCard who said it "opens up a world of financial inclusion for many South Africans who have previously not had access to banking products."

This marked a departure from the previous methods of payment that had been contracted to multiple entities, each with their own methods. The parastatal PostBank worked in Mpumalanga and Limpopo; AllPay, a subsidiary of the largest South African bank ABSA, had operated in the Western Cape, Eastern Cape, Free State, and Gauteng; Empilweni, a specialized grant delivery firm, had managed Mpumalanga; and Net1's CPS had delivered in Eastern Cape, Northern Cape, KwaZulu Natal, Northwest, and Limpopo provinces. While AllPay offered some recipients full bank accounts, the others typically paid beneficiaries in cash on a given day at a community paypoint where lines were long. Costs to government, too, varied, with cash dispersal at the paypoints costing up to ZAR30 (FinMark 2012).[6] Under the new system, all recipients would also be able to withdraw their grant at an extensive network of third-party retailers with whom Net1 CPS contracted or at any ATM across the country (though this would incur a standard fee). Additionally, the government would only pay R16 per grant payment, reportedly saving R800 million per year.[7]

Following the award to Net1 CPS, it soon emerged that in addition to the delivery of grants, the firm planned to offer financial services to the grant recipients. As the *Mail & Guardian* newspaper reported, they told shareholders of plans "to 'leverage' the social grant payment contract by selling financial instruments to about 10-million people who receive state grants" (McKune 2012). Net1 also has interests in a handful of microlending and insurance firms, and told investors "its financial products would be 'based on our understanding of [beneficiaries'] risk profiles, earning and spending patterns, demographics and lifestyle requirements'" (Mc-

Kune 2012). As the media and civil society organizations like the Black Sash and Legal Resources Centre quickly pointed out, these would seem to contravene rules against using administrative data for marketing, as well as prohibitions on deducting loan repayments or other fees from the social grants.[8] The Black Sash (2013) "urgently raised the issue of unlawful deductions from grants through formal submissions, monitoring reports and letters, and in meetings with decision makers." However, the payment provider's CEO, Serge Belamant, doubled down, defending the plans and arguing that "the cost is a lot higher than R16 [to deliver grants]. There has to be in the model some other means of being able to say, how am I going to be able to recover my investment and my losses?" (Belamant 2013).

The dispute would grow in the first half of 2013 as a number of pro-poor civil society organizations contested what they described as immoral and illegal actions by private financial service providers, including and beyond Net1 CPS. In what follows I describe and analyze some of the debates that characterized the dispute over how the social grants would be incorporated into the financial industry.[9]

Reckoning with (In)Formality

Studies of everyday economic behavior have cautioned against accepting too sharp of a divide between the so-called "formal" and "informal" economies. As originally coined by anthropologist Keith Hart (1973), the informal sector or economy sought to give attention to the rise of casual or self-employment in the Global South. However, Hart (2010) and others have more recently provided a more nuanced view of the interlacing between the supposedly distinct spheres. In South Africa, for example, Bähre (2012) has documented how major insurance firms instrumentalize social relations in townships to sell their services, and Hull (2012) has shown that "the formal" can give rise to "the informal" due to the contingencies of negotiating bureaucratic requirements (see also Neves and du Toit 2012).

Despite these empirical subtleties, for the individuals debating the relationship between social grants and financial services, "formal versus informal" was an emic categorization. Formal or "registered" lenders were often contrasted with informal *mashonisas,* a term meaning "moneylender" but often implying "loan shark." These informal financiers were understood to be prevalent, prone to violence, and likely to charge excessive interest rates (up to 100 percent). *Mashonisas* often congregate around social grant paypoints, plying loans to those in need or collecting repayments in the form of grants. As Versfeld (2012) has written in her ethnography of grant payments in Cape Town's Manenberg Township, "They seem to have a distinct style: natty fedora hats pulled low over their brows. . . . They sit in their cars or roam . . . available to make business from the desperate, or take [grant money] from the defaulters." These informal lenders often seize the SASSA card or national ID of their debtors, ensuring they control the material means of repayment.[10] As SASSA's CEO has noted, a cycle of debt means that many beneficiaries owe the full amount of their grant each month (Gerbi 2012).

Beyond encouraging grant recipients to maintain possession of their cards, conducting periodic police raids, and enforcing a rule that prohibited hawking within 100 meters of paypoints, government and civil society representatives with whom I spoke seemed unsure what more they could do to contain such a dispersed and widespread practice.[11] One option was to require would-be lenders to register with the government, in hopes that increasing the legibility of the microlenders would improve the government's ability to regulate them (cf. Scott 1999). Indeed, a SASSA official explained to me that the consolidation of previously distinct provincial payment systems into one national infrastructure did uncover a host of previously unknown grant deductions that were now visible in the new management information system. Another financial inclusion advocate pointed out that if electronic deductions were limited, perhaps pushing repayments into cash, regulators would be unable to monitor it effectively. But while supporters of formalization expressed support for the newfound legibility, in practice, the aspirations for panopticism were greater than the reality; although SASSA could now see the money disappearing each month, specifics were hardly clear: were they desired by recipients? Legal? Appropriate? For example, they did detect multiple recipients sharing a bank account – a practice not permitted in the formal regulations, though not obviously nefarious. This uncertainty would prove difficult for government officials who wanted to act quickly to protect the poor.

The exorbitant fees and often violent enforcement of repayment (cf. Bähre 2007) were frequently invoked as specters haunting the poor, pushing them into debt traps. In defending his plans to provide financial services to grant recipients, Cash Paymaster Service's chief was quick to cite the presence of informal and "other less scrupulous" lenders who, he argued, would not act as responsibly as his firm (Speckman 2013). While his argument may be self-serving, it was not an aberration, and others (without a profit motive) voiced similar opinions: maybe it was the *mashonisas* who were the real menace?

The *mashonisas* were cast as sinister characters, preying on the desperate poor and operating beyond the law. However, in at least one instance, an experienced community organizer made the case in favor of *mashonisas* vis à vis formal lenders. Responding to a suggestion that registered lenders were desirable because they could be legally regulated, she passionately raised fears about the power of formal lenders compared to informal ones. When the risk of *mashonisa* violence was raised, she downplayed the threat, arguing that because the informal moneylenders were part of the local community, they were more likely to understand their debtors' troubles and offer flexible repayment schemes. While she did not ignore the possibility of violence, in her mind, the alternative was worse: registered lenders would sue for repayment, potentially seizing a debtor's home and blackballing them more widely.[12] Although she did not use the term, in her understanding the *mashonisas* and grant recipients operated in a moral economy that did not include formal lenders (cf. Scott 1976).[13] In this dichotomy, the consequences of default in the informal economy were shorter lived and less durable.

Negotiating the Ethics of Financial Inclusion

While this argument in favor of *mashonisas* was not universally supported, within the networks of civil society organizations working on the conjunction of social grant payments and financial services, there was a general distrust of formal lenders, including the government's payment provider, CPS. As I have suggested, a crucial reason for their worry was the practice of automatic deductions that facilitated repayment through the electronic banking systems rather than physical cash. In contrast to the proponents' rhetoric of "empowerment," in this case, for many pro-poor civil society organizations, the legal and technical transformations that constituted "financial inclusion" were recognized as a reduction in the autonomy of the poor. As the prominent South African human rights organization Black Sash wrote, "After SASSA introduced an automated biometric-based payment system last year, we were horrified to find that grant beneficiaries were experiencing an avalanche of unauthorized and unlawful deductions from their social grants" (Black Sash 2013).

This fear was exacerbated by the lack of clarity about the functions and rules of the new grant payment system. Members of civil society organizations with whom I spoke were often unfamiliar with the technicalities of "the payments space" — a realm Maurer (2012a) has described as populated by self-described "payment geeks" who negotiate arcane legal and technical rules for the movement of money. For example, one of the concerns was that CPS, as both grant payment provider and financial service supplier, was positioned with an unfair advantage to be repaid ahead of others; CPS was, it seemed, both "officiator" and "player" (McKune 2012). For a few weeks, my interlocutors grappled to understand the alien terms of the payment infrastructure. One such phrase was "AEDO/NAEDO," an acronym for a relatively new payment system in South Africa that treats deductions in a randomized, non-preferential basis known as the "lottery system."[14] For those concerned with the fairness of the new system – here understood as equality of repayment opportunity – the use or non-use of this technical standard was crucial. Yet, the particularities of the formal banking system were not immediately obvious to these civil society organizations (let alone the poor they represented), a dynamic not dissimilar to the opacity of the popular economies mentioned above.[15]

The issue of fairness in repayment was one of a number of explicitly moral debates that fueled this contest. As economic anthropologists have emphasized, the particular cultural and ethical meanings attached to exchange and circulation differ widely (see, for example, Parry and Bloch 1989). In this case, competing moral claims and visions intersected with specific technical arrangements and legal definitions. More pressing than the impartiality of repayment for would-be lenders was the ethics of the relationship between grant recipients and microlenders. The views expressed were shaped by interpretations of South Africa's past and perceptions of the future, especially of potential risks to the poor.

Consider the case of Valerie, a representative of a pro-poor organization who spoke at a gathering of forty to fifty representatives of civil society, community organizations, and government, brought together to discuss changes in the grants payment infrastructure. Her motivation for addressing this issue, she began, was because she was "driven by what's right." Valerie exhorted the audience to think about the "ultimate goal of the grants," which she described as minimizing the financial needs of the poor and arising from South Africa's constitutional right to social security. This right was bound up with the country's apartheid history, and she asserted that the "grants are to right the wrongs of the past."

For Valerie, evidence that grant beneficiaries were not receiving the full amount of the grant – which she already believed was paltry – meant that the goals of the social grants were being undermined. She questioned the ethics of giving a loan on the basis of a social grant; if the government permitted this, it was tantamount to "giving with one hand and allowing it, through electronic banking, to be taken away." Or, as another individual told me, the risk is that you have a situation where "the government is paying social grants to the private sector, not the poor."

For Valerie and others, the law was quite clear: the Social Assistance Act requires the grants be paid to the recipients in full, except for specific categories of deductions as permitted by ministerial regulation: "a grant may not be transferred, ceded, or pledged or in any way encumbered and disposed of unless the Minister on good grounds in writing consents thereto." Furthermore, those exceptions must be "necessary and in the interest of the beneficiary" (RSA 2004). In reality, the only deduction that was legally allowed was for one registered funeral insurance policy per recipient, not to exceed 10 percent of the grant's value.

Despite such apparent clarity, from late 2012 members of civil society and the media documented examples of deductions from grants. In a typical example, an elderly woman in the town of De Aar found that the majority of her pension had been deducted before she withdrew it. It was unclear where this money was transferred or how to stop it, but investigations found the transfers were repayments to Net1 CPS subsidiaries.[16] In many cases, Net1's subsidiaries charged a service fee rather than an interest rate, seemingly avoiding National Credit Regulations. Critics rejected the salience of the service fee versus interest rate distinction, noting that "on an R800 unsecured loan, with a repayment period of six months, the service fee is R280 – equivalent to 70% annual interest. A loan of just R200 will attract fees of R100 – equivalent to 100% annual interest" (Steyn 2014). Entities, like the Legal Resources Centre, that advocate on behalf of the poor documented numerous such examples and raised alarm about the blurring of roles between paymaster and loan provider. For their part, the Black Sash launched a "Hands Off Our Grants" campaign. In response, the government said that it was exploring legal means of curtailing such activity. The politically influential Congress of South African Trade Unions (COSATU 2013) and the South African Communist Party (SACP 2013) also both condemned the alleged lending by CPS, with the latter putting it in the context of other "reckless lenders including the banks, who prey on the vulnerable and poor working class communities."

In some cases, these deductions were remnants from the previous system, where some provinces permitted deductions. In order to clear those cases, SASSA stated it would permit those loans to be repaid at up to 25 percent of the grant while prohibiting new lending against the grant. Other instances were perhaps improper and needed to be investigated individually. But other examples seemingly emerged from another technicality of the financial system. Due to the CPS partnership with Grindrod Bank, all grant recipients now had a formal bank account (even though few perhaps knew it, and they would rarely if ever interact with Grind-rod, which operates only a handful of branches). As far as the deductions were concerned, though, the importance was significant. Debit orders could be placed against the funds in a standard bank account. Thus, the grant may be fully paid into the recipient's account only to be subject to a debit order for, say, a microloan repayment. Some considered this fine distinction between *payment* of the grant and *receipt* of it by the beneficiary to be spurious. From the point of view of the recipient, after all, if the full grant reached their account only to be subtracted momentarily thereafter due to an electronic debit order, what difference does it make? Stories proliferated of pensioners who did not understand where their grant was going, and their unfamiliarity with the technology only magnified the confusion. In response to the backlash, the office of the Public Protector (a government ombudsman) opened an investigation that remains ongoing as of January 2014 (Waters 2013).

In his justification, Net1's chief, Serge Belamant, stridently laid out a vision for the grants to be unencumbered monetary value as soon as they reached the electronic account: "Once it's in his bank account. . . . If he goes to a microlender and signs a debit order, the debit order will be treated like anyone else's debit order." In his reckoning, Net1's lending was responsible. "The ethical issue would be that if you're granting them or giving them a loan and abusing them in terms of either interest rates or the way that you provide the loans to them – in other words . . . catching them in a system they can't get out of. We do the opposite" (Belamant 2013). He also defended a Net1 subsidiary selling airtime on credit to grant recipients (Jacobs 2013). Replying to a letter from the Legal Resources Centre alleging "that thousands of beneficiaries in the Eastern Cape and elsewhere have had deductions made from their grant," CPS "emphasized the right of beneficiaries to use their social grants as they deemed fit" and noted that the law "does not preclude third parties from enforcing the rights established by a debit order" (Ensor 2013).

In this view, the grants are less about "righting the wrongs of the past" or "human rights" than they are about unencumbered consumption. For the pro-poor advocates, the grants were also about consumption – usually under the term "basic needs" – but there was a symbolic value and practical purpose that they believed would erode if financialization proceeded unchecked. Even though the most vocal champion of the laissez-faire approach has a private interest in its promotion, it is worth taking this argument seriously, because it bears similarity to influential proponents of "financial inclusion" (like the World Bank's CGAP) who argue for responsible lending to the poor to use as they see fit. As Ananya Roy (2010) writes in her study of the "financialization of development," under "the watchful eye of CGAP, microfinance has been reinscribed as financial services for the poor, a new global industry that can be integrated into financial markets" (see also Elyachar 2005; James 2013).

It also aligns with a strain of support for the social grants in South Africa that anthropologist James Ferguson (2009) highlights as "surprisingly similar to the neoliberal rationality that we more usually associate with anti-welfare discourses." For many proponents of expanding the social grants, he notes, the recipient is "conceived, in classic neoliberal fashion, as a kind of micro-enterprise," while the state is imagined "as both omnipresent and minimal – universally engaged (as a kind of direct provider for each and every citizen) and maximally disengaged (taking no real interest in shaping the conduct of those under its care, who are seen as knowing their own needs better than the state does)" (see also Ferguson 2013). This junction has supported the design of the social grants as both unconditional and rights-based.[17]

This ambiguity was also reflected in the civil society debates. No one doubted the inevitability, and even the potential upside, of microlending. Rules that took too strong of a line against borrowing by grant recipients were a danger that was often raised. It was perhaps most relevant for pensioners: if the grant was their only source of income, and it could not be "transferred, ceded, or pledged" as collateral, would pensioners be blocked from borrowing? As one government official wondered aloud, "How do you give credit when the only income is a grant?" It was clear to all that a carte blanche rule against microlending, strongly enforced, was inappropriate.

Indeed, the existing exemption for funeral policies exhibited a similar balancing act. Why, I asked various interlocutors, should a particular type of insurance be treated differently than other financial products? Although some expressed ambivalence at this exception, in general there was agreement that funeral insurance policies were rightly exceptional and that the exception was narrow enough to avoid risks to the poor. This, too, was bound up with moral imaginaries. Invariably, I was told, funeral insurance was about avoiding the "indignity" of burial collections or, worse, a pauper's burial. Given that many of the grant recipients were elderly pensioners, as well as the high mortality rates due especially to HIV/AIDS, funerals are particularly salient in South Africa. Additionally, in recent years, funerals have grown in expense and flourish (Case et al. 2013), so the redistributive function of insurance was deemed appropriate.

Given the ambiguities facing would-be rule-makers, two camps emerged (though they were certainly not self-contained). Rather than regulation, for constituencies broadly in favor of the poor accessing formal financial services, the admitted risks, especially of debt, were to be solved through improving "financial literacy" (though the term was rarely defined). As one former banker now working for a financial inclusion consultancy told me, "access and consumer empowerment must go ahead together." This emphasis on individual responsibility is indicative of broader trends toward "responsibilization" that the literature on governmentality has noted (e.g., Shamir 2008; in South Africa, see Hull 2012; Krige 2012). As one government official put it, "The more we bring our beneficiaries into the banking environment, the more we need everyone to work together."

For others, the risks to the poor were too great, especially considering the asymmetric relationship between borrowers and lenders. Government action was needed, yet there existed the ability to overstep. For many involved, it was best to avoid too much prescriptive policymaking and instead focus on what was seen as particularly risky: automatic deductions. The use of automatic deductions for personal loans was the most problematic arrangement and should be curtailed. Two qualities in particular were deemed problematic. First was the aforementioned opacity of the system. A lack of understanding crippled the paths to recourse for grant recipients. While it is true that debit orders are supposed to require the consent of the debtor, the advocates with whom I worked marshaled numerous examples where the poor did not fully understand or were pressured into such contracts. Bähre (2012) has noted that low-income insurance customers in South Africa frequently cancel their insurance policies, often because they were pressured into signing up; similarly, James (2012) reports that the poor close down bank accounts to flee creditors using the oft-abused "garnishee orders" (which resemble automatic deductions; see Haupt et al. 2008). The opponents of automatic grant deductions recognized that the poor had limited capacity to take such options given the necessity of their grants. Such powerlessness would be increased by what might be called the "frictionless" aspect of automatic deductions (cf. Ratto 2007). Compared to monthly cash payments to a *mashonisa*, an electronic deduction doesn't require active participation.

In the view of well-respected pro-poor organizations, taken together, the opacity and frictionless nature of automatic deductions structured the terms of financial inclusion too much in favor of the creditors. As the Black Sash put it in a press release, "If deductions were to continue unchecked, we feared the systematic erosion of our social grants system by immoral elements of the private sector and called on government to take immediate steps to curb this potentially devastating trend" (Black Sash

2013). These individuals recognized that, as Elyachar (2002) writes, "even empowerment money has a price."

Social Citizenship and Cash Grants

Like many of the keywords in development circles, "financial inclusion" simultaneously posits a deficit and offers the solution (cf. Pritchett and Woolcock 2004). Once defined as a lack of access to financial instruments, poverty alleviation becomes, in part, the provision of those services. This instrumental logic is evident in studies and indices that equate access to financial services with development (e.g., CGAP 2010). The case explored earlier shows an alternative approach. Instead of financial inclusion *in general*, the participants in this debate considered financial inclusion *in particular*. Steeped in moral and structural considerations (albeit often imprecise and improvised), the civil society, government, and – to a lesser extent – industry engaged specific legal and technical minutiae to attempt to reformulate the conditions and characteristics of a particular financial inclusion regime. As one social security attorney working on behalf of grant recipients mused, "The world is moving towards financial inclusion. Are we simply on the bandwagon? Is it driven by demand, or is it driven by supply? SASSA has us all banked . . . are we being pushed to financial inclusion? Every grant recipient has an account somewhere, but they cannot use the banking system the way it should be used . . ." In her reckoning, the conditions of financial inclusion were variables to be changed through investigations, consultations, and activism.

This activist valence seems to reflect sensitivity to the structural constraints in which grant recipients are located, both through the worries of being pushed into debt traps and the unlikelihood of finding productive uses for microloans. In many ways, it mirrors prior debates around the National Credit Act, where similar opposition between contingents of capital, labor, and civil society resulted in "an uneasy truce" (James 2013: 9). In contrast to mainstream financial inclusion rhetoric, the civil society I observed knew instinctively that, to borrow from Bähre (2012), "The vocabulary of 'providing access' to the poor that is salient in development circles fails to take essential power inequalities into consideration." Here, then, was a collective effort to oppose the dangers of atomized financialization of everyday life through active government regulation – an effort that, interestingly, mirrors recent critical scholarship on these trends (Roy 2010; Martin 2002).

The elements of congruence between the recent scholarship on popular economies and the work of civil society recall anthropologist Annelise Riles's ethnography of networked women's rights advocates, where the subject of research "one encounters [is] already analyzed" (2000: xiv). An additional similarity is the relationship to what she terms "the Real." "At frequent intervals," she writes, "negotiators, staff members of international aid agencies, government workers, and networkers stopped to invoke a notion of the 'real world' or 'the reality of women' or simply what was 'real'" (Riles 2000: 143). Throughout the debates recounted earlier, social grant recipients were depicted and characterized in a representational contest that mattered deeply to the policy process. If they were uneducated and vulnerable, the justification for regulation would be heightened; if they were savvy, though needy, consumers, their financial activity should less readily be encumbered (cf. van Wyk 2012). For example, in a jab at civil society organizations, CPS's Belamant claimed "to talk to the pensioners themselves, not the people who claim to represent the pensioners. We meet with 10 million of them every month, so it is not difficult to get feedback from them in terms of what they actually want" (Barron 2013).[18] In contrast, Minister of Parliament Mike Waters, speaking on the deduction issue, said, "The fact that some of our most vulnerable citizens, who are in desperate need of assistance, are being treated this way leaves me angered" (Speckman 2013). And, of course, the nonprofit advocates with whom I coordinated were also involved in a representational contest (cf. Fisher 1997).

Though it was less commonly noted outright, the dispute was animated by an underlying tension in the relationship between the social grants, the state, and the market (cf. Barchiesi 2011). Consider, again, Valerie, the pro-poor community advocate. In her argument that lending to the grant recipients was unethical, she noted that, under the new payment system, "grantees are thus considered to be consumers as are other bank users, but the fact that the person qualifies for a grant makes them a special case." In her reasoning, "grantees deserve extra protection because they are in a vulnerable state." For Valerie and others, their poverty and associated marginalization was crucial, as was her understanding of the purpose of the grants as tied up with notions of citizenship and the collective harms of apartheid.

While social grants are a key realization of social citizenship in post-apartheid South Africa, they operate in a liminal zone between "the state" (where the norms and rights of citizenship rule) and "the market" (where citizens become consumers). The payment infrastructure is a crucial determinant of this liminality. In contrast to other social spending (e.g., primary education), cash transfers – especially unconditional ones – are more closely intertwined with market relations and their norms. Because they are means tested, the grants are particularly aimed at "income support," the act of improving the poor's ability to consume. Because they are unconditional, the grants do not require consumption of particular goods or services (such as education, in the case of Brazil and Mexico's similar cash transfers). Thus, the anti-paternalism that I earlier suggested was operating has a greater influence than it might otherwise (see also Ferguson 2009).

The state and market are also intertwined in this case due to the historically low bureaucratic capacity that helped to motivate privatization of grant delivery in the 1990s (Donovan 2015). Much of this occurred under the influence of Thabo Mbeki, first as deputy president and then as president from 1999 to 2008. The Mbeki government operated under what Marais (2003) called "the logic of expediency," under which there was a tendency to view governance as service delivery. In this approach, Hemson and O'Donovan (2006 argue, "citizens" become "customers" of one-way delivery. Framing the government's role in terms of "delivery" makes success dependent upon efficiency, not "to determine citizens' wishes and to secure their cooperation but to recruit the best 'delivery' techniques and personnel" (Friedman 2009).

A reliance on private firms to deliver grants has long been a source of critique due to their perceived reduction in responsibility to the grant recipients (Overy and Zuma 2004). Similar concerns were present in this case as civil society sought to stress the norms of citizenship rather than those of consumerism. As one high-ranking civil society representative concluded, "Grants should not open gaps between people and the state." She was particularly concerned that the use of third-party retailers, rather than community paypoints, would remove the street-level bureaucrats to whom grant recipients could turn with concerns. Under the new system, within the three months leading up to April 2013, the portion of recipients receiving their grant at retailers had jumped nearly 50 percent (Dunkerley 2013), and ATM providers reported a "huge injection" of new SASSA users (Moyo 2013). Indeed, during early 2013, the use of Shoprite (a major grocer) as a payment location would become controversial as reports arose of stores forcing grant recipients to spend a portion of it in the store (Davids 2013).

Entities like the Black Sash were engaged in an effort to extend the ethic of care from SASSA beyond mere delivery of the grant to moderate the risks they associated with the poor's location in the market. In Ferguson's (2013) terminology, it was an effort to move beyond "asocial assistance." However, given the relatively narrow remit of SASSA – predominantly to deliver grants – they began to find that doing so might require more extensive work, such as amending the National Credit Act (Black Sash 2013).

Discomfort with the use of private firms for delivery was also evident within SASSA. As its CEO has repeatedly said publicly, the current five-year contract with CPS is to be the last outsourced delivery method, and plans are underway to pay solely through government mechanisms (such as a potential SASSA bank). As one government official told me, "We do not want the private sector to see this as a lucrative opportunity when it is a government responsibility." Whether or not this tension can be resolved, however, remains to be seen.

Conclusion

In their introduction to a recent special edition on "popular economies" in South Africa, Hull and James (2012) astutely note, "These economies are situated, somewhat contradictorily, between global settings of financialized capitalism on the one hand and impoverished local arenas where cash-based economic transfers predominate on the other." These popular economies are the subject, Bähre (2012) writes, of economic contestation. As a complement, the case at hand demonstrates the type of policy contestations that emerge due to the relationship between financialization and social citizenship. In this case, underlying the dispute were conflicting visions for the social grants. While the unconditional, rights-based approach to income support was widely supported, many of the pro-poor civil society organizations imagined a more actively protective role for the state, especially given their understanding of the dangers of indebtedness facing South Africa's poor. For these activists and others, the particular manner in which "financial inclusion" had been enacted – especially electronic automatic deductions – represented a threat to the very goals that the social grants were meant to realize.

The debates about the institutional, legal, and technical arrangements for the payment of South African grants are particularly relevant given the global surge of interest in rearranging the means of exchange. As other chapters in this volume attest, payment infrastructures are shifting and attracting new entrants. Influential actors from industry and aid organizations are advocating *against* cash and in support of cashless or, perhaps more realistically, "cash lite" economies (cf. Bátiz-Lazo et al. 2014). For example, a 2011 academic conference entertained the idea of "killing cash" in favor of electronic payments such as debit cards and mobile money.[19] In 2013, entrepreneurs and technologists arranged the first Afri-Koin conference to discuss new financial innovations on the continent. The Better than Cash Alliance is a movement of development organizations, governments, and private companies that support the use of electronic payments, arguing that cash is costly, insecure, and unaccountable (see BTC 2013). The rapidly emerged motto is that "cash is the enemy of the poor" (for a discussion, see Maurer 2012b; Donovan 2013; Nelms 2013).

However, in South Africa, who or what exactly is the enemy of the poor is not entirely clear; the social grants are surrounded by various moral imaginaries, and changes in the technical and legal infrastructure of the grants serve to highlight the conflicts between them. New mediators (like e-payments) cannot be understood as merely a quantitative change (*more* efficient or *more* secure), but instead they transform the acts of exchange in subtle and unintended ways. They are technopolitical arrangements with concomitant ethical regimes (von Schnitzler 2013). As Maurer (2012a: 20) notes, "One needs to get into the technicalities of money, credit and payment in order to get at the status of value forms in practice." In South Africa, the particular technical arrangements (e.g., automatic versus manual withdrawals) were deeply consequential to the precarious lives of the grant recipients. Getting into these technicalities, though, was made more difficult due to the opacity of the privatized payments infrastructure.

It is in light of this that the full importance of this chapter's title is clear. When I was told "financial inclusion means your money isn't with you," the speaker was pointing to the change in autonomy that accompanies a shift away from government-backed cash to privatized electronic payments. As this case shows, without sustained attention and activism, financial inclusion and the movement against cash may, in the well-meaning pursuit of "innovation," "development," "efficiency," or another generality, lead to subtle but important shifts in the power dynamics of everyday financial activity. After all, if your money isn't with you, someone else probably has it.

Acknowledgments

I appreciate the comments from Jeremy Seekings, Erik Bähre, Natasha Vally, the participants at the UCT Social Protection Workshop in May 2013, and, especially, Ivan Small. I also appreciate the time and clarity of my various interlocutors. At various stages, the Institute for Money,

Technology & Financial Inclusion at UC Irvine, a Fulbright Fellowship, and Privacy International provided crucial financial support.

Kevin P. Donovan is in the programs in Anthropology & History and Science, Technology & Society at the University of Michigan. His research examines how smugglers, financiers, and politicians have unsettled the scales of economy and politics in East Africa since the 1950s. He has also published on the unwieldy border between states and corporations, humanitarian infrastructure, and the politics of surveillance. More information is available at http://kevinpdonovan.com.

NOTES

1. For a historical comparison, see Peebles's (2008: 235) discussion of efforts to replace "individual hoarding" with "pooled saving."
2. This chapter was written and revised from 2013 to 2014, and therefore does not reflect the continued disputes, particularly those that were widely circulated in the South African media in the first half of 2016 when this chapter was in press. For a discussion, see Neves and James (2017).
3. I have used pseudonyms for all private interactions but provided the actual names of people and organizations when those are already in the public domain.
4. Because one recipient (e.g., a low-income mother) may receive grants for multiple beneficiaries (e.g., three children), the number of *beneficiaries* is higher than *recipients* (of which there are around 10 million). See http://www.sassa .gov.za/Portals/1/Documents/905e088d-befd-42ae-b17f-84c6ae1c682f.pdf.
5. Notably, prior to this partnership, Grindrod was a relatively small bank, focused exclusively on high-net-worth individuals and institutional clients. Therefore, it operated only a few branches and lacked experience working with low-income clients.
6. In June 2012, USD1.00 was equal to a little more than ZAR8.00
7. The longevity of this arrangement, though, was thrown into question with the decision by the Constitutional Court in late 2013 that the tender for the contract had contravened crucial procedural requirements. While it was declared constitutionally invalid, the arrangement was not set aside (pending a February 2014 hearing) due to the importance of continued grant delivery to the poor (Froneman 2013).
8. The Black Sash and the Legal Resources Centre are prominent human rights organizations in South Africa that specialize in public interest legal services and other pro-poor advocacy efforts.
9. This episode is part of a larger history of political contests around debt and credit in South Africa. For divergent assessments, see James (2013) and Porteous and Hazelhurst (2004). Most recently, this has involved a hotly contested effort to enact a "credit information amnesty" bill that would remove some debtors' adverse records, though not their debts.

10. SASSA and others have sought to curtail this illegal practice through information drives and police raids, but thus far there has been limited prosecutorial follow-up.
11. This impotence is similar to that of the 2007 National Credit Act, which "has been largely powerless in the face of informal moneylending" (James 2012: 28).
12. The politics of "reckless" and "predatory" lending are discussed in James (2013).
13. James (2012) discusses the similarities and differences within and between "formal" and "informal" lenders in South Africa.
14. See http://www.pasa.org.za/more_aedo.html.
15. In a promotional video, Net1 CPS (2013) actually valorizes this opacity, though they oddly refer to the inscrutability of their black-boxed technology as transparent. "Net1's technology . . . is completely transparent to the end user, in other words they have no real experience or understanding of all the very clever things that happen in the background."
16. In one case, the government's regulatory Financial Services Board revoked the license of a Net1 insurance subsidiary named Smart Life due to a conflict of interest between Net1, CPS, and Smart Life, all of which were led by the same man (McKune 2013).
17. On the design of the largest grant – including debates around conditionality – see Lund (2008).
18. In matter of fact, there are 10 million grant recipients in total, most of whom are not pensioners. Furthermore, the prospect of receiving feedback from them is diminished by the fact that CPS pays most of grants through ATMs and third-party retailers.
19. See Killing Cash: Pros and Cons of Mobile Money for the World's Poor: A Look at Both Sides of the Coin. Boston: Tufts University. Retrieved from: http://fletcher.tufts.edu/killing-cash/.

REFERENCES CITED

Bähre, Erik. 2007. *Money and Violence: Financial Self-Help Groups in a South African Township.* Vol. 8. Leiden: Brill.
———. 2011. "Liberation and Redistribution: Social Grants, Commercial Insurance, and Religious Riches in South Africa." *Comparative Studies in Society and History* 53(2): 371–92.
———. 2012. "The Janus Face of Insurance in South Africa: From Costs to Risks, from Networks to Bureaucracy." *Africa* 82(1): 150–67.
Barchiesi, Franco. 2011. *Precarious Liberation: Workers, the State, and Contested Social Citizenship in Postapartheid South Africa.* Albany: SUNY.
Barron, Chris. 2013. "Belamant Hits Back at His Accusers." *Business Day,* 2 June. Retrieved from http://www.bdlive.co.za/businesstimes/2013/06/02/belamant-hits-back-at-his-accusers.
Bátiz-Lazo, Bernardo, Thomas Haigh, and David. Stearns. 2014. "How the Future Shaped the Past: The Case of the Cashless Society." *Enterprise and Society* 15(1): 103–131.

Belamant, Serge. 2013. "Net1 Welcomes Probe into Social Grants Loan Scheme." *Business Day.* Retrieved 3 November 2013 from http://www.bdlive.co.za/com panies/2013/05/29/summit-tv-net1-welcomes-probe-into-social-grants-loan-scheme.

Black Sash. 2013. "Unlawful, Immoral Deductions Should Stop." Black Sash. Retrieved 3 November 2013 from http://www.blacksash.org.za/index.php/me dia-and-publications/media-statements/1397-unlawful-immoral-deductions-from-social-grants-should-stop-says-black-sash-29-may-2013.

Breckenridge, Keith. 2005. "The Biometric State: The Promise and Peril of Digital Government in the New South Africa." *Journal of Southern African Studies* 31(2): 267–82.

BTC. 2013. "The Journey toward 'Cash Lite': Addressing Poverty, Saving Money and Increasing Transparency by Accelerating the Shift to Electronic Payments." Better than Cash Alliance. Retrieved 3 November 2013 from http://betterth ancash.org/wp-content/uploads/2012/09/BetterThanCashAlliance-Journey TowardCashLite.pdf.

Case, Anne, Anu Garrib, Alicia Menendez, and Analia Olgiati. 2013. "Paying the Piper: The High Cost of Funerals in South Africa." *Economic Development and Cultural Change* 62(1): 1–20.

CGAP. 2010. "Financial Access 2010." Washington, DC: CGAP.

COSATU. 2013. "COSATU Shares Bathabile Dlamini's Anger against Cash Paymaster Services." Politics Web. Retrieved 3 November 2013 from http://www.politicsweb.co.za/politicsweb/view/politicsweb/en/page71654?oid=4275 99&sn=Detail&pid=71616.

Davids, Nashira. 2013. "Shoprite's Grant Fiasco." *Times Live.* Retrieved 3 November 2013 from http://www.timeslive.co.za/thetimes/2013/03/05/shoprite-s-grant-fiasco.

Donovan, Kevin. 2012. "Mobile Money, More Freedom? The Impact of M-PESA's Network Power on Development as Freedom." *International Journal of Communication* 6: 2647–68.

———. 2013. "The Responsibility of Mobile Money Intellectuals?" *Information Technology & International Development* 9(1): 55–57.

———. 2015. "The Biometric Imaginary: Bureaucratic Technopolitics in Post-apartheid Welfare." *Journal of Southern African Studies* 41(4): 815–33.

Dunkerley, Dianne. 2013. "The Social Grant Payment System." CSSR Workshop on Social Protection, Cape Town, 27–28 May 2013. Cape Town: University of Cape Town.

Ensor, Linda. 2013. "Legal Challenge to Grant Distributor over Deductions." *Business Day.* Retrieved 3 November 2013 from http://www.bdlive.co.za/national/2013/06/10/legal-challenge-to-grant-distributor-over-deductions.

Elyachar, Julia. 2002. "Empowerment Money: The World Bank, Non-governmental Organizations, and the Value of Culture in Cairo." *Public Culture* 14(3): 493–515.

———. 2005. *Markets of Dispossession: NGOs, Economic Development, and the State in Cairo.* Durham, NC: Duke University Press.

Ferguson, James. 2009. "The Uses of Neoliberalism." *Antipode* 41(s1): 166–84.

———. 2013. "Declarations of Dependence: Labour, Personhood, and Welfare in Southern Africa." *Journal of the Royal Anthropological Institute* 19(2): 223–42.

FinMark. 2012. "The Payment Experience of Social Grant Beneficiaries." Midrand: FinMark Trust.

Fisher, William F. 2007. "Doing Good? The Politics and Antipolitics of NGO Practices." *Annual Review of Anthropology* 26: 439–64.

Friedman, Steven. 2009. "Seeing Ourselves as Others See Us: Racism, Technique and the Mbeki Administration." In *Mbeki and After: Reflections on the Legacy of Thabo Mbeki,* edited by Daryl Glaser. Johannesburg: Wits University Press.

Froneman, Johan. 2013. *All Pay Consolidated Investment Holdings (Pty) Ltd and Others v Chief Executive Officer of the South Africa Social Security Agency and Others* (CCT 48/13). Johannesburg: Constitutional Court of South Africa.

Garcia, Marito., and Charity M. T. Moore. 2012. *The Cash Dividend: The Rise of Cash Transfers in Sub-Saharan Africa.* Washington, DC: World Bank.

Gates Foundation. 2012. "Financial Services for the Poor: Strategy Overview." Seattle: Bill & Melinda Gates Foundation. Retrieved 3 November 2013 from https:// docs.gatesfoundation.org/Documents/fsp-strategy-overview.pdf.

Gerbi, Giovanna. 2012. "Clampdown on Micro Money Lenders." *Eyewitness News.* Retrieved 3 November 2013 from http://ewn.co.za/2012/10/12/Sassa-gets-serious-with-money-lenders.

Hanlon, Joseph, Armando Barrientos, and David Hulme. 2010. *Just Give Money to the Poor: The Development Revolution from the Global South.* West Hartford: Kumarian Press.

Hart, Keith. 1973. "Informal Income Opportunities and Urban Employment in Ghana." *The Journal of Modern African Studies* 11(1): 61–89.

Hart, Keith. 2010. "Africa's Urban Revolution and the Informal Economy." In *The Political Economy of Africa,* edited by V. Padayachee. London: Routledge.

Haupt, Frans, Hermie Coetzee, Dawid de Villiers and Jeanne-Mari Fouche. 2008. *The Incidence of and the Undesirable Practices Relating to Garnishee Orders in South Africa.* Pretoria: GTZ.

Hemson, David, and M. O'Donovan. 2006. "Putting Numbers to the Scorecard: Presidential Targets and the State of Delivery." *State of the Nation: South Africa, 2005–2006.* Pretoria: HSRC Press.

Hull, Elizabeth. 2012. "Banking in the Bush: Waiting for Credit in South Africa's Rural Economy." *Africa: The Journal of the International African Institute* 82(1): 168–86.

Hull, Elizabeth, and Deborah James. 2012. "Introduction: Popular Economies in South Africa." *Africa: The Journal of the International African Institute* 82(1): 1–19.

Jacobs, Marine. 2013. "CPS Accused of Exploiting the Poor." IT Web. Retrieved from http://www.itweb.co.za/index.php?option=com_content&view=article&id=68310:cps-accused-of-exploiting-the-poor.

James, Deborah. 2012. "Money-Go-Round: Personal Economies of Wealth, Aspiration and Indebtedness." *Africa: The Journal of the International African Institute* 82(1): 20–40.

———. 2013. "Regulating Credit: Tackling the Redistributiveness of Neoliberalism." *Anthropology of this Century* 6.

Krige, Detlev. 2012. "Fields of Dreams, Fields of Schemes: Ponzi Finance and Multilevel Marketing in South Africa." *Africa: The Journal of the International African Institute* 82(1): 69–92.

Latour, Bruno. 2002. "Morality and Technology: The End of the Means." *Theory, Culture & Society,* 19(5–6): 247–60.

Lund, Francie. 2008. *Changing Social Policy: The Child Support Grant in South Africa.* Pretoria: HSRC Press.

Marais, Hein. 2003. "The Logic of Expendiency." In *Thabo Mbeki's World: The Politics and Ideology of the South African President,* edited by S. Jacobs and R. Calland. London: Zed Books, 83–104.

Maurer, Bill. 2005. *Mutual Life, Limited: Islamic Banking, Alternative Currencies, Lateral Reason.* Princeton, NJ: Princeton University Press.

———. 2012a. "Payment: Forms and Functions of Value Transfer in Contemporary Society." *Cambridge Anthropology* 30(2): 15–35.

———. 2012b. "Credit Slips (but Should Not Fall). *Distinktion: Scandinavian Journal of Social Theory* 13(3): 283–94.

Martin, Randy. 2002. *Financialization of Daily Life.* Philadelphia: Temple University Press.

McKune, Craig. 2012. "Social Grant Contractor's Sideline Plan." *Mail & Guardian.* Retrieved 3 November 2013 from http://mg.co.za/article/2012-09-28-00-social-grant-contractors-sideline-plan.

———. 2013. "Financial Service Board Clamps Down on Net1's Insurance to Poor." *Mail & Guardian.* Retrieved from http://mg.co.za/article/2013-05-31-00-fsb-clamps-down-on-net1s-insurance-to-poor.

Moyo, Admire. 2013. "Social Grant Payments Boost ATM Transactions." IT Web. Retrieved 3 November 2013 from http://www.itweb.co.za/index.php?option=com_content&view=article&id=67312.

Nelms, Taylor. 2013. "Funny Money Roundup 5: Cashlessness." IMTFI Blog. Retrieved 3 November 2013 from http://blog.imtfi.uci.edu/2013/02/funny-money-roundup-5-cashlessness.html.

Net1 CPS. 2013. "Net1 Delivers on SASSA Responsibility." Retrieved 3 November 2013 from http://www.youtube.com/watch?v=otjiE0OqBf4.

Neves, David., and Andries du Toit. 2012. "Money and Sociality in South Africa's Informal Economy." *Africa: The Journal of the International African Institute* 82(1): 131–49.

Neves, David. and Deborah. James. 2017. "South Africa's Social Grants: Busting the Myths about Financial Inclusion. *The Conversation.* Retrieved from https://theconversation.com/south-africas-social-grants-busting-the-myth-about-financial-inclusion-74776.

Overy, N., and R. Zuma. 2004. *The Outsourcing of Social Security Grants in the Eastern Cape: Service Delivery Challenges and the Problem of Accountability.* Grahamstown: Public Service Accountability Monitor. Retrieved from http://www.psam.org.za/research/1183035633.pdf.

Parry, Jonathan, and Maurice Bloch, eds. 1989. *Money and the Morality of Exchange.* Cambridge: Cambridge University Press.

Peebles, Gustav. 2008. "Inverting the Panopticon: Money and the Nationalization of the Future." *Public Culture* 20(2): 233–65.

Pickens, Mark, David Porteous, and Sarah Rotman. 2009. *Banking the Poor via G2P Payments.* Washington, DC: CGAP.

Porteous, David, and Ethel Hazelhurst. 2004. *Banking on Change: Democratizing Finance in South Africa, 1994–2004*. Cape Town: Double Storey Books.

Pritchett, Lant, and Michael Woolcock. 2004. "Solutions when the Solution Is the Problem: Arraying the Disarray in Development." *World Development* 32(2): 191–212.

Ratto, Matt. 2007. "Ethics of Seamless Infrastructure: Resources and Future Directions." *International Review of Information Ethics* 8(12): 20–27.

Riles, Annelise. 2000. *The Network Inside Out*. Ann Arbor: University of Michigan Press.

Roy, Ananya. 2010. *Poverty Capital: Microfinance and the Making of Development*. New York: Routledge.

RSA. 2002. "Transforming the Present – Protecting the Future: Consolidated Report of the Committee of Inquiry into a Comprehensive System of Social Security for South Africa." Pretoria: Department of Social Development.

———. 2004. *Social Assistance Act*. Cape Town: Parliament of South Africa.

SACP. 2013. "Govt Must Urgently Review CPS' Contract with SASSA – SACP." Politics Web. Retrieved from http://www.politicsweb.co.za/politicsweb/view/politicsweb/en/page71654?oid=428383&sn=Detail&pid=71616.

Scott, James C. 1977. *The Moral Economy of the Peasant: Rebellion and Subsistence in Southeast Asia*. New Haven: Yale University Press.

———. 1999. *Seeing Like a State: How Certain Schemes to Improve the Human Condition Have Failed*. New Haven, CT: Yale University Press.

Schwittay, Anke F. 2011. "The Financial Inclusion Assemblage: Subjects, Technics, Rationalities." *Critique of Anthropology* 31(4): 381–401.

Seekings, Jeremy. 2007. "'Not a Single White Person Should Be Allowed to Go Under': Swartgevaar and the Origins of South Africa's Welfare State, 1924–1929." *Journal of African History* 48: 375–94.

———. 2008. "Deserving Individuals and Groups: The Post-apartheid State's Justification of the Shape of South Africa's System of Social Assistance." *Transformation* 68: 28–52.

Shamir, Ronen. 2008. "The Age of Responsibilization: On Market-Embedded Morality." *Economy and Society* 37(1): 1–19.

Steyn, L. 2014. "Cashing in on Social Grants." *Mail & Guardian*, 23 May. Retrieved from http://mg.co.za/article/2014-05-22-cashing-in-on-social-grants.

Speckman, Asha. 2013. "Madonsela Probes Social Grants Provider." *Business Report*. Retrieved 3 November 2013 from http://www.iol.co.za/business/companies/madonsela-probes-social-grants-provider-1.1522731#.UdB2oD6cXvg.

Van Wyk, Ilana. 2012. "'Tata ma chance': On Contingency and the Lottery in Post-apartheid South Africa." *Africa: The Journal of the International African Institute* 82(1): 41–68.

Versfeld, Anna. 2012. *AllPay and no Work: Spheres of Belonging under Duress*. Unpublished thesis. University of Cape Town, Department of Social Anthropology.

Von Schnitzler, Antina. 2013. "Traveling Technologies: Infrastructure, Ethical Regimes and the Materiality of Politics in South Africa." *Cultural Anthropology* 28(4): 670–93.

Waters, Mike. 2013. "Public Protector to Investigate CPS Loan Scheme." Demo-

cratic Alliance. Retrieved 3 November 2013 from http://www.da.org.za/news
room.htm?action=view-news-item&id=12332.

Zietsman, Dries. 2012. "More than 2.5 Million MasterCard Debit Cards Issued to
Social Welfare Beneficiaries in South Africa." MasterCard press release. Retrieved 3 November 2013 from http://newsroom.mastercard.com/press-re
leases/more-than-2-5-million-mastercard-debit-cards-issued-to-social-welfare-
beneficiaries-in-south-africa/.

CHAPTER 8

Social Networks of Mobile Money in Kenya

SIBEL KUSIMBA, GABRIEL KUNYU, AND ELIZABETH GROSS

Introduction

In 2010, among a Kisii polygynous family in Kenya, the oldest son used SMS messaging to organize a payment schedule among twenty-two siblings and half siblings for a father's prostate operation, which amounted to close to 300,000 Kenyan shillings (KES) (US $3000). Each child was expected to give at levels of 30,000 shillings (US $300), 20,000 (US$ 200), and so on. A sister in her late twenties named Julia explains:

> *Julia*: So now those who are able, they will pay 30,000, then they came to 20,000, 10,000, 5,000, 2,000, and 1,000. That was the least. Those who are looking for a job, they were told at least to look for 1,000 (US $10), and see that they have appreciated to contribute.
>
> *Sibel Kusimba*: Your sisters in the United States, how did you estimate their contribution, what did you decide?
>
> *Julia:* They were the ones given the highest of 30,000.

Julia went on to explain that her brother would use M-PESA, a mobile-money service based on text messaging, and a visit to Western Union to gather the contributions of his siblings, who live throughout Kenya and the United States.

In Kenya today, use of mobile phones and mobile-money services is creating new forms of social and communal life. Mobile-money systems, such as Safaricom's M-PESA money-sending service (Omwansa and Sullivan 2012), allow people to send money to friends and family securely and cheaply using mobile phone text messages. Using mobile money enables people to share resources and smooth uneven incomes (Suri et al. 2012). New forms of social interaction around mobile money recast long-standing traditions of reciprocity and are subject to cultural rules and debates;

in the example just mentioned, the oldest son took a leading role in organizing his younger siblings' participation but soon ran up against fault lines of resentment among half siblings in a polygynous family.

Kenya might be the only country in the world where mobile money has become a part of daily life. Five years after Safaricom first developed M-PESA in 2007, the government of Kenya reports that there are now more than 30 million mobile phones in this country of 40 million people and almost 20 million mobile-money accounts. Since May 2011, a Safaricom–Western Union partnership allows remittances from forty-three countries to the telephone handsets of M-PESA subscribers.

The purpose of this research is to examine cultural practices in the use of mobile money in Kenya, especially how remittances circulate in social networks and construct social relationships. Although mobile money has been implemented in Kenya and elsewhere in the hopes of financial inclusion and provision of banking services to the unbanked (Maurer 2012), most users in western Kenya utilize mobile money to access their social networks of friends and relatives. Although mobile-money technology is designed for person-to-person transfers, it is more accurately a tool of *individuals who see themselves as parts of groups or collectivities,* whether these be savings groups, groups of siblings and cousins, or extended families who amass contributions for public ceremonies. Sending and receiving mobile money is a part of a culture of entrustment (Shipton 2007) whereby people save through others, contributing to what effectively is a pool of resources. Mobile money strengthens and makes visible the ties among siblings, their mothers, and mothers' relatives in these patrilineal societies, revealing through "uterine kinship" (Wolf 1972) a support network of women and their children. These networks inspire questions about the relationship between mobile money and gendered flows of other forms of value.

Research reported here was conducted in the summer of 2012 in Bungoma and Trans-Nzoia Counties in Kenya, specifically the urban centers and agricultural hinterlands of Bungoma, Kitale, and Kimilili towns and in Naitiri market, a rural community. The region is Kenya's agriculturally productive and densely populated "breadbasket." About 80 percent of the residents are still rural farmers, although growing urban centers have important business communities and the civil service employs teachers and other government employees. Ethnically Bungoma County is dominated by the Luhya peoples, especially the Bukusu subgroup, although many other communities, including the Kikuyu, Luo, and Asian communities, participated. The research employed participant observation, research interviews, and survey questionnaires with more than three hundred Kenyans in and around the towns and agricultural hinterlands of Kimilili, Kitale, and Bungoma in western Kenya and the agricultural villages of Naitiri, a farming community about 60 kilometers (40 miles) northwest of Kitale in western Kenya. We also interviewed and collected questionnaire data from the United Kenyans of Chicago and the Kenyan Women's Support Group.

Mobile Phone Banking and Airtime in Daily Life

Safaricom's initial success with mobile-money transfer has spurred the interests of development economists, governments, and organizations in harnessing mobile phone technology for the purposes of "financial inclusion" of unbanked persons in developing settings (Donovan 2012). Mobile-money stakeholders such as development banks, development NGOs, and telecommunications companies have sought individual and female economic betterment through electronic money sending and payment services – the "Empowerment Story" (Maurer 2012). Safaricom and other companies have also developed other financial services for mobile phones. These include phone-to-bank money transfers, savings mechanisms such as mobile wallets or links to savings accounts, insurance, bill payment directly to utilities, companies and schools, pay-as-you-go solar power, and microloans. Most recently, a service called M-Shwari began offering mobile phone–based savings accounts and microloans in 2012. The hope of many mobile-money stakeholders in the private sector and in development organizations is to go beyond money sending to provide financial inclusion through bank-like or bank-lite services in a country where at least 60 percent of adults are unbanked.

Does mobile money serve financial inclusion? Our surveys in western Kenya show that a small number of Kenyans employ mobile-money services for diverse financial practices such as bank account access or direct payments to utilities or schools. In the Naitiri Village, where most people are subsistence farmers, we found only 1 to 2 percent of people have bank accounts. In Bungoma and Kimilili, where up to half of respondents report income to supplement or replace farming, from 8 percent of people had bank accounts. Most Kenyans explained that they did not have enough money to establish bank accounts, which are still seen as places to put large amounts of money not needed in daily life. Many were aware of prohibitive account fees. Our team found that at least 75 percent of transactions are used to send money to friends and relatives. Rather than using a mobile phone as an electronic wallet or bank liaison, people cash in and out quite quickly, and they purchase e-money in anticipation of sending, usually to a friend or relative. Johnson, Brown, and Fouillet (2012), working in Kenya's Central Province, found that on average users reported they kept about 300 KES (about US$4) on their phones.

Five years after the introduction of M-PESA, mobile money's persistent irony is its use in strengthening traditional economic support networks – friends and family – rather than its application to formal financial inclusion. The real "inclusion" twenty-first-century information and communication technologies (ICTs) provide is into a culture of entrustment (Shipton 2007) that is surely centuries old. In western Kenya men and women participate in frequent borrowing and lending of value in everyday and ceremonial contexts. Through these exchanges, value that is both economic and social is stored or saved through gifts to others until it is repaid at an unspecified time in the future – often in a different form or value. In practices of entrustment, ownership is a kind of temporary custody of wealth that circulates over time. In spite of an ethic of reciprocity, relationships are not equal – rights, obligations, and expectations of kin roles historically depended on seniority (especially among siblings), generation, and gender. Today prestige and its attendant responsibilities to carry others can also come from employment, education, assets, and urban or international migration. The use of mobile money in this culture of entrustment has a diversity of uses, including emergency or medical assistance, household consumption, school fees, investments, and contributions to savings groups, coming-of-age ceremonies, and funerals.

Effectively, mobile money circulates among individuals who see themselves as connected to extended families, savings groups, and other collectivities. Examples include groups of siblings who contribute to a parent's medical needs or to school fees for nieces and nephews; savings groups of neighbors, relatives, and coworkers; and extended families and communities who contribute at large ceremonies. Funerals and coming-of-age ceremonies amass contributions from hundreds or even thousands of people. The 2010 coming-of-age ceremony for one young man amassed livestock, gifts of blankets and clothing, contributions for a feast, and mobile-money gifts of 85,000 KES (about US$1,000), enough for his secondary school fees.

Financial inclusion and empowerment narratives seem to miss the mark on the fundamental importance of collectivities of people to the use of mobile money. Indeed, mobile-money systems were designed for person-to-person transfers, although they were avidly used by savings groups and by triads and collectivities to collect and pool funds. Furthermore the mobile phone handset allows people to make personal and private decisions about saving, sending, or cashing out mobile money, and to receive money directly and privately – features that are valued but that may produce conflict in African settings (Archambault 2013; Horst and Miller 2006; Kriem 2009; McIntosh 2010). We must turn to mobile communication and a study of social networks to understand the public and private spheres of remittances.

Mobile Money Is a Part of Mobile Communication

In its primary use to send remittances, mobile money is profitably understood not as "banking" but as an adjunct to the mobile phone as a social tool. First, consider mobile communication: it creates new kinds of relationships in a variety of cultural settings. In Kenya, as in many places and cultures, cellular phones strengthen close and intimate relationships, reach new connections, and help coordinate and plan the experience of time (Ling 2008; Shrum et al. 2011). Mobile communication creates an "absent presence" (Gergen 2002) and organizes community from moment to moment among a dispersed, transient, yet intimately bonded sphere of close contacts (Gergen 2010). Creative practices of mobile communication shape new communities and social bonds in Kenya and other societies (Hoflich and Hartmann 2006). For example, airtime gifts playfully enhance the intimacy of close relationships among Kenyan college students (Kusimba et al. 2013). Mobile technologies further individual privacy and agency, which are particularly appreciated but also potentially dangerous in African settings.

Mobile remittances strengthen the relationships of mobile communication. Anthropologists have long commented on the importance of economic transactions in Africa in the creation of social relationships. Remittances are a performance of kinship and friendship roles in many cultures, but in some African settings they actually create social relationships:

> [In East Africa] material transactions have long been considered very important to the creation of interpersonal relationships. . . . In contrast with the Western attitude that the emotional component in interpersonal relations is more important than any transfer of material goods involved (the latter being thought of as something incidental), Africans are frankly and directly concerned with the material transfer itself as indicative of the quality of the relationship. (LeVine, 1973)

That the material defines the social may explain the persistence of bridewealth, the importance of children in marriage, and other practices whereby people are equated with value (Guyer 1993). The equivalence of people and money is certainly relevant to the enthusiasm for e-money remittances among Kenyans, who will actually send a remittance in lieu of attending a wedding or funeral. That value that makes relationships "real" also explains the importance of remittances. For urban migrants from western Kenya in the 1960s, bringing or sending money home was often more important than physical presence in preserving relationships (Ross and Weisner 1977). In our study, a 62-year-old whose oldest son has lived in Kansas for twelve years described his ongoing presence in her life, insisting that "he is very useful around here – very useful. He bought me a gas cooker . . . and pays my workers."

By constituting an intimate sphere, the mobile connection may exclude others (Gergen 2010), as anyone who has been physically present but outside a mobile phone conversation can attest. Kenyan popular culture frequently satirizes the uncomfortable effects of mobile money sociality – disruption and exclusion. In a Safaricom television advertisement, a businessman appears to furtively sweet-talk several women via mobile while his secretary looks on suspiciously; the females are revealed to be egg-laying hens on his rural farm.

In western Kenya people relate to and understand mobile money for its social effects, which empower individuals to both create sociality and disrupt it. A woman farmer in her fifties had little to say about mobile money as an economic or financial tool. Instead, she passionately reproached the service M-PESA for disrupting relationships through inappropriate connections:

> Mostly marriages are breaking with this service. A man may send 1,000 without you noticing. . . . There is a bond that begins when you have sent the 1,000 to the other lady. It goes on until the marriage breaks. I wish it would be just for women. Or sometimes the SMS may get in; you find and say a certain amount has been sent to so and so. If you tried to inquire, that person is not related to him, not sister or cousin, how come you send money to her? It is really destroying marriages.

That mobile money is primarily social rather than economic in purpose has important implications for development. ICTs are rapidly diversifying and blurring the uses and meanings of telephones and computers in a variety of settings (Donner 2010). Many of these diverse uses are not instrumental but social or for pleasure or entertainment; a more holistic "capabilities" emphasis on personal value can better describe and understand peoples' engagement with these technologies (Rangaswamy and Cutrell 2013; Sen 1999).

Bitter Mobile Money and Marginal Gains

The culture of entrustment is not without its burdens. Part of the way in which people participate and shape mobile-money networks is not just in the maintenance or forging of connections but in the avoidance or refusal of ties. People use a variety of strategies to avoid the redistributive pressures of friends and relatives. Kenyans often have more than one phone or phones with multiple SIM card address books as a way of managing types of connections or types of requests. To avoid a call or connection, people will hide a phone, refuse to answer it, turn it off, discontinue their M-PESA registration, or feign having lost or misplaced a phone when the contact in question appears or finds them later on. One awkward meeting involved a claim that one's phone had fallen down the outhouse. On the international level especially, stay-behind relatives experience fear when they think their relations abroad have "become lost," which occurs when they no longer make contact or respond to phone or email messages. Excessive pressure to remit was thought to lead to "becoming lost," which can be countered by offering emotional support, starting a business for the relative, or building the relative a house on the family land as a symbol of belonging (see also Horst 2011).

"Nowhere to hide" and "It is a curse more than a blessing" are some of the sardonic idioms one hears about mobile money's relentless demands. Part of this ambivalence reflects the burden of dealing with requests from friends and relatives and the sense that people's affections have become monetized. Should one travel home or send the money one would use on transport to one's mother or brother? The ambivalence also emerges out of frustrated desires to make tangible and significant investments in the future: "the gift that keeps on giving." *Bitter Money* (Shipton 1989) described East Africans' mistrust of cash and capitalism in the early 1980s. The bitterness of e-money is the conflict it creates between personal and collective, between spending and saving. Many people avoid storing money on their phones, feeling that it leads to excessive purchases or capitulations to requests. Several people with bank accounts preferred to transfer money off their phones and into their bank accounts as often as possible, in spite of the significant fees for such transfers. A dentist in Kimilili earns about 2,000 KES a day—although he receives significant additional income from other sources—which he transfers into his bank account at the end of each day at a cost of almost one US dollar for each transaction. Most people explained to us that they keep very little money on their phones due to the temptation to cash it out and to respond to the many remittance requests they receive.[1]

In the face of the ubiquitous circulation of mobile money, another level of creative practice seeks to turn the culture of entrustment to one's advantage – that of using exchanges of different kinds of value to extract a small profit or "marginal gain" (Guyer 2004).[2] Unequal exchanges of value between mobile money and other kinds of currency or value – such as cash, airtime, and even their own persons in terms of their presence at family meetings or ceremonies – offer marginal gains.

The practice of airtime gifting can illustrate the concept. Kenyans go to great lengths to conserve their own airtime: many keep very little airtime on their phones regardless of economic station and grudgingly "top up" in small amounts of five to fifty shillings. Flashing (the caller hangs up after a few rings, saying "call me" without using airtime) can spur others with the appropriate social position or gender to pay for the call whenever possible (Donner 2007). Conserving airtime is also accomplished through short conversations with abrupt hellos and no goodbyes. Paradoxically, even as people seek to conserve their own airtime, they are avid senders of airtime gifts. A modest airtime gift is converted into a brief phone call to the sender, thereby rekindling a friendship or connection. Safaricom's advertising uses the image of a sliced cake to encourage people to use its *Sambaza* (Kiswahili: to spread) menu item to "Send airtime to friends and family!" Two internet advertisements aimed at Kenyans in the United States encourage them to "Send airtime to friends and family back home" and to "Surprise loved ones in Kenya: Recharge their mobile – fast and easy transfer!" The transformation of monetarily small amounts of airtime into valuable sociality and a preference for the gifting of airtime – and extracting greater social value at no extra cost – are examples of marginal gains.

The most entrepreneurial users will juggle the many registers of value to their advantage (Guyer 1993) – using marginal gains to lower the monetary costs of social networks while still staking their claim to the culture of entrustment. Wafula, a 50-year-old Nairobi resident, explained that at his age, he is reaching a high point of remittance demands, as nieces and nephews seek school fees and job placement and as elderly folk continue to need support. He explained that he has a "system" for dealing with celebrations. He explained how it worked during the 2012 circumcision of his nephew (who would refer to him as "father"), a ceremony that in western Kenya still draws hundreds or even thousands of attendees whose money and livestock gifts benefit the boy and his family:

> As the day approached I refused my brother's calls and those of my sister-in-law. I just kept quiet. I missed the whole thing. But then during the pass-

ing out [which took place three weeks later] I called my sister-in-law a few days before that. I asked her to prepare a shopping list of everything that would be needed for that meal. She sent me an SMS with the list that came to 6,000 shillings. I sent her that (via M-PESA). So there was a big feast, and that 6,000 paid for everything. My brother called me to say thank you.

By refusing to attend the ceremony, Wafula saved himself as much as 20,000 KES, avoiding the cost of transport and numerous requests for assistance before and during an event attended by several hundred people. He is expected to give money to older women for their "sugar"; many will need transport back home; churches will request donations; money will inevitably be short for food, the boy's medical costs, and so on. Wafula explained that his "system" allows him to extract maximum social capital with minimum expenditure. Initiating the call during the passing out and allowing his sister-in-law to set the price of the remittance makes him appear infinitely generous, even as his own estimates, he explained, would end up too high for the actual cost of groceries in the rural areas. All the attendees acknowledged his contribution of a public and shared feast.

Mobile money functions cannot be separated from the primarily social functions of the telephone of which they are a part. The conversion of the economic into the social and back again is one of the most widely appreciated functions of mobile phones and mobile money, and seems to be aimed at individual advantage. Through the creative use of mobile phones, social networks, and remittances, cobbled together into a "system," individuals extract marginal gains as they convert and balance their social and economic capital. Such conversions clearly have development impacts as people seek to keep more value for themselves and as ceremonies create more geographically dispersed, and perhaps less emotionally engaged, networks of contributors.

Social Networks

We use a social network perspective to examine how people are connected to others through mobile money transfers and how people's positions within social networks may influence their remittance decisions. A social network consists of a set of actors or nodes – in this case individuals – and the relations or a tie between them – in this case flows of mobile money transactions (Wasserman and Faust 1994). One approach to understanding how individuals create ties argues that individuals seek connections to maximize social capital, or "the sum of resources, actual or virtual, that accrue to an individual or group by virtue of possessing a durable network . . . of mutual acquaintance" (Bourdieu 1985: 248). Simply put, social capital is about seeking advantage for oneself or others (Burt 2005). Individuals and groups maximize the benefit of their positions within groups, which shapes the social network.

Remittance flows modeled as networks can reveal the density and patterns of social connections and document the potential for social capital associated with particular places in the social network. Two patterns in social networks imply social capital: closure and brokerage (Burt 2005). The more connections exist among a group of individuals, the more closure in the group. Groups of densely connected individuals are effective at distributing resources and information, evening out inequalities among the individuals concerned. These dense groups often represent the maintenance and strengthening of close ties (Lin 1998).

The second form of social capital in networks is brokerage. Weak connections – few ties – between groups are "holes" in the social structure. An individual whose network spans or connects the holes can broker flows of information or resources from one group to another, bringing information or resources across groups (Burt 2005; Lin 1999).

Social-network drawings were created for several families who send and receive mobile money by interviewing between three and ten individuals connected by mobile-money transfers. Each individual was asked to name relatives to whom they had sent and received money in the past year. Most individuals quickly named between five and nine individuals. Whenever possible, the individuals named by the first individual were contacted and the same questionnaire filled out, which resulted in the network diagrams that follow. Interestingly, several interviews the research team had with siblings demonstrated that many people in a group are aware of ties among their friends and connections; that is, they know quite a bit about who is sending money to whom within their close group of contacts. The resulting matrices were entered into the program R for the drawing of social networks.

For each individual, a list of persons they send money to and receive it from the most – in the past year – was collected. Figure 8.1 below allows us to examine the relationship between kinship and the sending and receiving of money. This polygynous family included twelve wives altogether, of which five (represented by large white circles) are part of the connections named by our ten interviewees. One wife (light gray circle) and her nine children form a dense network at the center of this diagram along with their children and in some cases their spouses. Certain indi-

Figure 8.1. The Bungoma Family 1 network is based on cousin, sibling, and maternal ties. It is centered on a woman (light gray circle) and her nine children (squares) and their children (triangles), with paths to four co-wives (white circles) and their children. Connections to fathers and paternal uncles are rare or absent; instead, men are mothers' brothers, brothers, or cousins.

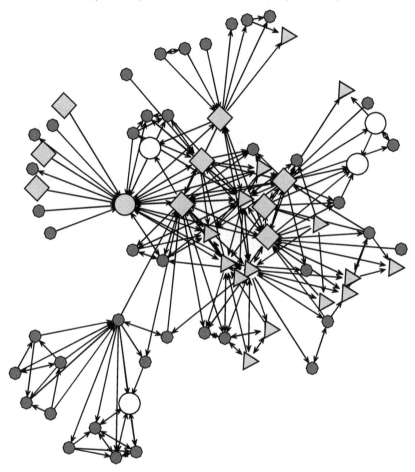

viduals are important bridges to other co-wives and their children and grandchildren.

Counting the types of kin relationships that form paths in Bungoma Family 1 allows us to see what kinds of kin relationships are especially associated with mobile-money transfers as drawn in figure 8.1. Cousin, brother, and sister relationships are especially common means through which people send and receive mobile money. The preponderance of cousin ties is especially interesting, as in most kinship systems in East Africa there is no commonly used word for cousin, the term "brother" or "sister" instead being used. Most informants explained that when brothers and sisters have a close relationship, their children will have a close relationship in which no distinction between siblings and cousins is made.

Relatively rare bridges exist between the dense networks of support created by the children of one mother. Mothers are more central than fathers, who are often not named in questionnaires at all. Brothers, sisters, cousins, and occasionally half siblings are all connected through the bonds of mobile money. Sibling ties, maternal ties, and in some cases cousin ties are the most important kin relationships, while marriage and in-law ties are relatively rare.

Ties in Bungoma Family 2 connect siblings to the children of these siblings and to their parents. Note that the dense group of three sisters and a brother form the basis of a clique connecting their children, and that they also connect to their three brothers and in turn to these three brothers' wives and children (figure 8.2; table 8.1). Finally, several patri-

Figure 8.2. In Bungoma Family 2, significant asset and income inequality exists among seven siblings (in white). Three sisters and a brother are part of a dense network of frequent ties (center), giving individuals several pathways to share resources. Paths connect them to three other brothers and their wives and children (on right side of the drawing) and to a sibling's husband and his relatives (left side).

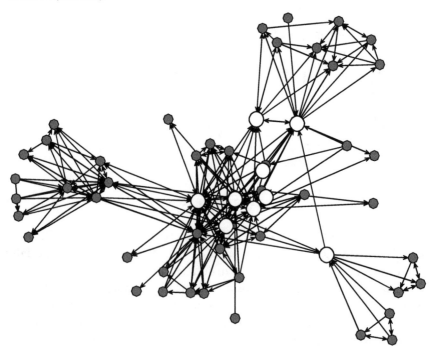

Table 8.1. Relationships of Receivers to Senders in Bungoma Family 2

Mobile Money Transactions in Bungoma Family 2			
Number of Female Ties to a . . .		**Number of Male Ties to a . . .**	
brother	17	cousin	22
son	12	brother	16
cousin	9	sister	13
mother	8	maternal aunt	9
nephew	7	nephew	8
daughter	6	wife	8
brother-in-law	5	maternal uncle	7
maternal aunt	5	mother	7
sister	5	niece	6
husband	4	sister-in-law	4
niece	4	other	39
uncle	4		
other	28		
Total Female-Sent MM Ties	114	Total Male-Sent MM Ties	139

lineal and in-law ties connect the central group to one sister's husband's family on the left side of the diagram. In field interviews, one of the three sisters' sons explained that he sees his patrilineal relatives at funerals but that the men who have helped him with fees and other investments in his future have been his mother's brothers. Three brothers are bridges in this network, spanning the closed groups of their three sisters and brother with that of their own wives and children.

The Naitri family includes as its matriarch a 67-year-old farmer, mother of eight, and grandmother of forty-four. In the network, she is a bridge connecting her network of children and grandchildren, including her sons- and daughters-in-law, to family of her deceased sister's oldest daughter, who in turn is connected through money transfers to her sisters and their children (figure 8.3). Her network also receives international remittances from two individuals in the United States.

In fact, the children of the two sisters in Naitiri Family have created a family association to collect school fees for the children and grandchildren of this pair of sisters. At the deceased sister's funeral (a type of event when social groups and generations often reconstitute themselves, and when discord is displayed and assuaged), the children of these two women, who live in Naitiri, Kimilili, Chicago, and Nairobi, discussed the high cost of education. On the spot, they formed a credit and savings group in which each of them agreed to contribute 1,000 shillings a month to a common savings account from which school fees would be paid on a rotating basis. The members meet once a month for a meal, where they also contribute 1,000 KES each toward a banked fund for school fees. Mobile-money services are used by some at the meeting to send mobile money to the treasurer; from Chicago, a daughter uses Western Union.

Figure 8.3. Naitiri Family is based in Naitiri, Nairobi, and Chicago. A 67-year old grandmother (triangle) is a broker (Stovel and Shaw 2012) connecting her children (pentagons), daughters-in-law, and grandchildren (dark gray) to her deceased sister's oldest daughter (light gray circle), her children (squares), and her other siblings (light gray circles). Her son and her daughter in Chicago are embedded within her network and send remittances via Western Union, sometimes directly to their relatives' M-PESA accounts.

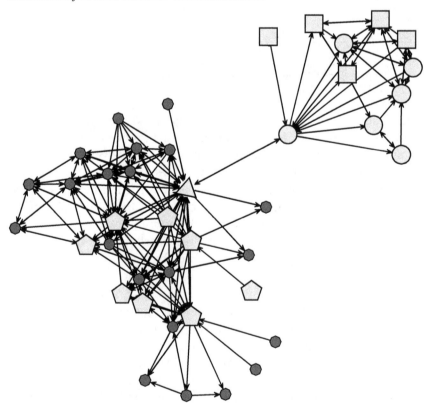

The three families mapped here show important similarities in terms of structure and types of ties. All show an emphasis on maternal and sibling ties. Sets of siblings show "closure" or dense ties and include mothers and their children. In many of these families, certain individuals have regular salaries or income from farming, shops, or rental housing, while others do not. Mobile-money circulations serve as an equalizing mechanism whereby individuals have a greater number of potential ties or links through which they can access the wealth of a family. In both Bungoma family networks, matrilineal kin create dense networks of closure. Although patrilineal and in-law ties are rare, they are important, as weak ties often are, in filling structural holes. Weak ties over bridges move resources into and out of tightly connected groups and bring new resources into groups. In Bungoma Family 1, these bridges are between half siblings; in Bungoma Family 2, bridges are in-law and patrilineal ties. Naitiri Family is predominantly made up of matrilineal ties.

Anthropologist Margery Wolf, in patrilineal Taiwan in the late 1950s, described how women in patrilineal societies build their own social networks based on establishing ties to friends, siblings, and children, which she called "uterine kinship" (Wolf 1972). Uterine kinship often exists outside the public, patrilineal sphere and describes flexible and personal mother- and sibling-centered ties. At marriage, a young woman newly moved in to her husband's community creates her own social ties through friendship, through her children, and through preservation of ties to her own siblings, particularly her brothers. Uterine kinship involves both men and women equally, through ties among siblings to mothers and mothers' relatives.

The mobile-money networks' emphasis on uterine kinship is in contrast to the ties of patrilineal kinship that have a high profile at public events. At coming-of-age ceremonies, young men are officially welcomed as adults into a circle of patrilineal kin. Patrilineal ties are still the basis of systems of inheritance and rights to land and other value in western Kenya (Nasimiyu 1997). Cellular phones and mobile money restore the relationships of uterine kinship and, in so doing, disrupt relationships of marriage and affinal ties. Among thirty-three women farmers in the rural outskirts of Kitale town, the privacy, secrecy, and autonomy of mobile money was used to strengthen friendship and kinship ties with blood relatives at the expense of spouses and affines. These women hide money from husbands and privately send money to their mothers and sisters to educate nieces and nephews. The common occurrence of teenage pregnancy means role overload for maternal grandmothers as their daughters' husbands reject children not biologically their own (Kilbride and

Kilbride 1997); women leverage uterine kinship to support their children or grandchildren born before marriage. In many families, especially Bungoma Family 2 above, the greater part of remittances to mothers is used to support illegitimate children.

Polygynous marriage networks like Bungoma Family 1 are rapidly fragmenting into networks like Bungoma Family 2 that develop around siblings. Historically, half siblings shared several "mothers" and were brought together by rights of residency, inheritance, and seniority (Wagner 1975). In Bungoma Family 1, half-sibling and co-mother ties are relatively rare, but this is because weak ties connect the central clique to co-wives and half siblings (figure 8.1). More commonly today, polygynous marriage is contested or practiced secretly (Kilbride et al. 2000), and the oldest son or *simakulu* often provides economic support when a father has "moved on." The absence of fathers and husbands is a feature of both Bungoma families, but particular resentment seems to exclude the polygynous father from remittance networks. A Kisii woman in her late twenties working as a secretary described her ambivalence about remitting to her ill father:

> My father had four wives. Mother is number two. We are twenty-two altogether. In our family the co-wives did not work together. They are not on good terms. In our family we were sidelined by our father. It was my mom who used to support us with her farming. My father could support the last two families. So us, we were dependent on our mother until our firstborn brother, second in the family, joined the university and started paying our school fees with the university boom. . . . He [Father] was unfair to us. Since we were his children, we didn't take it kindly. Sometimes there is an occasion – right now Dad is on treatment. He needs that support. When you call people to come together . . . we are so bitter. You get called. So now, we are called upon . . . you get so bitter. He didn't help us.

The centrality of women in their mobile-money networks of children and matrilineal kin could empirically support the gendered "Empowerment Story" (Maurer 2012). Social networks do demonstrate the social capital of certain women. Mothers are often visible in network drawings as receiving many ties from others (figures 8.1, 8.2, and 8.3). In Naitiri Family, a grandmother brokers a structural hole, connecting resources from her network, which includes large international remittances, with that of her sister's children.

Both women and men leverage the social and economic capital of uterine kin. However, the secret and illicit nature of these ties challenges the "Empowerment Story." Uterine kinship ties are more likely to be secret and illicit, disrupting the public and often patrilineal sphere, particularly when it supports illegitimate children. This and other studies have found that secrecy and privacy are salient aspects of women's phone usage (Hassan 2013). Women routinely keep secret phones and SIM cards from their husbands. In extreme cases husbands prevent women from accessing e-money services. For example, a 45-year-old lady is without an identity card, so she is dependent on her sister in Kansas for an account with M-PESA. Her husband destroyed the phone on which she received remittances from her sister, and she had to wait for that sister to visit and buy her a new phone, which she now hides from him. A second challenge to the Empowerment Story is the predominant use of remittances to circulate small transactions for consumption and emergency use. The average remittance among 47 people in Kimilili who reported 155 remittances in the past month was 1,800 KES (about US$20); in rural Naitiri 25 people reported 37 remittances, with an average value of 700 KES (US$9). Ethnographic data also show that at least one-third of remittances are sent for what are considered "emergencies," the asker being stranded without transport, sent home from school, or falling ill.

When I commented to one woman that she did not name her husband as an e-money contact, she clucked in annoyance – and pointed out her farm and chickens, entrusted to her by her husband and mother-in-law. Her reaction suggested that Kenyans themselves view remittances as a means of coping rather than true economic "empowerment" – what a 47-year-old father described as "a gift that keeps on giving: land and healthy animals . . . or a rental house . . . where it gives me something every month." A successful dentist in Kimilili town is nevertheless determined to develop farmland he inherited from his father. He explained, "With a real investment . . . you will never be poor." The visible and sharable wealth-building resources that the people of western Kenya truly value – such as productive farmland, real estate, or livestock – are still largely transferred through male inheritance (Budlender and Alma 2011; Nasimiyu 1997).

The uterine kinship of mobile money conveys the secrecy and marginality of connections to and through women as distinct from forms of wealth that are publicly entrusted, socially embedded, and appreciated on symbolic and emotional levels in this patrilineal society. In strengthening uterine kinship, then, mobile money may fix these relationships outside of the public sphere or even serve to justify exclusion. The relationship between the public and private sphere may hinge on the exchanges between them made by men, who participate in both the uterine and the public spheres of kinship. Time will only tell if mobile-money networks will eventually bring "the gifts that keep on giving" to the many who seek them in western Kenya.

Conclusion

Africans have long been comfortable with using different forms and registers of value through their involvement with regional, Indian Ocean, and European trade networks (Guyer 2004; Kusimba et al. 2005). Mobile money and airtime are the newest forms of value – value that can be offered in lieu of one's presence or emotional involvement, and that can be transformed one into the other or into goods, information, social relationships, or the emotional effect of connecting to a loved one. Traditions of entrustment – in which ownership is a kind of temporary safekeeping of wealth that circulates across the passing generations – reflect themselves in the new mirror of e-money. Using mobile money means storing or saving value through its entrustment to relatives, friends, or savings groups on a local, urban-rural, and even transnational scale. By recording one's gift in a public ceremony's record, a claim is staked toward a future recompense – as Mzee Nathan explained, this gift must be doubled upon its return. As long as Kenyan banks continue to charge prohibitive fees, the concept of saving through entrustment makes a great deal of sense.

Mobile money is an adjunct to the mobile phone and used in concert with the mobile phone. It is a social and economic tool (Donner 2009), used to shape social networks that express relationships and the economic value of entrustment (Shipton 2007) whereby people lend and borrow with others for needs great and small, thereby contributing to and drawing from what is effectively a pool of resources. Mobile-money networks make visible the ties among siblings, their mothers, and mothers' relatives in patrilineal western Kenya. Matrilineal flows of mobile money are often private and secret. The marginality of ties through women inspires doubts about the female betterment assumed by the Empowerment Story – yet they do not deny it outright. Mobile communication increases the redundancy of social networks and provides any mobile-money subscriber with the possibility of accessing and participating in the culture of entrustment, which has after all stood the test of time as real "financial inclusion."

Acknowledgments

We would like to thank the Institute for Money, Technology & Financial Inclusion (IMTFI) for the support that made this research possible and for the guidance this community of scholars gave us in conducting and interpreting the research. Support has also been provided to Sibel Kusimba by a faculty grant from Northern Illinois University. Dr. Chap Kusimba provided invaluable logistical support in the field and provided helpful suggestions that have improved this manuscript. Ivan Small of IMTFI read and made excellent helpful comments on drafts of this chapter. Finally, thanks go to John Terrell of the Field Museum for introducing Sibel Kusimba to Social Network Analysis.

Sibel Kusimba conducts anthropological and archaeological fieldwork in Kenya. She has studied mobile money in Kenya since 2012, and she has garnered three grants through IMTFI to examine digital money in Kenya. She has published numerous book chapters and articles. Her 2003 book, *African Foragers,* was named an outstanding academic book by the American Library Association. Her research conducted with funding from IMTFI is published in the peer-reviewed journals *Information Technology and International Development, African Studies Review,* and *Economic Anthropology.*

Gabriel Kunyu is an honors graduate of Egerton University in Njoro, Kenya. A historian by training, his honors thesis examined the role of ethnicity in the development of trading networks in western Kenya during the nineteenth and twentieth centuries.

Elizabeth Gross is an assistant professor in the Department of Mathematics and Statistics at San José State University. Before joining the faculty ranks at San José State, Dr. Gross was an NSF Postdoctoral Fellow at North Carolina State University and a visiting scholar at the Simons Institute for Computing at UC Berkeley. Her research interests include network models with applications to the social sciences, biology, and neuroscience.

NOTES

1. On the other hand, our team heard from women in ROSCAs that mobile money was an aid to earmarking or saving for merry-go-round contributions.
2. I would like to thank Ivan Small for pointing out the relevance of Guyer's concept.

REFERENCES CITED

Archambault, Julie. S. 2013. "Cruising through Uncertainty: Cell Phones and the Politics of Display and Disguise in Inhambane, Mozambique." *American Ethnologist* 40(1): 88–101. doi:10.1111/amet.12007.

Bourdieu, Pierre. 1985. "The Forms of Capital." In *Handbook of Theory and Research for the Sociology of Education*, 241–58. Edited by John G Richardson. New York: Greenwood Press.

Budlender, D., and E. Alma. 2011. *Women and Land: Securing Rights for Better Lives.* Ottawa: International Development Research Centre.

Burt, Roland. S. 2005. "The Social Capital of Structural Holes." In *The New Economic Sociology: Developments in an Emerging Field,* edited by M. Guillen, R. Collins, and P. England. New York: Russell Sage Foundation.

Donner, Jonathan. 2009. "Blurring Livelihoods and Lives: The Social Uses of Mobile Phones and Socioeconomic Development." *Innovations: Technology, Governance, Globalization* 4(1): 91–101.

———. 2010. "Framing M4D: The Utility of Continuity and the Dual Heritage of Mobiles and Development." *EJISDC: The Electronic Journal of Information Systems in Developing Countries*: Volume 44: 1–16. Retrieved March 1 2013 from http://dialnet.unirioja.es/servlet/articulo?codigo=3671001.

Donovan, Kevin. 2012. "Mobile Money for Financial Inclusion." In *Information and Communication for Development:Maximizing Mobile,* edited by T. Kelly and C. Rosotto, 61–74. The World Bank Group, Washington, DC

Gergen, Kenneth. 2002. "The Challenge of Absent Presence." In *Perpetual Contact,* edited by J. E. Katz and M. Aakhus, 227–41. Cambridge: Cambridge University Press.

———. 2010. "Mobile Communication and the New Insularity." *Qwerty* 5(1): 14–28.

Guyer, Jane. 1993. "Wealth in People and Self-Realization in Equatorial Africa." *Man N. S.* 28(2): 243–65.

———. 2004. *Marginal Gains: Monetary Transactions in Atlantic Africa.* Chicago: University of Chicago Press.

Hassan, Michelle. 2013. "Empowering Women with Mobile Money: The Kenya Report." Mobile Payments Today. Retrieved 1 March 2013 from https://www.mobilepaymentstoday.com/articles/commentary-empowering-women-with-mobile-money-the-kenya-report/.

Hoflich, Joachim. R., and Maren. Hartmann. 2006. *Mobile Communication in Everyday Life: Ethnographic Views, Observations and Reflections.* Berlin: Frank and Timme.

Horst, Heather., and Daniel. Miller. 2006. *The Cell Phone: An Anthropology of Communication.* Oxford: Berg Publishers.

Johnson, Susan., G. Brown, and C. Fouillet. 2012. *The Search for Inclusion in Kenya's Financial Landscape: The Rift Revealed.* Bath: University of Bath Institute for International Development.

Kilbride, Phillip., and Janet. Kilbride. 1997. "Stigma, Role Overload, and Delocalization among Contemporary Kenyan Women." In *African Families and the Crisis of Social Change,* edited by Thomas. S. Weisner, Candice. Bradley, and Philip. Kilbride, 208–23. Westport, CT: Bergin and Garvey.

Kilbride, Philip., Colette. Suda, and Elizabeth Njeru. 2000. *Street Children in Kenya: Voices of Children in Search of a Childhood.* Westport, CT: Bergen and Garvey.

Kriem, Maya. S. 2009. "Mobile Telephony in Morocco: A Changing Sociality." *Media, Culture and Society* 31: 617–32.

Kusimba, Chapurukha. M., Sibel. B. Kusimba, and David. K. Wright. 2005. "The Development and Collapse of Precolonial Ethnic Mosaics in Tsavo, Kenya." *Journal of African Archaeology* 3(2): 243–65.

Kusimba, Sibel., H. Chaggar, E. Gross, and G. Kunyu. 2013. "Social Networks of Mobile Money in Kenya," 1–19. Working paper. Irvine, CA: Institute for Money, Technology & Financial Inclusion. Retrieved 1 March 2013 from http://www .imtfi.uci.edu/files/imtfi/2013-1_kusimba_1.pdf.

LeVine, Robert. A. 1973. "Patterns of Personality in Africa." *Ethos* 1(2): 123–52.

Lin, Nan. 1999. "Building a Network Theory of Social Capital." *Connections* 22 (1), 28–51, 22(1).

Ling, Richard. 2008. *New Tech, New Ties: How Mobile Communication is Reshaping Social Cohesion.* Cambridge: Massachusetts Institute of Technology.

Maurer, Bill. 2012. "Mobile Money: Communication, Consumption and Change in the Payments Space." *Journal of Development Studies* 48 (June): 1–16. doi:10.1080/ 00220388.2011.621944.

McIntosh, Janet. 2010. "Mobile Phones and Mipoho's Prophecy: The Powers and Dangers of Flying Language." *American Ethnologist* 37(2): 337–53.

Nasimiyu, Ruth. 1997. "Changing Women's Rights over Property in Western Kenya." In *African Families and the Crisis of Social Change,* edited by T. S. Weisner, C. Bradley, and P. Kilbride, 283–98. Westport, CT: Bergin and Garvey.

Omwansa, Thomas., and N. Sullivan. 2012. *Money, Real Quick.* London: Guardian Books.

Rangaswamy, N., and E. Cutrell. 2013. "ICTs : Slums, Youth, and the Mobile Internet in Urban India." *Information Technologies and International Development* 9(2): 51–63.

Ross, Marc., and Thomas. S. Weisner. 1977. "The Rural-Urban Network in Kenya: Some General Implications." *Amerian Ethnologist* 4(2): 359–75.

Sen, Amartya. 1999. *Development as Freedom.* Oxford: Oxford University Press.

Shipton, Parker. 2007. *The Nature of Entrustment: Intimacy, Exchange, and the Sacred in Africa.* New Haven, CT: Yale University Press.

Shrum, W., P. N. Mbatia, A. Palackal, D.-B. S. Dzorgbo, R. B. Duque, and M. A. Ynalvez. 2011. "Mobile Phones and Core Network Growth in Kenya: Strengthening Weak Ties." *Social Science Research* 40(2): 614–25. doi:10.1016/j.ssresea rch.2010.09.015.

Stovel, Katherine, and Lynette Shaw. 2012. "Brokerage." *Annual Review of Sociology* 38(1): 139–58. doi:10.1146/annurev-soc-081309-150054.

Suri, Tavneet, William Jack, and T. M. Stoker. 2012. "Documenting the Birth of a Financial Economy." *Proceedings of the National Academy of Sciences of the United States of America* 109(26): 10257–62. doi:10.1073/pnas.1115843109.

Wagner, Gunther. 1975. *The Bantu of North Kavirondo.* Vols. 1 and 2. London: Oxford University Press for International African Institute.

Wasserman, Stanley, and Katherine Faust. 1994. *Social Network Analysis: Method and Application.* Cambridge: Cambridge University Press.

Wolf, Margery. 1972. "Uterine Families and the Women's Community." In *Women and the Family in Rural Taiwan,* edited by M. Wolf, 166–69. Palo Alto: Stanford University Press.

CHAPTER 9

Accounting in the Margin
Financial Ecologies in between Big and Small Data

JOSÉ OSSANDÓN, TOMÁS ARIZTÍA,
MACARENA BARROS, AND CAMILA PERALTA

Introduction

In the last years, researchers coming from a varied array of social scientific academic disciplines (such as anthropology, history, geography, and sociology) have started to show interest in the empirical analysis of finance. These developments have not run parallel with each other but have constituted a new multidisciplinary academic field – sometimes named social studies of finance (SSF) (Knorr Cetina and Preda 2012). SSF can be characterized by some shared emphases, notably an ethnographic approach and a special sensibility toward devices and sociotechnical assemblages. Simultaneously, within the finance industry and global policymaking, growing attention has been devoted to financial literacy, payment infrastructures, and new banking products targeting those at the so-called "bottom of the pyramid" (Collins et al. 2009). Like several of the chapters included in this volume, this one contributes to the growing literature at the intersection between these trajectories, where an increasing attention is being paid to practices of industry and policymakers targeting formerly excluded financial consumers around the world (Elyachar 2010; Guérin et al. 2013; Langley 2014; Maurer 2012; Ossandón 2012).

Existing social studies of *low* or domestic finance could be classified in two types: research on the changing financial practices of people facing new types of products and financial technologies (for instance Müller 2014; Villarreal 2014; Wilkis 2014) and research that pays more attention to technologies and practices enacted by financial providers targeting previously *excluded* financial consumers (Deville 2013; Ossandón 2014; Poon 2011). To use terms associated with the work of Michel Callon and

Florence Weber, research in this field seems to be split between those studying two modes of financial knowledge and practices, studies of "market devices" (Muniesa et al. 2007) (such as scoring, credit cards, or debt-collection experiments) developed by financial firms, and studies analyzing the new financial practices and modes of "ordinary calculation" (Weber 2009) being developed by economic users around the world. This chapter tries to bridge both sides. We believe social studies of *low* finance should not only be good at collecting detailed descriptions of the practices of users and financial providers but also be one (among others, for instance policymakers) of the channels connecting both sides. The site of social studies of low finance, in other words, is where both types of calculations, the *big* data of market devices and the *small* data of ordinary financial calculations, can be observed together.

While elsewhere we have tried to develop concepts to theorize this new epistemological position (Ossandón 2017), the current chapter focuses on some of the methodological challenges this position entails. More specifically, it describes the research strategies we developed in order to deal with two issues: how, by reusing one of the most mundane objects in everyday finance, monthly invoices, we embraced the information-intensive character of credits cards and how we visualized analogously one unexpected finding: networks of credit card lending. The chapter consists of four parts (one devoted to each challenge), a brief conclusion, and a brief introduction of our case of study.

Context: Department Store Credit in Chile

Consumer credit is a ubiquitous presence in the economic life of Chileans. Just go to any shopping mall, supermarket, or even medical center or university to realize that it is possible to buy almost everything with some sort of loan. As the Central Bank's Finance Survey of 2011–12 (Banco Central 2013) shows, while 58.3 percent of Chilean households have some sort of consumer debt, 43.5 percent have a debt associated with retailers' credit cards. Consumer credits are not only prevalent among middle-class households, normally associated to consumerism and over-indebtedness by the Chilean media, but also among low- and high-income households. Of course, Chile is not the only place where consumer credits and, particularly, credit cards have seen a significant growth in the last decades. However, the Chilean case shows an important particularity: the access to credits has neither been driven by banks (like in the United States; Guseva and Rona-Tas 2001) nor by specialized finance institutions (like in France; Ducourant 2009) but mainly by retailers such as supermarkets and department stores. As summarized elsewhere,

> In a country with a population of about 17 million, the amount of bank credit cards increased from 1,310,325 in 1993 to 4,499,627 in 2007, while retail credit cards expanded from 1,350,000 to 19,273,919 in the same period (Montero and Tarziján 2010). . . . In today's Chile, retail cards are not merely used to get installment credit, but they can also be used as credit cards in a growing network of associated stores and as medium to get "cash advances" and other personal loans. In a country where a large proportion of the population does not have a bank account, stores are becoming a main entry point for personal financing. (Ossandón 2014: 430)

Like bank credit cards in the United States (Montgomery 2006) or mobile money in Africa (Maurer et al. 2013), department store credit has transformed the financial landscape faced by those previously excluded to formal finance in Chile. This chapter discusses, more specifically, the results of our research project that studied the new "financial ecologies" faced by low-income Chileans in the context of the rapid expansion of department store credit.[1] We studied the ways in which store credit in low-income areas in Chile's capital city, Santiago, is complementing and/ or disrupting existing financial practices.

First Challenge: Collecting the Traces of *Big Data*

The expansion of consumer credit in Chile has not been invisible for social researchers (Ossandón 2011). By the end of the 1990s, sociologist Tomás Moulian (1998) published a critical essay discussing the side effects of a growing access to consumption not based on an improvement of salaries and work conditions but on the expansion of credit. A decade later, a national survey showed that Chileans have a dual relationship with consumer loans. Although these loans are seen as a key access to otherwise inaccessible goods, debts are a continuous source of stress (Barros 2009). Barros (2011) qualitatively complemented this picture, documenting how consumer credit is experienced as a – sometimes painful – learning process. More recently, Ossandón (2014) used interviews with key informants and industry insiders to reconstruct the sociotechnical history of consumer credit lending in the retail industry in Chile.

When attempting to reconstruct people's financial practices, two methods seem to be favored by social researchers. On the one hand, like Barros (2009) and Barros (2011), some have used individual and group in-

terviews to access the ways in which their informants signify and understand their relationship with financial providers and goods. On the other
hand, regulatory bodies have developed household financial surveys –
such as the already mentioned survey commissioned by the Central
Bank of Chile – to develop statistical indices (for instance, debt-income
ratio) that can orientate economic policies. Without denying that good
research can be (and has been) carried out with these two types of instruments, it is clear that these methods present clear limitations. Studies
centered on subjective perception tend to not to be very good in getting
the details of financial transactions, and household surveys extrapolate
a lot from one visit and are limited by their closed questions. An inter-
mediate, more successful, and increasingly influential technique is the
creation of financial diaries as developed by the authors of the book *Portfolios of the Poor* (Collins et al. 2009). However, even the diaries look very
pale if compared with the amount of information collected by credit
cards themselves.

In today's *Society of Big Data* (Savage and Burrows 2014), the production
of social quantitative information is not only located in state agencies or
social science research departments but increasingly in private organizations such as credit bureaus, online retailers, search engines, or social
network sites. In this context, credit cards are particularly intriguing objects of research. Like money (Luhmann 1982), credit cards bridge present
and future economic activities, but also, like a very efficient survey, they
collect and archive information of every single purchase. In the language
of recent "social studies of finance," cards are "market devices" (Muniesa
et al. 2007), objects located in complex sociotechnical assemblages where
transactional data and more or less sophisticated risk-scoring mechanisms play an important role in screening, pricing, and targeting loans
(Leyshon and Thrift 1999; Poon 2011; Stearns 2011).

The current *datascape* (Latour 2011) has been interpreted as a challenge
for social scientists (Savage and Burrows 2007) who have been trying to
find new ways of making themselves useful in a context where social data
is not necessarily produced by them. For instance, an increasing effort is
being made to trace, scrap, and reassemble social information produced
by big-data manufacturers (Marres and Weltevrede 2013; Savage 2009;
Latour et al. 2012). These strategies, certainly, are not free of problems.
Most of the time *big* data is also *private* data. Access is very restricted, and
research tends to be limited to ex-post "reverse engineering" of the traces
left online by search algorithms (Deville 2013). At the same time, and
despite their vastness, data collected by private firms do not always fulfil

the quality criteria required for academic research (Rona-Tas and Hiss 2010), or they might be too structured for the type of questions posed by qualitative social investigation.

So, how should we approach ordinary financial practices in the age of big data? Or, said in more practical terms, how can we embrace the informational nature of consumer credit, accessing and using some of the detailed information collected by store credit cards, without merely reproducing data already known in the industry, as well as collecting data that address the type of conceptual questions that inspire us? With amateur detectives' good luck, we found the solution to our dilemma in a very mundane object: monthly invoices.

Invoices

Perhaps as a consequence of the massive privatizations carried out since the 1970s, or maybe even earlier, the postal service has not been very present in the everyday life of Chileans. We rarely send letters to friends or family, not even at Christmas, and, accordingly, post offices and even mailboxes are quite difficult to find. The postal service, however, still carries out an important role: it is the main means to circulate bills. Monthly, every household receives letters with invoices or bills from companies providing water, electricity, phone, cable TV, internet, bank accounts and . . . department store and supermarket credit cards.

Figure 9.1 is an anonymized invoice of *Más,* the credit card accepted in the stores that make up the retail network of Cencosud, one of the biggest retailers in Latin America.[2] At the time of fieldwork, there were more than 2.5 million active *Más* cards in Chile. In order to illustrate the type of information contained in credit cards bills, the next paragraphs describe the information included in the invoice of the illustration. Readers already familiar with this type of document can skip directly to next section.

At the top left of the bill is a box that gives information about the time period of this specific invoice (until 20 July 2011); the total credit ceiling assigned to this card (Ch$1.258.000 – at that time, one US dollar was about 500 Chilean pesos, therefore about US$2.500); cumulated debt (Ch$853.421) and available credit (Ch$404.579); interest rates; next billing day (22 August 2011) and, in smaller letters, an average – in UF, an inflation indexed unit used in financial transactions in Chile – of the last three months of transactions. Below, there are two smaller boxes with advertisements. The box on the left shows the Nectar label, indicating

Figure 9.1. An anonymized credit card invoice.

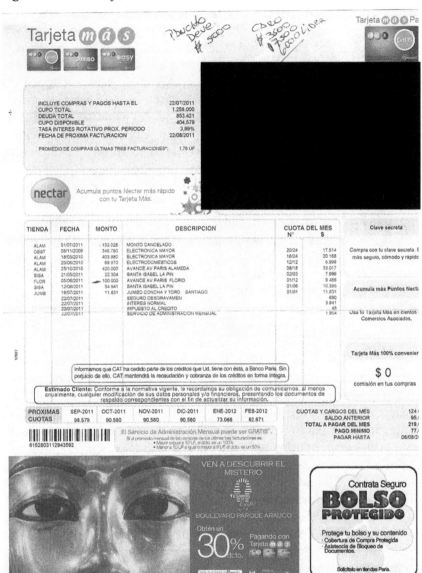

that *Más* is part of this global customer-loyalty program, while the box on the right reminds customers about the "exclusive discounts" available only for cardholders.

The box below has a table detailing transactions in five columns. The first column indicates, although in a slightly coded way, the place where the actual transaction was carried out (for instance, ALAM stands for Santiago's main street al.ameda, officially called Avenida Libertador General Bernardo O'Higgins, or OEST for a store located in a big shopping center called Plaza Oeste). The second column marks the dates of the transactions, and the third the amount of each of them (Ch$132.025, Ch$346.780, etc.). The fourth column is called *description* and details the types of transactions. For instance, the first row says *monto cancelado,* which means that at that date, the customer had paid Ch$132.000 of his or her previous debt. The second and third row say *Electrónica Mayor* (big electronic equipment), while the fourth refers to home appliances. The sixth, seventh, and eighth are purchases in the two supermarket chains, Jumbo and Santa Isabel, where *Más* can be used as a means of payment. Rows five and seven say *avances,* which means that this customer used the card to withdraw a cash loan, and the last four rows describe fees associated to the use of the card (payment protection insurance, interest, credit tax, and administration). The last two columns in the same box describe the installments, or *cuotas* in Spanish. The fourth column rates the total and paid amount of installments (for instance: 20 out of 24, 18/24, 12/12), and the last column displays the amount of money associated with each installment (17.514, 20.168, etc.). With this information, it is possible to understand each transaction. Consider for instance the second row of the table: on 8 November 2009 this card was used to buy electronic equipment at Plaza Oeste shopping center for Ch$348.780. This purchase was split into twenty-four monthly installments of Ch$20.168 each, eighteen of which have been already paid. Or the fifth row: on 25 October 2010 the same card was used to withdraw a cash loan of Ch$420.000 that has to be paid in eighteen monthly installments of Ch$33.017 each.

Still in the same box, but below, are two smaller boxes. The first mentions that CAT (Cencosud's card administration unit SA) has transferred part of the credits attached to this card to the bank of the group Banco Paris; the second reminds customers that they are obliged to inform in case of changes to their personal and financial data. Below, there is a table with one row and seven columns informing about the upcoming monthly payments (September 2011: Ch$95.579, October 2011 Ch$90.580, etc.). On the right-hand side, another box gives even more extra information (the total charges for the current month, the balance from the previous month, the sum of the last two, the minimum payment accepted, and the due date). Finally, the last horizontal strip on the page includes two advertisements: the first one shows a store where it is possible to get a discount using *Más,* and the second promotes an insurance policy against "handbag theft."

Bills That Talk

Despite their different graphic designs, the invoices distributed monthly by the different retail firms in Chile do not differ greatly from the one just described. It can even be argued that they don't differ much from bills circulating in other countries. As the example showed, bills, like a finance diary, include detailed information of each credit transaction carried out with a given card. Therefore, or so we realized – in a way that could resemble the data-collection method known as "photo elicitation" (Harper 2002), in which objects such as photos or other types of visual stimuli are used to trigger discussions in interviews – invoices could be turned into an instrument to start a conversation about financial practices.

The interview situation would be something like this: we would meet at our informants' homes and ask them if they would kindly share with us their credit card invoices. Of course, as invoices might be regarded as private documents and understandably not everyone is willing to share them, this implied a lot of trust and presented a big challenge for the fieldworker. In accordance to the ethical procurement agreed on for this research, we explained every time that we guarantee total anonymity and that we would not keep or record the bills, with the exception of some anonymized photos. We explained that we were after something else; we wanted to develop a conversation where they could tell us the story of each credit transaction and where invoices could be used as a sort of external memory providing hard details (dates, amounts, places of purchase) from where to start our conversation. Luckily, most of the people we visited were very willing to share their credit invoices and to start a conversation. But then we faced another difficulty, this time more practical. Not everyone keeps all their invoices. Some were particularly meticulous and filed everything. But others only had their last invoices or, in order to help our project, just started to keep them after we had met them for the first time.[3]

However, even in those cases where we could only access the very recent invoices, they contained a lot of information, and we could start the conversation. As already mentioned, credit invoices do not only have transaction information for that month included in the billing period; they also contain information for all the active loans. In other words, while we cannot claim that we are reconstructing the whole history of transactions carried out with each card, like the credit issuers can do, we do with invoices get a detailed description of past transactions from which we could start a conversation. At the same time, unlike credit issuers that can only access the details of the transactions carried out with the card of their company, we could see and reconstruct the stories of the transactions made with cards from store chains and other credit sources used by the informants.

And so we sat, for instance, in the living room or kitchen listening to the story of each of the transactions mentioned in the invoices, and this is how we reconstructed the credit practices of thirteen different households situated in three low-income/low-financial-inclusion areas of Santiago.

Accounting in the Margins

Like credit cards, monthly invoices turned out to be interesting mundane objects on their own. Bills are sometimes regarded as important documents that need to be carefully filed. Invoices can also be turned into "calculative devices" on their own. Like the handwritten notes at the top of the bill in figure 9.1 show, invoices are also pieces of paper where new calculations are performed.[4] Invoices in this sense are not only a printout of past card transactions but they also play an important part – together with shopping lists and cell phone calculators (Cochoy 2007) – in the household budget planning. In other words, bills are not only traces of big data collected by lenders with the use of each credit card, they are also devices of everyday calculation (Weber 2009) on their own.

Store credit certainly does not make household economic calculations simpler. Our informants did not only have to organize their monthly salary and expenses but they also had to consider the different temporalities associated with each credit transaction. In the invoice of the example, for instance, there were transactions using twenty-four, twelve, eighteen, and six installments, all starting in different months, and some associated with the purchase of particular goods (electronic equipment or home appliances), while others were associated with cash loans. The complexity multiplies if we consider that most of the people we talked to hold cards from three, four, or five different stores simultaneously. This makes a lot to calculate! Accordingly, we found several other instruments to help in this process. For instance, some used small pieces of paper stuck to the wall to remind them about paid and unpaid installments, and others kept financial notebooks that described the status of their various financial obligations in detail.

Second Challenge: An Unexpected Finding

Our first methodological challenge was how to access the rich memory of transactions recorded by credit cards. We found that the monthly invoices of the credit cards were a nice instrument. With the invoices we could access the history of every card and initiate a conversation oriented at reconstructing the stories associated with each transaction. At the same time, credit card bills turned out to be useful instruments on their own, as they were used to calculate the household budget and financial obligations. These calculations not only revolved around the many numbers printed on the invoices but they also considered handwritten numbers added in the margins. This "accounting in the margins," however, was not only used to make sense of the numbers in the bills but also to open a whole different type of story. Check the following quotations from two different interviews:

> *Patricia:* Imagine, for instance, each installment is Ch$10.200. I give my mom eleven or twelve *lucas* [Chilean slang for Ch$1.000], I always give her a bit more because they always charge my mom for the mail service, the use of the cards, whatever damn fee they add – a thousand for this, fifteen hundred for the other. It's the same with my dad, they are always charging him five *lucas* extra, so I always give some extra money on top [of the installment amount] to my mom.

> *Luisa:* Flor, my neighbor, was slow to pay, so now I don't lend them [cards] to her, because then she takes a long time to pay and I have to pay everything myself. And afterwards, they screw you over with the card.

Patricia (names have been changed in order to keep informants' anonymity) is worried about a matter that concerns many users of department store cards in Chile. It is very difficult to calculate in advance the real cost of each installment because credit card issuers do not only charge for the loan (i.e., the price of the goods plus the interest rate attached to it) but they also attach several fees associated with issues such as the administrative maintenance of the card and various insurance policies. But Patricia's concern with those fees has to do not just with her trying to limit her expenses; she also has to figure out how much she owes her mother, Lidia, the person under whose name the card she used to get that loan is registered. Luisa, on the other hand, explains that she does not allow her neighbor to use her credit cards anymore because it took too long for her to repay, causing Luisa to have to deal with late payment penalties.

Our informants, in other words, do not only use credit cards registered under their name; they also borrow (and lend) retail credit cards to one another. There are several reasons for this, perhaps at first view, strange behavior. Even though department store credit policies are much more inclusive than those of other financial institutions such as banks, some of the people we talked to did not have access to store cards. Most of the time, they were former credit card holders who had not paid past debts and were registered as "defaulters" in the credit bureaus and therefore rejected as new customers. These people might ask to borrow a friend's, neighbor's, or family member's card when they need to buy something that was out of their reach if not bought with installments. It is also possible that a person who has credit cards of certain stores might need to use the card of another store, for instance, in order to benefit from – a quite common marketing practice in Chilean stores – sales limited only to cardholders of a specific store chain. Or, it might also be that even if you have one specific card, your credit limit is not enough to buy a particularly expensive item (for instance a new TV). Because of the behavioral credit scoring methods followed by Chilean retailers, the credit limit of a given card increases with successful repayments. In this sense, lending a card can bring the side effect of increasing its available credit.

In our study, we encountered many stories like Luisa's and Patricia's. These stories, much like those recently described by Wilkis (2014) in Argentina, Müller (2014) in Brazil, and Villarreal and Niño (2016) on the border of the United States and Mexico, do not necessarily fit into the traditional categories associated with studies of popular finance. It is not exactly financial exclusion or informal credit, like in rotating savings and credit associations (ROSCAs). Neither is it purely formal finance. The handwritten stories partially registered in the credit card invoices pointed to a parallel circuit of debt developed *on top of* or para-siting the new payment and credit card infrastructure (Ossandón 2017; Elyachar 2010). A nice existing concept for expressing card lending is that of "circuits of commerce" developed by Viviana Zelizer (2010).[5] In fact, as shown in Luisa's citation, an important part of the interviews revolved around the edges or boundaries drawn when a commitment is broken and how the limits of these circuits can be reestablished.

But our main concern here is not to explain – or, certainly, judge – the rationality behind credit card lending, or to advance the conceptual consequences of these dynamics, but rather to discuss the methodological challenges we are dealt with while studying them. But how can we analyze the unexpected information found in the margins of the monthly invoice?

Knitting Circuits of Card Lending

Circuits of card lending are a type of network, more specifically a sociotechnical formation where different actors are connected through the common use of credit cards. Therefore, like other networks, circuits can be visually depicted. But how and what might we see were we to examine the lending of credit cards as a network? What are the nodes and types of relations? How to classify the types of actors involved? To solve these questions we decided to do a small visual experiment.

The following image visualizes the case of Luisa. The red pins represent her and her husband, and the blue pins depict her daughters and sons-in-law. The large pins represent retail store cards. In this case, Luisa is the only one with cards – one from the store chain Almacenes Paris, one from Corona, and another from La Polar. The threads represent uses of a card involving some form of credit, and they connect the person who receives the loan of the card with the credit card used for the transaction. We can see that Luisa has used her three cards for personal transactions, but the same cards have also been used by her daughters and sons-in-law.

Figure 9.2. Visualization of Luisa's card-lending circuit.

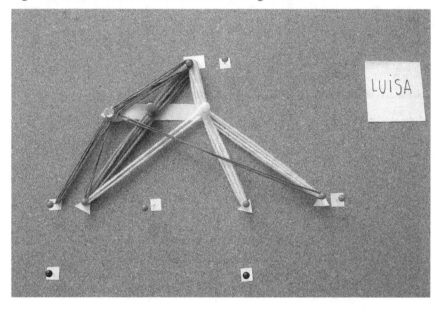

For example, Luisa lent her Paris card nine times to her daughter Andrea – three times for installment purchases of merchandise, another five times to purchase goods in the shop, and once for a cash advance consisting of six installments of Ch$15.000 each. In addition, Luisa lent her La Polar card to her daughter Andrea to buy a refrigerator and her Corona card for an advance of ten installments of Ch$10.000. Luisa also lent her La Polar card to her daughter Katya for a cash advance and for a furniture purchase and the Corona card to her daughter Paty to buy an iron in ten

Figure 9.3. Visualizations of card-lending circuits (12 cases).

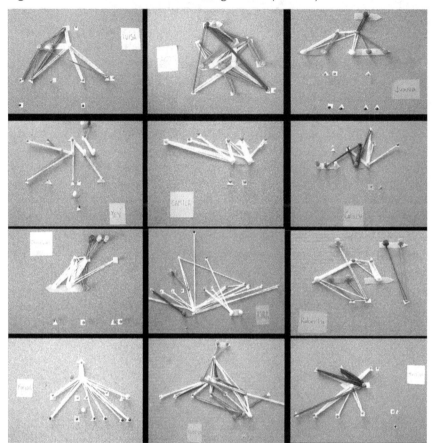

installments. On two other occasions, moreover, Luisa's son-in-law Rafael used her Corona card, once to buy himself sneakers and another time to buy a cell phone for his son.

We completed similar exercises with the other households.

Analogous Data Analysis

We are very aware that we could have used other ways to visually depict the circuits of card lending. We know our result would look more conventional and probably more convincing for an academic audience if we had used a format for our data that can be read by social network analysis software (as some of us have done in other research projects), or even if we had directly visualized the circuits digitally. But in this chapter our aim is not to black-box the manufacturing of our results; rather, our goal is the opposite: to illustrate the way we practically dealt with the methodological challenges we encountered in the process. And there were some reasons to do what we did that might be helpful for researchers dealing with similar issues in the future.

Network software packages are useful devices to work with massive amounts of data. They allow the visualization of networks composed by thousands or even millions of nodes and relations. But by using them, researchers are constrained by the affordances allowed by the software itself. As the amount of nodes and relations for each case in our study was quite small, limited to the amount of people and cards that connect them, we thought we could avoid the mediation of network analysis software altogether. Furthermore, in this research we used credit invoices to re-collect information tracked by store cards. Cards collect and produce digital data, and invoices are an outcome of this process of data production. But what we were trying to map out was not the digital information printed on the invoices but a type of data that has stayed outside the digital tracking, what we called "accounting in the margin." We thought that an analogous approach would be more consistent with the analysis of this latter kind of data.

Anthropologist Timothy Ingold (2013) has recently discussed the sometimes forgotten relevance of manual labor in social research. Research is not only sociotechnically distributed and equipped by technologies such as word processing or data analysis software, it can also be understood as a type of manual labor in which we continuously use our hands to *form* our concepts and hypotheses. Most of the time, social scientists carry out such types of activities individually (for instance when we take notes in class or when we summarize what we read in a library or café), but it is different in other fields, like architecture or design, where manual academic labor is performed in groups. We decided to embrace the flexibility afforded by using our hands and organized a way to collectively analyze our data. To find the particular way of doing that, we found inspiration in the description offered by sociologist John Law (2007) in an essay about the advantages of "pinboards" or bulletin boards as a means to think visually. In Law's words,

> My pinboard isn't of general interest, and I mention it only because it illustrates the permissive possibilities of working on a surface, flexibly, and without a very strong system of classification about what it is that goes (or doesn't go) with what. . . . The paradox is that a two-dimensional but otherwise unstructured surface is potentially quite permissive about the char-

acter of relations between the pieces arrayed upon it. Its two dimensions produce not two dimensions but many. (Law 2007, 113)

Armed with the necessary materials – cork bulletin board, yarn, and pushpins of different sizes and colors – we met in order to think visually, and tactilely, about our findings. We placed all the materials on a table, and with the notes and transcription we had collected for each case, we started finding a way to visualize the card-lending networks.

We tried different paths. For instance, we first used the large pins to represent the human actors in each case. But as we quickly realized, in these networks, the central nodes are the cards, so they should be the stronger pins. We ended up making a coding system where stores are represented with different colors and each credit transaction with yarn. Also, we ended up deciding to locate the actors as if they were in a family tree, with parents upstream and offspring downstream.

Figure 9.4. Coding pinboard.

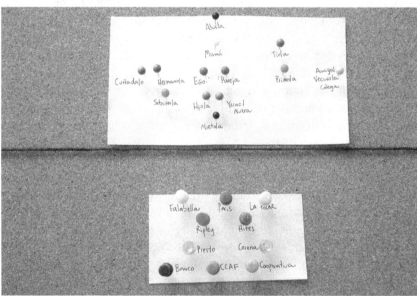

Conclusion: Studying Financial Ecologies
in between Small and Big Data

As Burrows and Savage (2014) have recently pointed out, the value of academic social research is being contested. Private firms – such as retailers, banks, or Google – or state agencies – such as the NSA as we have recently learned – produce, analyze, and visualize social data in such magnitude that is beyond the reach of the resources of academic social research. In their words, "Big Data does challenge the predominant authority of sociologists and social scientists more generally to define the nature of social knowledge" (Burrows and Savage 2014: 5). In this chapter we have shown the strategies we developed to analyze one area where social knowledge is massively produced by a complex ecology of private firms: consumer credit. More specifically, we have shown the ways in which we embraced the informational character of the cards by introducing in our inquiry a mundane trace of their activity, the monthly invoice, and how we visualized analogously the unexpected card-lending networks.

In this chapter we presented the ways in which we dealt with some practical challenges in our research. The chapter, although indirectly, deals also with a more substantive issue that we think social studies of *low* or domestic finances face more generally. Research in this field seems to be split between two types of approaches: those that, founding inspiration in recent literature on "market devices," try to reconstruct financial practices and modes of knowledge production developed by firms targeting population previously *excluded* of formal finance, and those that, inspired by recent economic anthropology, try to account or reconstruct those modes of ordinary calculation emerging with new financial products. We argue, instead, that social studies of low finance should be located *in between*: a position from where both types of knowledge and financial practices can be simultaneously observed. Elsewhere, we have discussed some of the conceptual consequences of this position (Ossandón 2017). The current chapter has focused on some of the methodological challenges. We have as yet begun to deal with the complicated ethical dilemmas this breaching position entails.

Acknowledgments

This chapter is the outcome of the research project "The Financial Ecologies and Circuits of Commerce of Retail Credit Cards in Santiago de Chile," funded by the Institute for Money, Technology & Financial Inclusion of the University of California, Irvine, whose main researcher was José Ossandón. We are very grateful for the time and help given by those who kindly shared their credit information and practices for this project. Many thanks to Orsi Husz, Morten Knudsen, Bill Maurer, Smoki Musaraj, Taylor Nelms, Trine Pallesen, and Viviana Zelizer for their comments and advice.

José Ossandón is assistant professor in the Department of Organization at the Copenhagen Business School, Frederiksberg, Denmark. He received his PhD in cultural studies from Goldsmiths, University of London.

Tomás Ariztía is associate professor of sociology at the Escuela de Sociología of the Universidad Diego Portales, Santiago, Chile. He received his PhD from London School of Economics and Political Science (LSE, London, UK).

Macarena Barros is research assistant at the Institute of Research in the Social Sciences (Instituto de Investigación en Ciencias Sociales) at the University Diego Portales, Santiago, Chile. She received her BA in anthropology from the University of Chile, Santiago.

Camila Peralta is research assistant at the Institute of Research in the Social Sciences (Instituto de Investigación en Ciencias Sociales) at the University Diego Portales, Santiago, Chile. She received an MA in social research methods from the Universidad Diego Portales, Santiago, Chile.

NOTES

1. "Financial ecologies" is a term used by geographer Andrew Leyshon and various colleagues (2004, 2006) meaning the uneven spatial distribution of financial inclusion. As they argue, close ethnographic inspection can show that behind aggregated national or regional statistics, it is possible to find, particularly, local "financial ecologies." In the same city there might be sectors of super inclusion – areas with many different bank branches and whose inhabitants comfortably pass the credit evaluations devised by the different types of financial institutions – and areas where branches are scarcer and it is still possible to find "relic" financial practices such as walking money lenders or rotating savings associations.
2. Cencosud is, in terms of sales, the biggest Latin American–owned retailer and the fifty-first largest in the world (Deloitte 2014). Cencosud is what in Chile is known as a multi-retailer (Calderón 2006), a multidivisional company made of firms that together comprise a full circuit of retail, including supermarkets, department stores, home improvement, bank, and insurance, all connected with their own payment means, in this case *Más*.
3. Some even agreed to try to recover past invoices and went to the stores to ask for them. Unfortunately, this latter project did not work very well, as the staff members that received them did not offer any help. We do not know the reason for this. It might have to do with practical reasons, for instance the people in the store did not know how to recover past invoices, or it could also have to do with the retailers' data policy. In Chile, banks are obliged to record every loan they issue in a centralized data system where other banks can see

the credit burden carried by their existing or potential customers. Retailers, instead, are only obliged to share what is normally called "negative" information – or data about defaulted loans – to the main credit bureaus of the country. Some regulators and representatives of the banking industries have been lobbying for years to change the current regulation and make both banks and retailers share positive and negative data. The retailers' representatives have defended themselves, arguing that such a change would be an illegitimate expropriation of the databases they have been collecting for years. In other words, as often happens with big data collectors, retailers see the information about their customers as one of their main assets.

4. The memory function of invoices is certainly becoming less relevant as online "banking" expands. The same is happening with department store cards in Chile. However, this feature was not yet widely used among the consumers we encountered. Future research could follow this transition.

5. Zelizer refers to circuits of economic transfers among a limited group of actors who bestow upon these transactions a shared meaning and make use of a particular means of payment, and she has paid attention to the work carried out by the actors to delimit these circuits.

REFERENCES CITED

Barros, Macarena. 2011. "Prácticas financieras en torno al uso del crédito en la industria del retail de Santiago." In *Destapando la Caja Negra: Sociologías de los créditos de consumo en Chile,* edited by José Ossandón, 113–32. Santiago: Universidad Diego Portales.

Barros, Paula. 2009. "¿Tres cuotas, precio contado? Observaciones sobre el endeudamiento de los Chilenos." In *Percepciones y actitudes sociales: 4o Informe de Encuesta Nacional UDP,* edited by Claudio Fuentes, 81–90. Santiago: Universidad Diego Portales.

Banco Central. 2013. "Encuesta Financiera de Hogares: Metodología y Principales Resultados EFH 2011-12." Santiago: Banco Central Chile.

Burrows, Roger, and Mike Savage. 2014. "After the Crisis? Big Data and the Methodological Challenges of Empirical Sociology." *Big Data and Society* 1(1): 1–6.

Calderón, Alvaro. 2006. "El modelo de expansión de las grandes cadenas minoristas chilenas." *Revista de la CEPAL* 90: 151–70.

Cochoy, Franck. 2007. "A Sociology of Market-Things: On Tending the Garden of Choices in Mass Retailing." *Sociological Review* 55(s2): 109–29.

Collins, Daryl, Jonathan Morduch, Stuart Rutherford, and Orlanda Ruthven. 2009. *Portfolios of the Poor: How the World's Poor Live on $2 a Day.* Princeton, NJ: Princeton University Press.

Deville, Joe. 2013. "Leaky Data: How Wonga Makes Lending Decisions." Charisma: Consumer Market Studies. Retrieved 12 November 2014 from http://www.charisma-network.net/finance/leaky-data-how-wonga-makes-lending-decisions.

Deloitte. 2014. *Global Powers of Retailing: Retail beyond Begins.* Retrieved 12 November 2014 from http://www.deloitte.com/view/es_CL/cl/industrias/8258448e031a3410VgnVCM2000003356f70aRCRD.htm#.

Ducourant, Hélène. 2009. "Le Crédit Revolving, unsucces populaire oul' invention de l'endetté permanent?" *Revue Sociétés contemporaines* 76: 41–65.

Elyachar, Julia. 2010. "Phatic Labor, Infrastructure, and the Question of Empowerment in Cairo." *American Ethnologist* 37(3): 452–64.

Guérin, Isabelle, Solène Morvant-Roux, and Magdalena Villarreal (eds.). 2013. *Microfinance, Debt and Over-Indebtedness: Juggling with Money*. London: Routledge.

Guseva, Alya, and Akos Rona-Tas. 2001. "Uncertainty, Risk, and Trust: Russian and American Credit Card Markets Compared." *American Sociological Review* 66 (5): 623–46.

Harper, Douglas. 2002. "Talking about Pictures: A Case for Photo Elicitation." *Visual Studies* 17 (1): 13–26.

Ingold, Timothy. 2013. *Making: Anthropology, Archaeology, Art and Architecture*. Abingdon: Routledge.

Knorr Cetina, Karin, and Alex Preda (eds.). 2012. *The Oxford Handbook of the Sociology of Finance*. Oxford: Oxford University Press.

Langley, Paul. 2014. "Consuming Credit." *Consumption Markets and Culture* 17(5): 417–28.

Latour, Bruno. 2011. "Networks, Societies, Spheres: Reflections of an Actor-Network Theorist." *International Journal of Communication* 5: 796–810.

Latour, Bruno, Pablo Jensen, Tommaso Venturini, Sébastien Grauwin, and Dominique Boullier. 2012. "'The Whole Is Always Smaller than Its Parts': A Digital Test of Gabriel Tardes' Monads." *The British Journal of Sociology* 63(4): 590–615.

Law, John. 2007. "Pinboards and Books: Learning, Materiality and Juxtaposition." In *Education and Technology: Critical Perspectives, Possible Futures*, edited by David Kritt and Lucien T. Winegar, 125–50. Lanham: Lexington Books.

Leyshon, Andrew, and Nigel Thrift. 1999. "Lists Come Alive: Electronic Systems of Knowledge and the Rise of Credit-Scoring in Retail Banking." *Economy and Society* 28(2): 434–66.

Leyshon, Andrew, Dawn Burton, David Knights, Catrina Alferodd, Paola Signoretta. 2004. "Towards an Ecology of Retail Financial Services: Understanding the Persistence of Door-to-Door Credit and Insurance Providers." *Environment and Planning A* 36 (4): 625–45.

Leyshon, Andrew, Paola Signoretta, David Knights, Catrina Alferodd, and Dawn Burton. 2006. "Walking with Moneylenders: The Ecology of the UK Home-Collected Credit Industry." *Urban Studies* 43(1): 161–86.

Luhmann, Niklas. 1982. "The Economy as a Social System." In *The Differentiation of Society*, Niklas Luhmman, 190–225. New York: Columbia University Press.

Marres, Noortje, and Esther Weltevrede. 2013. "Scraping the Social? Issues in Live Social Research." *Journal of Cultural Economy* 6(3): 313–35.

Maurer, Bill. 2012, "The Disunity of Finance: Alternative Practices to Western Finance." In *The Oxford Handbook of Sociology of Finance*, edited by Karin Knorr Cetina and Alex Preda, Oxford: Oxford University Press.

Maurer, Bill, Taylor C. Nelms, and Stephen C. Rea. 2013. "'Bridges to Cash': Channeling Agency in Mobile Money." *Journal of the Royal Anthropological Institute* 19(1): 52–74.

Montgomerie, Johnna. 2006. "The Financialization of the American Credit Card Industry." *Competition and Change* 10(3): 311–19.

Moulian, Tomás. 1998. *El Consumo me consume.* Santiago: LOM.

Müller, Lucia. 2014. "Negotiating Debts and Gifts: Financialization Policies and the Economic Experiences of Low-Income Social Groups in Brazil." *Vibrant: Virtual Brazilian Anthropology* 11(1): 191–221.

Muniesa, Fabian, Yuval Millo, and Michel Callon. 2007. "An Introduction to Market Devices." *The Sociological Review* 55(s2): 1–12.

Ossandón, José. 2012. "Quand le crédit à la consommation classe les gens et les choses: Une revue de littérature et un programme de recherché." *Revue française de socio-Economie* 9(1): 83–100.

———. 2014. "Sowing Consumers in the Garden of Mass Retailing in Chile." *Consumption Markets and Culture* 17(5): 429–47.

———. 2017. "My Story Has No Strings Attached: Credit Cards, Market Devices and a Stone Guest." In *Markets and the Arts of Attachment,* edited by Franck Cochoy, Joe Deville, and Liz McFall, 132–46. London: Routledge.

Ossandón, José (ed.). 2011. *Destapando la Caja Negra: Sociologías de los créditos de consumo en Chile.* Santiago: Universidad Diego Portales.

Poon, Martha. 2011. "Historicizing Consumer Credit Risk Calculations: The Fair Isaac System of Commercial Scorecard Manufacture, 1957–circa 1980." In *Technological Innovation in Retail Finance: International Historical Perspectives,* edited by Bernardo Bátiz-Lazo, J. Carles Maixé-Altés, and Paul Thomes, 221–45. New York: Routledge.

Rona-Tas, Akos, and Stefanie Hiss. 2010. "The Role of Ratings in the Subprime Mortgage Crisis: The Art of Corporate and the Science of Consumer Credit Ratings." In *Markets on Trial: The Economic Sociology of the U.S. Financial Crisis; Part A (Research in the Sociology of Organizations, Volume 30 Part A),* edited by Michael Lounsbury and Paul M. Hirsch, 115–55. Bingley: Emerald Group Publishing.

Savage, Mike, and Roger Burrows. 2007. "The Coming Crisis of Empirical Sociology." *Sociology* 41(5): 885–99.

Savage, Mike. 2009. "Contemporary Sociology and the Challenge of Descriptive Assemblage." *European Journal of Social Theory* 12(1): 155–74.

Stearns, David. 2011. "Electronic Value Exchange: Origins of the Visa Electronic Payment System." In *Technological Innovation in Retail Finance: International Historical Perspectives,* edited by Bernardo Bátiz-Lazo, J. Carles Maixé-Altés, and Paul Thomes, 221–45. New York: Routledge.

Villarreal, Magdalena. 2014. "Regimes of Value in Mexican Household Financial Practices." *Current Anthropology* 55(S9): S30–39.

Villareal, Magdalena, and Lya Niño. 2016. "Financial Practices on 'the Borderlands' (La Línea) in Times of Crisis." *Human Organization* 75(2): 151–58.

Weber, Florence. 2009. "Le calcul économique ordinaire." In *Traité de sociologie économique,* edited by Philippe Steiner and François Vatin, 367–407. Paris: PUF.

Wilkis, Ariel. 2014. "Sociología del Crédito y Economía de las Clases Populares." *Revista Mexicana de Sociología* 76(2): 225–52.

Zelizer, Viviana. A. 2010. *Economic Lives: How Culture Shapes the Economy.* Princeton, NJ: Princeton University Press.

Part IV

Design and Practice

JOSHUA E. BLUMENSTOCK

As mobile phones and related technologies become increasingly common in even the most remote parts of the world, new modalities have emerged to connect hitherto marginalized individuals and communities to formal financial services and institutions. This opportunity has not been lost on policymakers or the private sector, and hundreds of initiatives are currently underway that attempt to replicate M-PESA, the successful mobile-money program created by Safaricom in Kenya. However, most of these initiatives have struggled to attract and sustain an active base of customers. The reasons for such struggles are manifold, and in many instances the regulatory environment and other macro factors undermine carefully designed technologies for financial inclusion.

However, as the authors in this part each articulate in a different way, the tensions that arise most often at the technological interface between money and people occur at the micro level, when one size only fits some, and when design does not meet practice. Indeed, this is a theme that reverberates throughout this volume, so it is fitting to conclude with four chapters that bring into focus the many frictions, as well as the occasional successes, that arise when an existing financial interface is transported from one context to another. For, as these chapters show, many of the most evocative and powerful narratives around money, and the possible role for technology in such cases, exist at the margin.

Here we encounter four technologies enduring the growing pains of adoption, in four very different settings around the globe: game networks in Colombia, business correspondents in India, a conditional cash-transfer program in rural Philippines, and social payments in Ethiopia. In each case the authors move from careful ethnography to a set of insights that can inform the design of technologies for financial inclusion. What is quite remarkable is that despite the geographic and cultural distances that separate these different communities, the conclusions are markedly similar.

Echeverry and Cuartas dissect the success of Colombian game networks, a system of point-of-sale operators who initially facilitated ticket sales but now support a range of financial transactions. Through in-context interviews with street sellers in Medellin, the authors work toward a series of design guidelines for new financial applications. "Proximity, immediacy, and simplicity" is perhaps the most emphatic recommendation that emerges, in part because it resonates in each of the other chapters in this part. For the informal workers, microtransactions have tangible appeal and perhaps offer an entry point to credit and other financial services, but only insofar as they serve the need to "purchase, pay, send, and save in small amounts and without having to leave their workplace." For workers who are constantly on the move and who have little to save at the end of the day, a means to micro-accumulate is a promising complement to the existing formal services that are slow and laden with bureaucratic restrictions.

Nandhi's account of the EKO mobile banking system carries this same theme to the study of low-income workers in Delhi. Here, Nandhi documents the need for "convenience, efficiency, and flexibility," noting that 73 percent of those surveyed ascribe their increased savings to the fact that EKO has allowed them to make smaller and more frequent transactions. For instance, in one of the case studies in the chapter, we encounter a small shopkeeper who uses microdeposits to avoid temptation goods. Absent EKO, he tells us, the petty cash would have been kept on hand and used for more whimsical expenditures. Access to EKO, however, helps him to gradually accumulate microdeposits until he has sufficient funds to convert the balance into other savings instruments such as a ROSCA (rotating savings and credit association). In this way, Nandhi's shopkeeper exemplifies a second theme that all of the chapters in this part touch upon: the strong complementarities that exist between new financial technologies (in this case, EKO), and existing formal and informal systems (such as the group savings account or *gulak* piggy banks).

The juxtaposition of old and new systems of money is perhaps most striking in Gusto and Roque's account of indigenous people in the Philippines, where a government-aid program is providing several communities with their first regular and formal engagement with currency and banking. "Indigenous people beneficiaries," the authors note, "must be appreciated as a new and unique client segment that is economically vulnerable, with relatively low levels of education and who are still likely to be more comfortable operating in the informal sector." Yet here again we see that as currency is injected into the society, it is integrated so as to complement the existing barter-based socioeconomic ecosystem. Thus, "upon receiving the [cash transfer], they specifically spend it for their children's education and health expenses. When it is all used up . . . they go back to doing barter." The new system and the old thus coexist, though the complementarities are delicate and Gusto and Roque end on a note of caution. The critical juxtaposition here is not just between formal and informal but also between those who have access to both systems and those who do not. Thus far a strong sense of solidarity has encouraged the individual beneficiaries to redistribute newfound formal currency within the community; we are warned, however, that this may not be a sustainable equilibrium.

Complex systems of formal and informal exchange are likewise the focus of Woldmariam Mesfin's careful analysis of social payments among the poor in rural Ethiopia. In his account, Mesfin provides rich detail on the norms regarding gifts and payments around weddings and funerals, the processes that have evolved to document social debts and favors, and of how "families compete for social prestige" through the act of giving. When current practices of monetary exchange are so deeply enshrined in social interaction, it is perhaps difficult to envision a new technology that could capture such nuance. However, Mesfin's narrative follows a parallel trajectory to that of Echeverry and Cuartas, working from a detailed ethnography to a normative discussion around the design of appropriate mobile-money services. It is fitting, then, to observe several of the themes common to this part reflected in Mesfin's guidelines: the need for small and flexible contributions in Ethiopia, for instance, evokes the mandate for "proximity, immediacy, and simplicity" from the chapter set in Medellin.

Together, the chapters in this part thus provide a powerful glimpse into several communities struggling at the interface between money and technology. There are cases of successful integration – for instance, when strong communal norms stimulate redistribution or when microdeposits enable savings accumulation – but there are also many tensions and frictions. Each in a different way, we see the communities react against the rigid formalities of the current iteration of the technology. In Colombia it is the bureaucratic complexity and onus of documentation that overwhelms informal workers; in India, an illiterate rickshaw puller is intimidated by the user interface and for a long time is prevented from registering; for indigenous people in the Philippines, "it was hard to tell how many of the beneficiaries actually knew how to count or recognize the numbers on the ATM keypads. One thing was for certain: they . . . were scared that something might go wrong."

That such challenges materialize during a community's initial encounter with a new technology is not unexpected. Nor is it surprising that two parallel recommendations emerge: to remove complexity from the system and to ensure that new technologies complement existing modes of economic exchange and accumulation. However, to see these correlated insights resonate in four vastly different contexts is a powerful reminder of the chasm between current design and current practice.

Joshua E. Blumenstock is an assistant professor at the UC Berkeley School of Information and the director of the Data-Intensive Development Lab. His research focuses on developing new methods for using massive, spatiotemporal network data to better understand poverty and economic development. Previously, Dr. Blumenstock was on the faculty at the University of Washington, where he founded and codirected the Data Science and Analytics Lab, and led the school's Data for Social Good initiative. He has a PhD in information science and an MA in economics from UC Berkeley, and bachelor's degrees in computer science and physics from Wesleyan University. He is a recipient of the Intel Faculty Early Career Honor, a Gates Millennium Grand Challenge award, and a Google Faculty Research Award, and was a former fellow of the Thomas J. Watson Foundation and the Harvard Institutes of Medicine.

CHAPTER 10

Understanding Social Relations and Payments among Rural Ethiopians

WOLDMARIAM F. MESFIN

Due to the high cost and risks of running formal financial institutions in rural areas of the developing world, a large fraction of the population in these countries has been de facto excluded from the official financial sector (Duncombe and Boateng 2009; Kristof 2010; Rutherford 1999). In this context and given the rapid growth and penetration of mobile phone technologies across the developing world, the potential for mobile banking has attracted the attention of telecommunication companies, development and aid NGOs, research centers, and governmental bodies. For this conglomeration of actors, mobile money has the potential to provide the poor with alternative means of accessing financial services.

In a growing number of developing countries, policymakers, philanthropists, and industry professionals have claimed that mobile communication is enabling individuals to link their monetary needs and practices to various forms of financial services in unexpected and innovative ways (Kristof 2010; Maurer 2010). For these actors, the remarkable accomplishments of the pioneers of mobile-money systems, such as GCASH in the Philippines and M-PESA in Kenya, may be a sign of the future promise of mobile money (Kristof 2010). This digital revolution is creating tremendous possibilities within the space of money and finance (Mainwaring 2010). On a conceptual level, this shift toward mobile money also raises questions about the implications of this material transformation of money – from cash to digital – on everyday behaviors. But researchers and designers have yet to develop concrete frameworks and strategies for addressing these questions and for shaping this space of money and finance (Maurer 2010; Sterling and Zimmerman 2007). As noted in the introduction to this volume, to address some of these questions, it is crucial to pay attention to the ways in which the long-studied social, cultural, and religious meanings and functions of money come to bear upon the new designs of monetary forms.

In this chapter, I therefore explore existing monetary practices of individuals who live in mostly a cash economy in Ethiopia. I hope this study can provide a blueprint for future designs of mobile money or other forms of financial technologies aimed at financial inclusion.

Despite their lack of access to official financial services such as bank accounts and loans, people operating entirely in a cash economy also have developed elaborate ways of managing money and value (for example, see Guyer 1995; Maurer 2013). For instance, in the rural areas of Ethiopia where this study takes place, individuals differentiate their money based on color, physical size, and material. If electronic payment systems are to replace currency objects, it would then be crucial to gain a better understanding of existing practices of stashing, retrieving, sharing, spending, and saving as a means of designing more inclusive mobile-money systems that build upon (rather than substitute) existing financial practices and institutions.

Despite the abundance of studies in social science on the multiple social and cultural meanings of money and market exchange (Akin and Robbins 1999; Appadurai 1988; Carrier 1995; Guyer 1995; Hart 2001; Maurer 2006; Mauss 1922; Parry and Bloch 1989; Zelizer 1997), so far few studies and initiatives in the sphere of mobile-money services pay heed to the relationship between money and sociocultural institutions (Duncombe and Boateng 2009; Singh 1997). Motivated by this knowledge gap, I investigate in this chapter practices among the rural Ethiopians that illustrate the various forms, functions, and meanings of money in everyday life; specifically the systematic differentiation of payments for funerals and other social rituals into visible (documented) and invisible (undocumented) money-mediated transactions; the mediation of such payments (and non-payments) by the community savings clubs, the *edir*; the personalization of money gifts; the segregated cash-controlling practices; and the practices of refusal to accept some money "gifts." Better understanding of these practices enables providers to design new financial services and technologies (e.g., mobile-money systems) that fulfill a wider range of purposes.

Theoretical Framework

In order to meet life's challenges, individuals establish and constantly need to negotiate social relationships with the intention of generating both tangible and intangible social, psychological, emotional, and economic benefits in the short and long term (Foster 1963). Depending on the nature of the relationships and the kinds of things exchanged, Foster (1963) identified three different types of dyadic contracts/relationships. The first is one among individuals of a comparable socioeconomic status who exchange relatively similar kinds of goods and services. Such relationships are created during important life-cycle events, as when people are expected to share the costs of a funeral or a wedding or are bracing for the unexpected costs of a natural or man-made catastrophe. The second type of relationship can be created between individuals of unequal rank and/or wealth; this is also known as a patron-client relationship.[1] The third type of relationship is one between individual clients and supernatural beings and/or their manifestations. These also resemble the form of client-patron relationship, but here the deities play the role of the patron. Continuing patron-client contracts[2] with supernatural beings are best seen in daily prayers and the lighting of candles. In this chapter, I use these three types of relationships as a guideline for organizing the exchanges of monetary gifts and payments that I experienced on the ground during my field research in rural Ethiopia.

Traditionally, social exchange theory drew a stark distinction between commodity and gift exchange (for instance, see Gregory 1982; Malinowski 1922; Mauss 1922). One key contribution of Mauss's theory of the gift has been to broaden our understanding of gift exchange as involving much more than the simple equivalence of the goods transfer, seeing it also as mediating, negotiating, even creating relations. Mauss's analysis further claimed that gift exchange was not simply uninterested giving but an activity organized around the obligations to give, to accept, and to reciprocate a gift. Foster (1963) and Mauss (1922) theorize the different types of relationships discussed above as dyadic contracts that bind pairs of individuals through reciprocal obligations expressed in the exchange of goods and services. Each gift imposes an obligation over the receiver to give back to the giver.

Over the last two decades, however, the distinction between "gift" and "commodity" has been challenged at its core. Researchers across regions and disciplines have come to argue that commodity and gift forms of exchange are deeply intertwined. Noncommodity valuables are often used as a form of currency, while money itself serves multiple social, moral, and religious purposes (for instance, see Appadurai 1988; Maurer 2006; Parry and Bloch 1989; Zelizer 1997). Anthropologists of Africa, in particular, have underscored the point that (a) throughout history, various other valuables have been used as a form of currency and that (b) money itself is not just used for market exchange but also mediates social relations, rank, and hierarchies (Guyer 1995; Piot 1999; Shipton 2007).

The research conducted in rural Ethiopia echoes some of these findings and theoretical observations. To address these phenomena on the ground, this chapter draws on Bill Maurer's discussion of special monies, which broadly refers to "quasi-currencies, alternative currencies, and objects of wealth like land, livestock, vehicles, capital equipment, jewelry and special ritual items that can serve some or all of money's classic functions" (2010b:7). This chapter works with this notion of "special monies" (in commodity and noncommodity form) and the various functions and meanings of different types of monetary payments to explore the complex financial institutions and practices already existing on the ground. Thus, a number of items exchanged in the practices I observed fulfill the function of money, including cereals, labor and wood, food, spices, local alcohol, cash, coffee, tea, oil, sugar, cattle (sheep), honey, bread, cattle, umbrellas, candles, and church clothing. In the following I therefore explore how these are exchanged and how they organize the various types of relations in the communities discussed.

Study Site: Rural Ethiopia

This study focuses on rural Ethiopians. Research was conducted among the population living in an area 230 kilometers (around 140 miles) southeast of the capital, Addis Ababa. The research site has a population of more than 1,000 households. These households are largely dependent on traditional farming for subsistence. Their income comes primarily from the sale of cereals and cattle. Their farming is entirely dependent on rainfall, which varies from season to season. Whenever rainfall varies in its timing and quantity, farmers' productivity can decline significantly. The local population is composed of both Christians (Orthodox) and Muslims, but this study gathered data solely from key Christian informants, from the Amhara and Oromo ethnic groups. The respondents of the study also indicated that Muslims also have a similar practice.

The study site suffers from poor infrastructure. The informants in the study face a great difficulty in gaining access to financial institutions and services given that there are no banks or insurance companies within a 55-kilometer (34-mile) range. Thus, to deposit money in a bank account, one would have to travel a minimum of 110 kilometers (68 miles) (round trip), spend at least one night in another town, and often encounter difficulties arranging their return trip. In other words, in order to make a bank deposit, this individual would have to also pay for transportation to the nearest town and hotel accommodation. As a result of these costs, most farmers do not save money in banks. As a consequence, they noted during my conversations, they often spend money on trivial and unplanned things such as tobacco and alcoholic drinks.

Another infrastructural problem is lack of access to education, especially secondary and tertiary education. Students have to travel more than seventeen kilometers round trip on a daily basis. As a result, both students and their families prefer that they not go to school at all. This leads to an overall lack of reading, writing, or textual literacy. But, as the time goes, this is changing. Government is opening primary education schools proximate to farmers.

At the same time, individuals do have access to mobile telecommunication services even when lacking a fixed telephone line. The informants of the study indicated a high demand for mobile phones. Still, they also note that they frequently encounter problems with recharging their mobile battery and buying airtime, as there is no electrical service or airtime service providers nearby. Even the researcher could not recharge his mobile phone during the data collection.[3]

This study identified the following practices with regard to money exchange: (a) some money transactions are documented while others are undocumented; the former are often mediated by local savings associations, and the latter are usually remembered by the exchanging parties; (b) money gifts and other forms of "special monies" (Maurer 2010b) are frequently used to make payments for funerals, weddings, and other rituals; the distribution of these gifts follows the principles of obligations to accept and reciprocate as discussed in the classic form of gift-giving (Mauss 1922); yet, gifts may be also be refused; (c) individuals assign different labels and meanings to their monies in order to fulfill their social, cultural, and religious obligations. The following section discusses the major social relationship types and their money-exchange practices.

Social Payments among Individuals of Comparable Economic Status

Individuals with comparable economic status and rank create relationships to assist one another in times of emergency (such as death and crisis) and to share particular life experiences, such as weddings, birthdays, and other ritual ceremonies.

The Dynamics of **Edir**: *Saving for Funerals through Community Savings Associations*

Social support is most often associated with "strong" ties between kin, neighbors, and intimate friends. These ties generally provide individuals with emotional and expressive support as well as other forms of instrumental help such as loans, cattle, and rides (Dominguez and Watkins 2003). To assist one another during the event of a death within the family, individuals of the research site create formal association called *edir*, which can be established by male and female members of the households separately (male's *edir* and female's *edir*). In both types of *edir*, members make monthly contributions in cash or other valuable items such as wood, alcoholic drinks, spices, or cereals. In order to administer the association and monthly contributions and other assets, members nominate respected and relatively educated persons as their chairpersons and secretaries to serve the association for one or two years.

Edir helps members pay for the cost of funerals. The amount of *edir* contribution depends upon the nature of the death, i.e., whether the funeral is held in the home or when a person dies outside the local village and requires an out-of-household funeral. When the funeral is in the household, the male *edir* provides the family of the deceased with cash (the amount varies from *edir* to *edir*), cereals, labor, and wood, while the female *edir* will provide food, spices, local alcohol, cash, or labor. Cash collected from both the male and female *edir* is used to purchase items such as coffee, tea, oil, and sugar. These latter items are usually consumed by the visiting guests.

When a member of an *edir* experiences a death within his or her family, the chairperson and secretary of the *edir* will announce the event to other members so that they can bring in the noted items to the affected family. In addition, some individuals will be assigned to shoulder the dead body, and some others (usually women) assist with the cooking. Attendance will be taken in order to identify the presence or absence of members and discern who has contributed the necessary cash and other materials in the name of the *edir*. The money and materials that come from each member are also recorded or documented. In the event of an out-of-household funeral, families will receive only half of the amount allotted to an in-house funeral.

To become a member of an *edir*, one can simply apply at the members' monthly meeting where all the members have an equal say on accepting or rejecting the application. Before one is admitted, members verify whether the applicant has previously participated in another *edir*. Membership in an *edir* is nonexclusive, and one may be a member of many *edir* concurrently. The committee also verifies that the incoming person has no conflicts with any of its members. If a dispute is found between the incoming person and a member of an *edir,* the case is handled before the

Figure 10.1. Sample *mezgeb* recording monthly contributions to an *edir.*

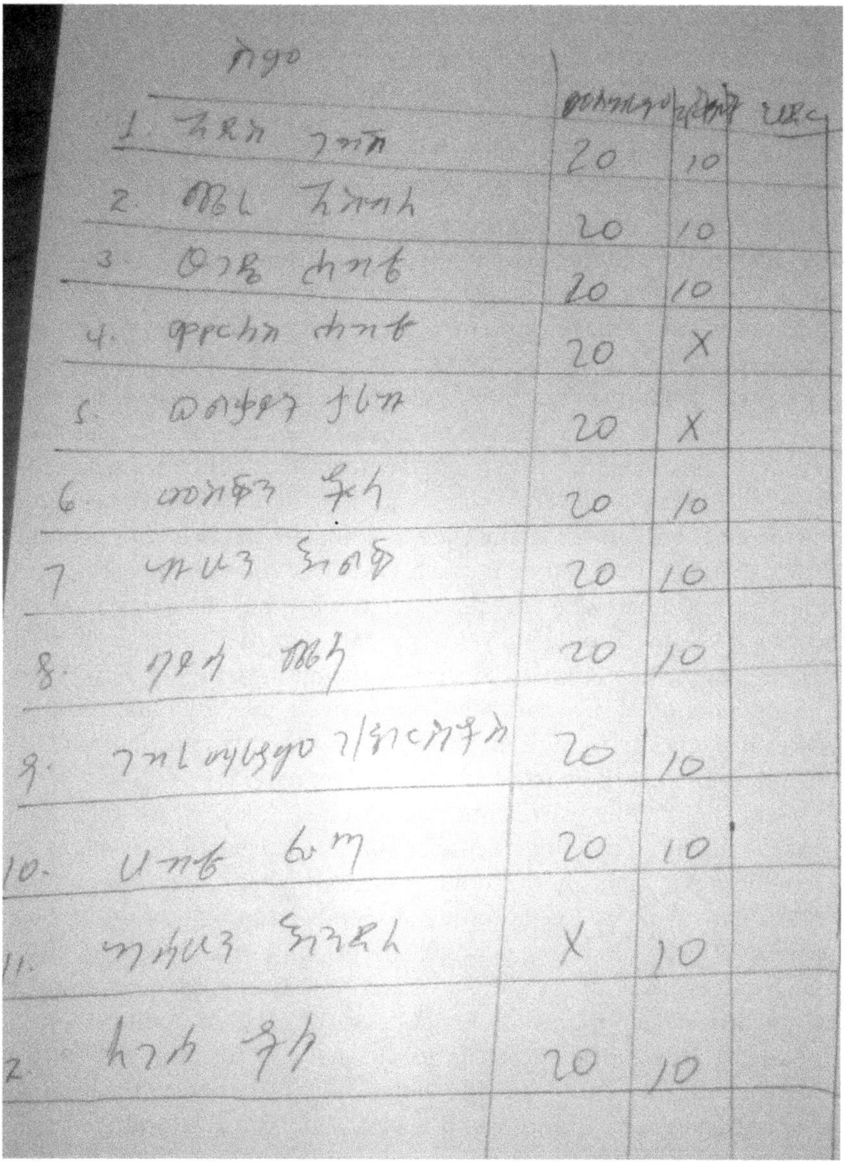

Photo by author.

admission of the applicant is finalized. Finally, the incoming person is required to pay the proportion of assets that members have contributed previously and that is currently available as inventory. The payment can be made in the form of installments. After completing this payment, the incoming person is entitled to get every benefit provided to the existing members.

Each month, members gather at one of their homes (on a rotating basis), hold a discussion, and make their monthly contributions. The host of this gathering will prepare food items and local alcoholic drinks. Meeting discussions focus on issues like deaths, new members, departing members, and monthly contributions. The monthly contribution is recorded in a book called *mezgeb* (see figure 10.1), which contains lists of members and monthly contributions. In the process, two individuals are involved: the chairperson and the secretary of the *edir*. These two individuals cross-check the contributed cash against the record, calculate total contributions made, announce the amount to the gathered members, and sign the *mezgeb* (which closes the contribution for the month, preventing latecomers from contributing after the meeting has ended). At the end, the chairperson retains the cash while the secretary retains the record, *mezgeb*. The names of absent members are marked with an X, and they are required to pay additional money in their contribution of the following month. Later the secretary announces where the *edir* will meet the following month.

At the end of the meeting, intimate friends or relatives leave the host's residence and invite one another out (often for the whole day). After accepting such invitations, individuals report that they feel they have invested too much emotionally in these social outings. Hence, being aware of the possibility of such extended invitations, some individuals send delegates (usually their children) to pay their monthly contribution. This technique enables them to avoid extended invitations.

Membership from an *edir* may be revoked due to work relocation, physical inability, repetitive abuse of rules and regulations (such as the inability to pay monthly contributions in cash or in kind), and conflicts with other members. In the event of membership revocation, the *edir* provides a written letter explaining the person's problematic behavior, effectively blacklisting an individual and preventing other *edir* from accepting his or her application should he or she apply for membership.

Based on these data, it is safe to say that *edir* function as a sort of insurance mechanism, organized along similar lines to other forms of informal savings associations in other parts of Africa and other regions of the world.[4]

Money Gifts and Social Relations in Funeral Payments

In the event of a funeral, individuals extend their support by giving cash to families of the deceased. The amount of these gifts of cash varies depending on the recipient's financial need and the intimacy of their relationship. Cash amounts usually vary from two birr (one U.S. cent) to ten birr (fifty U.S. cents).[5] The recipient uses this cash as a means to measure his reputation and community standing. This money is called *yazentega.*

Unlike payments to the *edir,* the amount of these money gifts and names of the givers are not documented formally on paper by the receiver. Even the act of paying the money gift is performed in secret manner. Further, the givers and the receivers do not count this money in front of others. The receiver memorizes this transaction instead of recording it formally on paper.

According to the respondents, there are many reasons for the secret giving and receiving process of *yazentega.* These include (1) not wanting to boast in public; (2) the fact that, as the gifts are made at different times and places, the recipient may not be able to easily record them; (3) concern that if the amount is somewhat small, individuals giving the cash will feel shame seeing it recorded; (4) the way that individuals visit the affected person because of moral obligation and, hence, if the money given is going to be recorded, individuals having no money will feel shame; and (5) because, in principle, this gift is not necessarily reciprocal.

Informants report that, in places such as Wolaita, such transactions are indeed recorded.[6] A pen or pencil and paper are provided to the giver to write his name and amount he would like to give. This document will be used as a reference to repay sometime in the future.

These explanations suggest that, although presented in a commodity form (cash), these money gifts take on some of the key characteristics of the classic forms of the gift exchange as outlined early on by anthropologists Marcel Mauss (1922) and Marshall Sahlins (1974). In particular, as I will discuss further, these accounts underscore the application of the three obligations intrinsic to the gift (to give, to accept, and to reciprocate the gift) (Mauss 1922) and of the generalized and balanced reciprocity (Sahlins 1974). At the same time, as I also suggest below, some of these rules are often broken, and when this happens, one gains insight into other aspects of organizing relations in the community.

When individuals give *yazentega,* they say *egziabher yatsngh,* which means, "Let God give you the strength to forget the death." In turn, the receiving person responds by *bealem yemeles,* meaning, "I wish your gift repaid on joyful events." This dialogue indicates that such a money gift is also a promise and obligation for a future repayment during other events such as weddings, birth dates, and college graduations (Homans 1958). In other words, the act of gift-giving here implies an obligation to reciprocate in an undetermined future and amount.

These gifts are not exchanged among pairs of individuals, but they are instead exchanged in a form of generalized reciprocity – individuals give with the expectation of some form of future return. Thus, not all individuals in the family receive *yazentega*. For example, when a wife or husband dies, their children (above the age of eighteen, married or unmarried) and the surviving spouse receive *yazentega* from their relatives. At the same time, the original families (mother, father, brothers, and sisters above eighteen) of the dead living outside the village can receive *yazentega* from their own local community. *Yazentega* is given anywhere (at the individual's home or at church during burial time) and any time after the burial, sometimes even more than a year after the death of a person, as individuals may come from a distant location when it is feasible for them.

When a family member dies, the surviving members do not eat anything before the dead is buried. After the burial, all individuals are expected to accompany the family of the deceased back home. When reaching the home of the deceased, accompanying individuals are offered food (*enjera, nifro, arkie*),[7] bread, tea, and coffee. These individuals express a feeling of shame if they are not able to give some money to compensate for what they have eaten and drunk, and so they give *yazentega*. Once again, this suggests that money gifts are obligatory and that they are seen as part of a system of reciprocal exchanges within the community.

Keeping with the principle of the obligation to accept a gift, one does not refuse *yazentega*. But if one does (and, as I found out, this happens frequently), the refusal can be understood in different ways. One common reason is that a serious dispute exists between the dead and the family member who survives them. The locals call this *ergiman*, which means these individuals had poor relations and both of them promised not to accept resources from each other or to their names. Thus, when one of them dies, they want to respect the oath and refuse to accept *yazentega* gifts. In this case, the person still living refuses gifts from all individuals. Another reason for a refusal of *yazentaga* is that some sort of quarrel may have occurred between the deceased and the family member. And finally, a less common reason is that relatively richer individuals sometimes refuse *yazentega* gifts from poor. This is considered an insult to the giver (Kochuyt 2009). In this case, members of the community assume they have been undermined and automatically alienate individuals who refuse gifts from other social affairs. In other words, irrespective of wealth, everyone has both a moral and practical obligation to accept *yazentega* and to reciprocate. "It is the attitude of the individuals, not the money, that matters," said one respondent. In addition, since the givers accompany the money gift with the wish *egziabher yatsngh,* refusing could be interpreted as an inappropriate expression of happiness about the death.

Although this cash gift is not recorded and repayment is optional in principle, Thomas and Worrall (2002) call it "uncertain counter reciprocity." In practice, individuals of this research site claim their repayments. If a person is financially capable of repayment but fails to do so, he risks losing his reputation and community standing and confronts possibly being sued in court or at *edir,* being badmouthed, and jeopardizing friendships. But if failure is due to real financial incapability and a good relationship persists, then the person may be given tasks so that he can repay through labor or with a more intangible asset like gratitude, love, esteem, and loyalty (Lebra 1975). In this scenario, the richer individual recognizes his power over the poorer, in which case such gifts reinforce the hierarchical relations between the two parties (Mauss 1922).

According to the rule of reciprocity, the nature and volume of the countergift determines the balance of power between the two individuals. If the return takes the form of cash but in a smaller amount, or if it takes a nonmonetary or even a noncommodity form (such as showing gratitude or loyalty), one implicitly resigns him- or herself to a relationship of dependency toward the other person (Kochuyt 2009). Reciprocity can have positive and negative effects: those who give more will receive more in return, and those who do not give much are also the poorest receivers (Homans 1958; Komter 1996).

Limited financial resources for some individuals can leave expectations for reciprocity unmet, generating increased tension and potentially leading to dissolution of relationships. This means that maintaining a balanced reciprocity of payments plays a crucial role in managing and sustaining relationships (Dominguez and Watkins 2003). To overcome the problem of financial incapability, givers assess the recipients' financial worthiness and capacity for repayment. A social relationship between individuals living in extreme poverty is frequently marked by ambivalence and distrust (Lee 1970). But sometimes situations arise in which individuals give more than the financial capacity of receivers. In this case, unless the receivers give something back, the relationship between the two will be affected; social gift-giving is a prerequisite for establishing good relationships (Mauss 1922; Kochuyt 2009).

There are two different attitudes toward attendance of individuals at funeral ceremonies in the course of this study. Within the Amhara ethnic group, physically able individuals should visit families of the deceased immediately upon hearing of the death and participate accordingly. But if one is working or living at distance, she or he can visit within a reasonable time period, usually within two months. This ethnic group does not accept any money sent through delegates. The researcher was informed that these ethnic groups value the physical presence of a person more than the money he gives. Hence, irrespective of distance, individuals must be physically present and express their concern to the family of the deceased. But for someone living outside the village, physical presence may be costly due to transportation and related expenses. Although these individuals value the physical presence of someone on such occasion, they will still expect the usual money gift of *yazentega*.

In contrast, informants of the Oromo ethnic group report that as long as individuals get *yazentega*, even if it comes through a delegate, families of the dead person might not care about the physical presence of distant people.

Money received in the form of *yazentega* is kept separately from the rest. This is to calculate how much the family received from the community. Once they have determined the total amount, a family pools this money and can use it without restrictions.

Social Relationships and Payments for Weddings

During wedding celebrations, individuals make social payments or gifts. Common forms of payment include (1) gifts to the mother and father of the groom and bride by their local community; (2) gifts to the groom and bride by their respective families (mother, father, sisters, cousins, grandparents, aunts, and brothers); and (3) gifts to the groom and bride by their respective colleagues. The following section discusses the types of money gifts given during weddings.

First, when planning a wedding, the respective families of the groom and bride inform their extended families well in advance to bring those gifts. Such gifts can be cash, cattle, or goods such as CD players, beds, blankets, chairs, and furniture. Unlike payments and gifts given during funerals (which happen suddenly), those given for weddings are prepared in advance, they are somewhat bigger, and it is obligatory for the receivers to repay at the time of other social events. Wedding gifts are consequently recorded on paper, something similar to figure 10.1. To make such collections, two individuals are assigned to record the amount of gifts and givers' names: one records the transaction, the other collects the cash. At the end of the ceremony (which can run for up to three days), these two persons cross-check the actual cash against the record and hand over the document and the cash to the families hosting the wedding. The document provides the event name (e.g., wedding), date, list of gift givers, and amounts given. After reviewing this document, a newly married couple or their parents are expected to return back the same amount or more than what they received. According to Lebra (1975), such a relationship is characterized as complimentary – mutual dependence exists between the gift givers and the newlyweds in whom both groups require the supply and demand in the two directions to match.

People planning a wedding leverage the practice of "balanced reciprocity" (Sahlins 1974) in calculating what items and amounts were previously given and what should be collected in return. Essentially, when people receive payments for a wedding, they assume the payment as debt and start thinking about repayment. If the recipients fail to repay, they will be taken to an *edir* and sometimes to court. As a result, their *edir* memberships may be revoked, and the wronged party may pursue the claim in court.

The other type of gift is given by relatives of the groom and bride. Contributions of this type include perfume, clothes, kitchen materials, and money to cover part of the wedding expenses. These gifts are covered with wrapping paper, and the giver personalizes the item by labeling it with their name. The giving and receiving of these of gifts usually involves some ceremony.

The informants of this study indicated some recent changes regarding social payments for weddings and funerals. As the cost of living has become higher, the community leaders have begun to advise individuals against spending too much (compared to the family's income level) for these important events. Some of the informants, however, disagree with such rules and insist on spending large sums of money anyway. For example, older individuals recall how their relatives celebrated funerals and weddings in the past and lament, "How can I spend less than those individuals?" According to one informant, some also assert that the very purpose of wealth is to use it during such events. Families compete for social prestige (Van der Geest 2000) by using large amounts of money for funeral and marriage ceremonies.

The attitude of the local community is that rich individuals should spend more for events like funerals and weddings. If rich individuals decline to spend much on these events, the community may undermine them, consider them to be greedy, isolate them from social affairs, and fail to assist them in difficult situations.

Social Payments among Individuals of Different Rank

The informants of this study stated that individuals of a lower class within the community want to establish relationships with higher-class individuals such as priests, cantors, and other people of power. These higher-class individuals are important and can play the role of a go-between for the individuals and deities. The following section discusses these relationships and payments therein.

Social Payments between Individuals and People of Power

Individuals who lack power and influence are continually alert to the possibilities of obligating a person of superior wealth, position, or influence. Relationships between these variously ranked individuals are organized similar to patron-client relationships (Foster 1963). Such higher-ranked individuals can help increase less well-off individuals' security during a variety of life crises such as illness, sudden need for cash, and legal disputes. Individuals approach higher-ranked people for different reasons, including solving their health problems, obtaining wealth, seeking aid to become successful in their activities (for instance, education or business), and other requests, including helping to search for a good mate or solving in-house disputes.

When individuals have their property stolen, victims report it to these higher-ranked individuals. These powerful and respected people will subsequently take some measures on account of the thefts. According to the informants of this study, such patrons take serious actions on defaulting persons (persons who do not act accordingly), even without any witnesses, to demonstrate how strong they are and to attract more individuals who believe in their power.

In exchange for services and support, beneficiaries (the clients) promise to give gifts to those in power. Common gifts of this sort include cattle (sheep), cash, local alcohol, honey, and bread. Individuals who do not have the above materials to give are expected to pay a cash equivalent of 1,500 birr, according to local respondents. If individuals promise to give cash, they keep it separately and promise not to use it for anything else. The cash and gifts also constitute a form of "special monies," in this case used as a type of payment for a particular service (protection, security, insurance). On the other hand, when these powerful individuals default and are unable to keep their promise or "contract," in whatever form it is, they cannot be sued in a court or an *edir*. If someone does bring such a case against a person of power, the community rejects the individual as a community member.

Money Donation to Church

The relationship between individuals and supernatural beings is important within the research community of this study. This relationship is usually facilitated when individuals face challenging situations such as health or family crises or when their animals are sick. They pray to deities or religious icons and make offerings to the spirits and gods in exchange for hope of receiving aid.

When individuals request assistance from deities, they promise to give gifts in return. Promised gifts can take different forms. A common form, for instance, is an offering of cattle as part of the transaction. Whatever the individual promises as part of the transaction, from this time onward, whether cash or cattle, the promised item becomes special money and is kept separately (Zelizer 1989, 1997). These items are called *yeselet genzeb*, which means "promised money," and individuals cannot use it for personal consumption. *Yeselet genzeb* must be kept separately and cannot be replaced with other items of similar type, as not all dollars are equal (cf. Singh 1997). The explanations given for this practice include statements such as, "As God has fulfilled my request, there is no need to change my promise, I have to respect my words too." But if the promise is made simply without specifying the form of payment, individuals can fulfill their promises by paying in whatever types of gifts they have in their possession. In this scenario, an individual has no need of keeping "promised money" separate.

Saints and the Virgin Mary, in some sense, are patrons (Foster 1963) in that contracts are made with them, but, ultimately, they are intermediaries within a religious hierarchy. They are seen as advocates who are easier to access than God. They handle cases when presented with them, but the fee must be paid and the petitioners must comply with the terms of the contract only if the cases are resolved. The payment is expected to be completed upon the fulfillment of the request. If the person assumes that his promise is not fulfilled, he is not supposed to deliver any gifts, and the relationship concerning the particular issue under consideration will terminate, but the relationship with the deity will remain.

In either case, the promise can involve different items for exchange such as cattle, children, umbrellas, or cash. As an example, individuals who are unable to bear children pray to saints for children and promise to give the child to the church or offer other materials in return. A child is given to a church in a sense that the child will serve the church of that saint. But this only happens after the child has grown and reached an age that he is able to understand the principles and procedures of the church.

In addition to promised gifts, other obligatory religious payments are required. One such payment is called *asrat bekurat*, which is required from every Christian Orthodox individual. "Ten percent of our earnings do not belong to us, and we should give it to the church," stated one informant. "When we give this to God, what we do on earth will be blessed, and we will get value from God or the church," added another.

Moreover, when individuals attend church over the weekend or on holidays, they place money into a designated vault called *mudye mitswat* (figure 10.2). In principle, individuals are not to count how much they give, but in reality they know the amount to give. The reason is that, as one informant explained, "God says, when your right hand gives, do not let your left hand see it." Such gifts are also not recorded or memorized. In addition to cash gifts, individuals can buy and give gifts such as candles and clothing to the churches.

During public holidays, churches also call on individuals to make donations or officially provide gifts. These donations are not recorded on paper. However, church officials announce to the public the total amount of donations and name of individuals who give significantly more compared to other participants. To make collection function smoothly, church individuals lay church clothes on the ground so that individuals can donate paper money or coins of any amount on the clothes. During fieldwork, the researcher also observed church representatives using an upside-down umbrella to facilitate donation collection. Once money is collected, a group of individuals counts the total donation and officially announces it to the crowd. Unlike individual donations, the group contributions are documented.

Design Implications

Following the lead of M-PESA's success in Kenya and of other mobile-money initiatives across Africa, a number of mobile companies in Ethiopia have partnered with local banks and credit and savings institutions to launch mobile-money products. These include, among others, public- and donor-funded initiatives such as mFarmer (funded in 2011–2012 by USAID and the Bill & Melinda Gates Foundation) and private partnerships such as M-Birr (a branch of the Irish company M-Birr Limited, itself an offshoot

Figure 10.2. A *mudye mitswat.*

Photo by author.

of the mobile software development firm NCL Technologies). While there has been an explosion in similar mobile-banking initiatives, their launch on the market is currently awaiting legislation that would allow for the types of transactions that these services plan to offer. An additional challenge for these new forms of money, savings, and transfers is reaching out to local people and enlisting them as clients.

As mobile companies and banks shape their new products, their success will depend upon their ability to incorporate existing local practices and institutions that enable savings and payments. This study therefore invites further investigation into design concepts that might provoke new inquiry, practice, experimentation, or development of new mobile-money systems for financial transactions.[8] For example, if money is digital, say in the form of mobile money, what will the effect be on money gift personalization, disclosure and secrecy, segregated controls, and refusal of money gift practices? How do we design a system that supports such practices? In the next sections I list some possible design concepts and features for mobile money services that incorporate current social practices.

Monthly Contributions

As discussed earlier, many of the informants make monthly contributions to community organizations such as the *edir*. Mobile-money services could therefore design services that would enable the following functions:

- Recording of monthly cash contributions (name of member, month, date, and amount contributed) in tabular format in a digital book.
- The possibility of flexible amounts for monthly contributions; charging of noncontributors.
- Summarizing the monthly contribution so that chairs can announce the total to members.
- Remote contribution by individuals so that they might not physically show up and engage in unnecessary drinks and parting.
- Closing of digital books at the end of every contribution period and scheduling the place to meet in the following month.

Payments for Funerals and Weddings

Given that payments for funerals and weddings seem to be at highest importance among the informants in this study, mobile-money services should attend to some of the existing practices around these payments, including:

- Enabling recorded cash gifts by individuals (secrecy or disclosure practices like *yazentega*). The record includes capturing information like date, name of giver, amount, etc.
- Enabling individuals to refuse to *accept yazentega* (as there could be some reason).
- Enabling monies to be labeled and differentiated; allowing remote and timed payments.
- Allowing people attach explanations and or reasons for remotely sent or contributed money.

Finally, the different illustrations like *mudye-mitswat* (figure 10.2), church clothes, and upside-down umbrellas filled with cash indicate some avenues to think about the design of hardware and graphic interfaces of mobile money.

Conclusion

This chapter documented monetary practices of rural communities in Ethiopia and then identified design insights that could sustain the practices of the community. The objective is to inform for designing culturally appropriate digital financial products and mobile-money services. This requires exploring how everyday money practices can be embedded into technical solutions and how the social relations and cultural values of a community can be embedded into technology solutions. For example, how can money practices in religious contexts or cultural contexts be affected by new forms of money? The ways money is earned, spent, exchanged, saved, stored and recorded are in fact symbolically charged and constantly contested. One of the main findings of the chapter is that for the Ethiopians studied, differentiating the uses (as well as sources) of money was extremely important. Based on the different practices in different contexts or environments, the chapter suggested possible design concepts. These concepts are interesting to investigate for digital financial systems.

Woldmariam F. Mesfin received his PhD in information systems from Addis Ababa University and has received research grants from the Institute of Money, Technology and Financial Inclusion (IMTFI); Addis Ababa University; the Ethiopian Ministry of Communication and Information Technology; and Creatic4Africa Project in Spain (consortium). He is based at Addis Ababa University Ethiopia, and his research focuses on financial inclusions and design issues related to new financial technology. His research is published by various journals and proceedings, including his most recent article "Monetary Practices of Traditional Rural Communities in Ethiopia: Implications for New Financial Technology Design" at the *Human-Computer Interaction Journal.*

NOTES

1. Foster (1963) defined a "patron" as someone who combines status, power, influence, and authority attributes useful to anyone in "defending" himself or in helping someone with lesser position.
2. In this chapter, the term "contract" is to be understood as always implying a "relationship."
3. Data were collected over a period of three months and consist of discussions with fifty key informants who were leaders of their local community in terms of their knowledge about their culture, tradition, and religion. For the most part, data were collected predominantly on Sundays. Discussions lasted between one and a half to two and a half hours. Questions were developed first in English but translated into Amharic or Oromifa during discussion, depending on the native language of the informants. All discussions were recorded.

    The purpose of this study is to investigate the financial practices in relation to various levels of social relationships. Discussions with informants are compared against one another in order to allow patterns regarding these practices to emerge. From this analysis, lists were generated of possible design concepts for potential mobile-money services.
4. See, for instance, Collins et al. 2009 for a review and discussion of various forms of informal, semiformal, or formal institutions of credit and savings for the poor, including funeral insurance associations (burial societies) in South Africa, and of the rotating savings and credit associations (ROSCAS) and accumulating savings and credit associations (ASCAs) in India and Bangladesh.
5. Birr is Ethiopian currency. The exchange rate as of January 2017 is 1 USD = 23 birr.
6. Wolaita is a small town in the southern part of Ethiopia.
7. Local food and drink items.
8. The design concepts are related to money transaction type and do not include physical wealth.

REFERENCES CITED

Akin David, and Joel Robbins (eds.). 1999. *Money and Modernity: State and Local Currencies in Melanesia.* Pittsburgh, PA: University of Pittsburgh Press.

Appadurai, Arjun (ed.). 1988. *The Social Life of Things: Commodities in Cultural Perspective.* Cambridge: Cambridge University Press.

Carrier, G. James. 1995. *Gifts and Commodities: Exchange and Western Capitalism since 1700.* New York: Routledge.

Collins, Daryl, Jonathan Morduch, Stuart Rutherford, and Orlanda Ruthven. 2009. *Portfolios of the Poor: How the World's Poor Live on $2 a Day*. Princeton, NJ: Princeton University Press.

Dominguez, Silva, and Celeste Watkins. 2003. "Creating Networks for Survival and Mobility: Social Capital among African-American and Latin-American Low Income Mothers." *Social Problems* 50(1): 111–35.

Duncombe, Richards, and Richard Boateng. 2009. "Mobile Phones and Financial Services in Developing Countries: Reviews of Concepts, Methods, Issues, and Evidence and Future Research Directions." Working Paper No 37. Centre for Development Informatics, Institute for Development Policy and Management.

Eisenstadt, S. N., and Louis Roniger. 1980. "Patron-Client Relations as a Model of Structuring Social Exchange." *Society of Comparative Study of Society and History* 22(1): 42–47.

Foster, M. George. 1963. "The Dyadic Contracts in Tzintzuntzan, II: Patron-Client Relationship." *American Anthropologist* 65(6): 1280–94.

Gregory, A. Christopher. 1982. *Gifts and Commodities*. Cambridge, MA: Academic Press Inc.

Guyer, Jane (ed.). 1995. *Money Matters: Instability, Values, and Social Payments in the Modern History of West African Communities*. Portsmouth, NH: Heinemann.

Hart, Keith. 2001. "Money in an Unequal World." *Anthropological Theory* 1(3): 307–30.

Hatch, J. Amos. 2002. *Doing Qualitative Research in Education Settings*. Albany: SUNY Press.

Homans, C. George. 1958. "Social Behavior as Exchange." *American Journal of Sociology*. 63(6): 597–606.

Kochuyt, Thierry. 2009. "God, Gifts, and Poor Individuals: On Charity in Islam." *Social Compass* 56(1): 98–116.

Komter, Aafke. 1996. "Reciprocity as a Principle of Exclusion: Gift Giving in the Netherlands." *Sociology* 30(2): 299–316.

Kristof, D. Nicholas. 2010. "Cash Is so 20th Century: I Have Seen the Future in Haiti." *New York Times*. Retrieved 31 March 2012 from http://www.nytimes.com/2010/12/05/opinion/05kristof.html?_r=1.

Lebra, S. Takie. 1975. "An Alternative Approach to Reciprocity." *American Anthropologist* 77(3): 550–65.

Lee, Rainwater. 1970. *Behind Ghetto Walls: Black Families in a Federal Slum*. Chicago: Aldine.

Mainwaring, S. 2010. Real Money and its Alternatives." In Cliver, M. (ed.) *New Organizational Models: Open-Source Financial Services Research* (pp. 42–43). Released at 2010 Ethnographic Praxis in Industry Conference (EPIC). Tokyo, Japan. https://issuu.com/melissacliver/docs/new_organizational_models_aug23_imtfi_sm.

Malinowski, Bronislaw. 1922. *Argonauts of the Western Pacific: An Account of Native Enterprise and Adventure in the Archipelagoes of Melanesian New Guinea*. London: Routledge.

Maurer, Bill. 2006. "The Anthropology of Money." *Annual Review of Anthropology* 35: 15–36.

———. 2010. "Monetary Ecologies and Repertoires: Research from the Institute for Money, Technology & Financial Inclusion." First Annual Report Design Principles. Institute for Money, Technology & Financial Inclusion, Irvine, CA,

January 2010. Retrieved 15 August 2016 from http://www.imtfi.uci.edu/files/articles/IMTFI_FirstAnnualReportDesignPrinciples.pdf.

Maurer, Bill et al. 2013. *Warning Signs, Ways Forward: Digital Payment Client Uptake.* Irvine, CA: The Institute for Money, Technology & Financial Inclusion. Retrieved 1 December 2016 from http://www.imtfi.uci.edu/files/docs/2014/imtfi-dpcu2-digital-lores.pdf.

Mauss, Marcel. 1922. *The Gift: Forms and Functions of Exchange in Archaic Societies.* London: Routledge.

Muhammad, Ozier. 2011. "Swiping Is the Easy Part: Paying for Items at Duane Reade with a Mobile Phone." Retrieved March 2011 from http://www.nytimes.com/2011/03/24/technology/24wallet.html?mcubz=0.

OECD. 2002. *The Future of Money.* Paris: Organization for Economic Co-operation and Development Secretariat.

Parry, Jonathan, and Maurice Bloch (eds.). 1989. *Money and the Morality of Exchange.* Cambridge: Cambridge University Press.

Piot, Charles. 1999. *Remotely Global: Village Modernity in West Africa.* Chicago: University of Chicago Press.

Rutherford, Stuart. 2000. *The Poor and Their Money.* Oxford: Oxford University Press.

Shipton, Parker. 2007. *The Nature of Entrustment: Intimacy, Exchange, and the Sacred in Africa.* New Haven, CT: Yale University Press.

Singh, Supriya. 1997. *Marriage Money: The Social Shaping of Money in Marriage and Banking.* St. Leonards: Allen & Unwin.

Sterling, Rhiannon, and John Zimmerman. 2007. "Shared Moments: Opportunities for Mobile Phones in Religious Participation." Paper Presented at the Designing for User eXperiences, DUX 2007 Conference. Chicago, Illinois, November 5–7.

Thomas, P. Jonathan, and Timothy Worrall. 2002. "Gift-Giving, Quasi-credit and Reciprocity." Volume 687 of CESifo working paper series. Munich: Center for Economic Studies and the Ifo Institute for Economic Research.

Van der Geest, Sjaak. 2000. "Funerals for the Living: Conversations with Elderly People in Kwahu, Ghana." *African Studies Review* 43(3): 103–29.

Walsh, Tanja, Piia Nurkka, and Rod Walsh. 2010. "Cultural Differences in Smartphone User Experience Evaluation." Paper Presented at 9th International Conference on Mobile and Ubiquitous Multimedia, MUM 2010. Limassol, Cyprus, December 1–3.

Zelizer, Viviana, 1989. "The Social Meaning of Money." *American Journal of Sociology* 95(2): 342–77.

———. 1996. "Payments and Social Ties." *Sociological Forum* 11(3): 481–95.

———. 1997. *The Social Meaning of Money: Pin Money, Paychecks, Poor Relief, and Other Currencies.* Princeton, NJ: Princeton University Press.

CHAPTER 11

Delivering Cash Grants to Indigenous Peoples through Cash Cards versus Over-the-Counter Modalities

The Case of the 4Ps Conditional Cash Transfer Program in Palawan, Philippines

ANATOLY "JING" GUSTO AND EMILY ROQUE

An indigenous woman, who is a beneficiary of the conditional cash transfer program, locally known as the "4Ps," put it: "We seldom handle cash except if it's from the 4Ps." The 4Ps stands for the Pantawid Pamilyang Pilipino Program, which loosely translates as "Filipino family tide-over program." It was set up to assist households during periods of financial difficulty. For the indigenous peoples who are beneficiaries of the program, handling bigger amounts of cash provided by the program is something new. Most live on the mountains or in areas where nonmonetary exchange of goods is still common and big denominations of cash are seldom used.

Conditional cash transfer (CCT) programs are increasingly regarded as an effective tool for fighting poverty worldwide. In Latin American countries, for instance, cash transfers have had a measure of success (International Development Economics Associates 2011). There has been a remarkable proliferation of such programs around the world, including, among other countries, Armenia, Bangladesh, Botswana, Brazil, Chile, Columbia, Honduras, India, Indonesia, Jamaica, Mexico, Namibia, Nepal, Panama, and South Africa (Fultz and Francis 2013). The Philippines created its own CCT program in 2008. The Department of Social Welfare and Development (DSWD) and the Land Bank of the Philippines (LBP) now act as the lead implementing agency and depository/disbursing bank of the program, respectively. The objective of the program is to promote investments in the education and health of children in order to help break the intergenerational transmission of poverty, by providing immediate financial support to the household. Beneficiaries are selected from households with estimated incomes below the poverty line who have at least three children zero to fourteen years of age and/or a pregnant woman during the assessment period. For beneficiaries to get a maximum of PHP1,400 (US$33.92)[1] per month, they have to fulfill certain conditions such as ensuring their children's attendance in school and getting a regular checkup at the community health center. Since its launch in 2008, the 4Ps has been scaled up rapidly and has become the cornerstone of the Philippine government's social protection efforts. It has been an important part of a renewed effort to address chronic poverty and meet the Millennium Development Goals (MDGs) to eradicate extreme poverty and hunger, achieve universal primary education, promote gender equality, reduce child mortality, and improve maternal health. By May 2012 the program covered approximately 3 million households across the country (Chaudhury et al. 2013).

The disbursement of grants of the 4Ps entails different means. Initially, cash grants were disbursed through the LBP cash card (interest-free debit card account) and could only be withdrawn from automated teller machines (ATMs). The transfer was deposited directly into the account of the beneficiary. The accounts were opened free of charge, and there were no fees to withdraw the cash transfer from LBP ATMs. However, the program recipients had to travel to the town center where the nearest LBP ATM was located to receive the cash transfer. At present, a portion of the grants are being released over the counter in LBP bank branches and through other conduits, including rural banks, cooperative banks, cooperatives, nongovernment organizations, pawnshops, GCASH Remit partner outlets, and the Philippine postal system (Phil Post).

Among the beneficiary groups, indigenous peoples (IPs) arguably pose the biggest challenge for the disbursement of the cash grants.[2] Because of geographical exclusion and resistance from the majority, most indigenous peoples are not reached by schools and are not familiar with reading or writing numbers or texts. To complicate things, the 4Ps program's grant disbursement entails the use of technology in obtaining cash grants via ATM withdrawal through cash cards or via GCASH. Given this, how does the 4Ps program work for indigenous peoples, and how has it affected their local practices? In what ways does it affect their day-to-day transactions and the handling of large amounts of cash?

The study presents findings drawn from a survey of sixty IP beneficiaries and six focus-group discussions with particular emphasis on spending patterns and points of interest in the area where community members usually go and transact their business. The indigenous people interviewed were members of the Palawan tribe living in Rizal and Brooke's Point in southern Palawan: lowland indigenous people who are cash-card beneficiaries and those from the upland who are over-the-counter beneficiaries. We also interviewed key officers and staff of DSWD and LBP as well as tribal leaders to validate the information gathered from the beneficiaries.[3]

Sharing Resources: A Sense of Community

The Palawan, like most indigenous tribes, have a strong sense of community; sharing is considered a valued trait. Studies show that in the face of external forces shaping indigenous tribes, this trait is still present. For example, mobile phones have been integrated into the life of several indigenous peoples in the Philippines, such as the Aetas from Zambales in Northern Luzon, the Tausugs from Zamboanga del Sur in Southern Philippines, and the Dumagats and Remontado tribes from Rizal in Luzon (Portus 2006). While consumerism entered these communities, there is no denying that the community incorporated local cultural values and practices in their adoption of the mobile phone. These phones have become a community tool whereby a unit is shared by everyone. According to Portus, this "socio-cultural development underscores the native ability of tribal communities concerned to adapt to the technological environment, but, more significantly, it reinforces the traditional custom or generous practice of sharing one's godsend or windfall with the community" (2006: 9). Portus also found that the Tausug and Aeta communities have at least two mobile phone owners who allow the use of their unit for a certain price. She called this "mobile-phone-for-rent" (ibid.).

Similarly, in the CCT program, beneficiaries share what they have received with their neighbors who were not part of it. According to one Palawan woman beneficiary, "If we have money left from what we have received from the program, we share it with our neighbors' children who are not part of the program. We give their children rice, or sometimes, money amounting to around PHP100 or PHP200."

It seemed that cash, just like any other resource, is meant to be shared with other members of the community who also need it. It can be argued that the 4Ps program created a divide within the indigenous tribe — beneficiaries and non-beneficiaries. Beneficiaries admitted that many non-beneficiaries in their community felt envious toward them because of their participation in the 4Ps program, but they also mentioned that the non-beneficiaries were somehow confused as to why not everyone was receiving support. Nevertheless, it was evident that the prevailing mind-set of the IPs is not about promoting personal gain or satisfaction of individual members of the group but that of the community as a whole. This was manifested in the way beneficiaries insisted on sharing their grants to avoid exclusion of others. When they receive their grants, they share some money or rice and coffee with their non-beneficiary neighbors.

Another instance where sharing is done by the IPs is when they travel to the disbursement sites. Program recipients in general incurred more costs in traveling from their residence to the payout site than from the payout site to the market. Transportation costs in the lowlands were far cheaper than in the uplands. Transportation costs for lowland recipients ranged roughly from PHP50 to PHP85 (one to two US dollars) for a round-trip tricycle ride from the lowland communities to the payout site, an amount equivalent to 6 percent of the monthly cash grant. The lowland recipients had shorter travel times going to the payout site and had access to more affordable modes of transportation. It took them about an hour on average to reach the payout site, as 60 percent of them took a tricycle ride while others opted to rent a motorcycle; no one walked to go to the payout area. Some lowland IPs belonging to the same community rented a tricycle owned by a beneficiary's husband. During one focus group, a participant shared that he would take several beneficiaries to the disbursement sites on a certain schedule in his tricycle. He would start at three in the morning, with his wife and a couple of beneficiaries as his first batch of passengers. Afterward, he would go back several times to take beneficiaries to the disbursement sites. After the payout, he would bring the beneficiaries back to the communities in the same order and charge PHP50 to PHP85 for a round trip.

On the other hand, upland recipients traveled by foot, rode a truck, or brought their own motorcycle to obtain their cash grants. By foot, it takes IPs three to five hours to reach the payout site. The site is "centrally located" to many communities, or *sitios,* and not just one, hence the distance for some IPs. The site can actually be reached in half an hour by motorcycle or truck. Other IPs preferred to ride a truck to and from the payout site. This, however, cost them PHP300 (US$7.27) for a round-trip ride alone, comprising almost 21 percent of the monthly cash grant they receive. Other upland IPs own motorcycles; however, this is rare. Nevertheless, IPs usually go together as a group either by foot or riding in a truck. The latter, however, is not a shared cost, as the truck driver dictates the price of the ride.

Behavior toward Cash

Our research supports the notion that the transfer program has contributed to an increased use of cash for both modalities. Even though very few people handled cash on a daily basis, as a result of their livelihood activities and the transfers being released only once every two months, the beneficiaries have begun to transact in cash more frequently since they started receiving cash transfers (see figures 11.1a–b).

Figure 11.1a. "How often do you handle cash through your sources of livelihood before 4Ps and now?" (Cash card)

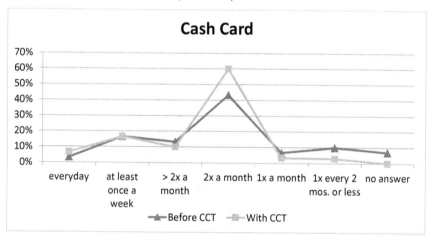

Figure 11.1b. "How often do you handle cash through your sources of livelihood before 4Ps and now?" (OTC)

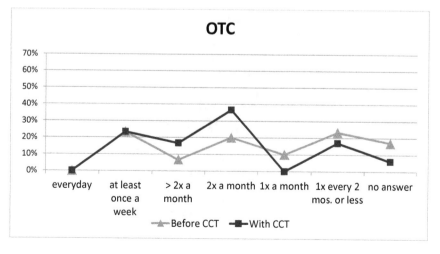

Not surprisingly, recipients are buying more goods as a result of the entry of "more cash" into their households. It is interesting, however, that neither disbursement modality led to a shift in consumption priorities among beneficiaries. As can be seen in figures 11.2a–d, both cash-card and OTC beneficiaries bought more of the same goods after receiving the cash grants, specifically 47–48 percent for food, 30–35 percent for education, and 6–10 percent for healthcare products.

Figure 11.2a. Cash Card/Lowland Households: Before Receiving CCT (General spending pattern)

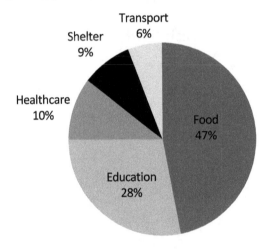

Figure 11.2b. Cash Card/Lowland Households: After Receiving CCT (General spending pattern)

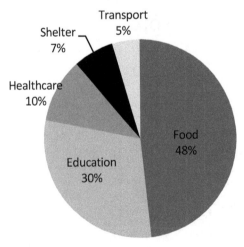

Respondents used the additional funds they receive mostly for food and education. They shared that they would not be able to support their children's education if the program was discontinued. One respondent said, "My children might stop going to school if there was no more support. We will need to spend on food first but I will try my best to earn a living to support their schooling."

Figure 11.2c. OTC/Upland Households: Before Receiving CCT (General spending pattern)

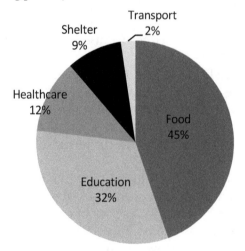

Figure 11.2d. OTC/Upland Households: After Receiving CCT (General spending pattern)

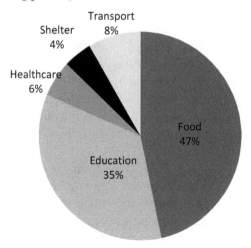

Both groups were similar in their spending patterns. They prioritized food items (US$20.60 for cash card; US$20.11 for OTC) over education items and healthcare needs, although the cash transfer was meant supposedly for supporting the family's expenses on education (US$21.81) and health (US$12.12) alone.

Cash-card households were increasingly likely to spend more on rice (US$15.66), meat (US$6.39), and vegetables (US$6.06), similar to the OTC households who were more likely to spend on rice (US$20.11) and meat (US$6.59). For education items, cash grants seemed to have the most effect on both groups' spending on school uniforms (US$9.92 and US$9.40, respectively) and school projects (US$9.07 and US$7.71, respectively). On healthcare and shelter needs, cash-card users were more likely to spend on medicine (US$3.81) as opposed to OTC users who were more likely to spend on vitamins (US$2.42). In terms of other nonfood items, the cash-card group was more likely to spend on airtime top-ups (US$2.39), the OTC group was more likely to spend on other items (e.g., plates), but both user groups were more likely to spend on clothes (US$10.23 and US$8.30, respectively). In terms of "temptation goods" or "vices," both beneficiary groups were more likely to spend on cigarettes (US$5.44 and US$1.11, respectively).

The beneficiaries we talked to during the focus groups validated the findings from the survey. When asked which items they normally use the cash grants on, they generally talked about the same food items (rice, vegetables, and meat or fish) as well as school items. One beneficiary shared, "My children used to have just one uniform and one notebook; but now, they have at least three pairs of uniforms and a notebook for each subject." Some beneficiaries also spent on other kinds of expenses, among which were housing repairs (roofs) and leisure expenses (commercial/paid cigarettes[4]). They also bought medicine/vitamins, cooking equipment such as pans and cooking oil, toiletries, flashlights, batteries, canned goods, and "relief clothes."[5] These relief clothes can be seen more in the upland indigenous peoples, who previously did not usually put on clothes.[6] The focus groups also revealed that the beneficiaries shared a portion of their grant with non-beneficiary neighbors by giving them some cash (usually around PH100 or US$2.42) or portions of what they bought, usually rice or coffee.

When the 4Ps money is used up, both groups go to their neighbors or other members of the community for rice or some food. During focus group discussions, lowland IP beneficiaries said they also resort to *utang* (informal borrowing from friends/neighbors/family members). On the other hand, in the uplands, most of the interviewed beneficiaries barter.

They usually barter goods such as sweet potato or banana in exchange for dried fish, a live chicken for one or two old relief clothes, and a *bolo* or knife for rice. Trading is done with relatives or close neighbors only. Their transactions are in large part converted into cash as a result of receiving some money from 4Ps. When the transfer comes in, they have cash to spend specifically for their children's education and health expenses. When it is all used up and they have nothing to eat, they go back to barter. As one beneficiary mentioned, "We seldom get the chance to use cash unless there is already money from the 4Ps. We are able to buy fish when we get the transfer. But when the money is all used up, we have no choice but to barter again."

Nevertheless, the entry of cash into their transactions did not create a change in values or a dependence on cash. Informants from both groups attached little importance to money itself, as most of them did not pay particular attention to where they kept it. At least in the areas we visited, cash is perceived as having little value beyond its function as a means of exchange. In fact, storing cash in conventional wallets or purses among indigenous groups is not a common practice, especially for the upland group. More generally, the concept of wallets was not really present. When asked where they keep their money, beneficiaries said they just put it in plastic bags or in an envelope containing their other 4Ps documents. In fact, they see more value in the baskets they carry on their backs, which they use for transporting goods they barter, sell, or purchase. Interestingly, one male beneficiary also showed us a wooden container around his neck where he kept some coins. He said that it was originally intended for keeping his homemade cigarettes (See figure 11.3).

In the areas we studied, many people preferred to keep their money in circulation rather than saving it. The only reason they would set aside some amount of cash was for paying or covering the future school-related needs of their children. For many beneficiaries the money spent on school projects tended to be for debts they incurred, knowing that the money would pay off the debts with the next cash disbursement. A stall across the disbursement area even has a sign, stating, "*utang sa school projects: pay here*" (payment for debts on school projects: pay here).

Introducing the ATM and the Cash Cards to the Upland and Lowland Communities

The cash card served as the first experience of a technology-based financial transaction for those in our study groups. It possessed comparative

Figure 11.3. A beneficiary uses an *alup* (bamboo cylindrical container) instead of a wallet to store his coins together with his homemade cigarettes.

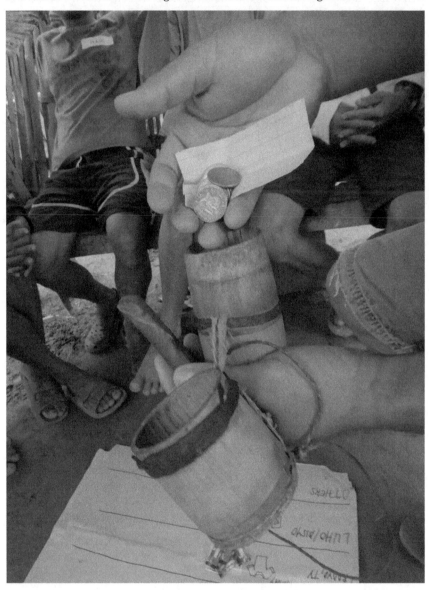

advantages, such as minimized cash-handling risks for the cash transfer proponents, faster transfer of the funds from the government to the accounts of the beneficiaries, and added opportunity to orient and capacitate IPs on alternative ways of conducting financial transactions. However, there were major implementation issues, in part because there was just one ATM available to the beneficiaries. Moreover, most recipients did not know how to perform ATM transactions on their own, and even when they were taught they preferred that someone else did it for them. It was hard to tell how many of the beneficiaries actually knew how to count or recognized the numbers on the ATM keypads. One thing was for certain: they lacked confidence and were scared something might go wrong: "I was afraid that the machine will malfunction and I can no longer get my money and cash card back if I press the wrong buttons." In most cases, municipal officials and parent leaders ended up doing the transactions for them.

It also became a practice for beneficiaries to keep their card together with the paper (the one provided by the bank) containing their default PIN, which implied very minimal effort to change the PIN or memorize the PIN as a precautionary measure.

Evolving Financial Transactions Once Exposed to Technology

Overall, the cash-card group put the transfers to a more diverse set of uses than the over-the-counter group. Access to markets could have played a role in these expanded consumption patterns. The presence of small market stalls in the payout venue was beneficial to the recipients as they suddenly had an option other than going to the town market. On the other hand, they were also exposed to other "unnecessary goods," which they did not actually need.[7]

There was also some indication that many of the beneficiaries went beyond withdrawal and spending of their money transfers and made an effort to open a savings account in the bank. When asked about their savings, recipients noted that noncash items remained the most popular mechanism, but we found that it was only the cash-card households that had some cash savings at home and, less commonly, had a bank account. Overall, 48 percent of IPs had other forms of savings, such as storing crops and livestock at home. The most common savings mechanism for both groups was noncash items (67 percent for cash-card households and 79 percent for OTC households). While it may be easy to assume that cash-card households are more likely to have higher usage rates of cash because they live closer to urbanized regions with banking and market infrastructures, there is an indication that increased usage of cash cards reinforces the utilization of cash for other purposes. Figure 11.4 illustrates the extent to which increased access of indigenous peoples to ATMs reinforces their usage of cash for savings and further suggests that areas with

Figure 11.4. Use of savings instruments among indigenous peoples in Palawan.

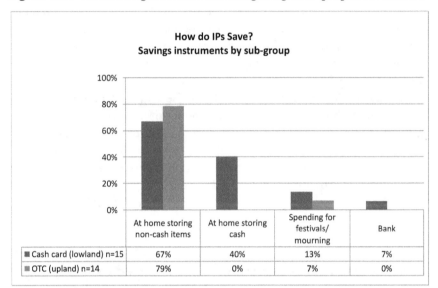

How do IPs Save?
Savings instruments by sub-group

	At home storing non-cash items	At home storing cash	Spending for festivals/ mourning	Bank
■ Cash card (lowland) n=15	67%	40%	13%	7%
■ OTC (upland) n=14	79%	0%	7%	0%

the most cash-card users are the ones that are likely to have the most deposit accounts.

There was one further use of the cash cards we heard about: in other municipalities, the cash cards were pawned, meaning that the lender agreed to keep the cash card and withdraw future transfer payments as payment for the loan to the beneficiary. Some beneficiaries allegedly did not utilize the cash grant as it was originally intended (for health and education). The DSWD staff thought that it would have been more secure if they were able to monitor the withdrawals of beneficiaries on the payout day.

Value Leakage

One interesting aspect to note is that the ATM in the study site only dispenses specific bills: PHP500 and PHP1,000 (see figure 11.5). We have observed that such payments made in high-denomination banknotes can pose challenges to accessing the entire amount of the grant during payouts. Supposing the beneficiary receives a transfer of PHP2,800. If the ATM only dispenses PHP500 or PHP1,000 notes, this is disbursed as two PHP1,000 bills and one PHP500, forcing a "leftover" of PHP300. Beneficiaries can only withdraw the remaining PHP300 or "whatever is left" during the next cash grant – as it is added to the last transfer paid to the account – but only if the new total balance is divisible by PHP500.

Figure 11.5. ATMs dispense only PHP500 and PHP1,000 bills.

Although the inability to provide recipients with immediate access to the exact amount of the grant can be considered a limitation of the technology, the focus groups uncovered practices and a growing mindset among beneficiaries that provides opportunities for mobile and electronic money development. The ATMs that dispense only high-denomination banknotes have forced the cash-card beneficiaries into "saving" amounts of their cash transfer between those denominations. Some reported satisfaction with this outcome, saying that it helped them to cover unexpected expenses in schools and buffer financial crises. Some beneficiaries stated that they were actually looking forward to the next payout because of the "bigger" amount of money that they will get. They attest to "feeling happy" when this happens. In a way, we found that beneficiaries had actually experienced saving, albeit unintentionally. In one instance, a recipient even inquired if it was possible to credit those funds to a deposit account.

Meanwhile, beneficiaries also stood out to lose some of the cash due to lack of change. Merchants eventually ran out of small bills and coins and were unable to give the exact change with beneficiaries all purchasing small items (e.g., items costing less than PHP100) with their high-denomination banknotes during payouts. In one instance, one merchant resorted to using candies in lieu of coins when he ran out of smaller bills for change.

Gender Roles

The implementation of the program has brought changes in gender roles and relations that proved beneficial for mothers. A 2013 evaluation showed that the conditional cash transfers had some empowering effect on women. "What we've seen is that when the woman has means to spend, they participate more in the spending decisions in the household. CCTs may have effects on improving the gender balance in intra-household dynamics. This in return translates into status improvement of women in the community (Handayani 2013)." In this study, women have also started to actively participate in the economic activities of the household such as going to the marketplace and buying goods, whereas before they largely stayed at home and took care of the children. Because 4Ps require women to be the main beneficiaries, they are the keepers of the program's documents. A female beneficiary summed up the role that she played in the collection and utilization of the cash grants: "I am the one who keeps all the 4Ps papers since I am also the one who receives/collects the money." It can be said that this is an expansion of the role of women from a private sphere, such as the home, to the public sphere, such as engaging in economic activities and being the frontrunners of the 4Ps program.

Before the program was introduced, it was primarily the men who conducted formal economic activities such as acquiring goods. Now, with the implementation of the program, men have also started taking on the traditional domestic responsibilities of women, such as taking care of the children. During the payout, husbands will usually accompany their wives to help carry goods purchased from the transfer. When we observed an actual 4Ps distribution, we saw women lining up inside the disbursement area while the men can be seen outside, waiting beside their motorcycles or hired tricycles. The men would only approach their wives after they had purchased goods to help carry and load them in the vehicle. It was only when their wives were not available to get the 4Ps money that men would line up with other women. Husbands seemed to have accepted their role as support to their wives. One male beneficiary shared, "It is my wife who receives the cash grants. I get to substitute if my wife is ill, but I still need to get an authorization letter from her to get the money."

Otherwise, the 4Ps disbursement areas, as well as the small market stalls beside them, are spaces clearly dominated by the women.

Conclusion

This chapter offers a glimpse into indigenous cultures and practices in the Philippines and how transfer channels and technology have affected them. The indigenous peoples discussed here might be seen as representing a segment of society that is on the margins and often located in places where people live, communicate, and consume differently. As the study shows, a majority of them originally had no or little exposure to cash, and only a few had access to mobile phones. The cash transfer program represented for most the first formal engagement with a bank, and the cash card served as their first acquaintance with a technology related to a financial transaction.

Despite the operational challenges, there are signs that the cash transfer program played an important role in introducing the concept of money, which has consequently affected the way IPs perform many of their transactions, from a mix of nonmonetary and minimal monetary exchange to more cash-based transactions.

Although our study was limited to a certain group of IPs in the Southern Philippines, the findings indicate that new technology and transfer channels can lead to a change in practices, especially a growing recognition of future financial needs and transactions. The denomination and divisibility of banknotes also open opportunities for savings and mobile- and electronic-money development.

The example of indigenous groups using ATM machines reveals that while there might be a relatively simple technology already available, the context with which the "target clientele" operates is still the same. Indigenous beneficiaries must be appreciated as a new and unique client segment that is economically vulnerable, with relatively low levels of education, and who are still likely to be more comfortable operating in the informal sector. These considerations will require that any new technology will need to include a significant training/financial education component that emphasizes both the benefits of using the service and the mechanics of accessing the service, mindful of the local practices (ways of using money) within the community.

Lastly, as much as conditional cash transfers are viewed as a vehicle for financial inclusion and are becoming tools to empower marginalized members of society, including indigenous peoples, the way they are implemented may actually lead to new layers of exclusion. In this study, it was evident that the cash transfer program in general and the cash-card modality in particular only benefited a few individuals within a tightly knit social unit whose members experience strong feelings of solidarity. With the program benefiting only selected individuals, CCT recipients manifested their strong sense of community by insisting on sharing their CCT resources with non-beneficiaries. While the CCT program rules prohibit this, the effect on the IPs, in turn, may be disruptive to the relationships in the community and may create or exacerbate feelings of enviousness and animosity within the group. Hence, it is important to be careful when incorporating technology in programs directed at indigenous populations to adapt to their local conditions and distinctive cultures.

Acknowledgments

The authors would like to express their deep gratitude to Director Rodora Babaran, national program manager of Pantawid Pamilyang Pilipino Program, and Director Wilma Naviamos, DSWD Field Office IV-B regional director. Their gratitude also goes to Mr. Vincent Dominic Obcena, Gloria Tuy, Veronica Arapeles, Faith Tabi, and Angelito Sanchez, who extended invaluable logistical support in the field. This research would not have been possible without funding from the Institute for Money, Technology & Financial Inclusion (IMTFI) at the University of California, Irvine.

Anatoly "Jing" Gusto currently heads the strategic initiatives of a Philippine thrift bank targeting micro, small, and agricultural entrepreneurs. He has more than fifteen years of experience in financial inclusion, digital financial services, and policy formulation. Through work with Bankable Frontier Associates, he contributed in the conduct of a diagnostic on electronic payment readiness of the Philippines for Bangko Sentral ng Pilipinas (Central Bank). Under a USAID-funded project, he assisted in streamlining the implementation of mobile phone banking applications and microfinance services for rural banks. He also has experience in policy development and analysis around capital market and nonbank financial institution regulation, having worked at the Securities and Exchange Commission (SEC).

Emily B. Roque, MA is currently a lecturer at the Department of Sociology and Anthropology in Ateneo de Manila University. She finished her master's degree in sociology and AB social sciences with a minor in development management at the Ateneo de Manila University. She did consultancy work with MICRA Philippines, the Institute of Philippine Culture (IPC), the Asian Institute of Management (AIM), and the Philippine Partnership for the Development of Human Resources in Rural Areas (PhilDHRRA). She has conducted research on topics such as street homelessness, social development, urban poverty, and budget and program monitoring and evaluation. She is currently engaged in consumer behavior and applying sociological and anthropological insights on marketing and business organizations.

NOTES

1. Average currency exchange rate during the study period: 1 USD = PHP 41.27
2. The Philippine state describes indigenous peoples as "a group of people or homogenous societies identified by self-ascription and ascription by others, who have continuously lived as an organized community on communally bounded and defined territory, and who have, under claims of ownership since time immemorial, occupied, possessed and utilized such territories, sharing common bonds of language, customs, traditions and other distinctive cultural traits, or who have, through resistance to political, social and cultural inroads of colonization, non-indigenous religions and cultures, become historically differentiated from the majority of the Filipinos" (NCIP 2013). IPs are also recognized to have "retain(ed) some or all of their own social, economic, cultural and political institutions, but who may have been displaced from their traditional domains or who may have resettled outside their ancestral domains" (ibid.).
3. Fieldwork for the study was conducted from September to October 2012 in two municipalities of Palawan, Philippines (Brooke's Point and Rizal). To help the beneficiaries articulate and express thoughts that may be difficult to talk about, we made use of a participatory rapid-appraisal tool adapted from

MicroSave's Market Research Tools (Wright et al. 1999), which included images of the most common expenses in the survey questionnaires as well as in our visual aid for the focus group discussions (FGDs) (large-sized paper) together with candies to act as markers for the amount they spent for each expense item. In the survey, the majority of the respondents are females, since 98 percent of the program beneficiaries are female. In the FGDs, three groups of female beneficiaries and another three groups of husbands of female beneficiaries were interviewed.

4. The IP males used to make their own homemade cigarettes by rolling up dried leaves or shredded dried leaves and rolling them in a paper and lighting them up. With the CCT money, they are able to buy commercial cigarettes.
5. Relief clothes are secondhand clothes bought at a cheaper price. Some relief might even cost less than a dollar.
6. Women used to have no upper-body garments, while men only wore their own version of "underwear."
7. Unnecessary goods are goods we categorized as non-basic goods. While basic goods mean rice, meat, food, and clothes, among others, unnecessary goods could be in the form of candies, junk food, hair dyes, and accessories such as fashionable bags, among others.

REFERENCES CITED

Aker, Jenny C., and Isaac M. Mbiti. 2010. "Africa Calling: Can Mobile Phones Make a Miracle?" *Boston Review.* Retrieved 6 January 2012 from http://bostonreview.net/BR35.2/aker_mbiti.php.

Aker, Jenny C., Rachid Boumnijel, Amanda McClelland, and Niall Tierney. 2011. "Zap It to Me: The Short-Term Impacts of a Mobile Cash Transfer Program." Working Paper 268, Center for Global Development. Retrieved 6 January 2012 from http://www.cgdev.org/content/publications/detail/1425470.

Brady, Fiona, Laurel Dyson and Tina Asela. 2008. "Indigenous Adoption of Mobile Phones and Oral Culture." *Proceedings: Cultural Attitudes towards Communications and Technology,* Murdoch University, Australia. Retrieved 6 January 2012 from http://www-staff.it.uts.edu.au/~laurel/Publications/IndigenousAdoptionOfMobilePhones&OralCulture.pdf.

Chaudhury, Nazmul, Jed Friedman, and Junko Onishi. 2013. "Philippines Conditional Cash Transfer Program Impact Evaluation 2012." World Bank. Retrieved 6 January 2012 from http://www.dswd.gov.ph/download/Research/Philippines%20Conditional%20Cash%20Transfer%20Program,%20Impact%20Evaluation%202012.pdf.

DSWD. 2011a. "DSWD Releases Cash Grants through GCASH Remit." Department of Social Welfare and Development. Retrieved 6 January 2012 from http://www.fo5.dswd.gov.ph/index.php?option=com_content&view=article&id=178:dswd-releases-pantawid-pamilya-grants-through-gcash-remit&catid=1:latest-news.

———. 2011b. "Pantawid Pamilyang Programang Pilipino: Program Implementation Status Report (Second Quarter of 2011)." Retrieved 6 January 2012 from http://www.dswd.gov.ph/index.php/pantawid-pamilya-accomplishment-report.

DSWD. 2011c. "Pantawid Pamilyang Programang Pilipino: Program Implementation Status Report (Third Quarter of 2011)." Retrieved 6 January 2012 from http://www.dswd.gov.ph/index.php/pantawid-pamilya-accomplishment-report.

The Economist. 2011. "Not Just Talk." Retrieved 6 January 2012 from http://www.economist.com/node/18008202.

Fultz, Elaine, and John Francis. 2013. "Cash Transfer Programmes, Poverty Reduction and Empowerment of Women: A Comparative Analysis" International Labour Office. Working Paper 4/ 2013. Retrieved 11 September 2017 from http://www.ilo.org/wcmsp5/groups/public/---dgreports/---gender/documents/publication/wcms_233599.pdf.

Handayani, Sri Wening. 2013. "Conditional Cash Transfers – Are they helping promote gender equity?" Social Protection Team, Asian Development Blog, 20 May. Retrieved from http://blogs.adb.org/blog/conditional-cash-transfers-are-they-helping-promote-gender-equity#sthash.ZV2YrVKc.dpuf.

International Development Economics Associates. 2011. "Cash Transfers as a Strategy for Poverty Reduction: A Critical Assessment." IDEAs Policy Brief No. 3/2011. Retrieved 3 March 2013 from http://www.networkideas.org/briefs/dec2011/PDF/03_2011.pdf.

Lariba, Aileen. 2011. "Badjao's Meeting School for the First Time," Philippine Information Agency. Retrieved 7 January 2012 from http://www.pia.gov.ph/?m=7&r=R07&id=20264&y=2011&mo=03.

NCIP. 2013. "Indigenous Peoples of the Philippines." Retrieved 1 June 2013 from http://www.ncip.gov.ph/indigenous-peoples-of-the-philippines.html.

Portus, Lourdes. 2006. "Connecting Indigenous Peoples: Mobile Phone Culture among Selected Indigenous Peoples in the Philippines." *Asia Culture Forum.*

Villa, Allen M. 2011. "Aeta Families Go Hi-Tech via Pantawid Pamilya ATM Cards." Philippine Information Agency. Retrieved 6 January 2012 from http://www.pia.gov.ph/?m=7&r=R03&id=51977&y=2011&mo=09.

Wright, G., S. Ahmed, L. Mutesasira, and S. Rutherford. 1999. "Focus Group Discussions and Participatory Rapid Appraisal for Microfinance: A Toolkit/Course." MicroSave. Retrieved 3 March 2013 from http://198.101.236.183/content/article/detail/1739/.

CHAPTER 12

Effects of Mobile Banking on the Savings Practices of Low-Income Users
The Indian Experience

MANI A. NANDHI

Introduction

Recent research into the economics of the poor demonstrates that low-income households manage to save money in one form or another, even if the amounts saved are small (Collins et al. 2009; Banerjee and Duflo 2011). A survey conducted by the National Council of Applied Economic Research (NCAER) and Max New York Life Inc. (Shukla 2007) found that over 81 percent of the Indian households save part of their earnings. Further, the survey indicated that over a third of the 205.9 million households still prefer to stash cash at home, even though this does not earn them any interest in return. Just as importantly, the survey found that poor households save about 40 percent of their annual income despite being in debt.[1]

The burgeoning mobile-money models in India target precisely this widespread demand for alternative forms of savings for people who are unbanked and financially underserved. Among such initiatives is one offered by EKO – a first mover in mobile banking platforms – that provides a pure cell phone–based model on a core banking platform called SimpliBank.[2] EKO's mobile-money campaign started in partnership with the State Bank of India (SBI) by launching the "SBI Mini Savings Bank Account" as a pilot in February 2009 in Delhi, Bihar, and Jharkhand.[3] EKO partners with a network of retailers – chemists, grocers, airtime vendors – known as customer service points (CSPs). In EKO's model, the mobile number is the bank account number of the customer, allowing individuals to transact in their No-Frills Accounts or NFAs (accounts that allow customers to have a zero minimum balance) by simply dialing numbers on their mobiles. The money a customer deposits remains with the bank and not with EKO, and the account holder gains a 3.5 percent interest per annum. The key advantage of using the EKO accounts as opposed to banks is the significantly lower transaction costs and the ease of access. By comparison to the average SBI branch transaction cost of INR 68 (US$1.45), EKO'S average transaction cost is only INR 10 (US$0.21) (Malhotra 2010).[4]

The booming success of M-PESA in Kenya has shown that mobile technology offers considerable potential for lowering transaction costs and providing secure banking services to vast numbers of poor people in the developing world. Given that large segments of the urban poor in India are financially excluded, EKO's SimpliBank mobile money may play a significant role in delivering cost-effective financial services to the poor. EKO's vision for building a low-cost financial services infrastructure for the unbanked depends on its outcomes. The full extent of these outcomes should be measured with respect to two sides of the same coin – that of the provider and that of the end user (customer). For the provider, the success of mobile money focuses on a macro perspective (namely, EKO's outreach, coverage, and customer base); for the end user, the impact of EKO's mobile money centers on the micro unit (that is, access, safety, and cost of transaction).

While EKO's mobile money serves as a phone cum savings account, thus enabling people without a formal bank account to engage in safer and more efficient savings mechanisms, it also becomes a medium of transaction in everyday economic life. Focusing on low-income EKO customers in Delhi, this chapter looks at the effects of mobile banking on their saving behavior and other informal savings practices. By way of example, the chapter also reflects on how efforts to financially integrate migrant rickshaw pullers using an innovative hand-holding support to get them mobile banked raised concerns that need to be addressed by the mobile banking industry.

Setting the Scene

India is a microcosm of a growing global phenomenon: the disproportionate ratio between the number of people with access to financial services versus that of people with access to mobile phones. As of 2010, 30 percent of India's population lived below the poverty line (World Bank 2011), and while bank account penetration is still relatively low in India, mobile phone usage is on the rise; recent estimates by the Group Special Mobile Association (GSMA) placed India as the second largest mobile broadband market (GSMA 2012b, 2016). India has attained near universal telecom access and has one of the lowest-cost retail distribution networks in the world. In this context, mobile money constitutes an opportunity for the financial inclusion of the poor. This is important because a prerequisite for poverty reduction and inclusive growth efforts in India rests on enabling the poor and underprivileged groups' access to formal financial services.

India has the second highest number of financially excluded households in the world – more than half of India's population is financially underserved.[5] A study on improving access to India's rural poor found that some 87 percent of the poorest households surveyed do not have access to credit and 71 percent do not have access to savings from a formal source. Among those with bank accounts, over 72 percent of rural households reported safekeeping of monetary assets as the primary use of the account, with little use for payments or checking services; further, there is limited demand for the use of these accounts to transact everyday spending because most transactions are cash based (Basu 2006). The Financial Sector Reforms Committee in 2008 indicated that 40 percent of India's earning population had no savings, with only 34 percent of the lowest income quartile having savings, and only 18 percent had a bank account. Data on the status of financial inclusion in India from the Global Findex 2014 indicates that while 53 percent of adults held an account at a formal institution, just 14 percent had savings at a formal financial institution in 2014 (World Bank 2014). More recently, the Indian credit agency CRISIL's Inclusix index (2015) evaluated India's progress on financial inclusion and described the country's performance as having improved with a score of 50.1 out of 100, indicating that there is underpenetration of formal banking services in most parts of India. While the Inclusix score has improved to 50.1 out of 100 at the end of Fiscal 2015 it also reflects that a large part of India's population remains outside banking network. One in three Indians still do not have a bank savings account; and with just one in seven having access to credit, the credit penetration (CP) score continues to be low.

In India, then, as in much of the developing world, "the financial markets are quite simply failing to meet the needs of a vast swath of society – those who are poor, and especially the poor living in rural areas – in a way that is affordable, convenient, and safe" (Mas 2009: 57). Banks shun the poor because they have unstable livelihoods; besides, they have unpredictable as well as low and uneven income flows. In short, the poor lack the means for achieving financial discipline in the eyes of the bankers. Consequently, the poor rely on a number of informal mechanisms and social arrangements that are costly (in both financial and social terms) but more convenient. The fact that the poor do save by relying on informal sources such as saving at home, ROSCAs, "money guards,"[6] or saving clubs is well documented (Rutherford 2000 and Collins et al. 2009). The financial ingenuity of the poor's saving and storing practices (against all odds) is documented in a recent study of cycle rickshaw pullers who form a sizeable segment of urban poor living on Delhi streets, in public spaces, and in slum settlements (Nandhi 2010). These include keeping cash on their person, where they stay, with neighborhood shopkeepers, with relatives or rickshaw contractors, and/or in concealed locations. The study also notes that these practices are found to be strong despite unstable local living conditions, fear of risk of losses, and an uncertain level of trust and availability in getting back the deposited money when needed. Similarly, Orlanda Ruthven's (2002) research among dwellers in Kalibasti, a squatter settlement in West Delhi, suggests that networks of relations are crucial to the financial security of the urban poor. The study found that, despite the lack of access to formal financial services, most respondents were regularly leaning on friends and neighbors to cover deficits and bridge cash flow; these respondents were saving by hiding money at home, they were giving interest-free loans, and/or they were taking private loans with interest or a wage advance. A valid question here is whether the use of mobile banking would benefit the poor. In particular, what are the effects of EKO's mobile banking on the savings behaviors and practices of low-income households?

To answer this question, the chapter draws on a survey of 160 customers/users who were interviewed in 2011 in three districts of Delhi (West, South, and East).[7] Also interviewed were key officials and field managers of EKO, seventeen retail agents or CSPs to cross-validate the information gathered from EKO customers. This was supplemented by focus-group discussions with non-users of mobile banking and case studies of EKO customers.

Users of EKO

The users of EKO's M-Banking include migrant workers (auto drivers, rickshaw pullers, handcart vendors, shop assistants), small business entrepreneurs (for instance, beauty parlour owners), street hawkers, daily wage labourers, vegetable/fruit sellers, petty traders, housewives, and students. EKO's potential target market includes cycle rickshaw pullers, as nearly a quarter of the sample (Nandhi 2010) was found to possess a mobile phone. Starting with an initial pool of five thousand customers and a network of two hundred agents, EKO has grown exponentially over time. As of 2014, it had served over 3 million customers through its three thousand customer service points (CSPs) across ten states (Joseph and Mazotta 2014; Mas and McCaffrey 2015). EKO has also launched a number of new initiatives. It has partnered with ICICI Bank, India's second largest private-sector bank, launching the "Apna Savings Account" scheme – rural savings accounts with a zero balance and no deposit requirement. Further, it has now moved beyond the No-Frills Account to the large domestic remittances market in north India by adopting *Tatkal*, a remittance facility introduced by SBI in mid-2010. According to Greg Chen, CGAP regional representative for South Asia, SBI-EKO *Tatkal* service had conducted 1.1 million transactions valued at over $800,000 within a time frame of nine months (Chen 2012).

From the wide pool of EKO customers, we interviewed 160 – 122 men and 38 women. The majority (54 percent) had attended up to middle school and 12 percent had no schooling. Of the group, 31 percent worked as daily wage/casual labor, factory workers, and domestic and professional workers; 19 percent were shopkeepers/petty traders; followed by sales assistants, housewives, and others. Nearly the entire sample owned a mobile phone. EKO users who were permanent residents numbered 78 percent, while 22 percent were migrants or temporary residents. At the time of the survey, the sample respondents had been EKO customers for an average of sixteen months. Of the EKO users in the study, 61 percent had a bank account and 39 percent had no bank account.

Users in the study had access to some form of financial services (formal or informal) before opening an EKO mobile account. Among the sizeable portion (61 percent) of the sample that had a bank account, 6 percent had not been using the bank account for various reasons, including inadequate ability to save because of low income. Further, 48 percent of the respondents had a Life Insurance Corporation (LIC) policy, while 19 percent were members of a "committee" or "kitty."[8] Among the non-users with bank accounts, three had a joint account with their spouses, three had an account in their village, and two rarely used their bank accounts.

EKO customers surveyed in the study were classified in three income brackets: 26 percent earned less than INR 5,000 (US$100) per month; 48 percent had incomes between INR 5,000 and 8,000 (US$100 and US$160); and 26 percent earned more than INR 8,000 (US$160). It should be noted that, assuming a household size of four members and an average inflation rate of 9 percent (and food inflation hovering around 11 to 12 percent by the end of October 2011), the first two income quartiles can safely be considered low-income consumers. While the sample mean and median income lies between INR 8,089 and INR 6,000, the range of minimum and maximum stood at INR 6,000 and 50,000.

Prior to opening their EKO mobile banking accounts,[9] 54 percent of the respondents were saving in formal institutions (banks, post office, and LIC), 81 percent were using informal savings mechanisms (hoarding at home, keeping with self or a money guard, contributing to a committee/kitty), and 11 percent of the sample had no savings.[10]

Findings

Four key findings emerged from the field survey:

1. Mobile banking improved the ability to save for a majority of our respondents, particularly by comparison to earlier practices such as keeping cash on hand. These informal forms of savings were seen as susceptible to unnecessary and trivial expenditures or claimable by friends/relatives.[11]

2. EKO mobile banking services have become a very effective, safe, and trustworthy savings instrument for its users; importantly, dependence on risky informal methods had decreased for a large percentage of customers who previously relied on these practices for lack of affordable and safe savings options.

3. Mobile banking is perceived as a good substitute to both traditional banking and informal forms of savings; however, it has not dispelled the need for these existing savings mechanisms. EKO mobile services were used as one among many other savings mechanisms – including informal methods – by a sizeable percentage of customers.

4. Users have diverging views regarding the preference of EKO mobile banking over other forms of savings. The majority consider EKO mobile-money accounts to be a preferred alternative for small savings. At the same time, in spite of an expressed preference for EKO mobile money, one-third of users became inactive[12] following the introduction of transaction charges for deposits and withdrawals.[13] In fact, a considerable minority of customers had concerns about a possible increase in the cost of EKO transactions. This would potentially make the service less attractive to those who are looking to save in small amounts.

EKO Mobile Banking Has Increased
the Capacity of Low-Income Users to Save

The survey indicated that 90 percent of users (N=144) found their "ability to save" has been improved by the mobile banking services of EKO. In response to a query about the extent of this improvement, 57 percent of users stated their ability to save had "definitely improved," and 41 percent noted that it had become "somewhat better" after opening an EKO account.

Users gave three important reasons for this positive effect from EKO mobile accounts on their overall savings behavior.[14] First, keeping money in the EKO mobile accounts is much safer than keeping cash on hand (84 percent). Second, having a mobile account enables users to avoid wasteful expenses and to save rather than spend, thus inculcating better saving habits. For instance, 66 percent of the users claimed that their EKO accounts had provided an incentive to deposit rather than spend their small amounts of extra cash. Third, their ability to save money frequently and in small amounts – as small as INR 10 (US$0.20) – has become more feasible with the No-Frills savings accounts offered on the EKO mobile platform. This finding was endorsed by 73 percent of the users in the study.[15] Similarly, Garg and Mehta (2010) found that the EKO clients reported more frequent savings, especially when people had extra cash that they deposited to their EKO savings accounts. Both EKO and M-PESA, which rely on a large number of small "corner shops," seem to encourage both deposits and withdrawals – as frequently as five times per week (Medhi et al. 2009).

Our users indicated that they were happy to use an EKO mobile banking account for a number of reasons. The top four reasons were as follows: it was "easy and convenient" (75 percent),[16] it was "easy to withdraw anytime" (69 percent), users "found a safe place to save" (65 percent),[17] and users could "avoid unnecessary spending" (63 percent).[18] A non-negligible number of users (22 percent – especially women) emphasized that EKO mobile money has been instrumental in keeping hidden their carefully saved money, thus giving them a "sense of financial control" (see case study 1).

▦ **Case Study 1**

Saving in Mobile Money: Secrecy and Route to Freedom

Leela, a graduate housewife, gets a monthly allowance for running her household and has a joint bank account with her husband. She opened an EKO account in 2009 (unbeknownst to her husband) and started to save between INR 1,000 and INR 2,000 regularly by managing her household expenses carefully. Around the same time she started a recurring deposit with the Indian post office for her children's future, and from what she saves in EKO she can withdraw some amount to deposit in the post office. She told us that her freedom to spend money or decide on her own about managing her savings has been a new experience. For instance, in May 2011 her brother asked her to get him a loan of INR 10,000 from her husband; instead she surprised him by withdrawing the money from her mobile account and lent it to him instead. She felt really good that she could help her brother on her own without her husband's aid or his having to know about her secret savings.

Source: Field notes of interview held on 28 September 2011.

EKO Mobile Account Is a Safe, Trustworthy and Useful Savings Mechanism

Three noteworthy findings emerged about the savings behavior of low-income users since opening their EKO accounts: First, EKO customers consider the services safe and trustworthy because their savings are securely deposited with the State Bank of India, whose brand name as a leading public-sector commercial bank in India lends credibility to the activities of their business correspondent, EKO. Second, after becoming EKO mobile banking customers, users were able to reduce their dependence on risky and costly alternatives in informal savings practices (keeping cash at home, under the mattress, or on their person) because their EKO mobile account became a safe saving option. For instance, dependence on informal savings practices such as "home savings" and "keeping cash on person" decreased by 54 percent; likewise, savings in committees and kitties dropped from 13 to 6 percent. Third, 11 percent of the respondents who had "no savings" were able to save after they opened their EKO accounts because it created an incentive to do so.

While all users in the study stated that they found a new saving mechanism in the EKO accounts, more than 10 percent of the users with bank accounts found it a better alternative and shifted to saving in mobile-money accounts. This was attributed to EKO mobile accounts having a dual benefit — that of a safe, reliable, and accessible savings option and its ability to keep money at arms' length to reduce temptation spending (see case study 2).

▦ Case Study 2

EKO Helps to Reduce Wastage of Money

Naresh has a small shop and repairs electrical items. In the past he kept his daily income at home and deposited a bulk amount in the bank once in a while. The downside to this was that many times the cash earnings were used up at home, making deposits into his bank account an irregular practice. However, an EKO mobile banking account changed this situation. He began to regularly deposit part of his earnings on his way home, keeping some cash on hand for routine expenses. EKO mobile banking enabled him to save by avoiding temptation expenses, and when his EKO savings accumulated, he transferred a lump sum to his bank account for converting to a fixed deposit mode.

Source: Field notes from interview held on 16 August 2011.

Of the users without bank accounts, 39 percent felt that they finally found a safe saving medium in EKO-SBI's mobile accounts. This savings mechanism improved their confidence in saving and managing money. For those users with bank accounts, EKO mobile banking offered a far more convenient method of saving, enabling them to save time, energy, and cost of transacting in a brick-and-mortar bank branch. Undoubtedly, speed of transaction and time saved at an m-banking agent store location (cash in/cash out stores for EKO, GCASH, and M-PESA) were important reasons for mentioning the convenience of these services (see Medhi et al. 2009). By comparison, non-users had not heard about saving through EKO mobile banking accounts; besides, they considered themselves ineligible for bank accounts either due to lack of sufficient "know your customer" (KYC) proof or a limited ability to save in a bank account.[19] Hence, they were dependent on informal social saving practices such as hiding money under the mattress or in a *gulak*.[20]

EKO Mobile Money Is a Good Substitute to Informal Savings Methods

The majority of low-income users in the study (95 percent) perceived an EKO mobile banking account as a good substitute for informal savings practices such as saving at home, cash on hand, or saving with a money guard (friends/relatives). Additionally, many remarked that an EKO mobile account was a good substitute for a bank account.[21] In effect, convenience, security of savings, efficiency of transactions, reliability, flexibility, safety, secrecy, and promptness of agent servicing were some of the main reasons why EKO mobile banking was considered a good substitute.

However, there was also a counterview to this dominant assessment: one-third of the users had negative perceptions about the prospects of EKO mobile money replacing existing savings mechanisms.[22] The two top reasons for dissatisfaction with EKO mobile banking accounts were the deduction of charges (33 percent) and server problems (18 percent).[23] The users (N=53) who expressed their unease about transaction charges included both active users (N=21) and inactive users (N=32). Delays in withdrawals, especially when needed immediately, as well as the loss of valuable time in transacting due to "server down" or "server not working" were also considered to be irritants in using EKO mobile banking service.

Coexistence of EKO Mobile Banking with Other Savings Practices

Mobile money was used by many of our interviewees alongside existing savings. One key feature of this ecosystem is the practice of earmarking specific types of savings for specific investments. For instance, "cash at home" and "cash on person" are used for everyday expenses on food, daily transportation, and other basic needs; committee/kitty contributions are used for buying assets or to cover "festival or ceremonial expenses"; finally, "money at home" and "EKO savings" are generally spent on recurring educational expenses.[24] Unsurprisingly, non-users in the study also exhibited similar behavior. In addition to educational expenditures, EKO savings were used extensively for emergencies or unexpected expenses – especially covering medical expenses or expenses related to death (N=87/120) as well for buying assets (for example, consumer durables).[25]

Interestingly, users also developed new applications of mobile money in their everyday transactions, including employing it as a complementary tool to existing savings practices. For instance, in order to make monthly savings contributions (payments to committee, kitty, or insurance premiums) in a timely manner, some users first made a deposit into their EKO accounts and subsequently made due payments from EKO savings. Some other users emphasized that, prior to their EKO accounts, when they set aside (as "cash at home") a part of their money for meeting these monthly contributions to other savings practices, they often failed to meet their due dates because the cash at home was easily spent on other purposes. However, when they started to save through their EKO accounts, they could ensure timely payment without a late fee. This finding runs against conventional views that easier forms of savings/payments (think, for instance, Paypal) generally lead to a decrease in individual control over expenditures and savings. The case of Neelam (see case study 3) amplifies how users hoard money informally before moving the built-up sums to an EKO account.

Case Study 3

Hoard Informally and Save Formally

Neelam is an apprentice at a beauty parlor earning INR 3,000 monthly. She tries to store her money in various ways by tucking it among her clothes, storing it in a *gulak,* keeping it on her person, or by giving it to a money guard. Her intention is to convert small sums into a big amount. With an EKO account (opened in January 2011) she had found a safe way to ensure her small savings can grow into a sizeable amount. Despite occasional hiccups in her informal storing practices, she finds it is easier to put small-denomination coins in a *gulak* till it fills or store money with a friend, because money on hand gets spent. At the end of each month, she deposits her informally stored amounts in the EKO account. She finds EKO is the best and most secure mechanism among her saving practices and is confident that she can build a large enough sum to be useful in the future.

Source: Field notes from interview held on 27 August 2011

EKO Mobile Banking Is a Preferred Alternative for Small Savers

Asked about their preference for saving in small lump sums of INR 1,000 to 2,000 (US$20 to US$40), 79 percent of the users in the study preferred EKO mobile banking accounts, while 26 percent preferred "saving at home." This number includes the 20 percent of EKO users who became inactive due to rising transaction charges. The study found that 31 percent of the overall users became inactive subsequent to the introduction of transaction charges by EKO on the grounds that the "sudden introduction of flat fee based transaction charges" was a disincentive to save.

They felt that the uniqueness of EKO mobile banking rested on the ability to make small deposits frequently and conveniently. However, a large percentage of this subsegment (thirty-two out of forty-nine) expressed their keenness to revert back to using the EKO mobile banking service if the transaction charges on deposits could be eliminated.[26] Their positive perception after using EKO mobile banking has been a binding factor in their desire to continue using the services in the future. Unlike former users who became inactive but are keen to restart saving in EKO mobile banking account, non-users did not think that mobile banking would help them save given their inadequate income.

Mobile Banking Initiatives: Catalyst in Financial Practices for the Poor?

In order to contextualize these findings and the use of mobile money, this section offers one case study from a recently concluded empirical study (Nandhi and Deepti 2013) in which a small group of fifty rickshaw pullers were helped to acquire both a personal identification card on the Aadhar platform and a mobile banking account. They were then monitored to observe the changes in behaviour around their financial practices. Based on personal narratives that chronicle their migratory lifestyles, Nandhi and Deepti (2013) illustrate the financial choices the migrant rickshaw pullers are forced to make or unable to make, enabling an understanding of their socioeconomic compulsions, needs, desires, and wants that define this marginalized group. These are illustrated in case study 4.

Case Study 4

Vinod and His Travails

Vinod Yadav, a rickshaw puller, attempted to open a bank account in his village by providing the necessary documentation (e.g., voter's ID, ration card), but his application was rejected because the fellow villager who signed his application form was not deemed eligible. Vinod could not find another person who could introduce him to the bank. When he learned about mobile banking, he was happy that he could open an account because he owned a mobile phone. On 26 October 2012 his ICICI-EKO mobile banking account was opened when he deposited INR 600 (about US$10). But he did not use the account subsequently because he lost his phone. Despite knowing that he had to get a duplicate SIM card to access his mobile banking account, he made a lot of excuses for not applying for it. After he ran out of excuses, it became clear that there was more to the story than met the eye. Over the course of a number of small personal meetings, the pieces of the jigsaw puzzle fell into place and we learned what kept him from using the eagerly opened mobile banking account.

Two months after *Deepawali* (a major Indian festival), Vinod had accumulated a total debt of INR 1,15000 (US$2,300) which he owed to many – his *tekedar* (rickshaw contractor) and a few fellow pullers – the result of playing *juwa* (gambling). To a query on how he would repay such a large amount, he said that while small amounts are taken on a reciprocal basis, larger amounts of money lent by a *tekedar* are repayable with an interest. For instance, a loan of INR 1,000 (US$20) would have to be repaid in a week's time with a high interest amount of INR 250 (US$5). His net earnings normally were about INR 500 per day (after basic expenses and rent for his rickshaw). So that would mean repaying the debt in seven to eight months. When asked if he was frightened about such a huge debt, he shot back: "Why would I be scared? I know I will have to earn and repay if I lose, but if I win I will be able to clear off some debts."

Vinod has regularly been depositing daily earnings with his *tekedar*, who treats the deposited earnings and the loans separately. The earnings deposited are also treated as collateral when a puller borrows from the *tekedar*. Of the eight *tekedars* in the slum settlement where he stays, three are frequent lenders. Vinod noted that they are happy to lend when the *juwa* is on, but rarely for other purposes. He said that in one of the games he won INR 40,000 (US$800). The stake was doubled in the next game by his *tekedar*, who encouraged him to gamble, and, unable to resist the temptation, Vinod played and lost INR 80,000 (US$1,600). Vinod explained that many pullers are tempted into playing cards and thus fall into a debt trap. Normally debts are squared between winners and losers when small sums are involved. If a friend wins big one week, he will lend to his friends who have lost and borrow from them the next, "like a moving wheel."

Though he was pressured by the *tekedar* to repay in ten days' time, Vinod explained that this was just one of a number of debts that would need to be settled at the same time: "I will repay each lender alternately because if I repay one and not bother about repaying another, I will face the wrath of the lender who is not getting back the loan from me." However, the challenge for pullers like Vinod is that when the stakes are high, they tend to borrow from sources with vested interests. This seems to reinforce their dependence on a "*tekedar* cum lender" pattern in their economic lives. And life goes on "by getting by" for many a puller like Vinod. Vinod has aspirations, but when gently reminded about saving in his newly opened mobile banking account, he simply replied, "How can I think of saving or bother about Rs.600 savings in my mobile banking account when my mind is concerned now only about returning the huge amount I owe people? Such things are far away in my mind." His answer echoed his life situation that dangles between desires and actual choices made under harsh circumstances.

Source: Based on field interviews from Nandhi and Deepti (2013).

Conclusions

Based on the sample, what can be concluded about the effects of EKO mobile banking on the savings behavior and practices of low-income users in the metropolis of Delhi? EKO mobile banking has improved the capacity of low-income users to save, particularly when compared to keeping cash-based savings; indeed, a majority of users rated the service as bringing about a definite degree of improvement in their saving ability. The EKO mobile banking service is considered a boon because of its safety, trustworthiness, and effectiveness for small savers and users who earlier depended on risky informal savings practices. These findings corroborate evidence from South Africa and Kenya, which showed that low-income customers positively value the mobile banking services for their convenience, safety, ease of use, and speed (Ivatuary 2006; Stuart and Cohen 2011; CGAP Brief 2009).

Notably, dependence on risky informal methods diminished for a large percentage of users, who were earlier dependent on them for lack of a safe saving option. In a related vein, a CGAP study in 2009 demonstrated how unbanked poor use M-PESA as a substitute for informal savings methods, especially keeping money at home – a practice that is notoriously susceptible to theft or claims made by family.

In addition, EKO mobile bank accounts have become a storage device for both unbanked and banked users, which resonates with a similar finding about M-PESA serving as a place to hold capital (Jack and Suri 2011). More importantly, it is considered as a healthy substitute to many informal savings mechanisms as well as a bank account. Yet, the savings behavior of users indicated that EKO mobile banking accounts have not

eliminated the need for some of the traditional savings mechanisms because different savings methods were perceived as having their own use-
fulness and purpose.

Another aspect of EKO mobile banking accounts is that a high percentage of users utilized it to save for emergencies. In a related vein, Stuart
and Cohen (2011) argue that the successful M-PESA in Kenya does not
appear to be a tool that low-income people use to accumulate savings;
however, they do use it as one among numerous tools to patch the holes
that routinely spring open in their regular cash flow. More critically, their
findings underscore that M-PESA is a valuable tool for these households
in meeting emergency expenses, especially hospital bills. This finding
is corroborated in other studies of M-PESA users who were found to be
keeping money for an "emergency" or unexpected event/expense such as
a funeral (see, e.g., CGAP Brief 2009; Zollmann and Collins 2010).

Contrary to expectations, EKO mobile money accounts also seem to
improve efficiency and regularity of other savings mechanisms, in addition to making payments and deposits easier and more accessible.
For instance, an interesting aspect of EKO mobile banking is that it has
become a convenient "fit-in" instrument among other savings devices,
including both informal and formal mechanisms–depending on the purpose and nature of saving goals (short term or long term). In fact, EKO
mobile banking is being blended with other savings methods as well as
being adapted as a complementary tool for an existing saving practice,
thus increasing the self-discipline of users in their savings efforts. Such
behavior is an indicator of a shift in the savings patterns to minimize the
risk of savings failures (for example, if carefully built-up "home savings"
are depleted due to its exposure to demanding relatives). Given that the
users were intermixing EKO mobile banking in their existing assortment
of informal savings methods and bank accounts, a key insight here is
that there is need for savings products that incorporate design principles
based on informal mechanisms (for example, like *gulaks*) to suit the needs
of low-income users who have low, irregular income streams and low
levels of savings.

Overall, the positive perceptions of mobile banking in the daily lives
of EKO account holders represent an encouraging sign of the potential of
mobile money for expanding the financial inclusion of large numbers of
low-income households in India. The negative perceptions that non-users
hold with regard to their savings capacity speak, on the one hand, to
their irregular income and, on the other, to their lack of awareness of the
potential of mobile banking for improving their financial opportunities.
This lack of awareness raises the need for more creative strategies for

reaching out to the poor in India and elsewhere. The lack of awareness about the benefits of saving in mobile banking is reinforced by Vinod's narratives in case study 4, which highlight that getting a mobile banking account is only the first step. Pullers new to banking need support to create a banking habit capable of overcoming all barriers to adopting the service. It is critical to show them how to translate the idea of having a bank account into practical ways of realizing their desires to save in a formal account through financial discipline. Toward this end, financial education has to be an essential component of a mobile bank account offered to disadvantaged populations; and more importantly, the "poor" need to be treated as "customers" with products that are designed with empathy and creativity. This alone will ensure their financial inclusion.

Mani A. Nandhi is an associate professor at the Department of Commerce at Jesus and Mary College, University of Delhi. She holds an MPhil in marketing from Delhi School of Economics and a PhD from the Faculty of Management Studies, University of Delhi. Her research on the urban poor and mobile banking has been funded by the Institute for Money, Technology & Financial Inclusion (IMTFI), University of California, Irvine. Her study *The Urban Poor and Their Money: A Study of Cycle Rickshaw Pullers in Delhi* was published by Pinnacle Learning in 2014. She has several publications in national and international journals and has presented her work in various national and international conferences.

NOTES

1. This behavior is in consonant with findings in other studies, which indicate that households often prefer borrowing – especially from informal sources like friends and relatives – over using savings, which is earmarked for specific needs. As Jonathan Morduch (2010) argues, while the phenomenon of "borrowing in order to save" is puzzling from the standpoint of traditional economics, it is a regular feature in the financial practices of the poor (see also Collins et al 2009).
2. Operated by EKO Aspire foundation/EKO India Financial Services Pvt. Ltd, New Delhi. EKO's SimpliBank is the application or the server that captures all mobile transactions, processes them, and then reconciles the same with the core banking systems. This middleware understands transactions done by customers at a retail point, and it is designed with the mobile phone as its primary transaction interface.
3. The State Bank of India (SBI) is the largest and most trusted public-sector bank in India with the greatest number of branches and accounts across the country.
4. The exchange rate of 1 USD is equal to INR 50 in the study.

5. "Underserved" broadly includes those who get partially some kind of financial service (one might have a no-frills account but no access to credit). "Unbanked" refers more narrowly to people without a bank account.

6. Friends or acquaintances who will take care of small amounts of money either for free or for a fee.

7. I used a structured schedule. The questionnaire included some open-ended questions that encouraged customers to respond freely. The terms "customers" and "users" are used interchangeably throughout the chapter.

8. A kitty is a group of members, usually women, pooling a certain amount of money every month, which is auctioned or is given in full to members in turn through a draw of lots. Kitties are also known as "kitty parties" based on their form of organization as social gatherings. These are popular among the middle-income urban women who join specific kitties based on their social networks. Regular meetings take place on a rotational basis and are hosted by the member that "wins" the lottery of contributions by all other members. Similar institutions are also common among working-class women in India. Similarly, "committee" is a popular method of saving among small/tiny business owners and is also known as a "lottery" system. Both fall in the purview of informal savings mechanisms. For a discussion of the similarities and differences among committees and kitties, see also Raj Mohan Sethi's (1995) seminal article "Women's ROSCAs in Contemporary Indian Society," as well as other chapters in this book.

9. This figure relates to the specific question: "Before opening the EKO account, where did you keep your savings/money?" It refers only to savings (both formal and informal). The cumulative is >100 percent due to multiple options.

10. Non-users were randomly selected and included three categories: those who had access to a mobile bank but no bank account, those who had both, and those who had neither. The non-user sample has an inherent limitation because the number of non-users does not proportionately match either the users sample or the non-users in the areas covered. In other words, it is not truly representative of non-users among low-income households in the sampled areas, and the researcher's bias both in the selection of non-users as well as in limiting their numbers is undeniable. Within a limited time frame, the intention was to capture the essence of perceptions of non-users about mobile banking and its use and related issues in order to get a comparative perspective.

11. In the Indian context and especially that of low-income households, "cash on hand" can often be used up either because it is claimable by demanding relatives (like husbands), children (emotional blackmail), or friends (who may justifiably expect [demand] a return favour for earlier money lent). Hence, the expression "claimable is situation specific."

12. Those users who stopped depositing completely for three or more months and withdrew most of their savings, leaving a nominal balance, were treated as inactive customers in the study.

13. EKO mobile banking service was initially offered free, but deposit as well as withdrawal transactions began to be charged a year after the service started. This led to users withdrawing from it, as the service proved too costly due to a

    flat-fee-based pricing structure. However, these inactive users expressed their keenness to restart using the service subject to a reasonable pricing policy by the mobile banking provider or the business correspondent (in this case, EKO).

14. In a CGAP study of nearly two thousand branchless banking customers in Pakistan (Easypaisa), India (EKO), and Mali (Orange Money), about three-fourths of poor users reported that the services had a positive impact on their lives and that the services were highly effective (McKay 2012).

15. This consisted of users with both bank accounts (61 percent) and no bank accounts (32 percent). By contrast, non-users of EKO showed a limited capacity to save either due to insufficient income or because the little that was kept on hand was spent and difficult to retain as savings.

16. A CGAP survey (Bold 2011) assessing whether branchless banking is reaching poor people found that 37 percent of the 814 EKO customers surveyed (especially the poor) used the service for savings primarily because of its ease of use; and, over three-quarters described the EKO service on a scale from 1 (not easy at all) to 10 (very easy) as an 8. Another study that explored how EKO's services have impacted its clients' saving practices (see Garg and Mehta 2010) found that convenience, ease of use, and trust in the nearby merchant were all reasons for preferring EKO's mobile banking service. Additionally, for a large portion of the low-income clients who were migrants with no or negligible documentation, the relaxed "know your customer" (KYC) norms gave an opportunity for opening an m-banking account, thus enabling them to start saving in a bank, a privilege they did not have earlier.

17. "Safekeeping of money" was the second most common reason for using EKO service in the CGAP 2011 survey.

18. The cumulative percentage is >100 percent due to the given choice of multiple answers.

19. Ivatuary (2006) similarly found low-income respondents in South Africa citing the lack of regular income as a main reason for not having a bank account.

20. *Gulaks* are piggy banks made of clay and commonly used in India among low-income households to save cash at home.

21. Garg and Mehta's (2010) study also indicates that those EKO clients with bank accounts have started to save smaller amounts in their EKO accounts as and when they have extra cash (as low as fifty rupees). Besides, those who were saving at home are now saving more frequently and in a more regular manner in their EKO accounts, which is also reinforced by the CGAP 2011 survey of EKO users.

22. Figures total to more than 100 percent due to multiple responses.

23. It is to be noted that the number of users who were "happy but not comfortable" (N=53) was analyzed as a percentage of all the users (N=160) in the study.

24. However, 10 percent of the users depended on "savings in a bank account" for meeting school fees in particular. Aligned with these results, M-PESA users were found to be integrating M-PESA into their savings portfolios (including informal and bank savings accounts) to decrease the risk of money being "wiped out" (see CGAP Brief 2009).

25. The two other key sources of funding for these same forms of investment are "borrowing from lender" followed by "insurance policy."

26. The fact that 74 percent of EKO and Easypaisa customers were apprehensive that losing access to the service would have a negative impact on their lives corroborates this view (see CGAP Brief 2009).

REFERENCES CITED

Bold, Chris. 2011. "Does Branchless Banking Reach Poor People? The Evidence from India." Retrieved 10 Septermber 2017 from http://www.cgap.org/blog/does-branchless-banking-reach-poor-people-evidence-india

Banerjee, Abhijit V., and Esther Duflo. 2011. *Poor Economics: A Radical Rethinking of the Way to Fight Poverty.* New York: Public Affairs.

Basu, Priya, and Pradeep Srivastava. 2005. "Improving Access to Finance for India's Rural Poor." In *India's Financial Sector – Recent Reforms, Future Challenges.* Edited by Priya Basu. 138–175. Washington, DC: MacMillan India Ltd for the World Bank.

CGAP Brief. 2009. "Poor People Using Mobile Financial Services: Observations on Customer Usage and Impact from M-PESA."

Chen, Greg. 2012. "EKO's Mobile Banking: Demonstrating the Power of a Basic Payments Product." CGAP Blog. Retrieved 31 August 2012 from http://www.cgap.org/blog/eko%E2%80%99s-mobile-banking-basic-payments-product.

Collins, Daryl, Jonathan Morduch, Stuart Ratherford, and Orlanda Ruthven. 2009. *Portfolios of the Poor: How the World's Poor Live on $2 a Day.* Princeton, NJ: Princeton University Press.

CRISIL. 2015. "CRISIL Inclusix – An Index to Measure India's Progress on Financial Inclusion." Volume III, June 2015. CRISIL Limited, Mumbai. Retrieved on 6 September 2017 from https://www.crisil.com/Crisil/pdf/corporate/CRISIL-Inclusix-Volume-III.pdf.

Demirguc-Kunt, Asli, and Leora Klapper. 2012. "Measuring Financial Inclusion: The Global Findex Database." Policy Research Working Paper 6025. Washington, DC: World Bank.

Garg, Nitin, Krishna Thacker, N. A. Venkata, Sachin Bansal, and Graham A. N. Wright. 2009. "Potential for E-M-Banking Enabled Migrant Remittances." MicroSave India Focus Note 29. October 2009. www.*MicroSave*.net

Garg, Nitin, and Swati Mehta. 2010. "Listening to Clients of Mobile Banking in India." MicroSave India Focus Note 37. April 2010 Retrieved on 6 September 2017 from http://www.microsave.net/files/pdf/IFN_37_Listening_to_Clients_of_M_Banking_in_India.pdf

Gartner. 2012. "Gartner Says India Mobile Services Market to Reach USD 30 Billion in 2016." Press Release, 27 March 2012. Retrieved 28 August 2012 from http://www.gartner.com/it/page.jsp?id=1963915.

Global Findex. 2011. "Financial Inclusion Data: India." World Bank. Retrieved 30 August 2012 from http://datatopics.worldbank.org/financialinclusion/country/india.

Government of India. 2008. "A Hundred Small Steps." Report of the Committee of Financial Sector Reforms, Planning Commission.

UNDP. 2009. "India: Urban Poverty Report 2009." Ministry of Housing and Urban

Poverty Alleviation and United Nations Development Programme. New Delhi: Oxford University Press.

Group Special Mobile Association (GSMA). 2012a. "History." Retrieved 4 September 2012 from http://www.gsma.com/aboutus/history/.

———. 2012b. "GSMA Announces That India Will Become the World's Second Largest Mobile Broadband Market within Four Years," 3 April. Retrieved on 6 September 2017 https://www.gsma.com/newsroom/press-release/gsma-announces-that-india-will-become-the-worlds-second-largest-mobile-broadband-market-within-four-years/

———. 2016. "The Mobile Economy: India 2016." GSMA Head Office, London, United Kingdom. Retrieved 6 September 2017 from https://www.gsmaintelligence.com/research/?file=134a1688cdaf49cfc73432e2f52b2dbe&download

Heyer, A, and Ignacio Mas. 2009. "Seeking Fertile Grounds for Mobile Money." Draft, 3 September 2009. Retrieved 6 September 2017 from https://www.gsma.com/mobilefordevelopment/wp-content/uploads/2012/03/fertile_grounds_mobile_money55.pdf.

Ivatury, Gautam. 2006. "Using Technology to Build Inclusive Financial Systems." *CGAP: Focus Note* (32):1–16 (January). Retrieved 6 September 2017 from https://www.cgap.org/sites/default/files/CGAP-Focus-Note-Using-Technology-to-Build-Inclusive-Financial-Systems-Jan-2006.pdf.

Jack, William, and Tavneet Suri. 2011. "Mobile Money: The Economics of M-PESA." Working Paper 16721. National Bureau of Economic Research, Cambridge, MA. Retrieved 6 September 2017 https://www.microlinks.org/sites/microlinks/files/resource/files/The%20Economics%20of%20M-PESA.pdf.

Joseph, Nikhil, and Benjamin D. Mazotta. 2014. "Frugal Finance: How Eko Helps India's Migrants Move and Manage Money." IBGC Working Paper 14-01. Institute for Business in the Global Context, Tufts University. Retrieved on 6 September 2017 http://fletcher.tufts.edu/~/media/Fletcher/Microsites/Cost%20of%20Cash/IBGC%20WP14-01%20EKO.pdf

Malhotra, Sarika. 2010. "Human ATMs: A Business Correspondent Model at Work." Open Forum. *Financial Express,* 23 May, 5.

Mas, Ignacio. 2009. "The Economics of Branchless Banking." *Innovations* 4(2) (Spring): 57.

Mas, Ignacio, and Mike McCaffrey. 2015. "Eko in India." Helix Institute of Digital Finance. Retrieved 6 September 2017 from http://www.helix-institute.com/data-and-insights/eko-india.

McKay, Claudia. 2012. "Do Poor People Use Branchless Banking Services?" Retrieved April 15 2016 from http://www.cgap.org/blog/do-poor-people-use-branchless-banking-services.

Medhi, Indrani, Aishwarya Ratan, and Kentaro Toyama. 2009. "Mobile Banking Adoption and Usage by Low-Literate, Low-Income Users in the Developing World." Microsoft Research India, Bangalore, India. Retrieved 6 September 2017 http://ww.w.gsmworld.com/mobilefordevelopment/wp-content/uploads/2012/06/hcii2009_medhi_ratan_toyama_d_26.pdf

Nandhi, Mani A. 2010. "Urban Poor and Their Money: A Study of Cycle Rickshaw Pullers in Delhi." Unpublished manuscript. Institute for Money, Technology & Financial Institution, University of California, Irvine.

Nandhi, Mani A., and Kc Deepti. 2013. "Evolving Participatory Relationships for Uplifting the Urban Poor Rickshaw Pullers: Next Step Forward." Unpublished manuscript. Institute for Money, Technology & Financial Institution, University of California, Irvine.

Planning Commission, Government of India. 2008. "Report of the Committee on Financial Sector Reforms – 'A Hundred Small Steps.'" New Delhi: Sage Publications.

Prahalad, C. K. 2008. "Leapfrogging the Digital Divide." *Microfinance Insights.* Vol 8 (Sept/Oct): 1215 https://issuu.com/microfinanceinsights/docs/30_aug_2008_-_final

———. 2010. *The Fortune at the Bottom of the Pyramid: Eradicating Poverty through Profits.* Noida: Dorling Kindersley (India) Pvt, Ltd.

Ruthven, O. 2002. "Money Mosaics: Financial Choice and Strategy in a West Delhi Squatter Settlement." *Journal of International Development* 14: 249–71.

Rutherford, Stuart. 2000. *The Poor and Their Money: Microfinance from a Twenty-First-Century Consumer's Perspective.* New York: Oxford University Press.

Sethi, Raj Mohini. 1995. "Women's ROSCAs in Contemporary Indian Society." In *Money-Go-Rounds: The Importance of Rotating Savings and Credit Associations for Women,* edited by Shirley Ardner and Sandra Burman. 163177. Washington, DC: Berg.

Shukla, Rajesh. 2007. "How India Earns, Spends and Saves: Results from the Max New York Life Inc. and National Council of Applied Economic Research (NCAER) India Financial Protection Survey." Max New York Life Inc. Retrieved 13 September 2017 from http://www.scribd.com/doc/17771523/MNYLNCAER-Book-How-India-Earns-Spends-and-Saves.

Srinivasan, N. 2008. *Microfinance India – State of the Sector Report 2008.* New Delhi: Sage Publications, New Delhi.

———. 2009. *Microfinance India – State of the Sector Report 2009.* New Delhi: Sage Publications.

Stuart, Guy, and Monique Cohen. 2011. "Dry Spells and Shocks: M-PESA as a Financial Management Tool." Financial services assessment, Microfinance Opportunities, Washington DC.

Thorat, Usha. 2007. "Financial Inclusion – The Indian Experience." HMT-DFID Financial Inclusion Conference, London, 19 June 2007.

UNCTAD. 2008. *Information Economy Report 2007–2008: Science and Technology for Development – The New Paradigm of ICT.* Geneva: United Nations Conference on Trade and Development.

World Bank. 2011. "India: South Asia." World Bank Development Indicators. Retrieved 29 August 2012 from http://data.worldbank.org/country/india#cp_wdi.

Zollmann, Julie, and Daryl Collins. 2010. "Financial Capability and the Poor: Are We Missing the Mark?" *FSD Insights* (2): 112 (December 1).

CHAPTER 13

Betting on Chance in Colombia

Using Empirical Evidence on Game Networks to Develop Practical Design Guidelines

ANA MARÍA ECHEVERRY
AND COPPELIA HERRÁN CUARTAS

Every evening, after leaving his sales cart at a nearby building, Juan, an informal seller, counts the money collected from sales that day. He makes sure to set apart ten USD for paying the daily rent for the room where he lives and the food he will prepare that night. He also takes a quarter of a dollar and walks to the closest betting kiosk. Every day he thinks that maybe this is the night he will guess the winning number of the Medellín Lottery that plays at 10:00 PM. Upon arriving at the kiosk, Juan tells the clerk to place a bet on the number 3567 and promises her that, if he guesses the winning number, he will give her a small commission from the three hundred dollars he gets. Juan also makes a secret promise to send a remittance of fifty dollars to his brother – from that very kiosk that would have proven to bring him luck.

Betting games have been a common practice among Colombians since colonial times (1600s–1800s). Whether lottery, cards, or dice, government authorities historically have tried to keep these practices under control through fiscal laws in order to prevent "the dissolution of hierarchies and the establishment." By the second half of the eighteenth century, city councils had already banned many of these practices, demeaning them as belonging to the common people and not appropriate for higher classes (Jiménez 2007: 92–93).

The game of Chance is a widely popular betting game in Colombia, especially among the poor. In a nutshell, this game is a more economical version of a lottery (around USD $0.25 per bet), in which a person tries to guess two, three, or four of the winning numbers in an official lottery. Although prizes are a lot less than winning a lottery (around USD $250), people have a greater chance of winning. Chance spread from Cuba to Colombia and became popular during the 1970s. This practice has been regulated by the state since 1982 due, in part, to the fact that illegal groups were using this betting game for money laundering ("Los Juegos que se Mueven tras el Chance" 2008). In 2001, the government took direct control of Chance as a "state monopoly" and created a strict legal framework that only allows electronically issued tickets, thus promoting the use of mobile devices for street sales (Sociedad Colombiana de Apuestas S.A. 2013).

While mobile-money services (MMS) have become a tool for financial inclusion for the poor in countries such as Kenya, India, and the Philippines, in Colombia cellular phones are mainly used for necessary calls, often through informal "minute-sellers" that offer lower-cost minutes than the prepaid plans (Ipsos – Napoleón Franco 2010). Although there are now more cellular phones than inhabitants in Colombia ("Colombia Tiene 46,1 Millones de Líneas de Telefonía Celular" 2011) and banks offer mobile banking services at no cost, by and large, the poor prefer to use game networks for conducting their financial transactions. Given that mobile and online financial services require clients to have a bank account, the low penetration of banking in Colombia represents a huge obstacle, especially for the poor (Villabona 2010). In contrast, game networks have specialized in offering a range of cash-based services that don't require previous affiliation. Since 2007 these networks have been expanding their services to the extent that nowadays people can send and receive remittances; buy insurance; pay utilities; reload prepaid energy, television, and phone services; among other things. They also serve as banking correspondents for people with bank accounts. Game networks have a nationwide presence through kiosks and independent sellers – via point of sale (POS) terminals located in city streets and rural areas.

Between 2007 and 2011, nonbanking correspondents, including retailers' chains such as Exito, small grocery stores, and corner shops, moved around US$7.7 billion ("De la Banca a la Titular" 2011). Meanwhile, game networks totaled about US$15.2 billion in remittances alone ("Giros Nacionales Casi Igualan Remesas" 2011). At the same time, mobile banking transactions represented only 0.5 percent of all banking transactions, an amount so small that the banking association Asobancaria does not even quantify it in its yearly reports because this channel is mostly used for checking balances (Asociación Bancaria y de Entidades Financieras, Asobancaria 2011).

The dramatic contrast between the game network's popularity and the sluggish adoption of other digital networks presents an interesting opportunity for identifying key aspects of users' needs that mobile services have failed to address. By using video-ethnographic methods, our team of social scientists and designers documented the activities of twenty-one informants who work in street sales in the city of Medellín, Colombia. Why, we asked, are these game operators preferable as financial service providers for the poor? What needs do they address? What can mobile-money service providers and microfinance institutions learn from these local institutions and practices? Although this study only covered a limited geographic area in Colombia, the findings and guidelines can be applied in different contexts affected by poverty in this country and beyond. Through an exercise in design thinking, we draw attention to criteria that should be taken into account when developing new products and services that are aimed at facilitating the use and exchange of money among people with scarce resources.

Proximity, Immediacy, and Simplicity

The business of informal sales relies on those small amounts of cash that people carry in their pockets and that can be quickly used to buy products and services on the go. In fact, as the monetary economy expands, there is an ever-growing use of fractioned money, which allows people to buy all sorts of things and feed the industries that live from this market (Simmel 1997: 243–55). Street sellers must have access to small amounts of cash; also, the gains in cash at the end of the day are used to buy the next day's goods. This situation leaves very little room for payment and saving options other than cash.

In other words, the informal workers who spend all day in streets and public spaces opt for payment and payment channels that allow them to purchase, pay, send, and save in small amounts and without having to leave their workplace. Transactional services that require a bank account are, therefore, not a feasible option. None of our informants found bank accounts useful or valuable given the inefficiency and inconvenience; there is no point in waiting in line to deposit cash that they would need to withdraw again the next day. Furthermore, most subjects felt that the bank account fees often amount to more than what they make in a day's work.

By contrast, game kiosks allow them to send money, buy reloads, and make payments from their workplace, without the hidden costs and through a simpler process. Kiosks have become a practical tool for these informal workers as they earn income; they can utilize the kiosks to set aside or use available resources in real time.

Importantly, the wide availability of kiosks, both in cities and in small towns, represents a great advantage for almost all subjects, who often send money to a close relative living in another location. For sending a remittance, users only need to provide identification, a phone number, and an address. Since kiosks specialize in small remittances, users do not need to fill out the long forms that banks use to prevent money laundering and terrorism financing. Furthermore, clerks at kiosks operate the terminals, exchange money, and answer questions so that users are not expected to own or know how to use a specific device to interact with them.

The behaviors evidenced here, which touch on the need for immediacy, proximity, and simplicity, present a challenge especially to traditional banking and financial service providers: How can they mediate or facilitate transactions of lower amounts, across multiple geographical areas, without the need of having a formal account? How can they enable transactions among unbanked individuals?

The Users' Income Cycles

Dependent on precarious and unstable sources of income, informal workers become accustomed to buying products and services in smaller units but at higher prices as a way of keeping open the possibility of using "unassigned" or "uncommitted" money to address unexpected needs. In other words, they prefer to pay a price in order to retain control over resources instead of committing these for future use. This need to keep control over resources, along with the uncertainty of a stable income, also leads many informal workers to avoid long-term payment commitments such as credit, rent, stay, and services; they fear defaulting on payments and facing legal consequences that would worsen their current living conditions.

Buying a cellular phone minute, half an hour of internet time, or a dollar of energy are some of the ways people manage spending and retain control over unspent resources. The value of being in control – of both what is used and what is saved – has become more evident with the expanding prepaid energy service offered by Empresas Públicas de Medellín (EPM), Medellín's public utilities company. This service is provided to low-income households that have difficulties paying their monthly bills (Empresas Públicas de Medellín 2011). The company installs an energy counter inside the home that, enabled with a pin pad, lets the user enter a reload code purchased at game kiosks for as little as one dollar. Users of this service feel that having the option to reload small amounts and monitor their energy use has enabled them to stay within budget and save resources. This reload system also shows that it is important to offer services that adapt to income patterns of users and give them control over usage. By adjusting payment cycles to usage patterns, users no longer fall behind payments or get cut off from services.

While formal workers receive regular salary payments that allow them to seek longer-term services, informal workers tend to avoid these commitments. Almost all of the subjects tried and failed to pay using credit for things such as a pair of shoes or a cellular phone, and they are now excluded from the formal credit sector.

Coming back to Simmel's concept that quick circulation promotes both spending and recuperating small amounts of money, these findings support the idea that financial service providers should always avoid the accumulation of amounts due by the user and rather promote a pay-per-use or consumption model. Quick cycles benefit people with unstable incomes, even if they lose the opportunity to save over the long run, because they value having control over the money earned each day to cover immediate needs. As game networks and utility companies have proven, profits can be made on both ends of the spectrum, from long-term as well as short-term circulations. Financial institutions should create new service models for informal workers that, unlike those provided for employed people with regular salaries, offer benefits based on quick cycles rather than on long-term deposits.

Reconfiguring Notions of Family and Practices of Value Transfer

As anthropologist Hernán Henao Delgado (2004) noted, Colombia has lived through ongoing fratricidal struggles during its nearly two hundred years of history as an independent nation-state. Over the past fifty years, the Colombian landscape has become increasingly urban, with peasants and country people moving to cities due to forced displacements. That expulsion process toward the cities has continued as the result of new actors and violence factors: guerrilla and narco-traffic in the 1970s and 1980s. Beginning in the 1980s, another new instigator emerged – paramilitary groups whose political and ideological stance is not yet clear. In this context, migrants, displaced or expulsed people, become inhabitants of a territory that does not belong to them. Migrants end up becoming unproductive beings and a financial burden to society and the state. External pressure generates a destabilization in the daily rhythm of the migrants' lives. Interaction and communication among each community weakens until it disappears at the moment of displacement. There is a process of uprooting parental bonds, family relationships, job occupation, patterns of consumption, and value systems, all of them marked by a deterioration of living conditions (Henao Delgado 2004: 201–14).

Migration due to displacement and the search for employment opportunities has separated and reconfigured most of the informants' families. Parental absence (due to abandonment, separation, or death) and the inability to survive on a single income also affect the roles and responsibilities of family members. "What characterizes this family's time, which seems to transcend into the next [twenty-first] century, is a typology or family modality that is complex in structure with interim adjustments due to agitated changes in institutions and principles in the Colombian culture" (Gutiérrez de Pineda 2005: 290).

The traditional paternalist family model, whereby the father is the sole provider and an authority figure, is uncommon among informal workers. "The masculine authority loses absolutism in favor of a democratic system: inside the family, authority lies on the principle that all decide, do and take responsibility, different from the patriarch system in which the father decides and takes responsibility while the wife and children obey and do" (Gutiérrez de Pineda 2005: 288). Instead, families ensure their survival through other familial arrangements: mothers, children, and older relatives all need to work and contribute to expenses. There are no quotas of fixed economic responsibilities, but each member is expected to help ameliorate the needs of the family.

Likewise, authority and decision-making are no longer parental roles but shared responsibilities. Family members gather their earnings in a common fund. The management and redistribution of that fund is often channeled through the person regarded as the most organized, responsible, and able of the group. Cohesion between family members remains in spite of physical distances, thus making remittances a crucial service for group survival. Family cohesion has been mentioned as an important coping strategy among displaced families who had to separate, relocate, and regroup away from their homes (López and Londoño 2007: 180).

In some cases, adapting to social and economic changes turn families into transient groups. New members join the family while others leave. Domestic partners, single mothers, relatives who can no longer survive on their own all affect family structures and the roles within the group. Then, when trying to assimilate these family groups in relation to the traditional model, family should be defined not only by the network of people that configure these groups but also by the contacts established among them (Parra 2005). In this context, families prefer to use services and tools that allow them to contribute, share, exchange, and transfer value easily among members. While cash is the predominant means for contributing and sharing, service reloads, remittances, and staples are also common ways that members help each other. In the vast majority of cases, money and expense management is a group activity, not an individual action.

Changes in family composition show that having blood ties or sharing a roof are no longer relevant factors to define a family group, thus presenting a new challenge for financial and transaction service providers. There is a growing need for offering services directed toward complex and changing family groups. The nature of services should change from a model based on the individual to a model that revolves around groups. For example, group credits, accounts that allow exchanges among family members, and incentives that promote the continuous use of services could benefit both the service provider and the client-group.

Alternate Channels for Saving and Borrowing

The lack of meaningful benefits from formal savings institutions and the high penalties these institutions charge drive the poor away from banks and toward informal services. Even though game networks offer banking services and are now nonbanking correspondents, informal workers do not use these services. These workers perceive banking services as useless, complex, and costly.[1] Despite the banks' efforts to project a more appealing image to the poor, the general distrust of banks makes it highly unlikely that informal workers would seek to use them for conducting their transactions. Our informants' experiences reinforce these perceptions. For example, almost all of them noted that the amounts of money they handle are so small that a bank account is not worth their while: interest rates do not cover the cost of fees, the security level is unnecessary, and access to a bank account does not guarantee access to credit.

With scarce and unstable income, most informal workers choose to save money out of sight – in cans, inside clothes, or in the back of a drawer – to cover occasional expenses or unforeseen needs. However, saving is not a habitual activity since it entails giving up a resource in addition to self-control or discipline. Skipping meals or walking long distances rather than using public transport are common ways to create saving opportunities. For many of our informants, keeping a shared fund among family members was done to set aside savings for covering monthly expenses such as rent or utilities, not for future needs or for improving their livelihood.

For credit or loans, informal workers rely on "payday" or "drop-to-drop" loans. These loans, provided mostly by criminal groups, come with 20 percent daily interest rates and must be repaid in a month or less. They are used by many of our subjects since they have no access to formal credit. Far from feeling at great personal risk, our subjects expressed appreciation for these lending services. Many mentioned that, unlike banks, payday loans offer quick credit evaluation, immediate cash availability, and on-site services. Some even noted that even if they had access to formal credit, they would still prefer payday loans because a bank would take days to process a request and can always reject it.

As economist Jairo Villabona (2010) points out, unlike other countries, Colombian *bancarization* – that is, the incentive for people to open at least a bank account so that all citizens use the formal financial system and pay taxes – has been closely linked to microcredit programs aimed at small businesses. It has not been consistent in strengthening other financial needs of the poor, such as savings, insurance, and money transfers. *Bancarization* cannot solely consist of, as is often argued, increasing the number of banking correspondents dedicated to collecting payments in distant communities to save the cost of opening offices. Rather, *bancarization* should also comprise allocation of resources, even if the state needs to guarantee or subsidize services (Villabona 2010).

These findings lead us to think that neither the *bancarization* initiative nor the services currently offered by formal credit institutions are solving the problems faced by the poor. On the contrary, it is the use of informal lending until "payday" that constitutes the main resource for financial services due to the speed, ease, and delivery benefits. This shows that the amount of paperwork, the need to have a credit history, and the length of time that formal institutions require to provide credit services have become significant barriers that the poor cannot overcome. At the same time, the popularity of the payday loans, even with abusive interest rates, demonstrate that there is room for developing new models of credit services that can serve the particular needs of informal workers. More flexible regulation that removes the "illegal" component of current informal lending would make it viable to offer short-term and lower-amount credit services. Also, it is evident that formal institutions need to rethink the necessary documentation, processing time, and mode of delivery in order to compete against the existing services that informal workers are using.

Public Space as an Intangible Asset

The need to access a wider customer base turns many informal workers toward public spaces as sites that can serve as a workplace and a source of income. Public space is at the center of an informal economy that provides sustenance for informal workers as well as profits for big companies and illegal groups. In this contradictory scenario, a conflict emerges between the state's need to protect public space and informal vendors' right to work by appropriating public property, which is considered an "invasion" by the state. While citizens lose their right to enjoy public space, formal merchants perceive informal vendors as unfair competition who do not pay taxes or any other cost associated with formal business (Blandón 2011: 14). The source of conflict for production and appropriation in public spaces stems from nomination processes, that is, the extent that a single agent or player has the ability to decide what is public, what belongs to all, and what is of general interest. Indeed, if any of the other players do not find those decisions natural or credible, decisions will be seen as lacking legitimacy (Vergara 2008: 147).

Obtaining the right to work in a fixed location on a busy street can mean years of struggle and persistence; it means reckoning with competitors, public officials, and, often, illegal groups that charge "protection fees." Local governments issue a limited number of permits to street sellers to keep in balance the rights to work and to move freely. However, the number of street sellers is so high that authorities resort to police operations in which merchandise is confiscated and the streets cleared. According to public officials, there are twenty-five thousand public space permits, but during the last ten years the number of street sellers may well have doubled (Zapata 2012).

For this reason, a public space permit has a value comparable to commercial real estate or exploitation rights that can be exchanged or traded in the informal market. For example, one street seller stated that he could sell "his place" for about US$2,500, while another was offered US$7,500 for his permit. None of the subjects with a legal permit would consider selling these permits for fear of losing their clients and sources of income. They are well aware of the value and protect their permits and places as a means to ensure their livelihood.

Some established companies have capitalized on the street sellers' ability to reach clients in public spaces. They provide carts, uniforms, and product training. Street sellers receive inventory in the morning and return unsold goods, profits, and carts at the end of day. Alternatively, as one street seller mentioned to us, he has to pay for dry ice and the melted popsicles that go unsold. If he loses or damages the cart, the company charges him US$250. He has no health insurance or benefits from the company because he is not an employee. As Alejandro Portes states, big companies can save on high costs of tax and labor codes by limiting the size of the declared workforce and by subcontracting the rest to informal entrepreneurs (Portes 2004: 42).

Public space permits carry invaluable information about its owner's work history, commitment to an activity, established commercial relationships, permanence in a community, and estimated income. In other words, the public space permit serves as an informal record of the worker's credit history – which is the only official way permitted vendors can demonstrate these things – but they cannot be used to gain access to other formal services such as bank loans.

As mentioned earlier, informal workers cannot be expected to meet a financial entity's requirements when those requirements are based on the assumption that clients will have stable jobs, own properties, and have an established credit history. Our findings reveal that there are other potential ways to assess and demonstrate an informal worker's capacity and commitment to use a financial service. The public space permit issued by city authorities is one document that financial entities can use as a replacement for employment history. Also, the purchasing history a seller has with his providers, which speaks for his stability and payment capacity, can replace formal credit histories. These alternate assets should be considered by financial service providers to create a different set of requirements that are easily quantifiable and could facilitate access to informal workers.

Bureaucratic Complexity and Financial Exclusion

Even though Colombia's Social Protection System offers a wide range of coverage – including healthcare, pensions, employment and professional risk insurance, as well as other subsidies – the reality is that informal workers have an extremely limited access to this portfolio. The growing complexity of urban practices and services can confuse and overwhelm informal workers who, lacking resources and education, give up on obtaining the benefits to which they are entitled. There are severe limitations in both the access to the aforementioned coverages, as well as the quality of the services received by state-funded programs (Gomez 2009: 130–33).[2]

Just obtaining a card for accessing basic healthcare services requires documentation, waiting in lines, filling out forms, home visits, and other procedures that are challenging for many people. Applying for state subsidies requires even more processing, sometimes lawsuits. Oftentimes the subsidies do not come regularly or are suspended without notice. Besides the difficulties in completing the paperwork, users feel poorly treated by state officials and find the state's inefficiency so overwhelming that they often prefer to go without the services.

For instance, we encountered an older woman who does not know why she stopped receiving a subsidy for the elderly, a single mother who has never heard of state-sponsored child assistance, and two displacement victims who survive without any support from the state. One of the latter sells ice cream from a well-known company that provides him with a cart and a uniform. He supports his family from sales commissions but gets no insurance or benefits. This is not an isolated case. In fact, there are a number of established companies that take advantage of street sellers through legal means. These companies achieve great savings in distribution costs and offer no protection to their informal sellers. From what we saw, not only do informal workers face difficulty negotiating with the formal sector but they also lack the protection, knowledge, and means to defend their rights.

If neither the state nor formal institutions provide basic social protection, it is unlikely that informal workers will trust other services such as banking or finance, since their experience indicates that these entities are not reliable. Moreover, as soon as banking and credit institutions ask them to bring forms and documents, informal workers lose hope and start looking for other options: game networks for remittances and payday loans for financing.

The complexity of current urban and state practices makes it worth considering services that (a) recognize informal workers as legitimate members of the community, (b) facilitate and simplify processes that require interacting with state and formal (state-like) entities, (c) improve the representation of informal workers in the community, and (d) promote offerings that better adjust to these workers' contexts.

Design Guidelines

Based on our research findings, we propose a set of concepts that, informed by the needs and values of informal workers, can serve as guidelines for designing and developing new applications that will promote financial inclusion. We have organized these concepts into four categories: access, creditworthiness, value, and reach.

Access

Leverage existing kiosks and points of sale as exchange nodes. For informal workers, especially street sellers, being able to easily exchange digital value and cash would be crucial for adopting mobile-money services. Since kiosks and shops usually collect money as part of their services, they would also be ideal places for cashing and receiving payments without having to visit a bank office. An additional benefit of this would be a reduction in the need for armored transportation, because kiosks and shops put the collected money back in circulation.

Offer multiple channels. In a context such as Colombia, a mobile phone is not a strictly personal device. Moreover, many users change numbers frequently because they buy preloaded SIM cards from whichever network offers the lowest price. These reasons, along with a high mobile phone theft rate, make it difficult to succeed through offering transaction services limited to mobile channels. There is room in the market for a provider that is willing to make services available through a variety of channels. Then, a user could choose to use whichever channel (mobile phone, kiosk, POS terminal) best suits his or her needs, according to the situation.

Offer a clear and transparent fee structure. Hidden costs, carrying fees, and multiple conditions can confuse and cause distrust among users. To promote the adoption of mobile-money services, the fee structure needs to allow easy recall, calculation and verification of charges. Furthermore, mobile payment and savings features should never be charged an additional fee because users would simply opt for cash.

Creditworthiness

Build a transaction history as an alternative to a credit history. Services should provide a summary report that groups and quantifies payments, purchases, and transfers without compromising the privacy of the user. Thus, people who lack a credit history could demonstrate economic or commercial relationships over time.

Minimize requirements to use services. Since remittance and credit services are core needs for informal workers, eligibility and affiliation become important issues. Therefore, transaction services should not be conditioned on having a bank account. For remittances, game networks only require senders and receivers to provide identification cards and contact information. Game networks only allow the sending of small amounts, thus eliminating the need to fill out forms for preventing money laundering and terrorism. Although mobile phones can serve as a transaction channel, it is important not to limit a service to a particular channel or a device. That way, users who do not feel comfortable using a mobile phone could still make transactions.

For credit services, the most important factor is to offer users alternate pathways to obtain a loan. Many informal workers do not have traditional assets, credit histories, or employment records, but they often have established relationships that demonstrate their income, spending habits, and commitment-to-pay obligations. For example, if a person has a public space permit, it means that they have spent years dedicated to an activity. It also means that they have developed economic relationships, kept an inventory, and managed expenses for a time period. It is unlikely that a street seller abandons a workplace to avoid paying a small loan since that place represents the only income source. Those who have not been able to get a permit may also have established relationships with providers, clients, and even formal businesses who can attest to the street seller's permanence at a location.

Privilege speed over amounts. Having immediate access to resources or benefits is key for people with scarce and irregular income. Unforeseen events, such as a serious illness or even a few days without good sales, create financial challenges that cannot wait for a week-long process at a credit institution to take its course. In such cases, speed becomes an eligibility issue. By focusing on smaller loans, financial services may be able to serve the needs of informal workers more quickly. Likewise, remittances of smaller amounts have fewer legal requirements and paperwork.

Value

Develop services based on short cycles. Nowadays, remittances are the most dynamic service offered by game networks. Nonetheless, for informal workers, access to small loans is their most critical need. In collaboration with microfinance institutions, it should be possible to offer short-cycle credit services that would be very useful to informal workers. Kiosks could facilitate both the disbursement and repaying of these loans. This option would provide many advantages over payday loans if the application process is simple enough. These services would address the critical needs of the poor that informal loans normally target.

Create out-of-sight saving opportunities. Even though informal workers do not find real benefits in banking accounts, they do set money aside and try to save small amounts to cover emergencies and unforeseen needs. A service or feature that allows users to set aside and save, for example, the change after a purchase, a reload, or part of a remittance can be a helpful alternative to a bank account. Instead of offering interest rates as banks do, this type of service can offer other incentives for reaching or keeping savings levels. While the users keep the value out of sight but ready to access and use, the network can count on those unforeseen future transactions.

Adapt payments to income cycles. To facilitate the payment of monthly obligations, a transaction network could offer advanced partial payments toward future monthly bills. It would work as a provisioning service. For example, a user could make small partial payments toward utilities or rent. By making provision for specific payments, users can get better control over cash and soften the economic impact when the bill arrives. Service providers could also use these provisions or advance payments as the basis for incentives and other rewards for positive behavior.

Serve user groups with shared services. Since most families manage income and expenses as a group, services should allow users to contribute, redistribute, and exchange value among members. As an example, a mother could use contributions recently made by her sons to pay the rent to the landlord. User groups could have some privileges over individual users such as larger loans and reduced costs per transferring value.

Reach

Legitimate informal workers' contribution to the community. Because cash transactions are not usually recorded or tracked, it is difficult to estimate and value the economic role of informal workers in a community. If street sellers' associations had more precise information, they could better articulate the guild's contribution, the number of families that depend on their activity, and the relationships with other industries that benefit from informal workers. A digital transactions network could provide information tools to guilds or associations that would help them to gain recognition from both the state and the private sector. In addition, these tools could enable the development of more targeted programs and also be used to measure the success of those initiatives over time.

Facilitate transactions for joint programs between the community, the state, and the private sector. Currently, inclusion programs are limited to providing public space permits and offering entrepreneurship credit, as long as informal workers have good credit reports and are willing to leave their places of work. These programs do not account for the informal workers' lack of means to manage entrepreneurial projects that could provide something more than a precarious income. Also, they do not take into consideration the families that depend on the street sellers' income. Instead of relocating sellers with individual projects, state programs should focus on promoting work opportunities with their families and the help from the private sector. Thus, initiatives could have a greater impact in the community and provide better work opportunities for the poor. As an example, hot-dog sellers could buy bread and ingredients from small suppliers owned or operated by street sellers' families. At the same time, private companies could help structure those suppliers' businesses as part of a social responsibility program. In collaboration with microfinance institutions, a transaction network could offer specific tools to manage and track transactions among members or their affiliated suppliers and sellers. The advantage of these services would be that they coordinate and facilitate transactions outside the formal banking system.

Guilds and associations have played a role in representing informal workers, but this has long been limited to mediating with the local government ("Dueños del desorden" 2012). These associations could play a significant role in promoting social and financial inclusion if they reached out to the private sector, especially those companies that have traditionally benefited by using informal workers as a distribution channel.

Final Thoughts

Game networks have challenged the traditional banking system in Colombia by using alternate channels to offer financial services to the poor. Despite the fact that remittances and payments are their main services, game networks are better positioned than banks to develop savings and credit services that fit the needs of informal workers. By developing alliances with microfinance institutions, game networks could create a complete range of financial and transaction services that are accessible via kiosks, POS terminals, and mobile phones.

Mobile-money services and digital transaction networks could make a significant contribution to financial inclusion in Colombia, as long as access is not limited to the use of mobile phones. Places where people can exchange money and get quick assistance with services are still the key to ensuring the wide adoption of services. If the regulatory environment becomes more conducive to mobile services, game networks could transform into digital transaction networks that could leverage mobile phone technology, kiosks, and POS terminals to facilitate transactions without depending on the banking sector.

Without a consistent follow-up from the state and appropriate regulations that foster financial inclusion, mobile-money services cannot be more, or less, inclusive than ATM machines. The dominant position of banks and telecommunication companies in the domestic market can negatively affect the development and availability of financial services to the poor. It is necessary to ensure that regulations allow multiple operators and service providers to compete and offer targeted services to specific groups, especially the poor, because they have a limited access to traditional banking and credit resources.

Ana María Echeverry worked as project lead through Toca LLC in Medellín, Colombia, on this project. She is an independent consultant and received her master of design from Illinois Institute of Technology.

Coppelia Herrán Cuartas worked as a co-researcher through Toca LLC on this project. She is a research professor at the Architecture and Design School at Universidad Pontificia Bolivariana and received her master in anthropology from Universidad de Antioquia in Medellín, Colombia.

NOTES

1. As Melgarejo does, we define perception as a means "by which human beings recognize, interpret, intercept and give meaning, judging and generating answers around feelings they get from a physical and social environment. Psychological processes, such as learning, memorizing and symbolizing also come into play here" (Melgarejo 1994: 48).
2. In a recent study about decent work, Alejandro Ordoñez, Colombia's attorney general, summarized the current situation with the following paragraph: "In Colombia, the persistent unemployment rates above 10%; the existence of an informal sector that generates around half the jobs; the discrimination of the job market against women, the young, people with disabilities, displacement victims, among others; the failure to meet labor standards; the abuse of figures such as those for cooperatives of associated workers; the low rates of union's participation; the precarious mechanisms for collective negotiation and the low proportion of affiliation to the social security system, reveal the high complexity of the problems associated to the job market, and make more evident the insufficient efforts the state has invested on overcoming them" (Ordóñez 2012: 16).

REFERENCES CITED

Asociación Bancaria y de Entidades Financieras, Asobancaria. 2011. *Informe de Inclusión Financiera 2011.* Colombia. Retrieved 13 December 2011 from https:// www.microfinancegateway.org/sites/default/files/mfg-es-documento-in forme-de-inclusion-financiera-colombia-2011-7-2012.pdf .

Blandón, Melquiceded. 2011. "El Trabajo En Las Calles: Territorialización, Control Y Política En El Centro De Medellín A Comienzos Del Siglo XXI." Magíster diss. Universidad de Antioquia.

"Colombia Tiene 46,1 Millones de Líneas de Telefonía Celular." 2011. *El Espectador* [Colombia], 26 August. Retrieved July 17, 2013 from http://www .elespectador.com/tecnologia/articulo-294636-colombia-tiene-461-millones-de-lineas-de-telefonia-celular

"De la Banca a la Titular." 2011. *Portafolio* [Colombia], 16 September. Bancarización section.

"Dueños del desorden." 2012. Editorial. *Universo Centro* (39) (October). Retrieved 12 July 2013 from http://www.universocentro.com/NUMERO39/Editorial.aspx.

Empresas Públicas de Medellín. 2011. *Programa de Energía Prepago en Medellín.* Retrieved 23 July 2013 from http://www.calicomovamos.org.co/calicomovamos/files/Red_de_Ciudades/Experiencias Otros CV/Energia prepago.pdf.

"Encuesta de Percepción Ciudadana.' 2012. Medellincomovamos.org (Colombia), 23 October 23. Retrieved 12 January 2012 from http://medellincomovamos.org/pobreza-y-desigualdad.

"Giros Nacionales Casi Igualan Remesas: Transacciones Mueven al Año Unos $7.2 Billones de Pesos." 2011. *Portafolio* [Colombia], 2 March. Economy section. Retrieved 17 December 2011 from http://www.portafolio.co/economia/giros-nacionales-casi-igualan-remesas.

Gomez, Ronald. 2009. *Independent Workers and Social Protection in Latin America.* Santiago: International Labour Office.

Gutiérrez de Pineda, Virginia. 2005. "Modalidades Familiares de Fin de Siglo." Edited by Enrique Valencia. Revista Maguaré. Universidad Nacional de Colombia. Number 19. Retrieved 25 June 2013 from http://www.revistas.unal.edu.co/index.php/maguare/article/download/10774/11238.

Henao Delgado, Hernán. 2004. *Familia, Conflicto, Territorio y Cultura.* Medellín: Editado por Corporación Región y el Instituto de Estudios Regionales (INER).

Ipsos – Napoleón Franco. 2010. "Percepción, Usos y Hábitos frente a las Tecnologías de Información y la Comunicación: Informe de Resultados." Ministerio de Tecnologías de la Información y las Comunicaciones, Colombia. Retrieved 23 July 2013 from https://www.slideshare.net/jmospina/encuesta-de-percepcin-del-uso-de-tics

Jiménez, Orián. 2007 *El Frenesí del Vulgo: Fiestas, Juegos y Bailes en la Sociedad Colonial.* Medellín: Universidad de Antioquia.

López, Olga L., and Luz María Londoño. 2007. *Desplazamiento Forzado en el Oriente Antioqueño: Estrategias Familiares de Sobrevivencia.* Medellín: Fondo Editorial Comfenalco.

"Los Juegos que se Mueven Tras el Chance." 2008. Investigative Unit. *El País* [Colombia], 6 April. Retrieved 3 July 2013 from http://historico.elpais.com.co/pai sonline/calionline/notas/Abril062008/cali02.html.

Melgarejo Vargas, Luz María. 1994. "Sobre el concepto de Percepción." *Revista Alteridades* (4): 8.

Montes del Castillo, Angel. 2001. "Filmes Etnográficos. La construcción audiovisual de las 'otras culturas.'" *Revista Comunicar* 16: 79–87.

Ordóñez, Alejandro. 2012. "Trabajo Digno y Decente en Colombia: Seguimiento y Control Preventivo a las Políticas Públicas." Bogotá: Procuraduría General de la Nación. Retrieved 17 June 2013 from http://www.procuraduria.gov.co/portal/media/file/Trabajo digno y decente en Colombia_ Seguimiento y control preventivo a las políticas públicas(1).pdf.

Parra, Hesley A. 2005. *Relaciones que dan origen a la familia.* Monografía, Facultad de Derecho y Ciencias Políticas, Universidad de Antioquia.

Portes, Alejandro. 2004. *La Economía Informal.* Santiago: Publicación de las Naciones Unidas.

Simmel, Georg. 1997. *Simmel on Culture: Selected Writings.* Eds. David Frisby and Mike Featherstone. London: Sage Publications.

———. 2010. *Cultura Líquida y Dinero: Fragmentos Simmelianos de la Modernidad,* trans. Celso Sánchez. México City, México: Universidad Autónoma Metropolitana.

Sociedad Colombiana de Apuestas S.A. "Normativa de conductas y Procesos." Retrieved 3 July 2013 from http://www.gane.com.co/index.php?p=quienes_somos/normativa_y_legislacion&.

Spicker, Paul, Sonia Alvarez, and David Gordon. 2009. *Pobreza: Un Glosario Internacional.* Buenos Aires: Consejo Latinoamericano de Ciencias Sociales, CLACSO.

Vergara, Marcela. 2008. "Urban Conflicts on Public Space Appropriation and Production." Magister diss., Universidad Nacional, Bogotá.

Villabona, Jairo. 2010. "Banca Colombiana, Alta Concentración y Sin Competencia." Centro de Investigaciones Económicas. Bogotá: Univesidad Nacional de Colombia. Retrieved 11 December 2011 from http://www.cid.unal.edu.co/cidnews/index.php/noticias/1781-banca-colombiana-alta-concentracion-y-sin-competencia.html.

Zapata, Rubén D. 2012. "Disputa por el Espacio Público." Periferia Prensa. Retrieved 24 March 2011 from http://www.periferiaprensa.org/index.php/edicion-actual/1080-disputa-por-el-espacio-publico.

Afterword

Monetary Ingenuity: Drink It In

BILL MAURER

> If you go drinking it's better to use MPESA because it's safer. Maybe you get drunk and you lose your money. If you find yourself unable to dial the number, it means that it's time for you to go home. (Iazzolino and Wasike 2015: 235)

One of Gianluca Iazzolino and Nambuwani Wasike's informants, a "family man" with a wife and two children, explained the benefits of using M-PESA when going out drinking with friends. M-PESA gave him control over his spending, or, rather, it prevented his spending when, due to drinking, he lost control. For the same reason, Iazzolino and Wasike find, married men prefer bank accounts over cash-only value storage or M-PESA because banks prevent easy access to your money. There are not very many ATMs, there are few branches, and this is a good thing – lack of access means more stability. The authors raise the concern that as electronic payment via cards becomes more ubiquitous in Kenya, this perceived benefit of bank accounts may fade. Perhaps M-PESA is better after all – at least you have to punch in some numbers rather than quickly and thoughtlessly swiping or inserting a card into a digital point-of-sale device.

Who could imagine payment could become so complicated, and interesting, and a site of such variegated social practices as documented in this volume? Payment has been backgrounded, made invisible, in so many accounts of development intervention, economic growth, trade and finance, marketplace dynamics. In many accounts, one often has to read twice, or more, to find out exactly how people are transferring value in a transaction, what technologies they use, what the kinematic and social dimensions of that use are, and which gestures, microinteractions, and verbal niceties occur. Only recently have payments, their infrastructures and social practices, seen significant scholarly attention (see Bátiz-Lazo and Efthymiou 2016). The beauty of the contributions in this volume is that they put the spotlight on the means of payment and thereby open up a whole world: a world of convention, practice, improvisation, and ingenuity. The lesson of this volume is that those who would remake payment or money with the aim of fostering financial inclusion, formalizing informal practices, providing additional safety and security for transactions, reducing crime or tax evasion – all reasons given from on high for reducing or eliminating physical cash – will fail unless they understand that ingenuity, and the myriad cultural and social forces in play whenever people pay.

The English term "ingenuity" has a muddled etymology. It derives from the Latin *ingenuus,* a sort of kinship term meaning "indigenous" but also "noble," because it also has the connotation of being inborn, the way nobility was presumed to be an inherent fact maintained through endogamy. It became associated with both creativity and simpleness (there are many lines to trace here, but I leave them aside for now), and thus the term "ingénue," borrowed from the French, entered the language, referring to a naïve yet good and virtuous young woman. Naïve, because possessed of the straightforward demeanor of one encountering the world fresh, as if for the first time; virtuous, because as-yet untainted by that world while superior to it.

Reading these chapters, witnessing the remarkable ingenuity of people navigating multiple systems of value and payment in multiple social, temporal, and geographic contexts, I have to pause and ask, who is the ingénue here? Is it the people described in these pages, having to grapple with the infrastructures of payment in rapidly changing economic and technological fields of power, regard, and recognition? Or is it those relatively well-off residents of the Global North who have enjoyed the luxury of not having to keep constant account of each others' debts and credits, or to worry about the reliability of the systems undergirding their economic well being, or to have concern over the day-to-day worth of their money? It is these same people, often in the role of experts or advisors, who have since before the financial crisis of 2007–8 advocated strenuously for "banking the unbanked" and have more recently been promoting an anti-cash agenda in the name of financial deepening and economic development. They imagine themselves above it all, noble and untainted by any market or mercenary interests. Yet this is part of their naïveté.

At the very first conference of researchers supported by the Institute for Money, Technology & Financial Inclusion at the University of California, Irvine, in 2009, Kenneth Omeje, a researcher from Nigeria, then based in Kenya, asked the gathering how many of them had lost money because of bank failures. At least half a dozen hands went up. He continued, pointing out how many of the researchers either came from or were working within active conflict zones where institutions and infra-structures could not be counted on to remain in full operation or even in existence from day to day or even hour to hour.

There are reasons, then, to doubt the ingenuousness of the experts of the North (myself included).

What does it mean to be at the margins, with money? I would literalize this bookish metaphor. Money is an accounting tool, a memory device, often centralized, whether in ancient temples that served as storehouses and recording houses or the contemporary Visa or Safaricom networks. Yet people write their own stories. They are on the margins and writing in the margins of the authoritative record. Thus, when the authoritative record says M-PESA is used for school fees, they simultaneously write the story that says, yes, it's for school fees, but those school fees sometimes come in the form of the thirteenth cow that must be given from the mother's brother to his nephew at the latter's initiation, more than a decade after a debt was first incurred through marriage, affirming the continuity of the patriline (Kusimba, Kunyu, and Wanyama 2015).

As we read these pages, we see a diversity of practices for everyday survival. As in biological evolution, diversity enhances the odds. I'd bring the biological metaphor into the domain of knowledge production and policy and industry application: we need a diversity of knowledge forms for survival, too. Randomized controlled trials might be great for now, or for one clearly demarcated set of interventions or circumstances. But what happens when the world changes? A little ethnography goes a long way. I think back to Kenneth Omeje, who asked his question at the first IMTFI conference. What happens when there is revolution? And there are all sorts of revolutions to be had, from political to religious to climactic, and always just beyond the horizon.

In a classic anthropological essay, Charles O. Frake described how to ask for a drink among the Subanun people on the island of Mindanao in the Philippines. While he is often read today as an exemplar of a certain perspective of culture that held it to be a code for action, an algorithm like a computer code, I am struck by the extent to which he emphasizes the style or panache with which one has to engage in the social interac-tions associated with drinking. Asking for a drink, Frake shows, is not just about getting that drink – and getting drunk. It is about "how to get ahead socially" (Frake 1964: 131). He writes:

> The Subanun drinking encounter thus provides a structured setting within which one's social relationships beyond his everyday associates can be ex-tended, defined, and manipulated through the use of speech. (Ibid.: 131)

Substitute money for speech, or mobile money, or any other means of payment, value transfer, or value storage in this book and you have a nice picture of what is happening whenever we decide how we would like to pay.

By going to the margins, going into the interstices, the places that are supposed to be the blank spots on the page (there's nothing there! Or else, "here be dragons!"[1]), IMTFI researchers have found that the question of adoption of digital financial services is never a simple one. There are not core variables here, knobs and levers that work in all times and places, or rationalities that can be boiled down to the simplicities of rational choice or even the irrationalities revealed by behavioral economics. No, there is, in a word, culture. There is the hurly-burly of practice, both semiotic and material. There is infrastructure, both social and technological. There are multiple timescapes taking place simultaneously – think of that thirteenth cow again.

This is not to say that everything is so complicated and particular that there is no point in trying to intervene. But it is to say that if one wants to intervene, perhaps one needs to enter into that flow first, to truly engage – in social practice, in meaningfully inclusive dialog – to drink it all in before jumping in with a "solution" to problems other than what those others out there in the "target geographies" of one's intervention might actually be experiencing. It is to say that the enterprise must be collaborative. This deep sense of collaboration is what IMTFI has sought to incite.

Figure 14.1. The thirteenth cow.

Bill Maurer is dean of social sciences and professor of anthropology and
law, University of California, Irvine. He is the author of *How Would You Like
to Pay? How Technology Is Changing the Future of Money* (Duke 2015), among
many other publications. The director of the Institute for Money, Technology & Financial Inclusion (www.imtfi.uci.edu), funded by the Bill &
Melinda Gates Foundation, he coordinates research in over forty countries on how new payment technologies impact poor people's well-being.
His work explores the technological infrastructures and social relations
of exchange and payment, from cowries to credit cards. His work has had
an impact on US and global policies for mobile payment and financial
access, and it has been discussed in venues ranging from Bloomberg Busi-
nessWeek to NPR's Marketplace. He was appointed to the Board on Behavioral, Cognitive, and Sensory Sciences of the National Research Council in
2015, recently received a grant from the National Science Foundation for
a new project on bitcoin, and consulted with the Department of Treasury
on the redesign of the US paper currency. He is a fellow of the American
Association for the Advancement of Science and received his BA from
Vassar College and his MA and PhD from Stanford University.

NOTES

1. The reference is to the European medieval practice of filling in the margins
   of maps with sea monsters.

REFERENCES CITED

Bátiz-Lazo, Bernardo, and Leonidas Efthymiou, eds. 2016. *The Book of Payments: His-
    torical and Contemporary Views on the Cashless Society.* London: Palgrave Macmillan.
Frake, Charles O. 1964. "How to Ask for a Drink in Subanun." *American Anthropol-
    ogist* 66(2), part 2: 127–32.
Iazzolino, Gianluca, and Nambuwani Wasike. 2015. "The Unbearable Lightness of
    Digital Money." *Journal of Payments Strategy and Systems* 9(3): 229–41.
Kusimba, Sibel, Gabriel Kunyu, and Alex Wanyama. 2015. "The Contingency Fund
    and the Thirteenth Cow: ICTs in a Coming of Age Ritual in Western Kenya
    (Part 2)." IMTFI Blog, 20 July. Retrieved 20 May 2017 from http://blog.imtfi.uci
    .edu/2015/07/the-contingency-fund-and-thirteenth-cow_20.html.

Index

CPSIA information can be obtained
at www.ICGtesting.com
Printed in the USA
LVHW051944100419
613667LV00017B/324/P

9 781789 200485